Plot Outlines Of
100 Famous Novels

Plot Outlines Of
100 FAMOUS
NOVELS

EDITED BY

ROLAND A. GOODMAN

THE NEW HOME LIBRARY
THE BLAKISTON COMPANY—PHILADELPHIA

An Original Publication of THE NEW HOME LIBRARY

THE NEW HOME LIBRARY is a series published by
The Blakiston Company, 1012 Walnut St., Philadelphia 5, Pa.

CL

PRINTED IN THE UNITED STATES OF AMERICA

Introduction

FOR SHEER ENJOYMENT novels are today and have been for centuries the most popular form of literature. A story dramatic and well told—with characters living their lives in moments of high adventure or meeting the familiar problems of everyday life with vigor and determination—is in itself an adventure for the reader. Few experiences are more thrilling than the reading of a good novel.

The novelists of today have much in common with the novelists of the past, and the pleasure derived from a new work of fiction is often increased by comparing it with a great work by an earlier writer. Yet many men and women do not have time to read the great masterpieces of fiction. Consequently there should be a place in everyone's library for *Plot Outlines of 100 Famous Novels.* In this book we have brought together the stories of the world's greatest works of fiction, each retold by the editor so that the whole plot stands out clearly and so that all the famous characters become familiar to the reader. This one volume gives you a satisfying acquaintance with the most famous novels of the past and with many outstanding novels of recent years. The fascination of these books will be evident from the plot outlines, and no doubt these accounts will lead many readers to turn to the novels themselves in their authors' own words.

The plot outlines go back in time to Cervantes' *Don Quixote,*

Bunyan's *The Pilgrim's Progress,* Voltaire's *Candide,* and Fielding's *Tom Jones.* The greatest novelists of the Nineteenth Century are all represented—Sir Walter Scott, Jane Austen, the Brontë sisters, Dickens, Thackeray, George Eliot, Trollope, Robert Louis Stevenson, Oscar Wilde, Du Maurier, Meredith, Hardy, and Kipling, in England; James Fenimore Cooper, Herman Melville, Hawthorne, Henry James, Samuel L. Clemens (Mark Twain), and William Dean Howells, in America; Victor Hugo, Balzac, Gautier, Flaubert, De Maupassant, Daudet, and Zola, in France; Turgenev, Tolstoy, and Dostoyevsky, in Russia. And from the recent period we have plot outlines of great novels by W. H. Hudson, J. M. Barrie, Ibañez, Romain Rolland, Marcel Proust, Joseph Conrad, John Galsworthy, H. G. Wells, D. H. Lawrence, Edith Wharton, Stephen Crane, Theodore Dreiser, Sinclair Lewis, and Ernest Hemingway.

The works of the great masters of fiction reflect in their mood and manner the characteristic point of view of their native lands. Consequently we have grouped the novelists represented in this volume under the headings: English, American, French, Russian, and Various Countries (including Spanish, German, Polish, Swedish). Within these national groups we have arranged the authors alphabetically, so that they may be most readily turned to; and all the novels by which any author is represented are of course grouped together in this way. A short biographical sketch of each author precedes the first of his novels presented in the book.

In selecting the 100 plot outlines, we have endeavored to include all the great favorites from among the tremendous number of important and interesting novels which we considered as possibilities. The reader may find that due to lack of space a few books that he would have liked included are not here. However, the same reader will undoubtedly discover here many absorbing plot outlines introducing him to books which he might not have looked for, but which will prove doubly welcome because they offer a wholly unsuspected fascination. The pleasure of recalling the details of old standbys, the thrill of discovering new treasures, and the opportunity for acquiring a wide familiarity with the masterpieces of fiction should make this book an almost inexhaustible source of information and entertainment.

R. A. G.

Acknowledgments

We wish to thank the following for their kind co-operation in giving permission to include plot outlines of books copyrighted and published by them:

Doubleday, Doran & Company, Inc., for *Lord Jim*, by Joseph Conrad, and *Gösta Berling's Saga*, by Selma Lagerlöf.

A. P. Watt & Sons for the Estate of Rudyard Kipling, and Doubleday, Doran & Company, Inc., for *The Light That Failed*, by Rudyard Kipling.

Charles Scribner's Sons, for *The Little Minister*, by J. M. Barrie, *The Man of Property*, by John Galsworthy, *A Farewell to Arms*, by Ernest Hemingway, and *Ethan Frome*, by Edith Wharton.

Harper & Brothers, for *Trilby*, by George du Maurier, *Peter Ibbetson*, by George du Maurier, *Tess of the D'Urbervilles*, by Thomas Hardy, *The Prince and the Pauper*, by Samuel Langhorne Clemens, *A Connecticut Yankee in King Arthur's Court*, by Samuel Langhorne Clemens, and *The War of the Worlds*, by H. G. Wells.

Henry Holt and Company, Inc., for *The Prisoner of Zenda*, by Anthony Hope, and *Jean Christophe*, by Romain Rolland.

Houghton Mifflin Company, for *Looking Backward*, by Edward Bellamy.

The John Day Company, Inc., for *The Good Earth*, by Pearl Buck.

D. Appleton-Century Company, for *The Red Badge of Courage*, by Stephen Crane, and *Mother*, by Maxim Gorki.

G. P. Putnam's Sons and Theodore Dreiser, for *An American Tragedy*, by Theodore Dreiser.

Harcourt, Brace and Company, Inc., for *Arrowsmith*, by Sinclair Lewis.

Random House, Inc., for *Swann's Way*, by Marcel Proust.

The Viking Press, Inc., for *Sons and Lovers*, by D. H. Lawrence.

Little, Brown & Company, for *All Quiet on the Western Front*, by Erich Maria Remarque.

E. P. Dutton & Co., Inc., for *The Four Horsemen of the Apocalypse*, by Vicente Blasco Ibañez.

R. A. G.

Contents

CONTENTS

AMERICAN NOVELS

FRENCH NOVELS

RUSSIAN NOVELS

NOVELS OF VARIOUS COUNTRIES

English Novels

Pride and Prejudice

By JANE AUSTEN

JANE AUSTEN, *daughter of an English country rector, spent her life away from cities, and never married. She was born on Dec. 16, 1775, at Steventon, Hampshire, and died on July 18, 1817, at Winchester, where she was buried in the cathedral. Her novels reflect her secluded life and the narrow range of society in which she moved, the circles of the country gentleman and the upper professional classes. She began writing early in life, although the prejudices of her times forced her to publish her books anonymously.*

IT IS A TRUTH universally acknowledged, that a single man in possession of a good fortune must be in want of a wife.

Thus the Bennet family in particular, as well as all Longbourn, was agape with excitement when Netherfield Park, the great place of the neighborhood, was let to a rich young bachelor called Charles Bingley, and it became known that Mr. Bingley and his party were to attend the forthcoming ball at the Assembly Rooms.

The Bennets, the chief family of Longbourn, had five unmarried daughters and only small portions for them. After 23 years of married life, the sarcastic humor, reserve, and caprice of Mr.

Bennet left him still something of a mystery to Mrs. Bennet, a still handsome woman of mean understanding, little information, and uncertain temper.

At the ball Mr. Bingley turned out to be a good-looking, unaffected gentleman. With him were his two sisters, and Mr. Hurst, husband of the elder, and Fitzwilliam Darcy, a young man who was much admired for his handsome features and his rumored ten thousand a year, until his haughty bearing turned the admiration into disgust. While Mr. Bingley danced every dance, Mr. Darcy took turns only with Mrs. Hurst and Caroline Bingley, and declined to be introduced to any other lady.

Elizabeth, second of the Bennet girls, obliged to sit out a dance, overheard Mr. Darcy tell Mr. Bingley that there was not a local woman in the room "whom it would not be a punishment to me to stand up with," and that Jane, the eldest Bennet, was the only handsome girl there. In fact, he glanced at Elizabeth and said: "She is tolerable, but not handsome enough to tempt me." Elizabeth did not feel cordial to Mr. Darcy for this, but her playful disposition led her to tell the story with great spirit among her friends.

Nevertheless the Bingleys and the Bennets soon established friendly relationships. Charles and Jane obviously were mutually attracted, and Charles' sisters liked Elizabeth, although they found Mrs. Bennet tedious and classed as impossible her daughters Mary, the plain one, and Lydia and Kitty, giggling girls who spent all their time running after men.

Mr. Darcy developed a sort of guarded interest in Elizabeth. He began to admire the expression of her dark eyes, found her figure pleasing, and was caught by the light ease of her manners. When they began to exchange little satiric speeches, Miss Bingley, who was angling for Darcy, asked him: "When am I to wish you joy?" and he replied: "A lady's imagination is very rapid."

The two elder sisters now paid a visit of some days to the Bingleys, Jane's being extended by a bad cold which her mother helped scheme into a longer stay. Elizabeth was less popular,

Caroline considering her too attractive, Mrs. Hurst deeming her too sharp-tongued.

Nevertheless Elizabeth had not overcome her prejudice against Darcy, and it was strengthened by her conversation with Mr. Wickham, a handsome and agreeable young officer in a militia regiment at Meryton, nearest town to Longbourn. Wickham told Elizabeth that he was the son of a trusted steward of Darcy's father, and that Darcy had cruelly disregarded his father's wish that Wickham be provided for.

Then, just as it seemed that Bingley was about to propose to Jane, the whole Netherfield party returned to town, with Elizabeth blaming the conduct of the Bennet family at a ball.

About this time the Rev. William Collins, heir to Longbourn, visited the Bennets. A pompous, tactless and humorless young man, he thought to make amends for the fact that some day he must dispossess the family, by offering to marry Elizabeth. She heard his long, set speech, then refused him. He insisted that she was merely trying to plague him, and was reluctantly convinced only after two more rejections—after which he married Charlotte Lucas, a prosaic girl who was Elizabeth's best friend.

Now Mr. Bennet found occasion for irony in reports that Bingley was showing an interest in Darcy's sister Georgiana. "Next to being married, a girl likes to be crossed in love a little now and then," he told Elizabeth. "When is your turn to come? Let Wickham be your man." Although Wickham had not yet become that intimate with her, he did turn his affections to a wealthier young woman. But Elizabeth parted with him on friendly terms to visit Mr. and Mrs. Collins at Hunsford.

Darcy also was a guest in that neighborhood, but Elizabeth's feelings against him were increased by her suspicions that he had caused Bingley to give up Jane. Therefore she was surprised when he suddenly told her that he loved her; nor was his case strengthened when he said that he had had to overcome a feeling that he would lower himself by marrying into her family. She rejected him, and told him why.

Darcy departed, but left her a letter in which he not only made some scathing but justifiable complaints against members of her family, but declared that he had not known that Jane was strongly attached to Bingley, and revealed that Wickham had been treated well but had repaid Darcy by idleness and an attempt to elope with Georgiana.

Two months later, while on a visit to Mr. and Mrs. Gardiner, an uncle and aunt in Derbyshire, Elizabeth was making an unwilling inspection of Pemberly, Darcy's home in that neighborhood, and was surprised to hear unstinting praise of him from his housekeeper. Unexpectedly Darcy himself appeared, and Elizabeth was just beginning to soften toward him when word arrived that Lydia, who had got herself invited to Brighton, had eloped with Wickham, whose regiment was stationed there, and was thought to be living unmarried in London with him.

Darcy seemed staggered by the news. The Gardiner party hurried to Longbourn, and Elizabeth's uncle went to London to assist Mr. Bennet in his search for the couple. While Mrs. Bennet worried about where Lydia would buy her wedding clothes, and Mr. Collins sent a mealy-mouthed letter of condolences, the Bennets' distress was eased by word that the couple had been found and it had been made worth Wickham's while to marry Lydia.

Arrangements were made for Wickham to enter the regulars and join a regiment at Newcastle, and Lydia invited her mother to visit them and bring along her unmarried daughters, saying: "I dare say I shall get husbands for them before the winter is over."

From Lydia's mention that Darcy had been present at her wedding, Elizabeth began drawing conclusions, which were confirmed by her Aunt Gardiner. It was Darcy who had found the couple, and had persuaded Wickham to marry Lydia by paying off a thousand pounds of his debts, buying him a commission, and settling another thousand on Lydia.

Meantime Bingley returned to Netherfield, and Elizabeth had the mortification of seeing her mother welcome him while treating Darcy coldly. When Darcy's aunt tried to make Elizabeth promise not to accept Darcy as a husband, the result was the opposite of that intended, for Darcy was informed of Elizabeth's refusal, proposed again, and was accepted.

The Bennets were dumbfounded, but in the end were all convinced. Bingley and Jane had become engaged, and Mr. Bennet announced: "If any young men come for Mary or Kitty, send them in, for I am quite at leisure."

The Little Minister

By J. M. BARRIE

JAMES MATTHEW BARRIE *was born on May 9, 1860, in Kirriemuir, Scotland. He was educated in Scottish schools and graduated from the University of Edinburgh in 1882. His natural bent was toward journalism and he worked for a few years for Edinburgh papers and periodicals. He soon became well known for his sketches of Scottish peasant life and his success was assured when "The Little Minister" appeared in 1891. He moved to England and started to write plays in 1892. In 1913 he was created a baronet. He died in London on June 19, 1937.*

WHEN Gavin Dishart came to the little Scottish village of Thrums as the minister of the "Auld Lichts" parish, he was only twenty-one, not a very tall lad, and not so far past boyhood as he liked to think himself. To him and to his gentle, loving mother, Margaret, who had willingly endured poverty that her boy might be educated, the manse where they lived and the eighty pounds a year that Gavin earned represented riches. And to both the ministry spelled the highest calling that a man could follow.

The people of Thrums were poor, hard-working and devout. They were weavers mostly; their lives rigorous, their pleasures simple, and their morals strait-laced. Only when their security was threatened did they cease to be docile. Even now the police were searching for the ringleaders of a recent riot.

The village was agog over the little minister's coming, and Thrums was soon completely won over by Gavin's earnestness, his eloquence in the pulpit and his love for his parishioners.

The man to whom Gavin's coming meant most was one whom the minister barely knew—Mr. Ogilvy, the schoolmaster, who long had loved Margaret and secretly watched her and her son with loving eyes.

Gavin's prestige with his parish was greatly increased by the incident of Rob Dow. Rob Dow, a great hulking brute whose vice was drink, entered the kirk one Sabbath noisy and intoxicated. The little minister, undaunted by Rob's size, forced the drunkard into silence, and later, through kindness, won him as a friend.

So for a while Gavin's life ran smoothly on. He was happy in his duties, happy in his mother's joy, and the love of his congregation.

But one night the militia came to Thrums to seize the ringleaders of the recent uprising. Somehow the soldiers' plans were discovered, for by a prearranged signal—a horn blast—the weavers were warned. Gavin was torn between duty, which told him to advise the culprits to surrender, and sympathy, which urged him to counsel flight. While he was exhorting his parishioners to drop the arms they had gathered, he was interrupted by a feminine voice shouting that the men must fight for their rights. The agitator was a beautiful gypsy girl. Flouting Gavin's authority, the men followed her, and when the militia arrived most of the men were safely in hiding, while the women covered their retreat, flinging earth and stones at the oncoming soldiery. Bemoaning her poor aim the gypsy girl, pressed a divit into Gavin's hand and, pointing to the captain of the militia, whispered, "Hit him!" Hypnotized, Gavin flung the clod of earth—and hit the captain on the head!

Later the gypsy was apprehended, but she escaped in the confusion and safely passed the sentries by posing as Gavin's wife. Furious at himself and the girl, Gavin grew more stern and preached a brimstone sermon against Woman. But he could not forget the gypsy's beauty.

The gypsy was to appear again. When poor old Nanny Webster was being taken, much against her will, to the poorhouse, the gypsy came to her rescue with promise of support. Astounded that a gypsy should have money, yet unable to disbelieve the girl's honesty, Gavin promised to meet Babbie—such was the gypsy's name—in the wood, and get a five-pound note for Nanny.

Babbie brought the money as she had promised. She was wilful and wild, teasing the young man about his calling and his lack of inches. They quarreled, but Gavin realized that he loved the gypsy girl.

That evening capricious Babbie came to the manse garden, swinging a lantern to frighten Gavin. He came out to chide her, kissed her instead, and she knew that she, too, loved.

Although he knew that marriage to a gypsy would end his career with his strait-laced congregation, Gavin determined that Babbie should be his bride. But the girl, fearing to be the ruin of her sweetheart, went away, and for a long time the little minister could find no trace of her.

Mr. Ogilvy, the schoolmaster, was the next to see Babbie. A rumor had arisen that Gavin had been killed while trying to stop a brawl in the public house. Mr. Ogilvy hurried to find out the truth of this, leaving Babbie to wait in Nanny Webster's cottage. He found the little minister unharmed and, touched by the young people's unhappiness, he was unable to forbear telling Gavin of Babbie's whereabouts.

After the first joy of their meeting was over, Babbie told Gavin the truth about herself. She was the ward of Lord Rintoul, who owned the castle on the hill. Years before the earl had found the little gypsy girl and, enchanted by her beauty, had reared her with every advantage. Now, loving only her beauty, he had determined to marry her. The wedding was to take place the next day. But Gavin refused to accept this. And while the bells rang for evening meeting and the angry elders denounced the absent minister, Babbie and Gavin were married by the king of the gypsies.

While this strange marriage took place, a storm broke and soon the lochs were in full flood. Babbie, separated from her husband, took refuge in the manse, and Gavin finally made his way to Mr. Ogilvy's house. Here he heard a strange story. Long ago, believing her husband drowned at sea, Margaret had married Mr. Ogilvy. Gavin was their son. But Margaret's man had returned and she had sent Ogilvy away heartbroken.

Gavin was beyond listening to the sorrows of others. Fearing that Babbie was in the hands of Rintoul, he went off through the flood to seek her. But when he came to the river he found that on a little island in the swollen waters his enemy, Rintoul, was marooned. In an effort to rescue Rintoul, Gavin too was trapped, and the two men awaited death together.

The townspeople stood helpless on the bank while the little island in the river was slowly washed away. While they waited, Gavin held his last service. Completely won over by his faith and courage, the people of Thrums forgave their little minister and took him back into their hearts. When all seemed lost Gavin's old friend the drunkard, Rob Dow, carrying a rope, leaped into the waves and saved the lives of Rintoul and Gavin at the expense of his own. Thus was the little minister restored to Babbie and to his people.

Lorna Doone

By RICHARD D. BLACKMORE

RICHARD DODDRIDGE BLACKMORE *was born June 9, 1825, at Longworth, Berkshire (England), where his father was rector. While very young he married a Portuguese girl. A long illness left him in difficult circumstances for years, but in 1860 he came unexpectedly into a fortune. He settled down to gardening and the writing of historical romances, becoming the pioneer of a new movement. He died at Teddington on Jan. 20, 1900.*

Two MILES below the farm of John Ridd's family at Oare, Exmoor, the Bagworthy water runs into the Lynn, but John hardly dared go fishing along those two miles, for that is where Sir Ensor Doone came with his tall sons and wild retainers when he was outlawed by good King Charles in 1640.

At first the newcomers did only a little sheep-stealing, but in the troublous times of the Great Rebellion they grew bolder, attacking men, burning farms and carrying off women, until all Exmoor stood in terror of this band of forty and more six-foot marksmen. Their worst deed was to murder John Ridd's father in 1673, when the boy was 12.

But when John was 14 he set out to explore the Bagworthy water. Spearing fish, he came to a great black whirlpool into which water thundered 100 yards down a cliff. Nearly swept away, he battled his way up somehow through the waterslide, but fainted when he reached the top. When he came to, a little girl with beautiful dark eyes, a primrose in her long black hair, was bending over him. She told him in her beautiful voice that her name was Lorna Doone. He kissed her, and she hid him in a hole in the rocks.

Frightened by the dozen fierce-looking men who came for Lorna that night, John stayed away. Working hard on his farm, he grew tall and strong, until he was the largest man in Exmoor and champion wrestler of the West Counties.

When John was 21, his uncle, Ben Huckaback, was robbed by the Doones and went to London to Lord Chief Justice Jeffreys, the most powerful and terrible man in England, "to get these scoundrel Doones shot or hanged." Ridd was sent to spy out the ground where the Doones lived. This time he climbed the waterfall without difficulty, and again he met Lorna, more beautiful than ever.

She showed him a cave which was her bower, and told him how angry she was with the violence and wickedness which surrounded her. Only a year before, she said, her cousin, Lord Alan Brandir, tried to rescue her and Carver Doone killed him. It was Carver who had slain John's father. John and Lorna agreed that if ever she needed help, she should hang out a black mantle as a signal.

John was called to London by Chief Justice Jeffreys, and when he returned saw Lorna's signal. He went to the waterfall, and found that Carver Doone was trying to force her to marry him. Lorna sat close to John, and he pleaded his love of her. At last she flung her arms about his neck, pledged herself to him "for ever and ever." Suddenly Carver approached the bower and only Lorna's presence stopped John from hurling himself on this tall, strong man with the cruel steel-blue eyes.

Returning home, John found troops waiting to attack the Doones. Wanting to warn Lorna so that she would be safe, he waited at her bower, and when she did not appear, set forth through a heavy snow for the Doone village. There he found Lorna a prisoner in her house. Sir Ensor Doone had died, and Carver was trying to starve Lorna into marrying him. Now she agreed to flee with John.

John hurried home, got a sled which he took as near as possible to the Doone village, then returned to Lorna. He was just in time, for a drunken Doone was threatening her. John choked him, and ran with Lorna in his arms. Soon John's mother and sisters were attending the exhausted girl in his home.

Young Ridd now prepared for the attack which would come as soon as the snow had cleared. The outlaws came by moonlight, and found troops waiting for them. John had his carbine against Carver Doone's breast, but found himself unable to take a human life. Instead he fought with a club, and knocked Carver down in the mud. The Doones broke and fled, with Ridd's warning: "I may not be your match in craft; but I am in manhood."

Emboldened by a victory over troops which tried to storm their stronghold, the Doones now entered the home of Kit Badcock, killed his baby and carried off his wife. Leadership against them was now thrust upon John. He led his men up the waterfall in a night attack, and burned Carver's logwood house before the enemy knew they were in danger. Every man in the band had some wrong to avenge, and no Doone escaped except Carver. John was vexed that this resourceful and desperate man was at large; he had ridden his horse through the guards posted to stop him.

In London, where Lorna had been sent, it was discovered that she was a great heiress whose true title was Lady Lorna Dugal. Related to the Doones, she had been carried off by Sir Ensor as an eventual bride for Carver so that her wealth might enable the outlaws to regain their position in the world.

This news made John Ridd sad, for there was too great a difference between her and a yeoman farmer like himself. But in the spring she returned to the Ridd farm with the joyful news that Lord Jeffreys, her guardian, had given her permission, for a certain sum, to marry John.

There was a joyful wedding, but as John stooped to kiss his bride, a shot rang through the church. Lorna fell across John's knees, her blood flowed out on the altar steps, and she grew cold.

John laid her in his mother's arms and went forth for his revenge.

Someone showed him the course, and he leaped unarmed on his horse, to discover whether in this world there be or be not a God of justice. Riding at a furious speed, at Black Burrow Down he saw, a furlong before him, a man on a great black horse. John knew he was strong and armed with gun, pistol and sword, but he had no doubt of killing him.

At Wizard's Slough, John Ridd came up with Carver Doone. A bullet struck John somewhere, but he took no heed of it. With an oak stick he felled the horse, and Carver Doone lay stunned on the ground. John bared his arms as for wrestling, and waited. Presently Carver gathered together his mighty limbs, and they closed. John was caught around the waist with a grip that cracked a rib, but he grasped Carver Doone's arm and tore the muscle out of it; then he had him by the throat and left him sinking into the black bog.

John returned to the farm, the thought of Lorna's death tolling in his brain. Into the old farmhouse he tottered, to hear his mother say:

"Lorna is still living, John."

She lived indeed, her beauty and gayness setting off the slower nature of him who is now Sir John Ridd. But he still can bring her to sadness by the two words, "Lorna Doone."

Jane Eyre

By CHARLOTTE BRONTË

THE ELDEST of three writing sisters, Charlotte Brontë was born at Thornton, Yorkshire, on April 21, 1816, and, being raised without companionship except her own family, lived in a world of the im-

*ugination that found her composing stories at the age of 13. Do-
mestic strain affected much of her writing, although her horizon
was broadened by a period in Brussels as a governess. She married
shortly before her death on March 31, 1855.*

ORPHANED IN INFANCY, Jane Eyre was left in the hateful care of an
aunt, Mrs. Reed of Gateshead Hall, where she was treated so
cruelly that she was grateful to be sent off to Lowood School, a
semi-charitable institution. There she spent eight not unhappy
years as pupil and teacher, leaving at the age of 18 to become
governess to Adela Varens, the ward of Mr. Edward Rochester,
at Thornfield Manor.

Thornfield was a fine old battlemented hall, and Mrs. Fairfax,
guardian of Adela and a relative of Mr. Rochester, was pleasant
to Jane. One day Mrs. Fairfax was showing Jane over the house,
much of which was unoccupied. On the way to see the view from
the roof, she mentioned that the quiet third floor would be the
haunt of a ghost if the hall had one.

Returning, on the third floor they heard a laugh—distinct,
mirthless and ending in a clamorous peal. "Some of the servants,"
said Mrs. Fairfax, and she called to Grace Poole, a square-built,
plain person, and warned her: "Too much noise." Not in-
frequently after that Jane heard Grace's laugh.

Late one January afternoon Jane, walking to the village nearby,
sat on a stile to rest. A rider on a tall horse passed by, then she
heard them fall on the icy road. The man's great dog summoned
Jane, but he refused help and limped to the fence. Though the
man had a dark face with stern features and a heavy brow, Jane
felt no fear of him; his very frown and roughness set her at ease.
He seemed perhaps 35; his expression looked ireful and thwarted.

When she refused to leave him at once, he questioned her,
found that she was the governess at Thornfield Hall, and permitted her to help him mount his horse. When she returned, she

found that the dog belonged to Mr. Rochester, who had just arrived.

Next day Jane was summoned to take tea with Mr. Rochester and Adela; there was an uncomfortable silence, then the master broke it by half-playfully accusing Jane of having bewitched his horse. When she stood up to him, he became less surly toward her, and by the time he had been at the hall eight weeks he always had a word for her, and sometimes a smile. She felt at times as if he were her relation rather than her master.

One night Jane's sleep was broken by a noise outside her room; she heard a demoniac laugh, then steps retreating toward the third floor staircase. Trembling, she opened her door and saw the gallery filled with smoke pouring from Mr. Rochester's room. She darted inside, found the bed on fire and him asleep, and waked him with the water by which she doused the flames. He said: "I must pay a visit to the third floor," and when he returned he swore Jane to silence. The household was told that a bedside candle had set the fire, and that the master had put it out.

While Mr. Rochester was away one day, a stranger named Mr. Mason, from the West Indies, arrived at the house. Rochester turned white when Jane informed him of it. "Jane, I've got a blow!" he gasped, then told her: "I wish I were in a quiet island with only you, and trouble was removed from me." But he would say no more, and Jane was relieved when she heard him speaking cheerfully after a long conference with Mason.

But in the dead of night the household was awakened by a fearful shriek from the third floor. In the chamber immediately above hers Jane heard a deadly struggle and a cry of, "Help!" Mr. Rochester appeared from the third floor and sent everyone back to bed, saying that a servant had had a nightmare. An hour later he quietly called Jane and took her upstairs to a room with an inner chamber whence issued snarls and that strange laugh. In the outer room lay Mason, unconscious and with one side bloody. Jane nursed him for two hours after he opened his eyes, then he was taken away before sunrise.

One splendid midsummer twilight Jane was intercepted by Mr. Rochester in the orchard. She admitted that she had become attached to Thornfield, and when he said: "Pity!" she concluded that he planned to marry the beautiful Miss Ingram, who had been a frequent visitor.

"In about a month I hope to be a bridegroom," he confessed. It was a blow to Jane, and soon she was sobbing and telling him: "Do you think I can stay to become nothing to you? Do you think, because I am plain and obscure, I am soulless and heartless?" Then he gathered her to him and pressed his lips to hers. She pulled herself away, and then he revealed that it was Jane, not Miss Ingram, that he loved.

"My bride is here, because my equal is here, and my likeness," he said gently. "Are you in earnest? Do you love me?" Jane asked. "I do. I swear it!" he said. The wind had risen, and the trees writhed and groaned and they hurried back to the hall.

There were no attendants, only Jane and Edward, as they stood at the communion rails in the church a month later. But as the clergyman was about to conclude the ceremony, a voice said: "The marriage cannot go on. Mr. Rochester has a wife living." And Mr. Mason stepped forward. He declared he was the brother of that wife, and that she was at Thornfield Hall.

A grim smile contracted Rochester's lips. "Bigamy is an ugly word," he said, "but I meant to be a bigamist." And he bade all at the scene to follow him to the hall. There, in the inner room beyond where Mason had lain wounded, ran backward and forward, seemingly on all fours, a creature that snatched and growled like some wild animal. It was covered with clothing, but a quantity of dark, wild hair hid its head and face.

Fifteen years before, said Rochester, he was tricked into marrying this woman, of a family of idiots and maniacs. Jane forgave him at the moment, but next morning she departed.

She found refuge at Morton, and accepted the post of village schoolmistress under the assumed name of Jane Elliott. The clergyman of that parish, Mr. St. John Rivers, soon offered her his hand in marriage, but one night she seemed to hear Mr. Rochester calling "Jane!" She could find no one near, so in the morning she set out for Thornfield—and found a blackened ruin.

At the inn she was told that Grace Poole had fallen drunk, and that the mad woman had escaped and set fire to the house. Mr. Rochester had got the servants outside, then had gone back for his lunatic wife. But she was on the roof, and killed herself leaping to the ground.

As Mr. Rochester had left the house, the staircase fell and he was taken from the ruins with one eye knocked out and one hand so crushed that it had to be amputated. Then the other eye became inflamed, and he lost the sight of that, too. Now he was living at Ferndean, a lonely manor house, with two servants. Jane hastened there.

Entering, she spoke to him and seized his groping hand.

"Is it Jane—Jane Eyre?" he cried.

"My dear master, I am Jane Eyre. I have found you out; I am come back to you!"

Wuthering Heights

By EMILY BRONTË

Born *July 30, 1818, at Thornton, Yorkshire, Emily Jane Brontë died 30 years later at Haworth, Yorkshire, on December 19, 1848. Except for brief visits terminated always by homesickness, she spent her life on those bleak North England moorlands whose spirit is embodied in her writings. Children of a clergyman, she and her sisters Charlotte and Anne found an outlet for their vivid imaginations in the stories and poems which they began composing in their teens. Emily died a year after the publication of her only novel, never knowing the fame it would attain.*

MR. LOCKWOOD, new tenant at Thrushcross Grange, met a surly reception from servants, dogs, and the landlord himself, Mr. Heathcliff, when he paid his first call. Mr. Heathcliff looked like a dark-skinned gypsy, but had the dress and manners of a country squire. Erect and handsome in figure, he was extremely morose and reserved.

Wuthering Heights, the landlord's home, was a well-built, battered old farmhouse, its name descriptive of the atmospheric tumult to which its exposed position subjected it in stormy weather.

The tenant, his interest aroused, called again next day and was forced by a snowstorm to remain overnight. He met the rest of this strange household—Heathcliff's widowed daughter-in-law, pretty and scarcely past girlhood, but silent and scornful; and a clumsy youth named Hareton Earnshaw, which was the same name as that carved over the door of the Heights along with the date "1500."

Put into a disused bedroom for the night, Mr. Lockwood found scratched in the wall the names "Catherine Earnshaw," "Catherine Heathcliff" and "Catherine Linton." And on the blank leaves of books in the room he found a scrawled diary with such entries as: "Hindley is detestable—his conduct to Heathcliff is atrocious —H. and I are going to rebel. . . . Poor Heathcliff! Hindley calls him a vagabond, and won't let him sit with us." Nightmares beset Mr. Lockwood, and he woke after dreaming that a pale child who called herself Catherine Linton stood outside the window and wailed to be let in, crying: "I've been a waif for twenty years."

Back at the Grange, Mr. Lockwood was told this story by Mrs. Nelly Dean, his housekeeper, who had long been a servant at the Heights and the Grange:

Old Mr. Earnshaw, Hareton's grandfather, brought back with him from a trip to Liverpool, a dirty, ragged, black-haired boy that he had found homeless in the streets there. They washed the child, gave it the single name of Heathcliff, and Earnshaw took a liking to this hard, silent boy who could absorb a blow without shedding a tear. Earnshaw's daughter Catherine soon became a constant playmate of Heathcliff, but her brother Hindley hated him for usurping his father's affections.

Earnshaw died, and Hindley returned from college with a wife who disliked Heathcliff and drove him to the company of the servants. Cathy clung to the youth, and they promised to grow up together as rude as savages. One night the pair were locked out for the night and Cathy took refuge with the Lintons at Thrushcross Grange—they wouldn't admit Heathcliff. She stayed there five weeks, becoming friendly with the Linton children, Edgar and Isabella.

Hindley's wife died in giving birth to Hareton, and the sorrowing husband abandoned himself to dissipation and fiendish torment of Heathcliff, who grew more savage as Catherine, now 15, developed into a headstrong beauty.

One day Cathy told Nelly that Edgar had proposed to her and that she loved him, despite his placid temperament. But Cathy added: "I'm convinced I'm wrong," that Heathcliff was "more myself than I am," though brought so low by Hindley that it would degrade her to marry him.

Heathcliff overheard, and bolted before Catherine, who added that she wouldn't have given Edgar a second thought except that this marriage would enable her to help Heathcliff.

That night she and Nelly searched the moors fruitlessly for Heathcliff, and next day Cathy went to bed with a dangerous fever. She recovered slowly, but not for three years did she marry Edgar.

After the marriage Heathcliff reappeared, tall, well-dressed and with ample money—where he got it and where he had been were never explained. Cathy welcomed him despite Edgar's frowns, and his old enemy Hindley was pleased to let him pay for lodging at Wuthering Heights.

Now came stories of gambling and drinking at the Heights, with Hindley going deeply into debt, while Heathcliff visited the

Grange regularly. Unexpectedly, defying all warnings that he was no man for her, Isabella Linton became infatuated with Heathcliff. One day Edgar ordered Heathcliff ejected bodily from the Grange, and Heathcliff took revenge by eloping with Isabella.

Eight weeks later the unhappy Isabella wrote to Nelly, now at the Grange, asking whether her husband was man or devil. Nelly went to see her and was induced by Heathcliff to arrange a meeting between him and Cathy, who had been ill in bed since the men had quarreled.

Heathcliff saw that she was dying. "You and Edgar have killed me," she told him, then sobbingly admitted that she had done wrong, after Heathcliff asked by what right she had left him when she loved him. That night she died in giving birth to her child, Catherine Linton.

Heathcliff dashed his head against a tree, calling on Cathy's ghost to haunt him and crying: "Only do not leave me in this abyss, where I cannot find you!"

Soon afterward Isabella fled to London, where her son Linton, a sickly creature, was born, and where she died a dozen years later. Linton was brought to Thrushcross Grange, about the time that Hindley Earnshaw finished drinking himself to death after mortgaging all his property to Heathcliff.

Now Heathcliff's purpose became apparent—to destroy the Earnshaw family and unite the Heights and Grange estates. He kept Hareton as a bemused dependent, ignorant that Heathcliff was his father's enemy. Heathcliff brought his son Linton home from the Grange, terrorized him into slavery, and arranged a marriage between him and young Catherine. Shortly came the deaths of Catherine's father and of her husband, who had been led to bequeath all his property to Heathcliff.

Thus came about the situation which Mr. Lockwood had found.

Some time later, on a trip north, Mr. Lockwood revisited the Heights. He found that Heathcliff had died. Catherine Linton had won over the untutored Hareton, and they planned to wed. Heathcliff had at first been angry at their friendship, then calmed down. "Nelly, there is a strange change approaching; I'm in its shadow," he said. And soon after he was found dead in bed.

The Last Days of Pompeii

By EDWARD BULWER-LYTTON

THE SON OF *Gen. Earle Bulwer, Edward George Earle Bulwer was born in London on May 25, 1805, and assumed his mother's family name of Lytton on her death in 1843. A precocious poet, he entered into an unhappy marriage when 22, which did not restrain his tremendous output of novels, poetry, and highly successful plays. In later years he served in Parliament and the British Cabinet, and in 1866 was made Baron Lytton. He died Jan. 18, 1873.*

POMPEII, the walled pleasure city of the great men of the Roman Empire, contained within its narrow limits every luxury of its day. In its minute shops, tiny palaces, its forum, theatre and circus, you beheld in miniature the energy and corruption of an empire.

On the glassy Bay of Naples were fishing and commercial vessels, the gilded galleys of the rich, and in the distance the fleet under Pliny's command.

Glaucus the Athenian, newly returned from Naples, sat on the beach with Clodius the aedile, who kept his purse filled with money won at gambling from the handsome Greek, who despised wealth as long as Rome held his city in thrall. They spoke of love, and Glaucus denied wanting to marry beautiful Julia, who was wealthy and adored him.

The Greek told of meeting several months earlier, in the

temple of Minerva at Naples, a beautiful maiden of Athenian descent who had been led away by a youth before Glaucus could learn her name. Unable to find her again, he had given himself up to pleasures.

But that night in Pompeii, Glaucus met Ione again, and knew that he loved her. The maiden and her brother Apaecides were the wards of Arbaces, a wealthy Egyptian, a sensualist and follower of the occult. Arbaces hoped to make Ione his, and sought to increase her confidence in him by displaying his store of knowledge. Arbaces put Apaecides among the priests of Isis, under the special care of one Calenus.

The Egyptian did not like to show himself too often to his ward, so he was not aware of the close bonds that grew between Ione and Glaucus, who were meeting daily. When Arbaces found out, he attempted to disparage the Athenian, and invited Ione to his home. There he greeted her with great respect, and she had no fear of him when he declared his love. "I love another," she said blushingly. Then Arbaces disclosed the violence of his nature, and said in a dreadful whisper: "Thou shalt go to thy tomb rather than to his arms."

A blind flower girl, Nydia, a Thessalian whom Glaucus had bought to save her from cruelty, was an attendant of Ione. Though she loved Glaucus, her loyalty to him was such that she warned the Athenian and Apaecides of the tryst at Arbaces' home. The lover and brother arrived barely in time to save Ione from the Egyptian.

Now Arbaces gave Julia a "love potion" for Glaucus which in reality was a poison which would drive the drinker mad. Nydia, jealous of Ione, stole the potion and herself gave it to Glaucus. He drank it in the evening, and began to leap about and babble, ending by running out into the starlit night.

The next morning the Egyptian encountered Apaecides in the street, quarreled with him and stabbed him. At this moment Glaucus came along and Arbaces knocked him down, dipped his enemy's stilus into the youth's blood, and loudly accused

Glaucus of the crime. Still under the influence of the poison, the Greek was jailed, while the Egyptian made prisoners of Calenus and Nydia, who knew of his plot.

Sentenced to fight a lion with his stilus in the amphitheatre, Glaucus was led before the multitude. He crouched to await the rush of the beast, but the lion seemed astonishingly unaware of his presence. It tried to escape from the arena, then returned listlessly to its cage.

As the keeper was about to goad the lion out again, a loud cry was heard at one entrance of the arena. All eyes turned in that direction as Sallust, a friend of Glaucus, appeared on the senatorial benches and shouted: "Remove the Athenian; he is innocent! Arrest Arbaces; he is the murderer!"

Challenged, Sallust pushed forward Calenus, haggard and starved, who faced the Egyptian, called him the murderer, and told the crowd: "These eyes saw him deal the blow."

"A miracle!" shouted the people. "Arbaces to the lion!"

This was the work of blind Nydia. Her efforts to escape having been in vain, she had bribed her keeper to carry a message to Sallust, and he had gone with his servants to Arbaces' house, freed the captives, and arrived with them at the arena in the very nick of time.

The crowd was rushing toward Arbaces when, right above them, he beheld a strange and awful apparition, and his courage was restored. He stretched his hand on high and shouted with a voice of thunder:

"Behold how the gods protect the guiltless! The fires of the avenging Orcus burst forth against the false witness of my accusers!"

The eyes of the crowd followed his gesture and beheld with dismay a vast vapor shooting from the summit of Vesuvius in the form of a gigantic pine tree; the trunk blackness, the branches fire—a fire that shifted and wavered in its hues with every moment, now fiercely luminous, now of a dull red. The earth shook. The walls of the theatre trembled. In the distance was heard the crash of falling roofs. The cloud seemed to roll toward the assembly, casting forth showers of ashes mixed with fragments of burning stone. Then the blazing mountain cast up columns of boiling water.

In this ghastly scene, all thought of justice and of Arbaces left the minds of the terrified people. There ensued a mad flight for the sea through the doomed city. A darkness as of the blackest night blotted out the daylight, and through it Nydia guided Glaucus, now partly recovered from the poison he had drunk, and Ione. Nydia's blindness enabled her to direct the others; to her alone was the scene familiar.

While Arbaces perished with the majority of the inhabitants of Pompeii, these three gained the shore and got aboard a boat. Utterly exhausted, Glaucus fell asleep on deck with Ione's head on his breast and Nydia lying at his feet.

Showers of dust and ashes fell into the waves, scattered their snows over the decks of the ships, and were borne by the winds into the remotest climes, startling the people of Africa, and whirling along the soil of Syria.

At last the dawn cast its light over the troubled sea. There was no shout of joy from the mariners—they were too wearied for that—but there was a low, deep murmur of thankfulness as the watchers of the long night took heart and felt once more that there was a God above them.

In the silence of the general sleep Nydia had risen gently. Bending over the face of Glaucus, she softly kissed him. She felt for his hand, and sighed when she found it locked in Ione's. With her hair she wiped from his brow the damps of night.

"May you be happy with your beloved one," she murmured. "May you sometimes remember Nydia! Alas, she is of no further use on earth."

She turned away, and a sailor, half-drowsing on the deck, heard a slight splash on the waters. He looked up, and fancied he saw something white above the waves, but it vanished in an instant. He turned round and dreamed again.

When the lovers awoke, they could find no trace of Nydia. They guessed her fate in silence, forgot their own deliverance, and wept as for a departed sister.

The Pilgrim's Progress

By JOHN BUNYAN

JOHN BUNYAN, *son of a tinker, was born at Elstow, England, in November, 1628. He had a scanty education, and fought for a year in the Civil Wars when only 17. Then he married a pious woman and, after a variety of religious experiences, in 1655 joined the Baptist congregation at Bedford, soon becoming its pastor and attracting great crowds. In 1660 he was thrown into jail as a dissenter, doing much writing while remaining there 12 years. After his release he resumed preaching. He died of fever on Aug. 31, 1688, while on a trip to London.*

As I WALKED through the wilderness of this world, I laid me down in a certain place to sleep; and I dreamed a dream. I saw a man, clothed with rags, turning away from his own house, a book in his hand, and a great burden upon his back.

He cried out that his city was to be burned with fire from heaven, but he could not tell what road to take. His relations thought some distemper had got into his head, but a man named Evangelist said: "Go knock at yonder wicket gate." The man began to run toward the gate, crying, "Eternal life!" but two neighbors pursued and overtook him.

"Friend Christian, why are you hurrying from the City of Destruction?" asked Obstinate. When Christian told of the fire to come, Obstinate returned home in scorn, but Pliable resolved to go with him. Not looking where they were going, they fell into the Slough of Despond, and Christian began to sink with the burden on his back. With a desperate effort Pliable got out and went back. Then a man named Help drew Christian out, and set him upon sound ground.

Now Mr. Worldly Wiseman turned Christian aside from the path to the wicket gate, telling him that Mr. Legality and Mr. Civility, in the village of Morality, could relieve him of his burden. But Evangelist came up to Christian, told him Mr. Legality was a cheat and Mr. Civility a hypocrite, and put him back on the true path.

At the gate, over which was written, "Knock, and it shall be opened unto you," a person named Goodwill pointed onward and told Christian: "Do you see that narrow way? Keep to it, and do not turn down any of the wide and crooked roads, and you will soon come to the place of deliverance." Up the narrow way Christian came to a cross, and his burden fell from off his back, and he leaped for joy. At nightfall he came to the House Beautiful, where four lovely damsels named Charity, Discretion, Prudence, and Piety fed him, gave him a peaceful bed, and in the morning clothed him in armor and gave him a good sword.

Then Christian went down into the Valley of Humiliation, where a foul fiend, Apollyon, blocked the way and said: "Prepare to die!" Wounded by flaming darts, Christian drove the fiend away after half a day by a last deadly thrust. Healing his wounds with leaves from the Tree of Life, Christian marched into the next valley, called the Valley of the Shadow of Death.

On the right hand was a very deep ditch, into which the blind have led the blind to perish in all ages; on the left a dangerous quagmire in which even a good man can find no bottom. Christian held to the exceeding narrow and very dark way, past the mouth of hell, whose hosts he banished by crying: "I will walk in the strength of the Lord God!" Day broke, and he got up with another pilgrim named Faithful, a neighbor from the City of Destruction.

They came to the town of Vanity, and could not avoid seeing Vanity Fair, which is kept all the year long, set up by Beelzebub and the other fiends. Everybody mocked at them, and when they answered gravely they were taunted, arrested as disturbers of the peace, and beaten. Christian escaped, with the aid of one called Hopeful, but Faithful was burned at the stake for high treason to Beelzebub; then the Shining Ones came with a chariot and horses, and carried off Faithful to the Celestial City. Hopeful went on with Christian.

They found much content in a delicate plain called Ease, but Hopeful had to be led away from the silver mine called Lucre, where many men had been smothered. Now they came to the River of Life, and drank the water and ate fruit and slept and were refreshed. But the way soon grew stony, and Christian persuaded Hopeful to turn aside into By-Path Meadow. Soon it began to grow stormy and dark, and they reached Doubting Castle, whose lord, Giant Despair, threw them into a dismal dungeon.

Though the giant flogged them, they lived, so he tried to persuade his prisoners to kill themselves. But Christian and Hopeful prayed earnestly; then Christian bethought himself of a key called Promise which he carried in his bosom. It opened the doors of the castle and the prisoners escaped, Giant Despair being unable to follow because the bright sunshine made him helpless.

Back on the rough and stony way, Christian and Hopeful came to the Delectable Mountains, where four shepherds led them to the top of the highest peak, called Clear, and showed them the gate of the Celestial City far off. Down the mountains the narrow way branched, and a black man in a white robe offered to lead them the true way. Instead they were entangled in a net, from which a Shining One let them out, telling them their guide was Flatterer, a false apostle. The Shining One chastised them, to teach them to walk in the good way.

Singing for very joy, the pilgrims now passed through the Enchanted Land, full of vapors that made them dull and sleepy, into the sweet and pleasant country of Beulah, where the sun shone night and day, and the air was so clear that they could see the Celestial City. As they drew near to the city their strength began to fail. It was built of pearls and precious stones, and the streets were paved with gold, and Christian and Hopeful grew sick with desire as they beheld it.

They came at last to the gate of the city. But before it was a river, and the river was very deep, and no bridge went over it. The Shining Ones told Christian: "You will find the river deeper or shallower, according to the depth or shallowness of your belief in the King of our city." The pilgrims then entered the river.

Christian at once began to sink and cried out: "The billows go over my head!" Hopeful answered: "Be of good cheer, my brother, I feel the bottom, and it is good!"

With that a great horror and darkness fell upon Christian; he could no longer see before him, and he was in much fear that he would perish in the river. When he recovered, he found he had got to the other side, and Hopeful was already there. The pilgrims went up the mighty hill to the city with ease, because they had left their mortal garments behind them in the river.

A company of the heavenly hosts welcomed them, and the gate was opened wide, and the two pilgrims entered and had raiment put on that shone like gold, and Shining Ones gave them harps to praise their King with.

And after that they shut up the gates, at the sight of which I had wished myself among them. Then I awoke, and behold! it was a dream.

The Way of All Flesh

By SAMUEL BUTLER

SAMUEL BUTLER *was born Dec. 4, 1835, in Nottinghamshire, England, the grandson of a Church of England bishop. He went through St. John's College, Cambridge, then did parish work among the London poor. Breaking away from this, he ran a sheep farm successfully in New Zealand from 1859 to 1864, then returned to London and won recognition as a painter, exhibiting some of his paintings in the Royal Academy. "The Way of All Flesh" is the best known of his books, which are iconoclastic in their attitude toward everything the Victorians cherished. He died in London on June 18, 1902.*

OLD JOHN PONTIFEX, carpenter in Paleham village, died moderately well off, leaving a son George who had made a comfortable fortune in London, publishing religious books.

George had five children, Eliza, Maria, John, Theobald, and Alethea. Like all middle-class parents of his day, he thrashed his boys to drive the self-will out of them.

Timid Theobald was packed off to Cambridge to study for ordination. He weakly attempted to rebel and was promptly put in his place, and took his holy orders.

Meanwhile Mr. Allaby, rector of Crampford, eight miles from Cambridge, had to find husbands for five unmarried daughters. He hired Theobald as an assistant, and the daughters played cards to determine who should have him. The winner was Christina, aged 27—four years older than Theobald.

The inexperienced Theobald was easy game. After several months' courtship there was nothing for him to do but propose, and to marry Christina, when, after a five-year engagement, he got a £500 living at Battersby-on-the-Hill. George settled £10,000 on the couple.

Theobald, grown in self-confidence, won the first argument, and thereafter Christina was his faithful servant, convincing herself that she was married to a paragon of virtue and scholarship. Their first son, Ernest, was born Sept. 6, 1835. Then old George died, leaving Theobald £17,500 after deducting £2,500 as a bequest to Ernest—for which Ernest's father never forgave his son.

Ernest was put to studying at 3, and at 5 was learning Greek and Latin. Beatings were his lot whenever he displeased his father—Mr. Overton, Ernest's godfather, witnessed one such scene when the boy, unable to pronounce "come," persisted in saying "tum." Ernest acquired only fear of his father.

At 12 Ernest was sent to Dr. Skinner's school at Roughborough. He went starved by an unbalanced diet of too much study and severity, and almost no kindness and understanding. He was sure that he was wicked for displeasing his father so much, and for preferring music to Greek.

Ernest found school not so unpleasant, but never lifted himself above the borderline between the reputable and disreputable boys.

Meanwhile Ernest's Aunt Alethea decided he was the only one of her relatives worth attention. She left her London literary circle and moved to Roughborough, where she gave Ernest his first happy days, encouraging his love for music and finding exercise for his puny body. But within a year Alethea died, leaving £15,000 to Mr. Overton, with the secret understanding that Ernest was to have it when he reached 28.

During a school holiday Ernest lost his last faith in his parents. Ellen, a Pontifex maid, found to be with child, was sent off summarily. Pitying Ernest gave her all his money and his watch. Found out, he was deprived of most of his allowance. This left him unable to pay his small debts in the Roughborough shops,

and his father forced out the whole story of petty schoolboy
iniquities—smoking, drinking beer, running up tiny debts. All
this, told in confidence, was passed on to Dr. Skinner by Theobald. Ernest, punished, became a school martyr, to his surprise.

Ernest went on to Emanuel College, Cambridge, where for the
first time he was consciously and continuously happy. He created
a stir by an article attacking the Greek dramatists, won a small
scholarship, and got his degree. Though he had come into £5,000,
his accumulated bequest from his grandfather, he did not comprehend that he was independent, and went on preparing for a
church career he did not particularly want.

After being ordained, Ernest fell into the hands of Pryer, a High
Church fellow-curate in the poor London parish to which Ernest
had been sent.

Hoping to increase his £5,000 and found a High Church college,
Ernest put it in Pryer's hands for speculation in stocks. Meanwhile Ernest moved into lodgings to be near the poor people.
Innocent of the world, he tried to convert a Methodist couple and
was nearly converted himself, and tried to reform a freethinker
and got his first doubts of the Bible's infallibility.

Then he decided to reform a dancer, was interrupted by the entrance of an amused former Cambridge fellow-student, suddenly
realized it was something else he wanted, visited another girl who
was reputed loose in her morals—and found he had been misin-
formed. In 10 minutes he was in a policeman's hands, charged
with assault, and Mr. Overton was unable to save him from six
months in prison.

The shock threw Ernest into a near-fatal illness, and when he
recovered he decided to start again in Australia. But Pryer had
absconded with all of Ernest's money. Ernest, unable to emigrate,
learned tailoring rather than attempt to be a gentleman on suffer-
ance.

Theobald and Christina, full of false forgiveness, waylaid him
as he was freed from prison—and were told he never wanted to
see them again. He had decided he could succeed only if he cut

himself away from a family that would insist on his being conventional, and trip him up if he tried to stand on his own feet.

Ernest met Ellen, his parents' banished maid, fell unwisely in love with her, and married her. With Mr. Overton's help he set up a tailoring shop that was a success until Ellen fell into drinking ways. The unhappy Ernest, nearly prostrated, was rescued by learning that Ellen had married him bigamously. He made Ellen an allowance, and put their two illegitimate children out to board with a simple poor family.

Low in mind and ill, Ernest was nursed back to health through Mr. Overton's care, and in a year and a half received his inheritance, grown to £70,000. His life had been a series of defeats until now, but he had learned from them.

Christina fell mortally ill, and Ernest went back to his family, annoying his father by being independently wealthy.

Ernest never married again. He filled his days with travel and publishing irreverent books that his money made it possible for him to write.

The Moonstone

By WILKIE COLLINS

WILLIAM WILKIE COLLINS *was born into the family of William Collins, an English painter, on January 8, 1824, in London. After studying for the bar Collins turned to journalism, in which he immediately enjoyed a fair success. He gained real fame with his novels, and may be called the father of the modern detective novel. Charles Dickens was a close friend of his, and the two collaborated on the writing of "No Thoroughfare." Collins traveled through America in the seventies, lecturing and reading excerpts from his works. He died on September 23, 1889.*

THE MOONSTONE, a yellow diamond appraised at 20,000 pounds, and once adorning the brow of a Hindoo Moon-god idol at the Indian city of Somnauth, was a fabulous gift for a young English girl to receive on her eighteenth birthday. But Miss Rachel Verinder did not realize when the gem came into her possession, that revenge, and not magnanimity, had prompted the gift; her profligate uncle, John Herncastle, who had obtained the Moonstone in India by murder and theft, and who was well aware that ill-luck attended possession of the jewel, bequeathed it to the girl to avenge himself for the slight put upon him by Lady Julia, Rachel's mother, when she refused to receive him.

But if Rachel was unaware of the danger threatening her, Lady Julia, young Franklin Blake, Rachel's cousin and suitor, and the trusted family steward, old Gabriel Betteredge, were not. They knew well the legend that hereditary Indian priests had followed the Moonstone to England and were waiting the opportunity to restore it to its original home, by fair means or foul. What was the consternation of old Gabriel and Franklin Blake when they discovered three Indian jugglers near the premises!

By the evening of Rachel's birthday dinner the household was tense and anxious and other circumstances had arisen to increase the ominous atmosphere. A maid in the house, Rosanna Spearman, lame, ill-favored and a reformed criminal, had fallen passionately in love with Franklin Blake; Rachel had refused an offer of marriage from handsome Godfrey Ablewhite, also a cousin, a serious young man greatly influential in charitable and religious circles. Despite the tension the birthday dinner passed without untoward incident except for the reappearance of the Indian jugglers, and the household soon afterward retired.

But in the morning it was discovered that the Moonstone had disappeared from Miss Rachel's room. Lady Julia and Franklin Blake immediately summoned the police but what was their surprise when Rachel refused to co-operate in any way! Her manner became secretive and bitter and she treated Franklin Blake, once her favored suitor, with marked coldness. After detaining the Indian jugglers, who were found to have an alibi for the night of the theft, and searching the servants' quarters, the police found themselves at an impasse.

Sergeant Cuff, a famous London detective, was called in; he was able to fix the time of the theft by a smear on a freshly painted door in Miss Rachel's sitting room, and started a search for the paint-smeared garment which should betray the thief. But once more Miss Rachel intervened, and the search was not conducted. Sergeant Cuff, suspicious that Rachel with Rosanna Spearman as confederate—Cuff was convinced that Rosanna had made away with the paint-smeared garment and had substituted a new one of her own making—had "stolen" the Moonstone to pay off secret debts, told Lady Julia of his theory and she declined to carry the investigation further. Rachel fled to London; and Franklin Blake, heartbroken by his beloved's sudden coldness, left the country to travel abroad.

Rosanna Spearman circumvented Cuff's efforts to learn her secret by flinging herself into the quicksand along the shore, leaving only a farewell note for Franklin Blake. Since no one knew the young man's whereabouts, Sergeant Cuff had to admit that the investigation was at a stalemate. So off he went, first prophesying that the Moonstone would next turn up in the hands of one Septimus Luker, a money-lender and not over-scrupulous dealer in gems.

For the next months no trace of the Moonstone was found and Rachel, residing quietly in London with her mother, still refused to explain her strange behavior at the time of the theft. But Luker, the jewel-fence whose eventual possession of the Moonstone had been predicted by Cuff, was observed to have placed in pledge for a year some valuable object, the exact nature of which could not be ascertained. And coincident with this deposit came a mysterious attack on Luker's person, during which he was overpowered and searched. But the strangest circumstance was that Godfrey Ablewhite, Rachel's respectable and charitably-minded cousin, had been made the victim of a similar attack.

Rumors arose questioning Godfrey's character, but Rachel, obviously unhappily possessed of some secret knowledge, announced herself ready to swear to Godfrey's innocence of the theft. To complete the girl's unhappiness Lady Julia died suddenly, and Rachel, in an effort to forget one whom she considered unworthy of her love—the absent Franklin Blake—promised to marry Godfrey Ablewhite. Then, finding that Godfrey had made secret inquiries concerning her financial position, she broke off the engagement and retired to live quietly with an elderly female relative.

And still no trace of the Moonstone! Those interested—old Gabriel Betteredge, Mr. Bruff, the Verinder family solicitor, and the three Indians who still lurked in the environs of London—waited eagerly for the day to arrive when Luker would redeem his pledge, and the Moonstone (if such Mr. Luker's mysterious object was) would once more be accessible.

Active interest in solving the mystery was revived when Franklin Blake, summoned back to England on his father's death, sought audience with Rachel and was refused! Determined to find the Moonstone and thus win back the girl's love, Franklin returned to the Verinder home to start his search there. He found waiting for him Rosanna Spearman's last note, declaring her love and directing him to where she had hidden a small box. Franklin eagerly opened the box, feeling sure it would contain a valuable clue—and discovered the paint-smeared garment which Sergeant Cuff had said would point out the diamond-thief. To the young man's horror he found that the name on the garment was—his own! And to his despair, Rachel, whom he finally managed to trick into an interview, declared that she had, with her own eyes, seen him take the Moonstone.

The explanation of this almost unbelievable occurrence was hit upon accidentally by one Ezra Jennings, a doctor who because of a painful disease had become addicted to the use of opium. By experimentation Jennings was able to prove that Franklin Blake, under the influence of opium administered by the former doctor of the village as a practical joke, had taken the gem in order to put it in a safe place. But where was the jewel now? How had it found its way into the hands of the redoubtable Luker? Rachel and Franklin, now reconciled, could only await the day when Luker was to remove his treasure from the safety vault.

When the day arrived Mr. Luker called for his pledge and was seen to pass it secretly to a dark and bearded sailor, who made off with it and was observed to put up for the night at a sailors' hostelry. But the next day, when Franklin Blake and Mr. Bruff arrived to snare their suspect, the sailor was found smothered, the treasure gone. Upon examination the murdered sailor proved to be none other than Godfrey Ablewhite disguised! Harried by debts and obligations (he was found to have been living a double life), he had stolen the stone from the drugged Franklin Blake the night of the birthday dinner. Thus the mystery was solved, but the diamond gone forever. The Indians had at last fulfilled their mission and had taken the Moonstone safely back to its home in the temple at Somnauth.

The Woman in White

By WILKIE COLLINS

THROUGH the good offices of an Italian friend, one Professor Pesca, young Walter Hartright, draughtsman and artist, found a position as drawing instructor at Limmeridge House. It was on the night before he entered into his new duties that Walter first encountered the woman in white. While wandering on the heath in the gloaming he was accosted by a lone woman, pale, beautiful, draped in white diaphanous garments. The woman asked to be directed toward the London road, evinced much fear of her surroundings, and with hesitating gratitude accepted Walter's escort to a carriage. She surprised Walter with a knowledge of the Fairlies, his new employers, and mentioned a baronet of Hampshire whom she obviously greatly feared. At her departure Walter was shocked to learn that she was an inmate escaped from a lunatic asylum.

Walter found his new position more than pleasant. Frederick Fairlie, master of Limmeridge, was a recluse and hypochondriac, but his nieces, Laura Fairlie, whose face was strangely familiar to Walter, and Marian, Laura's half-sister, were charming girls and apt pupils. Laura was a beautiful, fair-haired young woman, heiress to a great fortune; Marian was an independent, boyish, strong-minded person with whom Walter struck up an immediate friendship. The two girls were devoted to one another.

Walter's strange adventure with the woman in white haunted his memory, and he confided the story to Marian. She, in turn, told him of an old letter of her dead mother's which referred to the resemblance of the woman in white, one Anne Catherick, to Laura.

Walter's happiness at Limmeridge House ended when he learned that Laura, with whom he had fallen deeply in love, was shortly to marry Sir Percival Glyde of Hampshire. Laura received an anonymous letter warning her against Sir Percival, and Walter discovered that Anne Catherick had written it. To forget his disappointment in love Walter left for South America. What he did not know was that Laura, secretly returning his passion, had asked Sir Percival to release her from her engagement and had been refused.

Sir Percival Glyde admitted that it had been he who had had Anne incarcerated in a lunatic asylum but maintained that she was truly insane. He insisted that a settlement be made leaving him sole heir to Laura's estate should she pre-decease him. The unhappy marriage was concluded.

Six months passed and Marian visited Laura, now Lady Glyde, at her home in Hampshire. Laura had changed. Obviously her marriage was not a success and she hated and feared her husband. But far more fearsome to Marian than Sir Percival was a man who apparently had become a permanent part of the household—Count Fosco. Count Fosco was a huge man, soft-spoken, with strange magnetic eyes and an almost hypnotic power over his wife who was, incidentally, Laura's aunt and heir. Count Fosco seemed to have a great fear of his countrymen for he seemed relieved to learn that no other Italians lived in the neighborhood.

Events became steadily more mysterious to Marian. Anne Catherick, the woman in white, appeared again and promised to tell Laura a secret which would free her from the tyranny of her husband. Sir Percival's cruelty toward Laura stopped short of violence only through the intervention of the malevolent count. In need of money, Sir Percival was trying to get control of his wife's fortune and it was clear that he would not accept her refusal longer. Marian, overhearing a conversation between Sir Percival and Fosco, realized that there was a plot against Laura afoot, but before she could forestall it she became ill of fever and lapsed into helpless delirium. With Laura's friend and champion so neatly out of the way, Count Fosco proceeded with his plan unhindered.

Sir Percival and Count Fosco intercepted a message from Anne Catherick to Laura. Realizing that Anne was now a double menace—for she not only knew Sir Percival's secret, but was also aware of Laura's danger—Count Fosco abducted her and planned to pass her off as Laura. Meanwhile Laura was decoyed to London on pretext of being summoned by the ailing Marian and once there was committed to an insane asylum under the name of Anne Catherick. When the real Anne died she was buried as Lady Glyde. Escape for Laura seemed impossible.

But all was not lost. Marian, upon her recovery, was told of Laura's death. Convinced of foul play she determined to make Laura's "murderer" pay for his crime. In search of evidence she visited the supposed Anne Catherick at the asylum. What was her joy to find that Laura, although ill and despairing, was alive! Marian contrived an escape by bribing a keeper, and the two girls sought to prove Laura's identity. But they were frustrated when Frederick Fairlie refused to believe that Laura was any but Anne Catherick.

Walter Hartright, returning from his travels, was informed of Laura's supposed death. Bidding her a last adieu at her grave, he was approached by two women—Marian, and to his mystified joy, Laura!

The three friends set up a household in London and bent their efforts toward proving Laura's identity.

Walter's first clue came when he discovered that Anne Catherick's mother had had secret meetings with Sir Percival Glyde in the vestry of the church at Welmingham. Suspecting a liaison between Mrs. Catherick and the baronet, Walter found that such was not the case. By examining old records Walter discovered that the marriage between Sir Percival's mother and the old baronet had been falsified. That, indeed, Sir Percival was illegitimate and possessed no right to his titles and estates! This, then, was the secret which the Cathericks had held over Sir Percival's head. Sir Percival, realizing that Walter had discovered the forgery, sought to destroy the damning document, but while doing so, set fire to the church and perished in the flames.

Free of the man she hated, Laura married Walter. The two were very happy but Walter was still determined that his wife should have her rights. Suspicious of Count Fosco's fear of other Italians, Walter pointed out the nobleman to Professor Pesca. Fosco blanched with terror when he saw the professor, and Pesca confided to Walter that he and Fosco had been brothers in a secret society. The society had been betrayed by the count, and had ordained his death. Walter confronted Count Fosco with his knowledge, and, by promising him safe-conduct out of England, was able to exact a confession from him and thus establish Laura's identity.

When the dead Anne's resemblance to Laura had been explained by the fact that she was an illegitimate half-sister, the mystery seemed entirely solved. Fosco met his death in Paris at the hands of the secret society which he had betrayed, and the son of Walter and Laura took his rightful place as heir to Limmeridge House.

Lord Jim

By JOSEPH CONRAD

JOSEPH CONRAD *was born in the Ukraine on December 5, 1857, of a Polish family named Korzeniowski. He grew up in Cracow and spoke and read French fluently at an early age. Influenced by Fenimore Cooper's sea stories, he shipped as a sailor and at the age of seventeen found himself in Marseilles. The year 1878 found him in Lowestoft. He learned the English language easily, and became an officer in the British merchant service. He started to write while convalescing from a bout with Congo fever. Not immediately successful, nevertheless he retired to Kent to devote himself to literature. Toward the end of his life he achieved fame. He died on August 3, 1924.*

THE NATIVES called him Tuan Jim, that is to say, Lord Jim. But that was long afterward. Originally he came from a parsonage, and all through his life there clung to him that air of being "the right kind," of being a gentleman. He was trained on a mercantile marine ship, and it looked as though he were going to make an excellent officer.

Captain Marlow first saw Jim at the investigation of the disgraceful *Patna* affair. The other officers, vulgar and worthless, had run away, but Jim stayed to face the consequences. The officers who comprised the British set were rather distressed to see one of their own class in such a position. They would have preferred it if Jim had bolted—indeed, one of their number offered him enough money to take care of an escape. But it was no go. Some inarticulate obligation to himself made the boy stay on. At least, this was what Marlow could gather as Jim spoke.

Marlow made Jim's acquaintance as one of the sessions ended. Someone referred to a dog in the courtroom as "that wretched cur," and Jim turned around to Marlow in a rage. When Marlow had made him realize that the term had not been directed at him, he stumbled out of the courtroom sick with humiliation at the confession he had made of his own fears. Something about Jim's youth—he was no more than twenty-three or -four—and his clean, blond simplicity moved the older man. He insisted that Jim dine with him. Then he heard the story.

Jim had shipped as mate on the *Patna*. The ship was not seaworthy, and was captained by a dirty, drunken, cowardly old rascal. Its cargo was eight hundred Malayans on a pilgrimage. A suddenly bulging bulkhead warned the officers that the ship must sink almost immediately. It was night. The passengers were asleep. There were eight hundred of them. There were seven lifeboats. She might go under any second. There was no help for the eight hundred. What could help them? Without an alarm, without sound, the white officers—all save Jim—started to launch one of the small boats. They begged him to help them. He stood still, not knowing what to do. Finally the little boat was lowered. At the last moment Jim jumped to safety.

He hated his companions and himself, bitterly.

The *Patna* did not sink. A French gunboat noticed her drifting without direction and brought her into port. The inquiry resulted.

The inquiring board found that the officers of the *Patna* had conducted themselves "in utter disregard of their plain duty," and deprived them all of their certificates.

Marlow found Jim by the waterfront and took him to his room that he might have privacy for a little while. After awhile the

boy's misery abated. Marlow restored his faith in himself by rec-
ommending him to an old friend of his, a rice-mill owner.

Jim did very well in his new job. Marlow's friend grew fond
of him, and Jim's future was assured. Then, by the merest ill
chance, one of the other *Patna* officers drifted into the owner's
employ. Although the man said no word, his manner to Jim was
a torment and a reminder. Jim left abruptly.

Then began a wild and futile chase—Jim worked from town
to town in the East, well liked by all whom he encountered, but
always pursued by the demon within him. And although he tried
to escape the *Patna* incident and no one ever mentioned it to
him, still it was well known and he only deceived himself when
he thought people did not know. So he moved on from place to
place, and Marlow began to despair of his young friend.

As a last resort Marlow went and consulted Stein. Stein was the
head of Stein and Company. He was wealthy, honest, respected
and fearless. He was a merchant. He owed his wealth to an old
Scot, long dead, and was sentimental about the British. He
diagnosed Jim's case immediately. "He is romantic." This was
true. Jim had failed himself, had not lived up to his idea of
himself. This could not be forgiven.

Stein decided to send Jim to a remote island, Patusan, where
Stein and Company had a trading post. If Jim would not be
happy there, at least he would be away from the past. Stein sent
Jim to the island, gave him a ring to present to Doramin, an old
friend of Stein's, and went back to his study of entomology.
Marlow bade Jim good-bye with more emotion than he thought
possible.

When Jim arrived at Patusan the Rajah captured him and held
him prisoner for four days. Jim escaped and called upon Doramin
for help. The Rajah, who also engaged in trade, tried to kill
Jim, but old Doramin stood steadfastly by. Dain Waris, Doramin's
son, and Jim became close friends. A pitched battle on a hill
convinced the Rajah that Jim was there to stay.

When Marlow, two years later, came out to visit Jim, he found that already the young man was a legend. Stories of his invincibility had spread from village to village. The young man had changed. He was surer and graver. He had made a great success at the post.

Jim's predecessor was Cornelius, an abject old man who had been given his job because Stein admired and pitied his beautiful half-caste wife. This woman was now dead and her daughter by a former marriage lived on with the brutal old man because she had no way of escape. This girl was called Jewel by Jim. By the time Marlow arrived the two were already enormously in love. Their romance was full of gravity. They were dependent on each other, and the girl worshiped Jim blindly. Cornelius had offered for eighty dollars to help Jim to escape from the island and, refused, watched Jim succeed with hating eyes.

The girl instinctively hated and feared Marlow, who she was sure had come to take Jim away. When Jim assured her that he was not good enough for the outside world, she did not believe him. When Marlow left, it was with the feeling that he would not see Jim again.

The end came at the height. "Gentleman" Brown, a ruffian outlaw, needed food and money for himself and his crew. He landed on Patusan and tried to attack. But he was held off and finally beleaguered. After Jim had spoken to Brown he decided to let them go. But old Cornelius, with promises of wealth, showed the men a way to ambush the town instead of returning to their boat. In the fighting Dain Waris was killed. The people felt that Jim was responsible. Despite Jewel's pleas, he walked straight through the town and up to the father of Dain Waris, Doramin shot him dead.

Jewel found a refuge in Stein's house, bitter against her dead lover because he left her to die. But Marlow felt that probably the boy had been happy at the end. It was said that before he died he looked about him with a proud and unflinching glance.

Moll Flanders

By DANIEL DEFOE

DANIEL DEFOE, *born in London about 1660, has been called the first English journalist. Educated for the dissenting clergy by his father, a butcher, he became instead a political pamphleteer. At one time a confidant of King William III, he was thrown into prison when his satires became too effective. For a time he published his own newspaper. Always in debt, Defoe died in poverty on April 26, 1731, in Ropemakers' Alley, Moorfields.*

MOLL FLANDERS is not her true name, but it is the one by which some of her worst comrades knew her. Her mother, convicted of felony for a petty theft just before Moll was born, won a reprieve, and after Moll's birth was transported to the plantations, leaving the child with a relation. Moll went with some gypsies and was left by them at Colchester, in Essex, where the parish officers put her in the care of a woman who had a little school.

Terrified that she would be sent into service, when she was eight Moll told her nurse that she wanted to be a "gentlewoman" —by which she meant that she would support herself—and this story was told around, so that Moll became a favorite with the ladies of the town. Thus, when she was almost 14, she was taken to live at the home of one of the ladies, as companion to her two daughters. There Moll continued until she was between 17 and 18, sharing the girls' education and growing into a beauty.

Then the lady's elder son, taking notice of Moll, told her he loved her and by promising marriage made her his mistress, managing the affair with such secrecy that the family knew nothing of it. Moll was truly in love with him, and his generous gifts eased her conscience. Then Robin, her lover's younger brother, destroyed Moll's serenity by openly falling in love with her and proposing marriage against the will of the family.

Moll fell ill when her lover advised her to marry Robin, but at last he convinced her that it was to her interest, and her prudent conduct won the family's consent. Robin married Moll, and in the five years before his death Moll never gave him cause to complain. Robin never acquired much wealth, so Moll was left a widow with £1,200, her two children being taken off her hands by her parents-in-law.

The elder brother now being married, Moll sought a husband in London. She was not averse to a tradesman, but wanted one who was something of a gentleman, too. She was caught in her own snare and married a draper who spent her money in two years and a quarter, then was seized for debt. He promised she would never hear from him again, then escaped and fled to France, leaving Moll to retrieve what goods she could before the creditors got them. She found herself with hardly £500 left, and decided to dress herself as a widow and to take the name of Mrs. Flanders.

Settling with a friend in a part of town frequented by ship captains, Moll sought herself another husband. Her friend contrived a story that she had a fortune, and Moll picked out a man who seemed unlikely to inquire too deeply into such matters. When he protested his love, she declared she was poor and thus was under no obligation when she married him and went with him to his plantation in Virginia. Indeed, by bringing him a few hundred pounds in installments, she exceeded his expectations.

At first happy in Virginia, Moll was horrified to learn that her mother-in-law, who had achieved respectability after being transported to the colony, was in truth her own mother. Moll would no longer live with the husband who was her half-brother, and at length revealed what she knew and returned to England, leaving her two children behind.

On her own again after eight years, Moll Flanders went to live at Bath, while waiting for a cargo that her husband-brother had promised to send her. In a place where men may find a mistress but rarely look for a wife, she passed a season without loss of reputation, until she won the friendship of a gentleman whose wife was distempered in her head. He made Moll gifts of money, and treated her with great respect.

Her gentleman promised that he would take care of Moll if she were with child, and when she was delivered of a fine boy he moved them to London. For six years he maintained Moll in comfort, and then he was taken gravely ill. When he recovered he began to abhor his adultery, and would see Moll no more, though he took the child off her hands and made her a parting gift of £50 in exchange for a general release.

Moll was left in London with about £450 and a stock of clothes and linen. Friendless, she found a bank clerk who was willing to watch over her money for her; in fact, who offered to marry Moll as soon as he could divorce his wife, who had run off with another man. Moll was attracted by his offer, but first she wanted to try her fortune in Lancashire, where a woman friend had told her there was wealth to be found.

Courted by her friend's brother, a man who seemed to live on the scale of £1,000 a year, Moll consented to marry him, but they soon found that both had been cheated. Though they liked each other, Moll and her Lancashire husband agreed that they must separate, he telling her to marry again if she could.

Moll's man of business won his divorce, but she was with child by her latest husband. When her child, a boy, was born Moll put him out to nurse, and went to meet her bank friend, as though she had been in Lancashire the whole time. They married, and lived happily for five years, when the loss of most of his money stabbed Moll's husband so deeply that he died. Now 48, Moll was left with two children and little to live on, so that for two years she worried over every sixpence she spent.

Poverty and temptation were too much; seeing a bundle un-

guarded in an apothecary's shop, Moll carried it off. Other thefts
followed, until Moll fell in again with the woman at whose house
she had stayed before marrying her latest husband. Moll found
that this woman, whom she called her governess, was a pawnbroker and a confidante of thieves. Moll went to live with her,
and learned shoplifting, pocket-picking, and the theft of gold
watches from the ladies' sides.

So dextrous did Moll Flanders become at all kinds of thievery,
and so careful was she at concealing her true name and lodging,
that her name became legendary among the underworld. Indeed,
once she collected £150 in settlement for a false arrest. Although
in a few years Moll had enough money to live without stealing,
her trade had become so fascinating to her that she persisted in
it until disaster struck.

Being caught stealing a piece of silk from a wholesaler's shop,
Moll was unable to buy off the witnesses and was taken to New-
gate. At first sentenced to be hanged, she won a commutation
to transportation through the intercession of a clergyman. While
she was at the prison, she was shocked to see her Lancashire
husband brought in. She talked with him and learned that he
had turned highwayman and had at length been caught. He,
too, was able to win transportation, and they traveled to Virginia
together.

With the fruits of their thefts, Moll and her husband were able
to buy their freedom in the colony and to set up on their own
plantation, from which they returned to England when Moll was
seventy, resolving to spend the remainder of their years in penitence for their wicked lives.

David Copperfield

By CHARLES DICKENS

BORN *Feb. 7, 1812, at Portsea, England, where his father was a naval clerk, Charles John Huffam Dickens knew poverty early. His father was imprisoned for debt, and the boy had to work in a blacking factory. He taught himself shorthand, became a reporter on a London paper, and soon was writing fiction which was an immediate success. Thereafter his life was a series of literary triumphs and domestic crises until he died at Gadshill Place, Kent, on June 9, 1870, weakened by overwork.*

SIX MONTHS before David Copperfield was born, his father died, leaving his girlish wife Clara £105 a year and a servant named Peggotty. The night of David's birth his mother was visited by gruff Miss Betsey Trotwood, his father's aunt, who departed in a huff when she learned the baby was a boy.

For a few years David and his mother and the plump, plain Peggotty were happy together in their home at Blunderstone, Suffolk. Then one day Peggotty took David off to visit her brother Dan, a Yarmouth fisherman. Dan lived in an old beached boat with his nephew Ham, his niece Em'ly, and Mrs. Gummidge, "a lone lorn creetur" who was the widow of a partner of Dan. David grew to like little Emily and the cozy Peggotty home.

When he and Peggotty returned, David found that his mother had married Edward Murdstone, a dark, handsome gentleman who brought his sister Jane to live with them. David was treated with cruel discipline and his mother's gentle spirit was crushed. When the boy rebelled, Mr. Murdstone sent him off to school, where David found new ill treatment at the hands of Mr. Creakle, the bullying master. But he made one friend there, James Steerforth, a handsome fellow-student.

David's school days ended suddenly with the death of his mother, who had pined away under the tyranny of her second marriage. Peggotty was dismissed, and decided to marry Barkis, the town coachman, who had wooed her by sending through David the simple message: "Barkis is willin'." Now David was left in a state of neglect, which was finally broken when, at the age of 10, he was sent off to work in the counting house of Murdstone and Grinby, London wine merchants.

Half-starved, David washed and labeled bottles at the warehouse, and lodged with Mr. and Mrs. Wilkins Micawber and their brood of four children. Mr. Micawber was beset by creditors, but was always expecting something to turn up, though while waiting it was often necessary to pawn the silver. At last Mr. Micawber's affairs reached their crisis and he was thrown into debtors' prison. David had grown to love the impractical Micawbers, and when their home was broken up he resolved to leave London rather than seek another lodging.

Robbed of his money and belongings on the way, David at last reached his Aunt Betsey Trotwood's house at Dover, hungry and disheveled. He found his aunt curt and direct in speech and manner, but she fed and clothed him, and appointed herself his guardian when Mr. Murdstone tried to take him away.

Miss Trotwood soon sent him to school at Canterbury, where he boarded with Mr. Wickfield, her lawyer. The lawyer had a clerk, a carroty-haired, cadaverous youth named Uriah Heep whose groveling manner and clammy hands filled David with disgust. Mr. Wickfield had a sweet-natured, pretty daughter named Agnes, about David's age.

Dr. Strong's school was pleasantly different from Mr. Creakle's, and David graduated with honors. Before deciding on a profession, he went to Yarmouth to call on the Barkises and the Peggottys, meeting Steerforth on the way and taking him along.

They stayed a fortnight, with Steerforth ending by buying a boat and casting his eyes on Emily, now grown to pretty womanhood.

David chose the profession of proctor, and entered the law office of Spenlow and Jorkins. A meeting with Agnes revealed that Uriah Heep had gained such influence over Mr. Wickfield as to be taken into partnership. And in a meeting with Mr. Spenlow's daughter Dora, a girlish, graceful, bright-eyed creature, David lost his heart.

The last illness of Barkis took David to Yarmouth again, and while he was there Emily, who was to have been married to her cousin Ham in a few days, ran off with Steerforth, who she hoped would make her a lady. David, blaming himself for having first taken Steerforth to Yarmouth, returned to London while old Dan Peggotty set out on a search for his niece.

Arriving home, David found that Miss Trotwood had lost her entire fortune. Unable to recover the money that had been paid in for his apprenticeship, David obtained secretarial work and determined to learn shorthand in what time he had left.

Dora had reciprocated David's love, but when Mr. Spenlow found out he forbade the match. Mr. Spenlow died suddenly, and surprisingly left Dora nearly penniless. David, planning for their marriage on his tiny income, tried to induce Dora to learn to cook and manage a house, but her child-like brain couldn't comprehend such matters.

On a trip to Canterbury David found that Mr. Micawber, whom Heep had hired as a clerk, was as much under Uriah's control— as a result of accepting advances on his pay—as was Mr. Wickfield. And Uriah Heep dared to plan to marry Agnes.

David's income now being augmented by literary work and shorthand reporting, he was able to marry Dora shortly after he was twenty-one. They set up their own little home, but David's child bride—even with the help of a servant—couldn't cope with the problems of running it. After patient efforts to teach her, David at last became reconciled to having a wife whose ways were bewitching, though her housekeeping left something wanting.

When illness weakened her it only increased his tenderness toward her.

A disturbed letter from Mr. Micawber summoned David to meet him in London. There he revealed to David and his aunt that he had had enough of Uriah Heep and was ready to expose him as a scoundrel. In the week before the day set for the exposure, Emily reappeared in England after having been cast out by Steerforth, and was reunited with her forgiving uncle.

At the Wickfield home Mr. Micawber had the satisfaction of enumerating, in front of David, Miss Trotwood, Agnes, and Heep himself, the forgeries and thefts by which Heep had stolen Mr. Wickfield's and Miss Trotwood's property, and kept the Wickfields in his power. Her fortune recovered, Miss Trotwood financed a new start for the Micawbers in Australia, and they sailed on the same ship that took Emily and her uncle far from their scenes of sorrow.

But David's joy at this denouement was shattered by the death of Dora, whose body had proved as frail as her heart was light. Agnes comforted David, and induced him to go abroad to ease his mind. Before he left he paid a visit to Yarmouth, only to find a great storm battering a ship just off shore. Ham, Emily's cousin, lost his life in trying to rescue a man clinging to the wreckage. The man's body was washed ashore; it was Steerforth.

After three years in foreign lands, David returned to England. He began to realize that in his boyhood he had thrown away the treasure of Agnes' love, and began vaguely to think that some day he might marry her. But her love for him had been a sisterly love, he reflected, and so put such thoughts aside. Then Betsey Trotwood tricked him into seeing Agnes again, and she confessed that she had never loved any other.

They married, and as their family increased Agnes more than ever acted as the guide and inspiration of David, now a success-ful author.

A Tale of Two Cities

By CHARLES DICKENS

IT WAS the year of Our Lord one thousand seven hundred and seventy-five, and in both England and France it was clear to the lords of the State preserves of loaves and fishes, that things in general were settled forever.

On a cold November night Mr. Jarvis Lorry, of the London banking house of Tellson and Co., was on the road to Dover in the mail coach. There rose before him the wasted face of a man of forty-and-five, and over and over Mr. Lorry seemed to ask this specter: "Buried how long?" "Almost eighteen years." "I hope you are to live?" "I can't say."

At Dover he met a slender golden-haired girl of seventeen, who learned from him for the first time that her father, Dr. Manette, a French physician, was not dead, but had been secretly whisked off to prison before her birth; that her mother, to spare heartbreak for Lucie, when she died fifteen years before had left the child believing her father dead. The bank was the guardian of Lucie's few pounds. And now the doctor was released, and Mr. Lorry was taking Lucie to him at the home of an old family servant in Paris.

The Defarges kept a wine-shop in the St. Antoine district, and in an attic they sheltered Dr. Manette, who sat at a shoemaker's bench and stared blankly at all who spoke to him. To London and safety Lucie and Mr. Lorry took the feeble old man.

It was five years later that Charles Darnay, a young Frenchman, was on trial for his life in the Old Bailey, accused of spying against England. Called as unwilling witnesses against him were the Manettes—the doctor now restored in his mind by Lucie's tender care. The rigged-up case against Darnay was dark, but Sydney Carton, assistant to Mr. Stryver, the prisoner's lawyer, saved the day by pointing out that he and Darnay looked so much alike that mistaken identity could explain away the charges.

Carton was a brilliant and dissipated young man who, having thrown away his own career, lived by preparing the pushing Mr. Stryver's cases for him. Darnay had taken that name and the career of teaching and translating French for Englishmen, in preference to living off the estates of his father's noble family of Evremonde, which had earned hatred by its oppression of the poor of France.

Now Darnay, Carton, and even Stryver became regular visitors at the Manettes' little cottage in Soho, where the doctor again was practicing his profession, though in danger of slipping back into his shoemaking blankness if confronted by a shock. Both the young men were ready to give their hearts to Lucie, but it was Darnay that she chose. It was then that Carton opened his heart to her, asked to be allowed to visit them now and then, and told her: "There is a man who would give his life, to keep a life you love beside you."

Storms of unrest were brewing in France, and Madame Defarge produced much knitting into which she worked a register of those who were to pay for their offenses against the oppressed of her nation. But in England all seemed secure, as the Darnays found joy in a little golden-haired daughter.

Then the Bastille fell, with the Defarges leading those who assaulted it, and for three years blood was shed in France. In 1792 Mr. Lorry was called to Paris to care for the records of Tellson's branch there. And Charles Darnay followed to the same city to rescue the steward who had been arrested though he had tried to aid the peasants, as Charles ordered, from the proceeds of the Evremonde lands.

Mr. Lorry passed through safely, but Charles was seized as a returning aristocrat, and was thrown into lone confinement when it was learned that he was a hated Evremonde.

When word of the arrest reached London, Dr. Manette hastened to Paris with his daughter and grandchild, for he was certain that as a former Bastille prisoner he could exert much influence. They found the city in the hands of a bloodthirsty crew who, remembering years of tyranny, were little disposed toward showing mercy. Though the doctor was treated with immediate respect, and soon became physician to the prisons, he was unable to win his son-in-law's release. For a year Charles was kept alive in his cell, and then the Reign of Terror dawned. Lucie, feeding on hope, had been unable to see her husband.

At last Darnay was taken before the revolutionary tribunal. His life was demanded, and Madame Defarge sat knitting in the first row of seats in the court. Charles proved that he had voluntarily relinquished his station and estates in France, and there was an outcry in his favor when he said that Dr. Manette was his father-in-law. He had returned, he said, to save the life of a French citizen who was in danger. Dr. Manette added to the appeal, and there was a cheer when the jury voted to free Charles.

The Manettes bore Charles off triumphantly to their apartment for a celebration—they did not yet dare to flee to England with him—and then a new blow struck. Charles was arrested again and carried back to prison.

Implacable Madame Defarge had won her revenge. She had been a peasant, and the Evremonde family had destroyed hers by its cruelty. Dr. Manette had been imprisoned when he was preparing to accuse certain Evremondes of ravishing Madame Defarge's sister. She was determined to see the breed exterminated, even to Lucie's little daughter. Dr. Manette had known who Charles was, but had kept a forgiving silence, and Charles had not known what debt his family owed to his father-in-law.

Next day in court Defarge produced a letter which the doctor had written and hidden in his cell in the Bastille, telling the story of his imprisonment and pronouncing a curse on all Evremondes. This time there were no cries for mercy; the jury voted swiftly, and the sentence was death within four-and-twenty hours.

Sydney Carton had just arrived in Paris to see his friends.

He heard of Charles' second arrest, and met a man whom he recognized as an unsavory British character who was now a spy in the revolutionary prisons. Under threat of denunciation, he forced this man to agree to take him to Darnay's cell. Then he gave final instructions to Mr. Lorry, attended Darnay's trial, and gave a farewell kiss to Lucie, who had fainted.

That day, an hour before Charles was to go to the guillotine, Carton stood before him in his cell. They changed clothes, Sydney dictated a final message to Charles, and then the Englishman drugged his unwilling friend into unconsciousness. Charles was carried outside as the hangers-on jeered at the weakness of the English visitor they had seen go inside.

As the cart carrying the condemned left the prison, a coach passed out of Paris carrying Mr. Lorry and his charges—a blank-faced old doctor, a mother and her child, and the man who meant so much to them, carrying the papers of an English lawyer.

Madame Defarge, on her way to knit while Citizen Evremonde lost his head, sought out his wife. Lucie's servant, attempting to conceal that her mistress had fled, struggled with Madame Defarge and the Frenchwoman was killed by her own pistol.

So there was a vacant seat when among the knitting women the tumbrils rolled up to the knife. A young man sat smiling in one cart, comforting a little seamstress who sat beside him. And his face was peaceful as the knife was raised and the knitting women counted. His turn came. The murmuring of many voices, the upturning of many faces, all flashed away. Twenty-Three.

The young man Sydney Carton, so like Charles Darnay in looks that he could take his place, might have made this final utterance:

"It is a far, far better thing that I do, than I have ever done; it is a far, far better rest that I go to than I have ever known."

Oliver Twist

By CHARLES DICKENS

AMONG other public buildings in a certain town is a workhouse in which was born the boy whose name is prefixed to this book. His mother had been found lying in the street exhausted, her shoes worn from walking; the next day she gave birth to Oliver, then died without telling her name.

The orphan was farmed to a branch workhouse three miles off, where nine years of neglect and scant food left him a pale, thin child. On his ninth birthday, Mr. Bumble, the parish beadle, called to take back the boy he called Oliver Twist: "We name our fondlins in alphabetical order. The last was a S—Swubble, I named him. The next one will be Unwin."

Poor Oliver was set to work picking oakum for his education, and he and the other boys got three meals of thin gruel a day. Wild from hunger, the boys cast lots, and Oliver was selected; that evening he rose from the table and advanced to the master, basin in hand, and said:

"Please, sir, I want some more."

The horrified man seized Oliver and took him before the board, which promptly offered five pounds to anybody who would take him off their hands. Mr. Sowerberry, the parochial under-taker, thus acquired an apprentice whom he treated not un-kindly. Oliver, however, was at the mercy of Noah Claypole, the other apprentice, and finally was goaded to fight back when Noah spoke slurringly of Oliver's mother. Flogged for this, Oliver ran away next morning and took the road to London.

Hungry and tired, Oliver was fed by a strange boy who called himself Jack Dawkins, the Artful Dodger, and who took Oliver to a filthy house kept by a shriveled old Jew named Fagin. There were several other boys there, and Oliver was given a meal and put to sleep. The next day he watched the Dodger and a boy named Charley Bates play a game in which they slipped a watch, snuff-box and note-case from Fagin's pockets while he pretended to be a man looking into shop-windows.

Oliver also took part in the game, and after several days begged to be allowed to go to work with the other boys. At length Fagin sent him out with Charley and the Dodger, and Oliver was horrified to see the other boys steal a handkerchief from an old gentleman at a bookstall. In an instant he understood everything; and in his confusion he ran and was caught, while the others got away.

The old gentleman, whose name was Mr. Brownlow, took pity on Oliver when his innocence was established before a magistrate. Now seriously ill, Oliver was nursed back to health at Mr. Brownlow's home. Happy and tenderly treated, he was sent on an errand on the day that his benefactor intended to ask him his history.

But Oliver was seen on the street by Nancy, one of Fagin's crew, and was made a prisoner. Fagin was determined to involve Oliver in a crime in order to have a hold on him, so he turned the boy over to Bill Sikes, Nancy's lover, a hulking and cruel housebreaker. Bill and his accomplice, Toby Crackit, took the boy along to climb through the window of a house they had selected, but their plan went wrong and they had to flee. Oliver, wounded by a shot, was left behind.

The injured boy crawled back to the house and was given haven by the owners, Mrs. Maylie and her niece Rose, who could not believe him a criminal. There Oliver found love and happiness, though he was frightened once when he saw Fagin and a dark, evil-looking young man gazing at him, though no trace could be found of them afterward.

Meantime Mrs. Corney, head-worker of the workhouse where Oliver was born, had been called to the deathbed of the aged woman who had assisted at that birth. From her she took a pawn-ticket with which she regained a wedding ring inscribed "Agnes" and a locket which the old woman had stolen from the body of Oliver's mother. Mr. Bumble, the beadle, had married Mrs. Corney, and one evening the couple was approached by a Mr. Monks, the same man Oliver had seen with Fagin. For £25 Mrs. Bumble yielded the ring and locket, and saw Monks throw it into the river.

Now Nancy overheard Monks offering Fagin money to make a thief of Oliver, who had aroused in her a sympathy which had been submerged by her life of crime. Monks called the boy "my younger brother," vowed to do him harm yet, and laughed that of all persons, Oliver should fall into the Maylies' hands. At great risk, Nancy took this story to Rose, who was in London, nor would Nancy accept money for the information.

Oliver saw Mr. Brownlow again in London, and took the Maylies to him. After the happy reunion, Rose told Mr. Brownlow Nancy's story, and they resolved to discover Oliver's parentage and recover his inheritance for him. With the aid of Harry, Mrs. Maylie's son; Mr. Losborne, the Maylies' doctor; and Mr. Grimwig, Mr. Brownlow's friend, they laid plans to trap Monks. Rose blushed at the inclusion of Harry, for she had refused his hand because she feared an old scandal in her family might hurt his career.

Nancy was followed when she had another meeting with Rose, and on her return the angry Bill Sikes beat her to death despite her cries for mercy. Then Sikes, haunted by the memory of Nancy's eyes, fled into the country. But the murder was the end of Fagin's crew. The Jew soon was taken and hanged for his thefts, and the last ones still at large were trapped in an old hideout. Bill Sikes, who had returned to this refuge, strangled himself attempting to reach the ground with a rope.

Meantime Monks was taken captive by Mr. Brownlow, who recognized him as Edward Leeford, son of his best friend. Confronted by the evidence Oliver's friends had assembled, Leeford broke down and sullenly confessed. His father and mother were ill-suited and had separated, his mother going to the Continent with Edward, who soon fell into evil ways.

Edward's father was called to Rome on business and there sickened. He left behind him a letter to a young woman he had wronged, begging her forgiveness. And he left a will; half his property was to go to Edward, and half to the child of Agnes Fleming, except that if the child was a boy, he would forfeit his inheritance if he stained his name with any public dishonor. Mrs. Leeford burned the will and kept the letter.

Agnes, who was Oliver's mother, left her home and died as we have seen. And Agnes' little sister, left an orphan, was reared by some wretched cottagers, whom Mrs. Leeford hunted out to poison their minds against the girl, telling them she was illegitimate. Then a widow lady saw the child, took pity on her and took her home. The girl was Rose, now revealed as Oliver's aunt, and the widow Mrs. Maylie.

Leeford, living in a low haunt in London, had seen Oliver and recognized his features. While paying Fagin to try to corrupt the boy, Leeford had done his best to obliterate all proof of Oliver's identity.

There was £6,000 left of Leeford's fortune. Oliver took only half and allowed Leeford to go with the remainder to the New World, where he eventually died in prison. Mr. Brownlow adopted Oliver as his son, and Harry took a modest parsonage and married Rose. And Mr. and Mrs. Bumble, deprived of their situations, finally became paupers in that same workhouse where they had lorded it over others.

Pickwick Papers

By CHARLES DICKENS

ON THE MORNING OF MAY 13, 1827, Samuel Pickwick, Esquire, General Chairman of the Pickwick Club of London, set forth in a stage coach on a tour of the countryside. He was accompanied on his journey by the rotund Tracy Tupman, the timid Nathaniel Winkle, and the poetical Augustus Snodgrass. The object of their journey was to note down any interesting occurrences and observations to be reported to the club on their return.

In the same stage was a stranger, who introduced himself as Alfred Jingle. Mr. Jingle's mysterious background and colorful stories provided pleasant entertainment on the road to Rochester.

Arriving at Rochester, they found a grand ball in preparation for that evening. Desirous of attending, Mr. Jingle, unbeknownst to Mr. Winkle, borrowed the latter's dinner suit and wore it to the ball, where he succeeded in offending a certain Doctor Slammer. Early the next morning, Doctor Slammer's second waited on Mr. Winkle and frightened him by calling him out upon the field of honor. However, to Winkle's infinite relief, Doctor Slammer realized that he had the wrong man, and nothing further came of it, as Mr. Jingle had meanwhile disappeared.

Leaving Rochester, the little party journeyed next to pay a visit to the country home of one Mr. Wardle, a friend of Pickwick. In the course of their stay, Mr. Winkle contrived to fall madly in love with a beautiful girl named Arabella Allen, who seemed to return his affection. Then Mr. Jingle suddenly turned up again and, much to everyone's horror, managed to elope with Mr. Wardle's spinster sister, whom Mr. Tupman had been courting. Thanks to Mr. Pickwick's valiant actions, the couple was shortly apprehended in London, and Jingle was bought off for a round sum.

Mr. Pickwick, stopping at the White Hart Inn while arranging these matters, acquired a manservant called Samuel Weller, son of the fat old Tony Weller, coachman on the London stage. Together Mr. Pickwick and Sam returned to Mr. Pickwick's dwelling in Gosling Street, London. Mrs. Bardell, Pickwick's widowed landlady, on being informed of Sam's arrival, somehow managed to mistake Mr. Pickwick's explanation for a declaration of love and a proposal of marriage. She promptly fainted in his arms just as the door opened to admit his three Pickwickian friends.

Mr. Pickwick, deeming it advisable to quit London for a while, traveled to Eatonswill in the company of his friends. At Eatonswill the election was going forward with great rioting between the Buffs, represented by Mr. Horatio Fizkin, of Fizkin Lodge, and the Blues, who had as their candidate the Honorable Samuel Slumkey, of Slumkey Hall. After much excitement and commotion, the Blues came out victorious, and the Honorable Samuel Slumkey, of Slumkey Hall, was joyously returned. Here Mr. Jingle turned up once more, and prepared to elope with a wealthy young lady from a near-by boarding school. Through Mr. Pickwick's efforts, which included getting himself locked in a dark closet, the plan was foiled, and the young lady rescued. Thereupon Mr. Pickwick plainly revealed the rascally Jingle for what he really was, a strolling player in search of a fortune.

Meanwhile, in London, Mrs. Bardell had found two very clever attorneys at law, named Dodson and Fogg. Upon Mr. Pickwick's return to the city, he was immediately served with a legal writ, informing him that he was to be sued in the near future by Mrs. Bardell for breach of promise of marriage.

It was winter now, and Mr. Pickwick and his friends, with Sam Weller, once more visited the Wardle family in the country, this time to spend Christmas vacation with them. Mr. Winkle found himself more madly in love than ever with the attractive Arabella Allen, and they all witnessed the marriage of Mr.

Wardle's charming daughter to a young man by the name of Trundle.

On his return to London, Mr. Pickwick stood his trial in court for breach of promise of marriage. As evidence Sergeant Buzfuz, attorney for the plaintiff, brought forth a note written by Pickwick, requesting chops and tomato sauce for his dinner. The sergeant insisted that these were words of love intended to break the plaintiff's susceptible heart. Mrs. Elizabeth Cluppins was next called. Proceeding, as she put it, in a "permiscuous" manner up the back stairs, she overheard a conversation between the two which she related slowly and at some length. The next witness called was Mr. Nathaniel Winkle. He gave his name, which the little judge, Justice Starleigh, immediately wrote down as Daniel.

"Daniel Nathaniel, or Nathaniel Daniel?" asked the judge.

"Neither, my lord," replied Winkle, blushing, "just Nathaniel."

"Then why did you tell me Daniel?"

"I didn't, my lord."

"You must have," said the little judge, "or else how could I have got Daniel in my notes?"

The counsel for the plaintiff then proceeded to heckle and harass Nathaniel Winkle, who became suddenly too eloquent and managed to do a considerable amount of damage to Mr. Pickwick's case.

Sam Weller was next called, and with many loud promptings from his father, told his evidence, which turned out to be very unimportant, and did nothing at all to affect the minds of the jury. In reply to a question concerning why he did not see what was going on, Sam replied calmly that having eyes, and not a pair of patent double million magnifying-glass microscopes, of extra power, he was unable to see through a flight of stairs and a deal door.

The jury retired to consider their verdict, and the judge retired to his chambers, where he refreshed himself with a cold chop and a glass of sherry.

Upon the jury's return, they were asked for their verdict. The foreman announced that they found the defendant Pickwick guilty, and calling him before the bar, the judge pronounced heavy damages. Mr. Pickwick, furious at being thus condemned, stated plainly that he definitely refused to pay a pound, a shilling, or a penny, and they might sentence him to prison for the rest of his life before he would pay so much as a penny.

Mr. Pickwick left immediately for Bath, where he met some interesting people, and spent a quiet month, taking the waters daily.

Returning to London, he was shortly incarcerated in Fleet Prison for debtors. After a while he was able to get a room by himself, which he had furnished, and so lived fairly in comfort for three months. The faithful manservant, Sam Weller, arranged with his father to get himself locked up also, and so was able to attend upon him as before.

In prison they met the villainous Jingle, with his servant. The pair had sold all their clothes for food, and were near starvation. Mr. Pickwick, whose kind heart overcame his former sentiments, gave them money and food, and promised to help them when he got out of jail.

One day shortly thereafter, Dodson and Fogg, having failed to collect from Pickwick, had Mrs. Bardell and her son thrown into Fleet Prison also. This again touched the heart of the benevolent Pickwick, and he stood their bail.

At length he paid the costs and was set free, taking Jingle with him. Pickwick then went to the country to help Winkle elope with his love. Snodgrass married an attractive girl. Sam Weller married a housemaid and they both continued in Pickwick's employ.

Tired of traveling, Mr. Pickwick settled down in a house in the suburbs, and stood as godfather to all the children of his friends. Thus in peace and contentment he passed all his days, together with his friends and his faithful servant, Sam Weller.

Trilby

By GEORGE DU MAURIER

GEORGE DU MAURIER *was born in Paris on March 6, 1834. His father took his family to England when his son was quite young, but soon returned to France where George was educated in science. In 1856 his father died, and his scientific career came to an end. After that he studied art in Paris and Antwerp and then went to England where he began to contribute drawings to English magazines. He succeeded John Leech on* Punch *and also illustrated the serializations of many famous novels of his day. His first novel was* Peter Ibbetson, *which was followed by his greatest success,* Trilby, *the publication of which began in 1894. He died in London of an inflammation of the heart on Oct. 6, 1896.*

THE Latin Quarter of Paris in the middle of the last century was the mecca toward which every aspiring artist sooner or later wended his way. One fine, showery day in April, three Englishmen were enjoying the studio they had just furnished on the Place St. Anatole des Arts. One of them was a tall, athletic Yorkshireman, once a bearer of a commission in the Crimean campaign, but feeling within himself an irresistible avocation for art, had left the army for Paris and was now painting. He was called Taffy.

The second was called the Laird of Cockpen—a Scotsman of respectable parentage whose fondness for painting toreadors had taken him to Paris. The third was small and slender, graceful and well-built, and the possessor of a real talent, which could not be said for the other two. Little Billee had been brought up and educated at home; his widowed mother and sister now lived in Devonshire. He was the youngest of the three, and Taffy had an especially tender feeling for Little Billee because of his innocence and charm.

One afternoon the three Englishmen were visited by the musician Svengali and his sole intimate, Gecko, a little nondescript who played the violin. Svengali was a tall, bony individual, of Jewish aspect, well-featured but sinister. He was shabbily dressed and dirty, spoke a fluent French with a heavy German accent, had a sharp wit and enchanted his listeners with his playing of Chopin.

Suddenly came a loud rapping at the door, and a voice of great volume uttered the British milkman's cry, "Milk below!" In walked a young girl, clad in the overcoat of a French soldier, below which showed a short, striped petticoat. She had fine features, and the men saw at a glance that she was simple, humorous, brave and kind, and accustomed to a genial welcome wherever she went.

She introduced herself as Trilby O'Ferrall. And they soon learned that she modeled in the Quarter and was famous for her beautiful feet. To amuse them she sang the old song "Alice Ben Bolt." Though she sang off-key they were all astonished at the quality of her voice. Svengali especially seemed impressed by the voice, and he went on to tell them of his interest in singing and his long but frustrated ambition to become a singer.

Trilby returned to the studio many times. They learned from her that her father and mother were dead, and that she was taking care of her small brother. Her father was an educated man of good family, who had slowly drunk himself to his grave—her mother, a Scotch girl who had once been a barmaid in Paris. Trilby was no innocent, yet her natural sweetness had not been altered in her knocking about the Quarter.

Whenever Svengali met Trilby at the studio, he tried to persuade her to let him train her voice. But she scoffed at him, despised his cleverness, and thought him repulsive. As Trilby became better acquainted with the Englishmen, ties of affection were more closely knit. Sometimes she cooked for them, darned socks, and took care of the studio. Sometimes they all went on excursions to the country. Svengali never lost an opportunity to talk to her—soon he was pleading his love for her, frightened her with terrible stories. If it had not been for Little Billee and Taffy, Svengali would have made her quite unhappy.

Little Billee was one of the prize students in the classes of the famous Carrel. One morning he walked into the life class at Carrel's, and found Trilby posing in the nude. Little Billee rushed out of the class quickly. Later his friends caught him on his way to the station—all he would tell them was that he had decided to go for a month to the Barbizon to paint landscapes. Trilby later told the Laird what had happened and shortly gave up modeling and returned to her old work as a laundress. Taffy and the Laird both knew that Little Billee was deeply in love with Trilby. And Taffy knew that Trilby loved Little Billee with all her heart, since Taffy already had asked Trilby at the picnic to marry him and had been refused.

On Christmas day they rounded up all their friends and had a great dinner and supper. The dinner started at 10 P.M. and the party lasted until the next morning. It was a momentous occasion for Little Billee, because, "for the nineteenth time" he proposed to Trilby—and this time was accepted. And for the first time in his life he got drunk.

On New Year's day Taffy and the Laird were at work in the studio when their landlady announced visitors. Downstairs were Little Billee's mother and her brother-in-law, a clergyman, the Rev. Thomas Bagot. Followed a painful interview in which Taffy and the Laird were subjected to some searching questions about Trilby. In the midst of all this, Trilby herself came in. Mrs. Bagot recognized her at once. Trilby acknowledged her consent to marry Little Billee a terrible mistake, and promised to give him up. After she had gone, Mrs. Bagot was quite overcome by her discovery of the kind of girl Trilby *actually* was, but very happy that her mission had been a success.

The next morning Taffy received a letter from Trilby. It was a touching farewell: she thought she had not made a mistake, told him she was leaving Paris with her little brother—she did not say where she was going. When Little Billee returned to Paris and heard what had happened, after a furious outburst, his sensitive nature gave way under the shock, and he became violently ill. Months later he went back to Devonshire with his mother and sister. Trilby had not been heard from; indirectly Taffy learned that her brother had died from scarlet fever.

Five years later the paintings of William Bagot, *alias* Little Billee, were well known throughout European art circles. But ever since his illness he had lost his power to love—in his heart was a small spot which was deadened to all affection. He had not married, and he had not fallen in love. At this time the capitals of Europe were in ecstasies over a new singer known as La Svengali. And Little Billee was soon in Paris again with the Laird and Taffy to attend her forthcoming concert. That evening they entered their stalls early. When the orchestra filed in, they saw that the first violinist was their old friend Gecko. Then Svengali came out to conduct the overture. Time and prosperity had wrought a wonderful alteration in the man.

As the curtains parted a woman came out in a dress of classical design in cloth of gold, her face thin and rather haggard, but tender, sweet and simple.

It was Trilby!

Words could not describe that performance. Her magical powers of evocation seemed enhanced in the simple old songs that she sang. The next day Little Billee spied Svengali at a table in the post office. On the way out Little Billee spoke to him. In response Svengali called him an ugly name and spat in his face. At that moment Taffy bounded up the steps and took a good pull at Svengali's nose and gave him a resounding smack on the face. They exchanged cards, but they saw no more of Svengali in Paris.

On their return to London, they could think of nothing but Trilby. Her London concert was awaited with the greatest impatience. Before the concert, a bit of sensational news came out. Svengali had been slashed with a penknife by Gecko during a rehearsal. On the night of the performance the three friends noticed that Svengali did not conduct the overture, and that the first stage box remained unoccupied. Just before Trilby's appearance, Svengali entered that box. Trilby could not sing for the substitute conductor. When she tried "Alice Ben Bolt," it was only as she had sung it in the old days. A clamor broke out. The poor girl did not seem to realize why all these people were aroused by her inability to use her voice. Svengali had played a grim joke—and his last one. As she was led from the stage, Svengali collapsed in his box, dead of heart failure.

Little Billee and Taffy took Trilby under their care at once, but it was plain to the doctors that nothing could be done to arrest her decline. Some considered her a mental case since she had no knowledge of her international fame as a singer. She spoke of Svengali as an old friend, but she said that she had only loved Little Billee. Her death was a sad occasion for everyone who had known her, but especially for Little Billee, since she died looking at a picture of Svengali. And just before that she had once more sung with the golden voice while staring at that portrait.

The shock was too great for Little Billee. The sight of Trilby had restored his powers of affection; her new loss was too cruel a blow. He died not long after Trilby.

Some years later, Taffy, now wedded to Little Billee's sister, came across Gecko on a trip to Paris. Gecko told him the story of how Svengali had trained Trilby's voice. He had been the mind, she had provided the instrument. After long training, he had been able to put a sort of spell on her and project his mind into hers to control that marvelous instrument. But the arduous training, the shock of the successive ordeals of singing had at last worn down her health. Her love and kindness had been the one thing that had redeemed Gecko's life. And he had tried to kill Svengali because he could not bear to see Trilby hurt during their awful rehearsals.

Peter Ibbetson

By GEORGE DU MAURIER

THE RECORD of a man incarcerated in an asylum for the criminally insane may have interest for the sensation-lover. But it was because of Peter Ibbetson's dying request that his memoirs be published exactly as he had written them that Madge Plunket, his only living relative, did not allow the story to die a natural death. Madge Plunket recalled Peter Ibbetson, whom she had known only as a child, as the most beautiful boy she had ever seen; his qualities of mind and spirit were as great. In the manuscript left to her, Madge Plunket changed the names of persons and places and omitted some unnecessary detail; otherwise all was left as the author penned it.

Pierre Pasquier spent his early childhood in Passy, a suburb of Paris. These years were blissfully happy. His handsome parents, their friendly neighbors, his own playmates, were gay and lovable. Those sunlit years were with him all his life. The thought of them evoked memories of lilting French songs, the adorable garden where he romped, and the Mare d'Auteuil, the most beautiful silvery, secret pool in the world.

The Seraskiers were the favorite friends of the Pasquiers. Dr. Seraskier, his extremely tall and divinely beautiful Irish wife, and their sickly but plucky little daughter, Mimsey, were almost part of Pierre's family. The little boy was nicknamed Gogo, and to frail Mimsey, Gogo was a god and the love of her life. The Pasquiers and their circle were happy and beautiful and good.

Joy ended abruptly for the little boy when his happy-go-lucky father was killed experimenting with an invention which was to make their fortune. Mme. Pasquier soon followed her husband to the grave, and Pierre was alone. He passed into the protection of a cousin of his mother's, Colonel Roger Ibbetson, an Englishman who had loved Mme. Pasquier and lost her to Gogo's father. Mimsey nearly died of grief when Pierre left her. The boy was taken to England. His guardian insisted that the lad take his name, and Gogo Pasquier became Peter Ibbetson.

Peter was wretchedly unhappy in England. He hated his guardian, who was snobbish, pompous, vicious and, as Peter learned as he grew older, utterly immoral. He lied about supposed conquests of women and aspersed many an excellent reputation. A Mrs. Deane, a handsome and respectable young widow, was led a dance by this man who not only had not the slightest intention of marrying her, but also had hinted falsely that she was not all she ought to be.

As soon as he reached young manhood, Peter left Colonel Ibbetson to enlist for a year in Her Majesty's Household Cavalry. When his term of enlistment had expired he was apprenticed to Mr. Lintot, an architect, and studied and worked in the dull little town of Pentonville.

Peter had grown to be an extraordinarily handsome young man, nearly six feet four inches in height with a slim, strong body and a perfectly proportioned face. But his extreme shyness and sensitivity had made him friendless. He was bitterly unhappy, despising England, his work, himself. He flung himself into an appreciation of the arts but nothing could long still the pain of loneliness within him.

It was at a concert in an aristocratic house that he first saw the Duchess of Towers. From the moment that this tall, slim, beautiful, unhappy woman walked into the room Peter Ibbetson was irrevocably hers. He said no word to her and never hoped to see her again, but she haunted his every waking moment.

Peter at last was able to afford a trip to France. When he returned to Passy, the scene of his childhood joy, no one recognized him save the senile Major who had told him stories long ago. In Paris he saw his lovely Duchess of Towers drive by, and he thought he saw recognition on her face.

That night in a dream more real than reality Peter Ibbetson met and spoke with the Duchess of Towers. She taught him how to "dream true," and he returned to his childhood. When in his dream he touched his mother's skirt she faded away and he awoke. But from that night on he could project himself into another world when he wished, and return to the happy days he had loved.

Back in England he received another invitation to the house in which he had first seen the Duchess of Towers. He learned here that Mary Towers had been a Miss Seraskier—none other than his little Mimsey. At an interview with the Duchess he unwillingly identified himself as Gogo grown up. But Mary was less surprised than he—she had noticed the resemblance on first meeting. The two were astounded to find that the dream he had had the night they had met in Paris had been shared by Mary. Mary confessed to him that all her life she had remembered and loved him and that during her unhappiness (she was the wife of a drunken brute and the mother of an idiot child), the dream of her childhood love had sustained her. She, too, was able to "dream true" and had found escape that way for many years. But she forbade their meeting in further dreams since she was bound to her husband.

Peter returned to his wretched existence, haunted by thoughts of Mary but dreaming no more. It was at this point that Mrs. Deane, now Mrs. Gregory, caught sight of him walking alone, and showed him a letter that she felt he must see. The letter, to Mrs. Deane, and signed by Colonel Ibbetson, conveyed the malicious lie that Peter's mother had been his mistress and Peter was his illegitimate child. Mad with rage at the slur cast on his good and beautiful mother and the happy days so sacred to him, Peter confronted Colonel Ibbetson with the letter and, upon being taunted by the man, felled him with his stick and accidentally killed him.

Peter refused to repeat the slander that had induced him to strike Ibbetson, and was condemned to death. But that night he dreamed again. In the dream Mary told him that his sentence was to be commuted to life imprisonment, also that her husband and little son were dead, and that now, though they were separated by prison walls, they could be together by dreaming true.

What Mary told him happened. For twenty-five years Peter lived quite happily in the prison. Each night as soon as he fell asleep he and Mary were together in their beautiful childhood home. In a cipher they invented while dreaming they communicated in the everyday world. The years of joy flowed swiftly. They grew so adept at dreaming true that they were able to project themselves centuries back, and, always together, visit the people from whence they had sprung.

But one day the door was closed. Mary had died. Insane with grief, Peter attacked his keepers. They believed him mad, and he was removed to an asylum. He was ill of a brain fever and wished only to die. But he lived, and one night dreamed again. Now an old man—before, in his dreams, he was ever young—he wandered desolate by the shore of Mare d'Auteuil. An old woman waited there for him—Mary! She had returned from the beyond to bid him have hope. One day they might be together again. So he lived the rest of his life in dreaming true. Each night he returned to the scenes he had loved so well, and sometimes Mary returned to him for a little while. He was happy and knew that all would one day be well.

Adam Bede

By GEORGE ELIOT

MARY ANN EVANS, *who wrote under the name of George Eliot, was born Nov. 22, 1819, on the Arbury estate in Warwickshire, of which her father was the estate agent. She studied at home, and her first important literary work was a translation from the German. In 1851 she became assistant editor of the* Westminster Review, *thereby making many friends among authors. With one, George Henry Lewes, she lived until his death in 1878. Eighteen months later she married J. W. Cross, but in a few months she died, on Dec. 22, 1880.*

SIX O'CLOCK came in the roomy workshop of Mr. Jonathan Burge, carpenter and builder, in the village of Hayslope on the 18th of June, 1799. Tall, muscular Adam Bede set off for home, but his brother Seth went to the village green, where gentle Dinah Morris was preaching at the Methodist services.

Seth saw Dinah home, and on the way asked her to be his wife, but she said tenderly that her call from God did not leave her free to marry. He went home sadly, to find Adam at work on a coffin which their father, who had taken to loitering at public houses, had forgotten to complete.

While their mother, Lisbeth, complained about her life, Adam hammered on. The brothers delivered the coffin early the next morning, and on the way home they found their father drowned in a brook. He would not be a burden in his old age, Adam sadly realized.

At the home of Dinah's aunt, Mrs. Poyser, lived another niece, distractingly pretty Hetty Sorrel, a curly-haired girl of 17. Though she knew Adam Bede could be made to turn red by a word from her, Hetty had eyes only for Captain Arthur Donnithorne, grandson of the squire, who had no foolish ideas about marriage, but did have an eye for a dimpled arm. Hetty's uncle wanted her to marry Adam, but she dreamed of the luxuries he could not give her. Meantime Dinah went off to work and preach in a mill town.

That summer Arthur went away, and Adam thought that Hetty might return his love. Then Arthur came home on leave from his regiment, to celebrate his 21st birthday. It did not occur to him that big, sober Adam loved Hetty.

One August night, Adam, returning home from working on the Donnithorne estate, saw two figures standing with clasped hands in a grove of beeches. They separated when Adam's dog barked, and the girl hurried away. Arthur, flushed and excited, walked toward Adam and said carelessly that he had met Hetty by chance and had asked for a kiss.

Adam harshly called Arthur "a selfish scoundrel," and when the young squire tried to pass it off lightly, Adam said: "You've robbed me of my happiness when I thought you my best friend. You're a coward."

They came to blows, and the delicate-handed gentleman proved no match for the powerful workman. When Arthur had revived after the fight, Adam demanded: "Either tell me you're lying when you say you haven't harmed her, or else write her a letter, telling her you won't see her again." Arthur struggled, then promised, convincing Adam that there had been only an innocent flirtation.

Hetty gave way to dull despair when she received Arthur's letter. Seeking only some change in her life, she thought: Why not marry Adam? So, when in November Adam was offered a share of Mr. Burge's business, and he put the question to Hetty, she accepted. Mr. and Mrs. Poyser were overjoyed that their niece at last was to marry the man they admired.

The wedding had to be delayed until a house could be found, and in February Hetty told her uncle that she was going to visit Dinah, who was then at Snowfield. Instead she was determined to find Arthur, whose regiment was at Windsor. But Arthur meanwhile had been transferred to Ireland.

Ignorant of the country, Hetty wandered about, and in a strange village Arthur Donnithorne's child was born. Hetty left the baby in a wood and later returned to find it dead.

Arthur's grandfather died and he returned home, to learn that Hetty had been arrested and was in prison charged with the murder of her child. She was sentenced to pay the capital penalty.

Dinah went to visit Hetty in the condemned cell, and helped her cousin to pray. And their prayers were answered. Two days later, in the shadow of the scaffold, Arthur Donnithorne, full of remorse and shame, brought a reprieve. But Hetty's sentence was commuted only to transportation, and a few years later she died on her way home.

Adam Bede, squaring his shoulders again, returned to his work-bench. For him all the joy of life seemed over.

In the autumn of 1801, Dinah Morris again was living with the Poysers, only to leave them once more for her work in the town. Her aunt noticed that Dinah, who never used to change color, flushed when Adam said: "Why, I hoped Dinah was settled among us for life."

Mrs. Poyser remarked that "I suppose you must be a Methodist to know what a Methodist 'ull do," and Mr. Poyser declared that it was like breaking her word; but Dinah, trying to be quite calm, insisted that she had agreed to stay only to comfort her aunt for a while.

Now Dinah set off with Adam, for Lisbeth was ailing and wanted Dinah to sit with her a bit. On the way Adam remarked: "You know best, but if you could ha' been my sister, and lived wi' us all our lives, I should ha' counted it the greatest blessing."

Dinah made no answer and they walked on in silence, until Adam saw her face flushed and with a look of suppressed agitation. "I hope I've not hurt or displeased you," he said. "I'm satisfied for you to live thirty miles off if you think it right." Poor Adam! Thus do men blunder.

Lisbeth opened Adam's eyes on the next Sunday morning, when Adam sat at home and read from his large pictured Bible. For a long time his mother spoke about Dinah, and how they were losing her when they might keep her, until Adam at last told her she would have to make up her mind to do without Dinah.

"Nay, but I canna ma' up my mind, when she's just cut out for thee. What's it sinnify about her being a Methody? It 'ud happen wear out on her wi' marryin'."

Adam leaned back in his chair and looked at his mother. He understood now what her talk had been aiming at. He tried to drive the notion from her mind, but was amazed at the way in which this new thought of Dinah's love had taken hold of him. He felt that it had an overmastering power that made all other feelings give way before the impetuous desire to know that the thought was true.

Adam spoke to Seth, who said quite simply that he had given up all hope of marrying Dinah, and would rejoice to see his brother happy. "Thee might'st ask her," said Seth. "She took no offense at me for asking."

When Adam did ask, Dinah answered that her heart was strongly drawn toward him, but that she must wait for divine guidance. So she went back to the town, and Adam waited. Then he went after her for an answer.

"Adam," she told him, "it is the divine will. Now you are with me, and I feel that our hearts are filled with the same love, I have a fullness of strength to do our Heavenly Father's will that I had lost before."

Adam looked into her sincere eyes and said: "Then we'll never part any more, Dinah."

And they kissed each other with deep joy.

The Mill on the Floss

By GEORGE ELIOT

DORLCOTE MILL was located on the River Floss. For five generations it had been in the hands of the Tullivers. The present owner, Edward Tulliver, was honest, generous, and quarrelsome. His great weakness was a passion for lawsuits, and he believed that the man who had the smarter lawyer was likely to find the law on his side.

Mr. Tulliver was very fond of his two children, especially his nine-year-old daughter Maggie. Maggie was an active girl who loved outdoor play and was a constant companion of her brother Tom, three years her elder. Her mother was a Dodson, an eminently respectable English family of near-by St. Ogg's. The Dodson plan for the upbringing of young girls had already aroused Maggie's rebellious instincts.

Mr. Tulliver was now faced with the problem of his son's education. Talking the matter over with his friend, Mr. Riley, Tulliver said, "I want to send him to a downright good school, where they'll make a scholard of him." Behind that remark was Mr. Tulliver's desire that his son should be a match for the lawyers with whom he had become involved.

If Tom had been consulted, he would have preferred the village school and the companionship of Maggie. He loved the outdoors, fishing and boating on the Floss, and had no mind for Latin and geometry. Maggie was quick, clever, imaginative where Tom was slow, obstinate, and practical. She would have taken more kindly, her parent realized, to the kind of education he was planning for Tom.

It was decided that Tom should go to a school kept by the Rev. Walter Stelling at King's Lorton, fifteen miles from the mill. Mr. Stelling was not a hard master, but he found Tom exceedingly slow to unravel the mysteries of Caesar and Euclid. Though he was not unruly and wanted to gain the approval of the master, Tom was unhappy and missed Maggie and the pleasant life at the mill.

At the end of his first half-year at King's Lorton, Mr. Tulliver drove over with Maggie to visit Tom. In spite of the boy's protests, Mr. Tulliver insisted that Tom should stick it out at Mr. Stelling's.

In the second term, Mr. Stelling acquired a new pupil, Philip Wakem, the son of lawyer John Wakem, whom Tulliver considered his chief enemy. Because of an accident to his back in infancy, Philip was deformed. Tom thought of him as a hunchback, and the prejudice he had already developed for the Wakems was increased by his antagonism to Philip's character. Philip was sensitive and somewhat shy, quick at learning, and unlike Tom in almost all respects.

But Maggie had touched Philip's heart. He had grown very fond of her. Upon her departure, she told him that she wished he was her brother, too, and assured him by a kiss that she would not forget him. Shortly thereafter Maggie was sent to a boarding-school.

When Tom was sixteen, misfortune descended on the Tullivers and Dorlcote Mill. A lawsuit, long pending against Mr. Tulliver, over water rights on the Floss, was decided against him. Mr. Tulliver's ruin was complete. The shock was too much for him. That day he fell off his horse, a victim of an apoplectic stroke. During the two months he was in bed, he showed no recollection of the things that had happened.

The mill and the property were taken over by Wakem—even some of the household goods were put up at public auction, to the humiliation of Mrs. Tulliver and of the Dodsons, who did nothing to help the Tullivers. But the Tullivers were not dispossessed from their house. Wakem offered Tulliver employment as manager of the mill. In the meantime Tom, who had begun to work for his Uncle Deane in the firm of Guest & Co. at St. Ogg's, wanted his father to refuse Wakem's offer. However, Tulliver thought he could save enough out of his salary at the mill to make a second payment to his creditors.

He brought out the family Bible. He would serve Wakem as an honest man, he told Tom; but he asked Tom to write in the Bible that he would never forgive Wakem, that he hoped evil would befall him, and that he should resolve to repay the Wakems for the suffering inflicted on his father. To no avail, Maggie urged her father not to demand this of Tom. But Tom was all eager to carry out his father's wishes.

After the failure of her father, Maggie resolved to lead a life of self-renunciation. When she was seventeen, she met Philip Wakem again. She had been taking long walks to an old quarry, the Red Deeps, and there Philip had encountered her.

This meeting stirred her old feelings of affection for him. Philip tried to assure her that his father had not plotted Tulliver's ruin, and that he had no desire to continue the feud. Later he declared his love for her, and Maggie mistook her affection toward Philip for love.

Philip went abroad, but he saw Maggie again the following spring. Tom learned of their meetings and confronted her coldly with the choice of never speaking to Philip again or having him tell her father of her love for Philip. For her father's sake, Maggie gave in to Tom.

Mr. Tulliver saved all he could from his salary, and Tom became an energetic trader to gain additional funds for the payments. At last the time came when they could clear the debt. On the day of a dinner they had planned to celebrate the payment of the last of the old debt, Tulliver met Wakem outside the mill. Tulliver's excitement led to an argument, and in his fury he attacked the lawyer. Wakem was uninjured, but the excitement was too severe for Tulliver, and brought on another stroke. Dying, he begged Tom to look after Maggie; this world, he had found, was too much for an honest man.

After her father's death, Maggie went away to teach at her old boarding-school. Now at the age of nineteen she had grown into a beautiful young woman. Her cousin Lucy Deane became interested in her, and asked her to visit at St. Ogg's. And for the first time Maggie had a taste of the social pleasures of girls of her age.

Her cousin's suitor was Stephen Guest, the handsome young son of St. Ogg's wealthiest family. Stephen was attracted to Maggie at once. In spite of the fact that Lucy was trying to bring Maggie and Philip together again, Maggie fell in love with Stephen. One day they went boating together on the Floss. The current carried them far downstream, and Stephen then proposed that they run away and marry.

In spite of her love for Stephen, Maggie would not yield to his proposal of marriage. But when she returned to her family, Tom had already heard about her running away with Stephen, and he refused to forgive her. Tom turned Maggie out of the house.

Guest & Co. had in the meantime purchased Dorlcote Mill and had installed Tom as the manager. Maggie had found it impossible to find an occupation, but she had been taken into the home of her Aunt Jane Glegg.

In September of that year the floods came. Realizing the peril of her brother, Maggie set out in a boat for the mill. The water had already reached the first story, but Tom was able to climb out of a window into the boat, and he tried to row the boat toward the shore. A treacherous current carried them into the middle of the stream and swept them along toward the wreckage of machines that had fallen with the wharves into the Floss. There was no saving themselves now. Grasping each other, brother and sister were pulled down into the swirling waters, brought together for the last time and reconciled in death.

Romola

By GEORGE ELIOT

ONE MORNING, in the year 1492, the usual crowd was gathering on the Mercato Vecchio, or Old Market, of Florence. The news of the death of Lorenzo de' Medici had just reached the populace. In their midst walked a handsome young man to whom the hubbub of conversation sounded quite strange. He was a Greek, and had just made his way to Florence after a series of adventures.

His name was Tito Melema, and he was revolving in his mind the disaster that had overtaken his foster-father, Baldassarre Calvo. On a trip to the Greek island of Delos, their boat had been attacked by pirates. Tito had escaped by swimming away from the boat, but his father had been captured by the pirates. Luckily Tito had concealed on his person a fortune in gems which belonged to his father. The old man expected him to arrange for his ransom as soon as he could get word to Tito.

At the moment Tito was hungry, and when he saw a pretty girl eating alone, he begged her to share her breakfast with him, playfully saying it was "for love." She told him that her name was Tessa, and although she was only a contadina, he was attracted by her pretty face.

Tessa, in turn, introduced him to Nello, a barber by trade, but a man who knew every important artist and patron of art in Florence; his shop was a resort of the *eruditi* of Florence. Nello was completely captivated by Tito's charm and beauty, and when he learned that Tito was a scholar trained in Greek, he resolved to take him under his protection and try to advance his fortunes. With this thought in mind, he introduced him to Bardo de' Bardi, a blind scholar of the famous Florentine family, the Bardi, and also the possessor of a magnificent library.

Bardo gave Tito employment as his secretary and assisted him in selling the gems of his father. Soon Tito won his confidence and the esteem of Bardo's beautiful daughter, Romola. Romola had led a secluded life as a helper of her father in his library. She fell in love with Tito almost at first sight, and in giving him her trust and affection, never doubted that he had the same high ideals as she had. She did not know about his affair with Tessa.

Several months later, at the San Giovanni celebration, Tito was given a letter by a monk, which the monk had received from a man who had seen Baldassarre Calvo. The letter begged Tito to speed the ransom of his father. By this time Tito had made great progress in Florentine society. He had been awarded a professorship of Greek, and he felt that soon his engagement to Romola would be announced. He had no desire for his treatment of his father to come to light.

The monk was Fra Luca, Romola's brother who had returned from the East broken in health. He did not convey to Romola his knowledge of Tito, but, on his deathbed, in the presence of the great Savonarola, he gave her a mystical warning which she could not understand. In the meantime, Tito had gone through a mock-marriage with Tessa, who, because of her naïveté, never suspected its fraudulence. Shortly thereafter, Tito and Romola were married.

Tito's fortunes continued to prosper. In 1494 when Charles VIII, the King of France, entered Florence, Tito was one of the citizens chosen to be present at his reception. Brought into Italy with the King's army were the prisoners of the French. One of them was old Calvo, and though his mind was now affected, he recognized Tito as the guards led the captives through the streets. Breaking away from them, the old man ran up to Tito, who recognized him, but denied his pleas. Later on, by accident, he found refuge with Tessa, for whom Tito had taken a house. When Tito visited Tessa one evening, he was surprised by his foster-father and attacked, but his chain-armor kept him from being wounded.

In the meantime, Bardo de' Bardi had died. His final desire was that his treasure of books, which he had spent a lifetime in collecting, would be preserved for the use of the people of Florence. But, to raise money, Tito decided to sell the collection. For the first time, Romola's eyes were opened to the true nature of her husband, for Tito was willing to violate what she regarded as a sacred trust.

Completely disillusioned, she considered that her marriage vows no longer bound her to Tito. She had decided to leave him, and was on her way out of Florence in disguise when she was recognized and stopped by Savonarola. He exhorted her to return to the city, insisting that it was wrong for her to place her personal wishes above the services she could perform for others in Florence.

At this crisis in her life Romola yielded to the judgment of Savonarola, returned to Florence, and went on living with Tito. But she devoted her life to good works and became one of Savonarola's most devoted workers, although she could not accept all of his ideas.

Tito continued to rise in Florentine politics. He had no firm loyalties and could serve all parties in the guise of his pretended partisanship for each. Baldassarre Calvo again tried to air his grievances against Tito, and this time openly accused Tito at a great dinner in the Rucellai Gardens. But Tito's influence was strong enough to have the old man cast into prison, where he remained for two years. Calvo, however, told Romola about Tessa, who now had two children by Tito.

Tito became deeply involved in the Medicean conspiracy of 1497. Through Tito's treachery, Bernardo del Nero—Romola's godfather and the man who had been most interested in helping her father carry out his plan for the library—was arrested as a party to the conspiracy. When Romola could not get the aid of Savonarola for Bernardo, he was executed, and Romola fled from Florence.

She stopped at a plague-stricken village, and working there

amidst disease and death, she regained her hold on life. While she was away, Savonarola had been arrested, and Florence was in an uproar. Tito's treachery was at last ferreted out by Dolfo Spini and his followers, and they aroused a mob against him. By jumping into a river, Tito got away from them; exhausted, he crawled up on the opposite bank. There he was found by Baldassarre Calvo, who strangled him, and then died himself.

Romola returned to Florence and learned about her husband's death. She was present at the martyrdom of Savonarola. Later on, she sought out Tessa and her children and took them into her house. . . . Many years later she was still devoted to the memory of her great master Savonarola.

Tom Jones

By HENRY FIELDING

HENRY FIELDING, *great-grandson of the Earl of Desmond, was born at Sharpham Park, near Glastonbury, England, on April 12, 1707. He began to study law, but lack of money caused him to start writing for the stage, and in the nine years after 1727 he saw eighteen of his plays produced. Much of his work was done under the pressure of poverty, even after he won appointment as a justice of peace for Westminster in 1748. Fielding, having lived a full life, died on October 8, 1754.*

IN SOMERSETSHIRE there lately lived a gentleman named Allworthy, a favorite of both nature—for his sound constitution and benevolent heart, and of fortune—for his inheritance of a large estate.

He lived in the country with his beloved sister Bridget, now somewhat past thirty, one of those women you commend for good qualities rather than beauty.

Returning much fatigued one evening from a full quarter of a year in London, Mr. Allworthy was prepared to step into bed when he beheld, to his great surprise, an infant wrapped up in some coarse linen between his sheets. Feeling compassion for the little wretch, he ordered a servant, Mrs. Deborah Wilkins, to find a nurse for it in the morning, and her arguments for leaving the boy on the churchwarden's doorstep were outpleaded by the gentle grip of the tiny hand on Mr. Allworthy's finger.

In the morning he showed the infant to his sister, who commended him for his charity and gave as liberal orders for providing for the child as she could have had it been her own. Mrs. Wilkins pursued inquiries about the village, and when Jenny Jones, a maidservant, admitted that the child was hers, the squire sent her from the neighborhood.

Miss Bridget marrying Captain Blifil, a half-pay officer, she became the mother of a boy. At Mr. Allworthy's request, she had consented to bring up the foundling, whom his foster-father had named Thomas Jones. Soon afterward the captain, who had depended on inheriting Mr. Allworthy's wealth, died of apoplexy; so the two children grew up in the squire's home.

By the time he was fourteen, Tom Jones—who, according to universal opinion, was born to be hanged—had already been convicted of robbing an orchard, stealing a duck, and picking Master Blifil's pocket of a ball. Tom had taken the food for the use of his friend the gamekeeper, but Jones alone was discovered and bore the whole blame. His vices were heightened when opposed to the virtues of Master Blifil, who was sober, discreet and pious beyond his age.

The Rev. Mr. Thwackum was engaged to instruct the two boys, but though he had frequent orders to make no difference between them, the divine was as kind and gentle to Master Blifil as he was barbarous to the other. Blifil had greatly gained Thwackum's affections by learning his phrases by heart, and maintaining his religious principles. Tom Jones was not only deficient in respect, but unmindful of his master's precepts.

At the age of twenty, however, Tom had become a favorite hunting companion of Mr. Allworthy's neighbor Squire Western; and Sophia Western, the squire's only child, lost her heart to him before she knew it. On his side, Tom, who admired her accomplishments and tenderly loved her goodness, had never entertained any thoughts of possessing her though he had a much stronger passion for her than he knew.

Hurt on the hunting field in saving Sophia from her mettlesome horse, Jones was confined for some weeks in the Western house, and not only found that he loved Sophia with an unbounded passion, but plainly saw her tender sentiments for him. Yet he despaired of obtaining the consent of her father, nor would he pursue her by any base method.

But the news that Mr. Allworthy was dangerously ill drove all thoughts of love from Tom's head, and he hurried back with all haste.

On the night that his patron was pronounced out of danger, Jones was thrown into an immoderate excess of rapture which he fortified so freely with the bottle that he very soon became literally drunk, and fell into immoderate good-humored disorder. Blifil, whose mother had died during her brother's illness, was highly offended, and told Jones so, at which Tom apologized and offered to shake Blifil's hand in pardon. At this Blifil made an insulting allusion to Jones' birth, and a scuffle resulted.

Now Squire Western discovered that his daughter loved Jones, and at once decided she should marry Blifil, whom she abhorred. Blifil seized upon the opportunity to present the story of Jones' drunkenness in the worst light to Mr. Allworthy; and Tom, full of grief at Western's discovery of his affair, made the poorest possible defense of himself.

Mr. Allworthy told Jones that he was determined to banish him from his sight forever, speaking of "your audacious attempt to steal away a young lady." Tom, overcome by tears, could only kiss his master's hands before obeying. Mr. Allworthy sent him away with £500, which was promptly stolen from him.

Hardly had Jones left in agony and despair than Sophia Western resolved that only by flight could she escape from marriage with the detested Blifil. Mr. Western loved his daughter, but thought her inclinations of little consequence, and through deceit Mr. Allworthy had been led to approve the match. So Sophia sent her maid to an appointed meeting place, and, after a final awful scene with her father in which filial devotion almost led her to abandon her secret scheme to flee, stole away from the house at midnight.

Both Sophia and Tom set out for London; she to her aunt there, Jones to the home of Mrs. Miller, a pensioner of Mr. Allworthy. Once they stayed at the same inn, unbeknownst to Tom.

Tom had many adventures on the road, among the chief of which was the rescue of a handsome woman of middle age, a Mrs. Waters, who was being beaten by a man in a wood. They stopped at an inn together and she lured him into bed with her, Jones never realizing that this was the same Jenny Jones who had been driven from his native village.

In London, when his fortunes were at the lowest, Jones was forced into a quarrel with one Fitzpatrick, wounded him with his sword, and was carried off to jail. Soon afterward Mr. Allworthy, Mr. Western, and Blifil reached the city.

Mrs. Miller defended Jones before Mr. Allworthy, and declared that Tom was not at fault in the fight, which Fitzpatrick himself, having unexpectedly recovered, acknowledged.

Then Mr. Allworthy discovered that Blifil had been arranging with a lawyer to get the men who had arrested Jones to bear false witness against him, and further learned that on her deathbed his sister Bridget had left a message for him, confessing that Tom was really his child, a message which her son had suppressed. The old man's affection for Tom then returned, and he called on Sophia to apologize for Blifil's having been encouraged to annoy her, and to inform her that Tom Jones was his son and heir.

Mr. Western, a man overviolent in his disposition, was now as eager for his daughter to marry Jones as he had been to couple her with Blifil.

There were touching scenes of reconciliation between Jones, Mr. Allworthy and Mr. Western; while Blifil was sent away with an income of £200 a year and turned Methodist in the hope of marrying a very rich widow.

Tom married Sophia promptly on the welcome command of her parent, and there is not a neighbor or a servant who does not bless that day.

The Man of Property

By JOHN GALSWORTHY

JOHN GALSWORTHY *was born in Surrey in 1867. He was educated at Harrow and went to New College, Oxford, where he received an honor degree in law in 1889. For two years he traveled and read widely, not settling down to the practice of law. He was encouraged by his wife to write, and published his first novel in 1899. In 1903 he began writing the Forsyte series, of which* The Man of Property *is the first. Between 1906 and 1918 he devoted himself to writing for the stage, but thereafter he returned to the Forsyte saga. In 1930 he came to the United States for a while. He died in Hampstead, London, Jan. 31, 1933.*

ON JUNE 15, 1865, the Forsyte family gathered at the home of old Jolyon Forsyte to celebrate the engagement of June Forsyte, old Jolyon's granddaughter, to Philip Bosinney, a young architect without fortune. All of Jolyon's brothers except Timothy were present, along with Jolyon's sisters, Ann, Hester, and Julia. From the point of view of the elder Forsytes, the man they were going to meet that afternoon seemed a little dangerous. Philip Bosinney was a stranger to them, and they had already formed the opinion that he would never do any good for himself.

June, who had lived with her grandfather since she was four, was to inherit all of old Jolyon's property. June's father, young Jolyon, had been disinherited fourteen years before and he was completely estranged from his father. Old Jolyon had often wondered whether he had been too severe with his son.

After the party June went to visit Philip's family. During June's absence, old Jolyon finally gave way to his desire to see his son; so one evening he stopped at young Jolyon's club. Their meeting was surprisingly cordial, and their conversation continued the same evening at the old Forsyte home on Stanhope Street. Jolyon found that his son was getting along better than he had expected and was happy with the woman whose affections had first cost him the anger of his family.

Philip's introduction to the Forsyte family began for him a series of social engagements. At these teas, receptions, and dinner parties he had many occasions to talk to Irene Forsyte, the wife of Soames, one of old Jolyon's nephews. The interest that developed between Philip and Irene was not lost on other members of the family.

Soames had decided to build for himself and Irene a new home in the country. He chose Philip Bosinney as his architect, and Philip soon submitted plans and figures. During the construction of the house, Philip saw Irene frequently, and they were discussed in the family circles more than ever. Finally the costs of the house began to exceed Philip's original figures, much to the irritation of Soames. He had also begun to pay attention to the gossip about his wife. June, too, was aware of Philip's attachment for Irene, and the increasing tension broke up her long friendship with Irene.

In the meantime old Jolyon had visited his son at his home in the suburbs of London and had met his two grandchildren. He began to consider altering his will; the fact that his brothers considered that young Jolyon had got just what he deserved by being cut off from the property rankled in him, and he decided that he had been quite unfair to his son.

One day old Jolyon took out his will again and read it. He went down to his lawyer after making a note and told him that he was going to take the trusteeship away from James Forsyte and his son Soames. Then he went to young Jolyon and informed him that he was settling £1,000 a year on him at once, with £50,000 to June on his death, the remainder to go to young Jolyon.

Soames Forsyte, in the meantime, had decided to attempt Philip's ruin through a lawsuit against him for his excessive expenditures in the construction of the house. Actually he was moved by the fact that he felt that Philip had won an affection from his wife that he had never been able to gain. Philip did not contest the suit and made no appearance in court.

On the day of the suit, June Forsyte was in court and was not surprised that Philip did not appear. After the judgment was handed down in Soames' favor, she took a cab to Philip's rooms. He was not there, but she knew that his key was under the mat and made use of that. While she was waiting, Irene came in. She told June that she had left Soames. All of June's anger came out; she accused her of being a false friend. Irene left—though she seemed to have no place to go.

That same night June urged her grandfather to buy the house that Philip had constructed; they both knew now that Soames and Irene would never live in it. The next morning a policeman brought the news that Philip had been run over in the fog the night before by a cab. There was a rumor of suicide. . . . Old Jolyon bought the house from his nephew. Irene returned to her husband.

The Vicar of Wakefield

By OLIVER GOLDSMITH

OLIVER GOLDSMITH, born Nov. 10, 1728, in rural Ireland, was educated at Trinity College, Dublin, where he displayed his lifelong characteristics of brilliance, improvidence, and playfulness. He studied medicine, then vagabonded for a year on the Continent to make a precarious living as a hack-writer and teacher. Dr. Samuel Johnson, whom he met in 1761, helped him settle down to serious work as a poet, essayist, dramatist, and novelist. He died in London on April 4, 1774.

DR. PRIMROSE, the Vicar of Wakefield, chose his wife for such qualities as would wear well. Their children, educated without softness, were well-formed and healthy. His daughters were beautiful, Olivia open and sprightly, Sophia soft and modest; his four sons hardy and active. He had £14,000, and made the profits of his living over to the more needy.

The day had been fixed for the nuptials of his eldest son George, just out of Oxford, to Miss Arabella Wilmot, but the fathers quarreled and just then Dr. Primrose's fortune was made off with by the merchant to whom he had entrusted it. Mr. Wilmot broke off the engagement; George was sent to London to make his way; and Dr. Primrose became curate of a small community at £15 a year in a distant neighborhood.

On the way the family fell in with a Mr. Burchell, a pleasing companion who told them of young Squire Thornhill, their wealthy, pleasure-loving new landlord, who was the nephew of the great and good Sir William Thornhill. Mr. Burchell rescued Sophia, who had fallen into a rapid stream, and soon afterward took leave of them.

One autumn afternoon Squire Thornhill, out hunting, stopped to chat with the vicar, and found favor in Olivia's eyes. Soon he became a frequent visitor, lured by Mrs. Primrose's venison pasty as well as her daughters' charms. Mr. Burchell, too, called often, though he was less welcome after the visits of a person of superior station.

One evening young Mr. Thornhill came with two young ladies, richly dressed, whom he introduced as women of fashion from town. Though they once or twice mortified the Primroses by slipping out an oath, they inspired the girls to emulate their finery, and the vicar's preachings against display soon were ignored.

The women now wanted to sell the family's clumsy colt and purchase a harness horse, so Moses, the vicar's second son, was sent to a neighboring fair to make the transactions. He sold the colt for a fair price, but a sharper sold him a gross of green spectacles for the money, so the family was worse off than before.

The young squire's two ladies offered to take Olivia and Sophia to town as companions, and Mrs. Primrose was overjoyed at the good fortune. But Mr. Burchell argued against it so strongly that he became estranged from the family, and soon afterward Squire Thornhill told the Primroses that reports from some malicious person had prevented the project. Discovery of a warning letter from Mr. Burchell to the squire's two ladies soon fixed the blame.

Though Mr. Thornhill now called oftener than ever, it seemed that his fine sentiments had more of love than of matrimony in them. One evening the vicar's son Dick came running and told of having seen Olivia go off with two men in a carriage. She had cried very much, but had been persuaded.

The vicar vowed to pursue her and save her. His suspicions at first fell on Squire Thornhill, but that young man swore he had nothing to do with it. Then the finger of guilt seemed to point at Mr. Burchell. The vicar fell ill on his search, but three weeks later found his daughter abandoned at a little country inn. To his shock he learned that it was the squire who had lured her away into a false marriage, and that Mr. Burchell had tried to prevent this.

Arriving home next night, the vicar found his little house on fire. The family escaped, but the building was destroyed, and they had to move into a wretched little shack. And the vicar's wife greeted their daughter with words of scorn, but was silenced when her husband told her: "I have here brought you back a poor deluded wanderer—her return to duty demands the revival of our tenderness."

Olivia's grief was increased by the news that Mr. Thornhill was to be married to the rich Miss Wilmot. When Dr. Primrose denounced the squire to his face, the young man demanded his rent, which the vicar was unable to pay, and on the following day the clergyman was taken to the county jail.

The fortune of the vicar's family, who were lodged in the town, was now wholly and distressingly adverse. While he was in the jail, he was brought the dreadful news that Olivia, who had been ill, was dead. And then his wife came weeping to tell him that Sophia had been seized by ruffians and carried off.

The sum of his miseries was now made up, the vicar thought; but then his son George, to whom he had written, went to Thornhill Castle to punish the family's betrayer. Attacked by the servants, he injured one of them and was brought to the very prison where his father was confined.

The vicar, now extremely ill, rested his only hope in a letter he had written to Sir William Thornhill, telling him of his nephew's misdeeds. Meantime he began to prepare his soul for eternity.

At that darkest moment, Mr. Burchell entered the cell with Sophia. "Here, Papa," she cried, "is the brave man to whom I owe my delivery." The vicar told Mr. Burchell that, humble though he might be, he knew of no man so worthy of his daughter's hand. Then a message brought in from Mr. Thornhill revealed that

Mr. Burchell was none other than the great Sir William, the squire's uncle.

Confronted by the two villains he had hired to carry off Sophia, the young squire shrank back in terror. And then one of the men, the same sharper who had cheated Moses and, in another horse deal, the vicar himself, revealed that Mr. Thornhill and Olivia had been truly wed. The squire's agent had procured a true priest instead of a false one, so that he might hold it over his master's head.

The vicar now learned that Olivia was alive, and that he had been told otherwise so that he might consent to the young squire's wedding to Miss Wilmot, which at that time had seemed the only way out of prison for him.

Now Mr. Thornhill, his assurance gone, fell on his knees and implored his uncle's compassion.

"Thy vices, crimes and ingratitude," said the baronet, "deserve no compassion; but a bare competence shall be supplied thee, and thy wife shall possess a third part of that fortune which once was thine."

On the next day Sophia was wedded to Sir William Thornhill, and George, now free, led Miss Wilmot to the altar. And that morning came word that the vicar's merchant had been arrested at Antwerp, and that his fortune was recovered.

The vicar now had nothing on this side of the grave to wish for. It only remained, he said, that his gratitude in good fortune should exceed his submission in adversity.

The Return of the Native

By THOMAS HARDY

THOMAS HARDY *was born June 2, 1840, near Dorchester, England. For the most part self-educated, he worked in an architect's office as a young man and later practiced architecture independently. From the year 1871 until 1897 he published the series of novels for which he is chiefly known; after 1897 he devoted himself almost entirely to the writing of verse. He continued to live in Dorchester, where he died on Jan. 11, 1928.*

LATE on a Saturday evening in November, Diggory Venn, an itinerant purveyor of reddle for marking sheep, was driving his cart over the hills and hollows of that somber, impenetrable tract of land in southern England known as Egdon Heath. In his cart slept a young girl, Thomasin Yeobright, to whom two years previously he had made a proposal of marriage. And now he was passing a group of merrymakers getting ready to celebrate a marriage which they mistakenly thought had already taken place— between Thomasin and Damon Wildeve.

In truth, Damon Wildeve was an unhappy victim of his own indecision. The mistake he had made about the license had given him an opportunity to reconsider his relations with another woman far different from his simple, sweet near-bride. This woman, Eustacia Vye, dark, full-limbed, and passionate, was sustained by a longing for the full experience of a great love, for which, she knew at heart, the affair with Wildeve was a poor substitute. They had one thing in common—an intense dislike of the heath. Eustacia was the orphaned granddaughter of a retired sea captain. Wildeve, once an engineer, had now declined to the state of rural innkeeper.

Mrs. Yeobright, Thomasin's aunt, in the meantime had gone to see Venn. When she discovered that he was still in love with Thomasin, she had another interview with Wildeve and got him to promise not to stand in the way of Thomasin's marrying another man. And Wildeve at his next rendezvous with Eustacia on the heath told her that now they might think of going away together. Yet she disdained a prize so easily won; her ears had already quickened to the news that Clym Yeobright, after several years in Paris, was returning to the heath.

Meeting Clym was not easy. Though she walked the heath in the neighborhood of the Yeobrights, her hopes for a casual encounter were defeated. So she bribed one of the boys who was taking part in the traditional Christmas play of St. George at the Yeobrights, to let her take his part.

Clym singled her out; though she refused to remove her mask, she knew that she had at last aroused his curiosity. Her next step was to terminate her relationship with Wildeve. A curt note of dismissal to Wildeve was borne by Diggory Venn, who was selfless enough to value Thomasin's happiness above his own; and with Eustacia out of the way, it was an easy matter for him to convince Wildeve that he should go through with his marriage to Thomasin.

Clym was fascinated by Eustacia, and in frequent meetings on the heath love ripened between them. To his mother's profound disappointment, the strongly intellectual turn of Clym's mind had led him to give up forever a promising post in a diamond house in Paris. His new purpose in life—to establish a school which would embody the new ideas which had brought him to a turning point in his life—seemed to his mother a sad step backward. And when she learned that he was in love with Eustacia Vye, the rift between them widened. She made no attempt to conceal her dislike of Eustacia. "Clym," she said, "if she makes you a good wife, there has never been a bad one."

Clym's mind, however, was fully made up; he proposed to Eustacia that they be married at once, and that they take a small cottage near the heath while he finished his preparation for his work. Their marriage took place, and Eustacia accepted Clym's plan for life on the heath—although she was still convinced that her secret hope, to get Clym to return with her to Paris, would be realized.

In his eagerness to complete his studies, Clym strained his eyesight so severely that he was forced to stop reading; and in order to avoid living solely on his small savings, he began to work as a furze-cutter on the heath.

A chance meeting with Eustacia at a village festival revived in Wildeve the old attraction. One day he came to Clym and Eustacia's cottage. Clym was asleep, but Eustacia admitted Wildeve. A knock at the door was heard; Eustacia looked out and saw that Mrs. Yeobright had come to pay a call. She decided to show Wildeve out the back way because she thought that Clym was waking up. When she came back, she found Clym still asleep and no sign of Mrs. Yeobright. Later in the afternoon Clym decided to walk to his mother's house. Halfway across the heath, he stumbled over his mother, lying prostrate and fatally sick beside the path. At a near-by cottage he and some of the villagers discovered that she had been bitten by an adder.

Other people arrived soon—among them Eustacia and Wildeve together. When Eustacia saw that Mrs. Yeobright was dead, she turned to Wildeve and said, "I am to blame for this. There is evil in store for me."

Eustacia withheld her knowledge of the events of that fateful day; and when Clym, racked by grief, a sense of guilt, and illness, stumbled upon the truth, he released a torrential fury on his wife. Eustacia admitted her guilt and left her husband. Her only hope now was to get away from the heath entirely.

She knew that Wildeve was willing to run away with her, since he had recently come into a small fortune, and she decided to get him to drive her to Budmouth. In the meantime, Clym wrote a letter to Eustacia offering a reconciliation; it was delivered on a November night as she was preparing for her journey.

However, she did not see the letter on the mantel, so quickly had she fled from her grandfather's house. At the spot on the heath where she was to meet Wildeve, she realized that she had no money, and also that she did not want to break her marriage vow by turning to a weakling like Wildeve.

Not long afterward Clym met Wildeve searching the heath for Eustacia. When they saw a dark form swirling in the weir, Wildeve jumped in. Yeobright tried to save them, but only through the assistance of Diggory Venn was he himself saved from drowning.

Many months later Thomasin decided to marry Diggory. And Clym finally found a vocation in preaching to the villagers on the heath.

Far from the Madding Crowd

By THOMAS HARDY

"Far from the madding crowd's ignoble strife" the little Wessex village of Weatherbury, tenanted mainly by shepherds and a few small farmers, lived the unsophisticated life of a place separated more by years than by miles from the modern city.

The villagers were well acquainted with the personal histories of the country gentry in the environs. At the moment they were greatly concerned with the arrival of Bathsheba Everdene.

Bathsheba Everdene, at the time that she learned that she had inherited the manor house at Weatherbury, was very poor. Her beauty and wit had won her the love of Gabriel Oak, a small sheep-farmer; somehow Gabriel, huge, simple, devoted, was not the husband that Bathsheba wanted—if, indeed, she wanted one at all, which she doubted—and she refused him. Then her lucky inheritance called her to Weatherbury and she had no time to think of her unhappy suitor. Gabriel's ill fortune continued—he lost a valuable flock, then his farm, and was forced to go forth and seek employment on the farms of other men.

The villagers were greatly interested in the handsome new mistress of the manor. To their surprise Bathsheba turned out to be an intelligent and capable manageress, and it seemed as though the farm would continue to prosper under her.

About the time that Bathsheba had come to Weatherbury, the graybeards of the village were shocked at the conduct of one of their girls. This lass, Fanny Robin, had been a good and dutiful girl who worked as a maid at the manor-house; the silly creature had been seduced by a handsome soldier, and one night she disappeared.

Bathsheba's entire farm was gravely endangered when her wheat-ricks were nearly burned down. The fire was extinguished by Bathsheba's old friend Gabriel Oak, who had wandered into Weatherbury in his quest for employment. Bathsheba prevailed upon Gabriel to stay and work on her farm, and the man consented in order to be near the woman he loved.

Bathsheba's capricious charm soon enslaved all who knew her. She even won the love of cold, aristocratic William Boldwood, who resisted her beauty so long that he piqued the high-spirited young woman. By sheep-shearing time, Boldwood was completely under Bathsheba's spell. It was clear that she also was not indifferent. Gabriel Oak realized that his Bathsheba must soon be another man's wife; but, sensible of Boldwood's worth and desiring only the happiness of the loved one, he determined to accept the blow bravely.

A shearing supper was held in the barn, and it was clear that Boldwood would soon declare himself. But that night tragedy in a most attractive disguise first approached Bathsheba. It was the custom of the young mistress of the manor to inspect her houses and grounds personally each night before retiring. In an isolated part of the farm, Bathsheba felt her skirt caught, heard a man's voice. Her momentary fear left her when she found that the object impeding her progress was a spur caught in the material of her dress. The spur was attached to the boot of a handsome young soldier.

Sergeant Troy was gay, debonair, romantic. Gabriel knew that this was the man who had seduced Fanny Robin, but Bathsheba did not. Troy's fine dark eyes and quick wit attracted the emotional young woman, but Gabriel hoped that Bathsheba's better sense would soon reassert itself. It might have, had not William Boldwood, fiery and passionate beneath his cold exterior, created a dreadful scene and insulted the young redcoat. Bathsheba impulsively sprang to Troy's defense, then married him.

From the very beginning even Bathsheba was aware that the marriage could come to no good. At a wedding supper in the barn, Troy became hopelessly intoxicated. He lay helpless with drink while his wife's lands were menaced by storm and fire. All night Bathsheba and Gabriel Oak worked to save the farm, and at last they were successful due to the efforts of the man whom Bathsheba felt she could never love but must always turn to for assistance in time of stress.

Despite Bathsheba's efforts her marriage brought her only unhappiness. She soon learned that Troy, besides being irresponsible, was also wicked. Fanny Robin, the little maid whom he had seduced, returned to Weatherbury after having wandered for many months homeless and in disgrace. The baby, whose father Troy was, died with its young mother. The two unfortunates were to be buried from the manor house.

When Troy saw the girl whom he had ruined lying in her coffin with his child in her arms, he was overcome by remorse. Bathsheba realized that despite her beauty and wealth, she was no rival for the dead girl whom her husband had loved. All hope of making her luckless marriage succeed then left Bathsheba. And Troy, finding his surroundings unbearable now, abandoned his wife and left Weatherbury.

Gradually the scar left by Bathsheba's marriage started to fade.

Rumors that Troy had been drowned reached the young woman. William Boldwood renewed his wooing, and Bathsheba promised that at the end of seven years she would be his. This lapse of time was necessary before it could be proved that Bathsheba was really a widow.

Happiness, more mature joy than the gaiety of her girlhood, seemed very near to Bathsheba at the Christmas Eve party which Boldwood had planned to celebrate their "engagement." The festivities were at their height when a ghost appeared among the revelers. Sergeant Troy, brutalized by drink and suffering, had returned to claim his wife.

Mad with rage at the thought of once more losing his love, Boldwood seized a gun and shot Troy dead. The soldier would trouble his beautiful wife no more.

Boldwood was tried and condemned to life imprisonment and for many, many months Bathsheba was an invalid without will to live. But she was restored to strength when she learned that Gabriel Oak was about to leave Weatherbury. Feeling that Bathsheba no longer needed him and wishing to avoid the scandal that was beginning to result from the villagers' discussions of her dependence on him, Gabriel was about to bid her good-by. But Bathsheba came to his cottage and, realizing that his fidelity had finally aroused in her heart the emotion he wished, promised to be his.

Their marriage was very happy and Bathsheba found peace and contentment with Gabriel, her unromantic first love.

Tess of the D'Urbervilles

By THOMAS HARDY

ON AN EVENING in the latter part of May, a middle-aged man named John Durbeyfield was walking toward his home in the village of Marlott. He was a cottager there who provided rather meagerly for his large family by doing odd tasks in the neighborhood. Tonight his gait was somewhat unsettled by drink. Overtaken by the village parson, Durbeyfield was amazed at his greeting.

"Good night, Sir John," the parson said.

The parson, a noted antiquarian of local lore, went on to inform Durbeyfield that he was the last of a noble family, the D'Urbervilles, whose male line was supposed to have died out long since. But the name went back to a Norman knight of William the Conqueror.

The next day, John's wife Joan called to mind a family of D'Urbervilles that had a house in near-by Trantridge. She supposed at once that this family was related to her husband, and proposed sending her oldest daughter, Tess, to find out whether they might not take an interest in her. As a matter of fact, this family had merely selected the name for their use and had no blood connections with John Durbeyfield.

In view of the recent misfortunes of her father, Tess thought it her duty to do something to help him, and the next day she set out for the district known as the Chase where Mrs. D'Urberville's house was situated. On the lawn of the estate she was met by a young man who presented himself as Alec D'Urberville. He was attracted by her beauty at once, and asked her many questions, but he did not take her to see his mother.

Very soon a letter came to the Durbeyfields offering Tess a

place with Mrs. D'Urberville as a tender of her fowls. They were informed that a cart would be sent for her things, but on the day of her departure Alec himself appeared in a smart gig hitched to a spirited mare. On the way to the house, Alec took advantage of Tess' fears about riding downhill in the gig to tease her and to annoy her with unwanted attentions.

Tess learned that Mrs. D'Urberville was blind; she was taken into her presence very seldom. But her work was light, and on Saturdays she went into town with the work-folk to shop and to attend the dances. One Saturday night her group started back to the Chase much later than usual. An argument arose among the women, and one of them began to take her spite out on Tess. At that moment Alec came by on horseback, and Tess was glad enough to accept his invitation to ride home with him.

As before he tried to make love to Tess. This time she was fatigued; her answers to him were somewhat confused. He went on past the usual turning-off point and had to get down to find his directions. Overcome by her long walk and her tiredness, Tess fell asleep by the roadside. There Alec found her. . . .

In late October four months after Tess' arrival at Trantridge, she was walking back to Marlott—a basket on one arm, a bundle on the other. Alec drove after her in his gig, but he had no power to persuade her to return. She had not loved him, and she never could. When she got home, she told her unhappy mother the whole story. She had dreaded Alec, but she had succumbed to the advantage he took of her helplessness; then, temporarily blinded by his ardent manners, she had been stirred to surrender for a while. Suddenly she had despised him and had run away.

About a year later, Tess was working in the fields with the harvesters. Since its birth, her baby had been weak and sickly and she wanted it baptized. That very night the baby grew worse, and in her terror she went through the baptismal ceremony herself. The child died before morning, and the vicar refused it a Christian burial. After that Tess decided that she must leave Marlott, yet she found no opportunity until the following May, when a letter informed her that a dairy-house many miles to the southward needed a milk-maid.

At Talbothays dairy a new and happier life began for Tess. The head dairyman, Mr. Crick, and his wife took a liking to her, and the milkmaids, girls her own age, were friendly; Tess became very skillful in her work with the cows. The thoughts of the past gradually receded in her memory.

Staying at Talbothays as a student of agriculture was Angel Clare, the son of the Rev. Mr. Clare, a devout and earnest minister of near-by Emminster, whose evangelical, low-church leanings were disliked by his fellow clergy, and not shared by his sons. Angel Clare, like his brothers, had been intended for orders, but a rationalistic skepticism and a dislike of upper-class society had turned him toward the land. He had planned, after a period of observation and study, to begin farming.

His attraction to Tess was immediate, yet it took him some time to translate this into a serious love. Tess was soon aware of his predilection for her, as were her three friends, who had all fallen in love with Angel. Yet they were straightforward girls and were not spiteful and jealous. When Angel finally spoke to Tess of his love, he was resolved to marry her. Though she was deeply in love with him, she withheld her consent.

In the meantime Angel went to see his father and mother to tell them of his intentions. In spite of their misgivings about Angel's not choosing a "lady" for his wife, they gave him their consent.

Tess at last yielded to his persuasions. She had intended to tell him everything that had happened to her in the past, but when she got to the part about the D'Urberville connection of her father, he mistook that for her "secret" and passed it off lightly.

The day before New Year's was set for the wedding—some seven months after Tess had come to Talbothays. Angel planned to take Tess with him to study some near-by mills and then he was going to try to find a farm. After the wedding—to which neither of the families came—they drove to Wellbridge, where Angel had engaged rooms.

On their wedding night Tess told her husband the story of her relations with Alec D'Urberville. At first Angel could not believe her. "You were one person; now you are another," he told her.

The more he thought about it, the more estranged he became from Tess. After a number of long discussions, he decided that at present he could not live with her. The fourth day after their marriage, they separated, Angel to think over the future, and Tess to return to her family. Soon afterward Angel set out for Brazil, to try his fortune on the new lands then being opened up to settlers.

Tess, eight months later, after working at several dairies for short intervals, was again walking the countryside in search of work. When her old friend Marian, one of the milkmaids of Talbothays, told her of work at a farm called Flintcomb-Ash, she set out for the place. There she was hired to do hard, rough work in the turnip-fields.

One Sunday she decided to call on her husband's parents. After she had walked to Emminster, she found that they had all gone to church. Her courage deserted her when she overheard Angel's brothers talking. On her way back to Flintcomb-Ash she stopped to listen to an itinerant preacher. He was Alec D'Urberville.

He followed her and demanded that she talk to him. He explained that he had given up his old ways after being converted by Mr. Clare. From that time on, he kept trying to see her, and at last one day he came to the farm dressed once more as a fine gentleman. Her influence, he told Tess, had decided him against preaching; all he wished now was to restore her as his wife, and to bring her and her family what happiness he could.

Tess loathed him more than ever. Her father had died and left his family in a precarious position. She had not heard from Angel. She felt it was necessary for her to do something for her family. And Alec kept jeering at her husband. In desperation Tess wrote a long, passionate letter to Angel, which was sent on to Brazil by the Clares.

When Angel got home from Brazil, there was an even more urgent note from Tess—as well as an anonymous letter from Tess' old friends warning him of her desperate plight. Through her mother, Angel traced her to Sandbourne, where he found her living in lodgings with Alec D'Urberville.

He was too late, she told him. Yet an hour later he found her on a road outside Sandbourne, running away from the city. She told him that, after he had left, she had stabbed Alec to death. For two days they wandered through the country, settling for a time in an uninhabited dwelling. The hours spent there with Angel were the tenderest that Tess had known. On the evening of the fifth day, when they had got as far as Stonehenge, the police closed in on them.

On a warm day in July a gallows was erected in the prison of the old town of Wintoncester. From a distant hill, Angel Clare watched a black flag ascend the shaft. "Justice" was done, and the President of the Immortals had ended his sport with Tess.

The Prisoner of Zenda

By ANTHONY HOPE

ANTHONY HOPE HAWKINS *was born on February 9, 1863, the son of the Vicar of St. Brides, Fleet Street, London. He was educated at Marlborough and Balliol College, Oxford, and was called to the bar in 1877. Literature was only his avocation at first, but later took all his time. In May, 1894,* The Prisoner of Zenda *was published. It enjoyed great and immediate success and was the prototype for many less successful imitators. In 1903 Hawkins married Elizabeth*

Sommerville Sheldon of New York City, and in 1918 he was knighted. He died in 1933.

ADVENTURE was part of Rudolf Rassendyll's heritage. Scandalous tradition had it that Rassendyll's fine old English house of Burlesdon bore a royal blot on its escutcheon. Six generations before a duel between Lord Burlesdon and King Rudolf of Ruritania had been fought over a question involving Lady Burlesdon's honor. Whatever the truth of the matter, from that time on the Burlesdons were at intervals embarrassed by the appearance of a child bearing a startling resemblance to the royal Elphberg line of Ruritania.

Blue-eyed, tall and straight, with the long, characteristic Elphberg nose and hair of the true Elphberg red, Rudolf Rassendyll was such a one. Blessed also by the courage, quick wit and careless charm of his royal connection, he shared the illustrious foibles too. At twenty-nine his lack of ambition appalled his brother, Lord Burlesdon, and his pretty sister-in-law, Lady Burlesdon. To placate Lady Burlesdon, Rassendyll promised that if at the end of six months nothing better had turned up he would join the consular service. Meanwhile he was off to the Tyrol to fish and perhaps—here Lady Burlesdon brightened—write a book.

But Rassendyll's true destination was not the Tyrol. Rudolf the Fifth was to be crowned king at Ruritania's capital, Strelsau, and the young Englishman intended to satisfy a lifelong curiosity concerning the Elphbergs and Ruritania. Telling no one of his plans, he set out for the tiny country which figured so greatly in the history of his house.

En route he learned that all was not happy in Ruritania. Michael, Duke of Strelsau, the old king's son by a morganatic marriage, was more popular in Ruritania than the young king; and Black Michael—as his enemies called him—looked to the throne with a longing eye. It was said that his ambition extended to the person of beautiful Princess Flavia, who was the intended of the young King Rudolf.

While about to entrain from Paris to Dresden, Rassendyll noticed a lovely but tragic-eyed woman whose destination was apparently his own. Rassendyll's companion described this woman as Antoinette de Mauban, and suggested that she and Michael of Strelsau were something more than friends.

Rassendyll's immediate destination was Zenda, a small town some fifty miles from the capital. Zenda, the Englishman soon learned, supported Black Michael, who owned much of the land in the environs of the picturesque village. The Duke's castle on the hill was a formidable fortress—the modern chateau where Michael lived was backed by this ancient moated building.

Next day Rassendyll set out to explore the dark forests of Ruritania. He tramped for hours over the hills until, exhausted by fresh air and exercise, he fell asleep under a tree. He was awakened by two gentlemen who seemed to find him in some way amazing. The older identified himself as Colonel Sapt, the younger as Fritz von Tarlenheim, both in the service of King Rudolf. Rassendyll was further astonished by the arrival of a fourth man. Except for being beardless this man was almost the exact double of himself! The gentleman was the King!

Far from being annoyed at this living proof of the old indictment, the King was highly diverted, and invited his new-found cousin to dine at his hunting lodge. The gentlemen dined rather too well and when a special bottle of wine was brought to the King with the compliments of half-brother Michael, His Majesty was too befuddled to be suspicious and drank the bottle straight off.

The next day, the coronation day, King Rudolf lay in a drugged stupor fifty miles from Strelsau.

Here was the last blow to Rudolf's tottering throne. Michael need only press his advantage and the kingdom was his. But Rassendyll's astonishing resemblance to the King seemed like an act of Providence. Sapt prevailed upon the Englishman to pose as the King until the crown was safely upon an Elphberg head. As soon as the King had recovered, Rassendyll could be smuggled out of the country. Rassendyll consented. The three men hid the unconscious King in the cellar; Rassendyll shaved his beard and donned the royal uniform; and the fantastic journey to Strelsau began.

With Sapt continually at his elbow, Rassendyll somehow got through the coronation. Of all whom he met Rassendyll could afterward remember only one person—beautiful Princess Flavia with her pale face and hair of Elphberg red.

Late that night Rassendyll and Sapt rode to the hunting lodge. But the old place was silent—in the cellar they found the King's servant murdered, the King gone! Black Michael had scored!

After the first moment of horror old Sapt soon recovered his wits. Black Michael did not dare harm the King nor yet proclaim Rassendyll's imposture lest he implicate himself. Until one side or the other moved, the game was stalemate. Until the King could be found, the masquerade must continue!

Rassendyll found himself successful in the role of King. None—save Black Michael and "the Six," Michael's notorious cohorts led by villainous young Rupert of Hentzau—suspected that he was not what he seemed. And Flavia showed Rassendyll a graciousness she had never vouchsafed the King.

The next move came from Michael and "the Six." Rassendyll received a note from Antoinette de Mauban bidding him to a tryst. Pretending innocence, Rassendyll obligingly fell into the trap and kept the rendezvous in a dark summer-house near the palace. Here he learned from Antoinette that the King was in the Castle of Zenda, a fact which shrewd old Sapt had suspected. Michael's "Six" tried to entice Rassendyll forth with a bogus bribe, but, using an iron tea-table as a shield, the Englishman forced his way out.

As the days passed Rassendyll realized that he was hopelessly in love with Flavia and she with him. To strengthen the devotion, long withheld, which the people were at last beginning to feel for "the King," it was necessary that the betrothal of the royal pair be announced. Now Rassendyll knew that he must liberate the King swiftly and be gone before his love for the Princess tempt him into disloyalty.

A shooting party was arranged as camouflage while Sapt and Von Tarlenheim made plans to rescue the King from Zenda. Johan, a spy, was placed in the castle, and while ostensibly confined to his bed by wounds inflicted by Rupert of Hentzau, Rassendyll made a secret tour of the castle and found that by swimming the moat he could gain access to the lower part.

A note smuggled in to Antoinette gave her word to create a disturbance at a given hour. At the same time Rassendyll would try to seize the King and Johan would open the gate to Sapt and reinforcements.

But they reckoned without fate. Antoinette, who long had been the object of Hentzau's desires, screamed for help long before the appointed hour; Michael, rushing to her aid, was slain by Hentzau. Under cover of the ensuing confusion Rassendyll reached the King. Sapt and his reinforcements arrived and only Hentzau escaped. Far more bitter than the pain of the wound he had suffered was the anguish Rassendyll felt when Flavia learned that he was not really the King.

The rightful King now rules in Ruritania. Rudolf Rassendyll has returned to England. But each year he journeys to Dresden, there to receive a little box from Fritz von Tarlenheim. In the box lies a red rose, round the stalk of the rose a piece of paper. On it these words are written: "Rudolf, Flavia, Always."

Green Mansions

By W. H. HUDSON

A NATURALIST *as much as he was an author, William Henry Hudson was born Aug. 4, 1841, at Quilmes, near Buenos Aires. He lived on the pampas of South America until 1874, when he moved to England. During many of the years in London his wife Emily kept a boarding house, and their means were extremely limited. A civil list pension granted in 1901 helped him somewhat, but it was not until years later that belated recognition of his work enabled him to relinquish such aid. Hudson died Aug. 18, 1922.*

ABEL GUEVEZ DE ARGENSOLA, 23-year-old member of a well-to-do Venezuelan family, fled into the interior after the failure of a political conspiracy. Resolved to go across country by way of the Rio Negro into Brazil, he turned aside to the Parahuari mountains, far into southern Venezuela, in search of gold.

Abel reached the last of the Indian settlements there without encountering a trace of gold. Discouraged, he sat down to rest beside a stream called the Curicay, and found the scene so beautiful that he decided to stay in this calm, peaceful region for a season. He gave a tinder box, almost his last possession, to Runi, chief of the 18 Indians who lived there, in exchange for shelter and food.

Hunting with the Indians, eating and sleeping in their single hut, teaching fencing to a youth named Kua-ko, Abel passed his time pleasantly. But one day he discovered that two miles west of the village lay a forest covering five or six square miles. He found that the Indians had an apparently superstitious fear of these delightful and varied woods, which were full of animal life.

Next day, alone in the woods, he heard a new sound, an exquisite bird-like melody, wonderfully pure and expressive, but he could never find the singer behind the leaves. Abel induced Kua-ko to go with him, hoping the Indian could identify the sound.

The Indian showed great fear, and refused to shoot his blow-pipe at any game, letting slip his belief that "the daughter of the Didi would catch the dart in her hand and throw it back" and kill him. Suddenly Kua-ko ran, and Abel fell when he tried to follow. Ashamed of his panic, Abel went back, and then he heard the mysterious song for the first time that day.

A few days later, Abel came silently on a clearing, and saw a girl reclining on the moss playing with a bird. She was about four feet six or seven inches tall, and wore a shimmering chemise of whitish-gray. Her hair falling about her shoulders seemed iridescent in the sun and shadow, as did her white skin. Her hands and bare feet were small and delicately shaped. Suddenly she realized that he was there, and faded into the woods.

Abel was horrified when the Indian's savagery showed through as he said that if Abel would kill this girl, the evil being who kept them out of the woods, he would be greatly honored. Abel angrily refused.

Next day, meeting a poisonous snake, Abel was about to kill it when the girl appeared and stopped him. Fascinated by her face, the loveliest he had ever seen, combining intelligence and a wild alertness, and by the play of colors in her hair, skin, and eyes, Abel stepped on the snake accidentally. It bit him, and he ran in panic until he fell from a precipice into unconsciousness. He woke in a hut where sat an old man, dark as an Indian but with a beard. The man, whose name was Nuflo, called out in Spanish for his grandchild, and a girl of 17 answered. It was the child of the woods, now shy and spiritless like a caged bird. She spoke Spanish and would not talk about her musical language.

Abel learned that the girl's name was Rima, and that she would not let her grandfather kill animals or fish for food; but beyond that the old man was secretive. When he was able to walk once more, Abel went into the woods with Rima, and again she was like a wild creature, warbling and moving about out of sight. When he induced her to sit down, she was reluctant to talk in Spanish, though she did say that her mother was dead and would not answer when Rima tried to call to her. She wondered that Abel could not speak her bird tongue.

Only when Abel caught her and held her hand did she seem altogether human, but then she turned shy again and for days avoided him. One day Abel discovered that Nuflo went across the next range to hunt his forbidden meat. Abel's feeling of remorse at sharing this feast made him realize that he loved Rima deeply.

One day Abel returned to the Indian village and found all away on a hunting expedition except one old woman. He learned that he had been given up for dead. When he got back, Rima led him to the top of a mountain and asked him to tell her about the world. She wanted to know whether there were other people like herself, and he sadly told her that he knew none. Then he mentioned that in a faraway part of the Venezuelan wilds there were mountains called Riolama, and Rima cried that she had been named for those mountains, that her mother had been found there. She said angrily that her grandfather had known it all the time, and had deceived her.

Nuflo believed that Rima had supernatural powers and could insure his entry into heaven, so he yielded when Rima demanded that he lead her to Riolama. On the difficult eighteen-day trip, Nuflo at last told Abel the story of Rima. An outlaw, he had saved Rima's mother from his gang at Riolama. A beautiful woman in a garment woven like Rima's from spider webs, she was lamed by a fall. She could speak only in the bird language, and was soon to become a mother. At the nearest settlement, Voa, Rima was born. Her sad mother, who shrank from the

Indians, died after seven years. Nuflo took the girl to the Parahuari mountains. At first they lived at Runi's village, but the girl had her mother's horror of the Indians. Then the Indians grew hostile when Rima prevented them from killing animals, and decided she was a daughter of the Didi when a poison arrow shot by one Indian killed another as they tried to hunt down Rima.

At Riolama, Abel sorrowfully restrained Rima from searching for her people, explaining that her mother would have told Rima if any survived. They must have been wiped out by the Indians, Abel said, or her mother would not have consented to end her days in Voa. Rima, unwillingly convinced, fainted. When she recovered, she told Abel that she had wanted her people to explain to her this strange new sensation she felt. Abel told her it was love, and she now responded to his kisses, and said that they must return to their woods. Impatient of Abel's and Nuflo's slow pace, she set out alone.

When the men arrived, they found the hut burned and no trace of Rima. Leaving Nuflo, Abel returned to the Indians, whom he found surly and suspicious. They told him there was no daughter of the Didi in the woods now. He told them he had been away in search of gold. Distraught, he forced himself to use the patience necessary to get the story out of the Indians. At last Kua-ko told him.

The Indians had learned that Rima was gone, and began hunting in the woods again. Then seven days before Abel returned they saw her again and trapped her in a tall isolated tree. They set the tree on fire, then danced about it, shouting: "Burn, burn, daughter of the Didi!" At last the flames reached the top and Rima cried: "Abel! Abel!" Then, through leaves and smoke and flame, she fell like a great white bird killed by an arrow, and was burned to ashes.

Abel killed Kua-ko, and fled in a vengeful frenzy to Runi's enemy, Managa, whom he goaded into wiping out Runi's village. Half-insane with sorrow, Abel succeeded in recovering the burnt bones of Rima, and, carrying them with him, made his way to Georgetown, British Guiana. He died there several years later and was granted his final wish that his ashes might be mingled with those of Rima.

Westward Ho!

By CHARLES KINGSLEY

A CLERGYMAN *and author, Charles Kingsley was born June 12, 1819, the son of the rector of Chelsea, London, and died Jan. 23, 1875, canon of Westminster by appointment of Queen Victoria. Besides winning fame as a writer, he taught history at Cambridge and took part in the Christian Socialist movement of 1848, aiming to improve living conditions among the British working people.*

ONE BRIGHT SUMMER'S AFTERNOON in the year 1575, a tall, fair boy, lingering along Bideford Quay in North Devon, came upon a group of sailors listening to this speech: "I tell you, as I, John Oxenham, am a gentleman, I saw it with these eyes, and so did Salvation Yeo there," and heard of great heaps of silver to be found along the Spanish Main. Oxenham was recruiting men and boys for another voyage, and when he learned that the tall youth was Amyas Leigh, son of an old friend, he sought Mr. Leigh's consent to take the boy along.

But neither Mr. Leigh nor Amyas' godfather, Sir Richard Grenville, would let the 15-year-old student go a-voyaging. A year later Mr. Leigh died, and, Amyas turning rebellious at school, his godfather let him sail with Captain Francis Drake.

Three years passed, and Bideford was holding a triumphal

celebration. Church bells tolled, and there was a pageant, and in the midst of the crowd there strode forth four weather-beaten mariners, led by a tall, beardless boy. It was Amyas, back from sailing around the world, coming to church to give God thanks at the side of his mother, who wept for joy.

While Amyas was absent Rose Salterne, daughter of Bideford's honest mayor, had grown into such a beauty at 18 that every gallant in North Devon had lost his heart to her. When the time came for Amyas to fight the Spanish-led Irish rebels, he and his brother Frank, who was a favorite at Queen Elizabeth's court and had won honor abroad, concocted a dinner at Bideford's Ship Tavern. There sat down together seven old schoolfellows, all rivals for Rose's hand, including young Will Cary, and they swore fealty to the Brotherhood of the Rose, vowing ever to stand by each other and her, and to win honor in the wars in her name. The seven found an eavesdropper, John Brimblecombe, piggish son of the schoolmaster, and when he vowed that he, too, loved Rose, they jestingly admitted him as chaplain of the brotherhood.

In Ireland Amyas captured a Spanish grandee, Don Guzman, and sent him to stay with Sir Richard Grenville until his ransom should be paid. And then, the Irish campaign being ended, Amyas sailed with Sir Humphrey Gilbert on his ill-fated voyage to Newfoundland, from which he returned in rags.

Landing at Plymouth, Amyas learned that Don Guzman had made love to Rose and fled with her. The Spaniard had been made governor of La Guayra, port of Caracas, and his ransom had been paid. Some said that the harshness of Rose's father, arising from his desire to protect his beloved girl, had led her to go off with Don Guzman.

The bowed-down Mayor Salterne, filled with hatred for the Spaniard, offered to spend his whole fortune if Amyas would go in pursuit of him. He outfitted a good ship, and Amyas assembled a brave crew, led by scholarly Frank, brave Will Cary, and faithful John Brimblecombe. Salvation Yeo was chief gunner, eager for revenge against the Inquisition which once had held him prisoner.

A hundred men on board, the good ship *Rose* sailed westward ho! and after a brave voyage came to La Guayra, at the foot of the cliff which parted the sea from the interior. Spanish warships and a strong land force made it impossible, Amyas concluded, to reach the governor's house where they expected to find Rose, but Frank insisted on making the attempt. The brothers, with six seamen, made their way ashore at midnight and climbed the path to the house. They found Rose there, but she refused to abandon her husband, although they invoked her religion as an argument.

Suddenly they were discovered, and had to flee to the beach, pursued by the governor's guard. Amyas, blinded by blood, staggered out to the boat with Frank in his arms, then was hit by a stone and remembered no more until he woke on the way to the ship. Only two of the seamen were left, and Frank, who had fallen into the surf, was given up for dead. The *Rose* was forced to weigh anchor and dash for safety.

Now came more than two years of weary, costly adventuring through the interior, in search of a phantom Inca city where Amyas hoped to find gold that would reward his loyal followers. All they discovered was a half-English, half-Spanish girl named Ayacanora, grown up wild among the Indians, who proved to be the "little maid" for whom Yeo had long mourned after she had vanished from the expedition on which he once fell into Spanish hands.

Struggling back to Cartagena on the Caribbean, after capturing a Spanish gold train, Amyas and his men seized a rich Spanish galleon by trick. Before setting back for England, he learned that Frank had been taken alive and had been burned to death with Rose by the Inquisition. He swore a dreadful oath for revenge on Don Guzman, who had resigned his governorship, and vowed that as long as he had eyes and hands he would kill all the Spaniards he could.

Amyas brought back his gold and his sad tidings to a mother grown old, and to a William Salterne who soon died, leaving money to Amyas to sail a new ship, to be called the *Vengeance,* against the Spaniards. Mrs. Leigh took Ayacanora into her home and transformed her into an English girl, although her wildness never left her completely. She would have made herself his slave, but Amyas had no eyes for her—his thoughts were only of vengeance.

In the summer of 1588, Spain raised her great Armada, and Captain Amyas Leigh went out with England's other seamen to deal a death blow against their mortal enemy. He had his especial prey—he had learned that Don Guzman was aboard the *Santa Catherina.* The English guns and the storms of the North Sea shattered the Armada, but Amyas pursued Don Guzman up to the Orkneys and around England to Lundy Island, on the south.

There the *Santa Catherina* struck on the rock called the Shutter, and vanished into the sea.

"Shame!" cried Amyas, hurling his sword into the water, "to lose my right, when it was in my very grasp!"

The sky was rent by a bright flame, and the world went dark for the young captain. He had been struck blind by a bolt of lightning.

Amyas was led home, hatred gone at last from his heart. His mother urged him to respond to Ayacanora's love, and now he consented.

"It is true, after all," said Amyas to himself. "What God has joined together, man cannot put asunder."

The Light That Failed

By RUDYARD KIPLING

BORN IN *Bombay on Dec. 30, 1865, the son of a British artist who was a museum executive in India, Rudyard Kipling was educated in England and began his writing career at 17 in India on the Lahore* Civil and Military Gazette. *By the time he was 24 he had won acclaim for his poems and short stories. He lived for a few years in the United States, where he married Miss Caroline Starr Balestier in 1892. In 1907 he was awarded a Nobel Prize. Kipling died on Jan. 18, 1936, in London.*

"WHAT do you think she'd do if she caught us?" said Maisie; and Dick answered: "Beat me, and lock you up in your bedroom."

The two orphans had bought a revolver and cartridges from their allowances without the knowledge of Mrs. Jennett, their guardian. For the six years Dick Heldar had been with her, she had given him hate and ridicule instead of love and sympathy, and her version of religion had caused him to hate his God. At least he had learned to live alone, a power that was of service when he entered a public school and the boys laughed at his mended clothes.

For holidays he went back to Mrs. Jennett, and one autumn he found a companion in bondage, a long-haired, gray-eyed and silent little atom whose chief friend was her goat Amomma and who controlled Mrs. Jennett by threats to "write to my lawyer-people." Their misery drove the children together, though Maisie stayed as independent as ever.

They walked far up the beach, near Fort Keeling, for their

pistol practice, which was almost interrupted when Maisie fired accidentally and nearly struck Dick in the face. On their return she confided that she was being sent to study in France, and Dick suddenly found that he minded this very much. An awkward first kiss proved more eloquent than words, and Maisie agreed when Dick told her: "You belong to me for ever and ever."

Up the Nile, below where Gordon was fighting for his life at Khartoum, Dick was initiated into syndicate work by Gilbert Torpenhow, a war correspondent who had found him sketching at Suakin, on the Red Sea. Torpenhow had said: "You're right to take your first chance," and thus Dick was started on the career for which he had prepared by following trouble about the East. Caricatures of his masters had been his only achievement at school.

Seated on a sandbank patching his trousers while soldiers struggled to repair one of the whaleboats carrying supplies up the Nile, Torpenhow was bantering with Dick when the Mahdi's men suddenly attacked their column. The British formed a square in the stifling heat as three thousand naked warriors charged. Then the weak side of the square yielded, and a native's saber cut Dick across the helmet. Dick killed his attacker, and one who threatened Torpenhow.

Dick's wound healed, the campaign over and a draft on account having come from the syndicate, Dick went to Port Said, to set down in black and white and color all the races congregated there to practice all the world's iniquities and vices. Then a telegram arrived from Torpenhow in London: "Come back, quick: you have caught on."

Dick found that his work was in demand; he had a fresh touch, a new way of drawing things. Torpenhow installed him in a studio overlooking the Thames, and looked on in admiration as Dick cowed the plump syndicate manager who didn't want to return his original sketches.

Believing Dick to be a self-taught artist—he didn't reveal that he had studied two years in Paris—the public bought everything he could paint, and in three months he was well off. Eager for success, he started doing the slick things the editors wanted, in spite of all the protests of Torpenhow and the Nilghai, the fat chief of the war correspondents.

One evening on Westminster Bridge Dick met Maisie, the dark gray eyes and firm mouth unaltered.

He found that she, too, was painting, but without his success. And his old love for her returned. He could not conceive that she should refuse sooner or later to love him, although she said: "I've got my work to do, and I must do it." He took to reveries that cut down his output, and called faithfully on Maisie every Sunday. She accepted some of his advice on painting, but not him, which was beyond the understanding of the red-haired girl with whom she lived.

Then Dick was overtaken with an idea for an excursion to Fort Keeling, over the very ground they had trodden together ten years before. He congratulated himself on his cunning. But when they sat and looked out at the sea, all the answer he could get was: "I despise myself because I take everything that you give me and I give you nothing in return. But I don't feel that I care." Indeed, she turned the tables by telling Dick to promise not to do bad work for the sake of money.

Restless at the sight of the sea, Dick did no more work the rest of that week, and was dismayed to learn on Sunday that Maisie was going to France to paint a Melancolia with which she hoped to storm the gates of the Salon. He saw her off with a farewell kiss so long that she wrenched herself away angrily.

Back home, he found that Torpenhow had been feeding a hungry servant girl whose name turned out to be Bessie Broke. Her pretty, frightened face made Dick resolve to use her as the model for a Melancolia of his own. But when he found her imploring Torpenhow to take her in with him, Dick interfered and won her hatred, though his fees made her continue to sit for him.

One day a haze before Dick's eyes seemed to blot out part of the studio, and Dick went to an oculist to learn that the old sword-cut had damaged his optic nerve. He had at most a year before he would go blind. Frightened, he set to work in earnest on his painting, the idea at last clear in his mind. He painted day after day, drinking to chase the spots from his eyes. Torpenhow returned from a holiday, was shocked at his drunken condition, then more deeply moved by the explanation for it, and by the magnificent Melancolia.

Dick finished the painting and fell asleep exhausted. Vengeful Bessie got her money and went to work with turpentine and palette knife. When she slipped away, the picture was a scarred muddle of colors. That night something cracked inside Dick's temples like an overstrained bowstring, and he found himself in the dark. He raved for three days in a delirium, and Torpenhow heard Maisie's name for the first time.

From slender clues, Dick's friends found Maisie, told her he had gone blind, and brought her back from France to Dick. She found him sitting brooding by the window, her unopened letters in his hand. He rejected pity, and told her: "I'm down and done for." She realized that he was no longer a man to be looked up to —only some blind one that seemed on the point of crying. She felt pity for him, not love.

Maisie burst into tears, and Dick told her: "It would be kindest not to see me any more," and sent her away after showing her what he thought was his Melancolia. Maisie fled, and that was the end of her.

Torpenhow, not knowing that anything had gone wrong, went off the following day to the new campaign in the Southern Sudan, and Dick was left in the thieving hands of Mr. Beeton, the caretaker. He was unshaven and slovenly, finding it a task to dress, counting lumps of coal for amusement, everlastingly thinking of Maisie and might-have-beens.

On one of his rare walks out-of-doors with Mr. Beeton, he encountered Bessie again and took her home with him. Though she still despised Dick, she could not stand to see him defrauded. She began to dust his rooms, and Dick decided to pay her to look after him, though he told himself that it would hurt more than anything else to fall so low as to live with Bessie.

Bessie learned that he had a little more than four thousand pounds, the fruit of his year's work. The Melancolia was to be sold, he told her—and she giggled and confessed what she had done. Dick gripped her wrist and thought; he did not hit Bessie, but he realized that his project was useless.

"The Lord is a just and terrible God, with a very strong sense of humor. It serves me right," Dick said. Then he cashed his odd pounds, made a will leaving the four thousand to Maisie, sold his furnishings and gave Bessie the money, and took passage to Port Said on a mail boat.

Even in his blindness, Dick's money and his knowledge of the East got him to Suakin and to the troops on duty in the desert past there. At dawn he reached the camp on camel-back, and called to Torpenhow as shots rang out from the sands. His friend cried: "Come down, you damned fool." And Dick came obediently, but as a tree falls. His luck had held to the last, even to the crowning mercy of a kindly bullet through his head.

Sons and Lovers

By D. H. LAWRENCE

DAVID HERBERT LAWRENCE, *son of an impoverished coal miner, was born September 11, 1885, at Eastwood, in Nottinghamshire, England. Educated at Nottingham on scholarships, he passed the teaching examinations with the highest marks in all England. A weak chest made it difficult for him to work regularly, but he began writing novels, and with the publication of his first book in 1911 the emergence of a powerful and original new talent was hailed. His work was influenced by the psychoanalysts, and later by his travels in Italy, New Mexico, and Australia. He died at Vence, near Nice on the Riviera, on March 2, 1930.*

GERTRUDE COPPARD, daughter of an impoverished engineer, married Walter Morel, a coal miner, when she was twenty-three and he was twenty-seven. He was vigorous, with a rich natural laugh, a handsome dark man, without education. She was small, pretty and proud, well-read and fond of intellectual conversation. For six months they were happy in their miner's cottage at Bestwood in the coal field north of Nottingham. But Mrs. Morel found that they could not talk seriously together, and disillusionments piled up—poverty, Morel's return to drinking, the refusal of his sensual nature to face the obligations which her morality sought to impose on him. He became irritable, and a lifetime battle between them began.

Mrs. Morel took refuge in her children. The first was William, and she had to protect the boy at times against his father's quick temper. And she tortured Morel about his shortcomings, though their love was at an end and he was an outsider to her. William had come two years after their marriage, and Annie came two years later. Another five years, and Paul was born. He was a delicate baby, a serious one, on whom she lavished her love. Then Morel fell ill, and his recovery brought a period of tenderness which brought a fourth child, Arthur.

William became a shorthand clerk and night-school teacher, and turned socially ambitious. He went to dances, which Mrs. Morel disapproved, although she was proud when he got a situation in Nottingham. It was painful to her to have him go off to London at 120 pounds a year when he was 20 years old, for he would be lost to her, she felt.

Meantime Annie had been studying to be a teacher, and Paul was learning French and German and algebra with the aid of his godfather, the town clergyman. Paul grew stronger as he grew older, but he remained pale and quiet, sensitive to what other people felt, and always attentive to his mother. His father's drinking disturbed him; Paul shared his mother's suffering, and grew to hate his father's brutality. Morel was shut out from the family except on occasional jolly moments.

William, doing well in a lawyer's office, came home a gentleman on his holidays. He did not forget his family, but London life left little money for him to send home. Then he became engaged to an empty-headed brunette, Lily Western, who lorded it over the Morels when he took her to Bestwood for a visit. William began to dread marriage to this frivolous girl, but his problems ended in his death from pneumonia. Mrs. Morel brooded over his death for months, then began to root her life in Paul.

At fourteen Paul went to work for Mr. Jordan, a Nottingham maker of surgical appliances. He lived at home, riding to his job by train. His eight shillings a week left little money over, but he found that the factory was not an unpleasant place to work.

The Leivers family, friends of the Morels, had taken isolated Willey Farm. Paul began going there often to see the Leivers boys, and then began to take notice of their sister Miriam, a year younger than he. She had a shy, dark beauty, and was mystically romantic and religious. She began to half-worship Paul, who was gentle and clever, although as manly as her coarser brothers. Mrs. Leivers' religiousness had permeated Miriam, who had a constant intensity about her. An illness kept Paul idle for ten months, and he saw a great deal of Miriam. They fell in love, though her inability to be just "ordinary" made him almost hate her at times. He began to teach her mathematics and French, and her French exercises became outpourings of her love for him. Yet at times she seemed more deeply interested in looking for his soul in the drawings at which he was beginning to excel than in Paul himself. Indeed, she set up a barrier of spirituality between them that seemed to keep Paul from bringing their love to the point of physical contact. And Mrs. Morel showed an antagonism for this girl who wanted to possess her son completely, who made Paul so morose as he repressed his passions.

Mrs. Morel's health was failing. And she reproached Paul with spending so many hours with Miriam, though he insisted that he did not love her, but only liked to talk with her. Instinctively he realized that he was life to his mother. And she was the chief thing to him. With her he never felt the uncertainty that possessed him with Miriam. Once she cried: "I could let another woman— but not her. She'd leave me no room." And when he repeated that he was not in love with Miriam, his mother kissed him fervently.

Miriam, confident of Paul, did not believe him when he said he did not love her. She told herself his soul wanted her. And she wanted to cry when he offered to stop calling on her so that she could find another man. He did call less often, and Miriam confidently decided to put him to a test. She introduced him to Mrs. Clara Dawes, a handsome, well-built woman who had become a suffragist and was living apart from her blacksmith husband. Paul was to be tested by a choice between the "higher" and "lower" things—Mrs. Dawes' physical attractions being the "lower" in Miriam's mind. Paul joked freely with Clara, feeling an ease that he had never known with Miriam. But still he acquiesced in Miriam's faith that he belonged to her.

Interspersed with Paul's emotional life were other events. Annie married; Arthur, having enlisted in the army, was bought out and took a wife. Paul progressed with his painting, and began winning prizes. And Morel's leg was crushed in a mine accident which left him a bit lame; he was beginning to grow old.

The passions ran high in Paul though at twenty-three he had not had any actual experience of love. His closeness to his mother remained; she had continued proud and courageous in spite of illness and poverty, and her life was bound up in his. She felt that Miriam had undermined Paul's joy, and her heart broke for him. Paul stayed away from Miriam for months, but when spring came he went back to her for a test of his own. He had never been able to kiss her, make love to her. Now he forced his way through the barrier. One evening in the woods she relinquished herself to him, but it was a sacrifice in which she felt something of horror. This thick-voiced, oblivious man was a stranger to her. Paul felt that she was clenched against him. For a moment he loved her utterly, but the feeling never came again.

Now he turned to Clara's warmth. He had helped her get work in Jordan's factory, and he saw much of her. His eight years of Miriam he ended with a last conversation which left her bitter. He and Clara walked together, and one day he took her to the banks of the Trent, and spread his rainproof on the moist earth between two trees. He sunk his mouth on her throat; everything was perfectly still, and there was nothing in the afternoon but themselves. Clara told him of her husband, Baxter Dawes, with whom she had never attained understanding in their three years together. Mrs. Morel welcomed Clara as she had never accepted Miriam. Dawes learned of their affair, and Paul hurled beer in his face in a tavern when Dawes made a scurrilous remark about them. The blacksmith vowed revenge, and Clara was angry when Paul refused to carry a weapon to defend himself. The physical feeling was the chief link between Paul and Clara, and Paul drew from her the confession that she thought Dawes still belonged to her. She said Baxter gave her all of himself; she could never get all of Paul. Then one night Dawes intercepted Paul and beat him terribly in spite of Paul's instinctive fighting back. After this Paul found himself avoiding Clara.

Then Mrs. Morel fell ill at Sheffield, on a visit to Annie, and they learned that she could not recover. In deep pain she was brought home to await her slow death. Meantime Paul made friends with the tortured Dawes, and restored Clara to him. Paul could not bear to watch his mother's slow death. Realistic, she willingly ate little so that the end might be hastened. But it was horrible watching her waste away, and at last Paul and Annie fed her an overdose of morphia. He kneeled beside the bed, embraced her wasted body, and whispered: "My love—my love—oh, my love!" Paul felt he could never let her go. This love had stood out above all his others. For months he went about in a gloomy daze, unable to draw, unwilling to live. He met Miriam again in Nottingham, but she was still capable only of sacrificing herself to him, not of sharing his burdens. Leaving Miriam's lodgings, Paul thought of his mother. She was the only thing that had held him up. But no, he would not give up. He shut his fists against the desire to join her, and walked quickly toward the city's glow.

The Ordeal of Richard Feverel

By GEORGE MEREDITH

BORN *at Portsmouth, England, on February 12, 1828, George Meredith always tried to conceal the fact that his father was a naval outfitter. Orphaned early, he was raised as a ward in chancery. He studied in Germany, and at 21 began to eke out a living as a poet and journalist. He married the daughter of Thomas Love Peacock, and had two children by her. Recognition came late to him, although as literary adviser to Chapman and Hill, the publishers, he helped Thomas Hardy and others to their first fame. Meredith died on May 18, 1909, at Mickleham, Surrey.*

THE CLEVEREST WOMEN IN ENGLAND pursued Sir Austin Feverel, Baronet, of Raynham Abbey on the Thames, because he had published "The Pilgrim's Scrip," a book of aphorisms in which he deftly and coldly dissected womanhood. But Sir Austin was well armored, for his wife had run off with his best friend, a poet, and the baronet's heart was wrapped up in all that remained to him—his son, a graceful, handsome boy. The baronet called his loss his ordeal—he said every Feverel must have one.

Sir Austin intended to make Richard into a perfect man by rearing him according to a System which would hedge round the boy's youth from corruption, building up his animal health and moral fortitude so that he would act properly by instinct on the day when he should have to face the world.

Every October there was a festivity for little Richard's birthday. The family came together, including the boy's uncles; his cousin Adrian Harley, a wise, cynical youth who was part of the Raynham household; his cousin Austin Wentworth, a gentle young man at whom society shuddered because he had atoned for an error by wedding his mother's housemaid; Mrs. Doria Forey, Sir Austin's sister and the female head of his house, and Doria's quiet little daughter Clare, who adored Richard.

It was on his fourteenth birthday that Richard ran away from the celebration with his friend Ripton Thompson, the son of Sir Austin's solicitor. Richard, as shy as a girl, fled as one insulted when asked to disrobe for the annual physical examination on which his father insisted. The boys, hunting through the woods, unknowingly poached on the farm of independent Giles Blaize, who horsewhipped them. His hot pride stung, Richard paid Tom Bakewell, a farm youth, to burn Blaize's rick. Tom was caught. Blaize and the Feverel men knew well what had happened, but the farmer said he would withdraw charges only if Richard himself apologized. At last the boy yielded to his bitter duty; as reward, Tom was hired as his servant.

Richard retired into himself as he passed into adolescence. Handsome, strong, intelligent, well-bred, he blossomed into a youthful poetry-writing that normally would have passed of itself. But Sir Austin pressed the issue and asked Richard to burn his writings. Richard did—but it was the end of true confidence between father and son. The baronet, thinking himself all-wise, knew less of Richard than did the servants.

Sir Austin, with Richard nearing eighteen, set out for London to find a perfect girl whom his perfect youth could marry when he was five-and-twenty. But Richard, rowing on the Thames, met a simply-dressed girl with blue eyes and long golden curls who was eating dewberries on the bank. They fell in love without knowing it was love. The girl was Lucy Desborough, a Catholic, the orphan niece of farmer Blaize.

Informed of this affair by Heavy Benson, the butler—Richard beat Benson half to death when he learned of the spying—Sir Austin called Richard to London. When they returned in three weeks, Blaize had sent Lucy off to school. Richard learned that it was at his father's request; he had been denied even the opportunity of showing his father that Lucy was lovely. Though Lady Blandish, a widow who humbly loved the baronet while waiting for him to melt to her, had told Sir Austin of Lucy's beauty and fine behavior, Sir Austin had conceived a personal antagonism for this person who had interfered with his experiment.

Richard learned where Lucy was; he started after her, was stricken ill, and when he recovered long weeks later he was cold and reserved, and did not mention Lucy. Sir Austin decided London was the cure, and Richard was sent off in the care of his dyspeptic Uncle Hippias. But at the London station Richard encountered Lucy. He spirited her off to a lodging house which turned out to be operated by Mrs. Berry, his childhood nurse. Nineteen-year-old Richard's love conquered 17-year-old Lucy's wisdom, and she consented to marry him. With the aid of Mrs. Berry and Ripton Thompson, Richard deluded Hippias and kept up his visits to his London relatives—who now included Mrs. Doria and Clare, who still loved him—all the while he was getting the license and engaging the church.

Then, leaving Ripton to tell Sir Austin, Richard married his Lucy and took her off to the Isle of Wight for a honeymoon.

To Lady Blandish, Sir Austin's surface reaction to the smashup

of his system was too coldly philosophical to seem genuine. He
told her: "It is useless to base any system on a human being,"
and his concern seemed for the loss of his plan, while his son
took the blame for all the failings of the human race. Richard
was still sure that his father would welcome Lucy if only he
would meet her, but the baronet refused to answer his son's
letters, though he kept Richard supplied with money.

Then Adrian Harley and Lady Blandish decided to attempt a
reconciliation. Richard was glad to go to London, but the baronet,
though he did not say no, was in no hurry to meet his son again.
Lucy was left behind on the island; she wanted Richard to meet
his father alone. The weeks and then the months dragged on,
while Adrian invented new promises and amusements to keep
Richard from hurrying back to his bride. At a party the youth
met the notorious Mrs. Mount, whom in his innocence he regarded as a woman misunderstood by the world. She was wise
enough not to use her tricks on Richard, and he spent long
hours talking with her, scorning all warnings from his friends.

Three months passed; Richard made a last effort to get an
answer from his father, then told Mrs. Mount he was going back
to Lucy. She unloosed her charms at a farewell dinner, and
Richard fell an easy victim.

Lucy had not told Richard she was with child. Thus, when she
did not hear from him for two weeks, she believed he was off
looking for his father, while Adrian believed he had gone back
to Lucy. Then Mrs. Berry took matters into her hands and
fetched Lucy to London, where Sir Austin finally had arrived.

Two weeks later Richard suddenly reappeared without a word
of explanation, greeted his father with restrained calm, but made
no move to go to Lucy. Clare had married a man twice her age;
now Richard was summoned to her deathbed. He went with Mrs.
Doria, and learned from Clare's diary for the first time that she
had loved him. Richard refused to go back to Lucy. He said:
"I have killed one. I cannot go to my wife, because I am not
worthy to touch her hand." Instead he went off to the Continent,

while Sir Austin waited austerely at home for his son to return before he would see his daughter-in-law.

Honest Austin Wentworth returned after five years abroad, learned how matters stood, and cut a Gordian knot by taking Lucy—who meantime had had her child—from Mrs. Berry's to Raynham. Sir Austin found he had a sweet and wise daughter-in-law, and a sturdy grandson, and capitulated with the words: "She is extremely well-looking."

Richard had burned all his letters from England, so that when Austin sought him out in the Rhineland, he learned for the first time that he was a father. Heroism faded, and he started back.

But in London Richard found a letter from Mrs. Mount revealing that her rake of a husband, Lord Mountfalcon, had paid her to keep Richard occupied while he tried vainly to seduce Lucy. Burning with anger, Richard forced Mountfalcon to accept a challenge to a duel, then went on to Raynham. It was midnight when he entered Lucy's room. They embraced hotly, and then his patient wife asked what she had done to incur his anger. Richard burst into tears, told her he had broken his marriage oath, and begged her forgiveness. When he told Lucy he had never loved any other, she replied only: "Darling! Kiss me." Then Richard tore himself away to go to his duel, leaving Lucy fainting.

The end came quickly. Wounded, but not mortally, Richard lay in a village on the French coast. Lucy, kept from him lest the excitement of seeing her impede his recovery, fell ill of a cerebral fever, and died while her husband was recovering. His father told Richard, and the youth listened and lived, though it was plain his heart was broken. Lady Blandish summed it up: "If Sir Austin has saved his son's body, he has given the death blow to his heart. There are some who are worse than people who deliberately commit crimes."

Diana of the Crossways

By GEORGE MEREDITH

ENGLISH SOCIETY first became aware of the charm and loveliness of Diana Merion at a ball given in Dublin to honor the Irish soldier, Lord Larrian. Diana was a young girl then—not yet twenty—but already possessed of the dark statuesque queenliness that was her Irish heritage. Her wit was a foil to her beauty; vivacious, intellectual, infallibly amusing, and poised beyond her years, she shared the honors of the evening with the old soldier-hero who, himself, confessed that he was captivated by her charm.

More enraptured by Diana's success than the girl herself, was Lady Emma Dunstane. Older by a few years than Diana, "Emmy" was the young woman's dearest and most faithful friend. A fever contracted in India had left Emmy a semi-invalid whose greatest consolation was her vital and beautiful young friend, "Tony"—a contraction of Diana's middle name, Antonia.

Diana made a reputation for herself at the Irish Ball; more than that she acquired two devoted friends—Lord Larrian, himself, and Thomas Redworth, a solid young Englishman who, despite his immediate capitulation to Diana's charm, was too strongminded ever to seem fully in accord with the capricious and radical young Irishwoman.

Feted by society, admired by all, Diana was nevertheless not contented. Her tastes were simple: she loved nature, books and conversation, her beloved friend Emmy, and Crossways, the home of her childhood. She found the position of an unprotected beauty in society precarious and often unpleasant. She was most happy living with Emmy on the latter's estate in Surrey; here she particularly enjoyed the intellectual companionship afforded her by their neighbor, Thomas Redworth. She did not suspect that this gentleman refrained from proposing marriage to her only because his limited income—he was in a Government office—could provide her with no luxury. Redworth, in an effort to augment his resources, started to engage in Railway investment. Diana, who spurned commerce in favor of the more romantic profession of War, was unimpressed by this speculation, and despite his small but immediate success, Redworth postponed speaking to the young woman about marriage.

Meanwhile Diana's serene happiness at Emmy's home had been disrupted. Sir Lukin Dunstane, Emmy's good-natured but insensitive husband, inflamed by Diana's beauty, made overture to the girl in an uncontrolled moment. Although he immediately repented his rashness, Diana knew that the sanctuary of her friend's home could no longer be open to her. Distraught and disgusted with society, she sought refuge in a marriage with a cousin, Augustus Warwick.

Emmy was horrified at her friend's choice. Correct, cold, a gentleman of leisure and fifteen years Diana's senior, Warwick's only claim to being the proper husband to the high-spirited Irish girl was his promise not to sell the old family home, Crossways.

The marriage was doomed from the first. Chilly, opinionated, unloving and suspicious, Warwick soon even went back on his promise about Crossways and threatened to let the old place. Finally the innocent friendship between Diana and Lord Dannisburgh, an influential politician and twice the girl's age, led Warwick to the final step. He sued for divorce. Emmy learned that Diana planned to flee the country rather than stay and prove her innocence. In desperation Emmy sent Tom Redworth to the Crossways, whither she knew intuitively her friend had fled, and the stalwart Englishman brought Diana back to face her detractors. Diana's admirers stood staunchly by. Emmy, Redworth, Lord Larrian—who sent a gigantic Newfoundland dog, Leander, to be her protector—Danvers, her faithful maid, and others all upheld Diana's innocence. Gradually Diana returned to society. She took lodging in London with her maid, supported herself by her pen, and even attended parties where her beauty and wit charmed as before. Warwick lost his suit against her, and she was left absolved of guilt but tied to a man whom she hated and refused to see.

It was in Italy while travelling with an English party that Diana encountered Percy Dacier. He was a brilliant young man, handsome, intelligent, and already a noted and influential figure in Parliament and his party. When he met Diana he was reported to be interested romantically in Miss Constance Asper, a beautiful, pious, insipid young heiress. Diana at first impressed only his intellect. Her growing popularity as a novelist—she had had a success with her second novel, "The Princess Egeria"—intrigued him. But when on the death of Lord Dannisburgh, an uncle of his, Diana complied with the last request of the deceased and kept watch by his body, Dacier's admiration insensibly increased to love. Dacier's passion gained expression when he followed Diana to Caen whither she had retreated and there declared himself. Although she discouraged him, Diana felt more for Dacier than she guessed. The passion grew. When, her husband falling ill, she feared that he might force her to return to him, Diana admitted to Dacier that she loved him, and even consented to plan an elopement.

But the next day Dacier waited in vain at the railway station where he and his beloved had planned to meet. Emmy had suddenly been forced to undergo a dangerous operation; Diana had been summoned, and, forgoing all other considerations, had fled to her friend's bedside. Emmy survived. When Diana and Dacier met again, their passion had cooled to sanity and they abandoned their scheme. For a year afterward, they did not meet. Then Diana invited Dacier to her London home, and he became a constant visitor there. Their relationship was, except within their own hearts, one of friendship only, and, until the ailing Warwick should die, must continue so.

But the extravagant salon that Diana maintained to further Dacier's political career drained the beautiful Irishwoman's re-

sources. At her wits' end she sold some political information
that Dacier had given her to a journalist, unaware that what she
gave away was of extreme importance to Dacier's career. Infuriated, Dacier abandoned her and married Constance Asper.
Although Diana abruptly found herself freed by Warwick's death
in a street accident, she had lost her will to live. Shut up in her
bedroom, refusing food and warmth, Diana was near death when
Emmy arrived at her house. She prevailed upon Diana to regain
her hold on life. Diana finally found happiness where she
least expected it—in a marriage with the sturdy, faithful Thomas
Redworth.

The Cloister and the Hearth

By CHARLES READE

NOVELIST *and dramatist, Charles Reade used his pen to combat
the evils of his time, as did many other Victorian writers. He was
born June 8, 1814, at Ipsden, Oxfordshire, the son of a squire,
won honors at Oxford, and was educated for the bar. From 1851,
when his first play was produced, until his death on April 11,
1884, he produced a steady succession of novels and plays. The
lunacy laws and prison conditions were among the matters he
helped to reform.*

IT WAS past the middle of the fifteenth century when our tale
begins in Holland. Elias and Catherine, his wife, had a comfortable trade in cloth and curried leather in the little town of
Tergou, and four of their nine children were set up for themselves. Two others were unable to work, and Cornelis and
Sybrandt were too lazy.

There remained young Gerard, destined for the Church, who was taught by the monks until one day they discovered that he was teaching them. Then he took to illuminating on vellum, in which he was helped by old Margaret Van Eyck, sister of the famous brothers, who was ending her days in Tergou. Gerard sent in some of his work to a competition in Rotterdam, and his mother gave him a crown to go see the prizes given.

On the road a league from Rotterdam, Gerard found an old man and a comely young woman sitting exhausted. Their clothing denoted both dignity and poverty, and Gerard shared his food with them. Ghysbrecht Van Swikten, burgomaster of Tergou, came by at this moment and recognized the pair as Peter Brandt and his daughter Margaret, whom he had defrauded of rich lands, though they did not know it. Gerard fell in love with the girl.

Now began a tale of trouble. Through Margaret Van Eyck, Gerard was promised a benefice as a priest, but when he returned home he sought out young Margaret Brandt at Sevenbergen. The burgomaster, fearing the young man would learn of certain documents which would reveal his fraud, told Gerard's parents of the attachment. Gerard's father threatened to have his son imprisoned until he became a priest, and the youth swore that he would run away rather than enter the Church while young Margaret lived.

Now Margaret Van Eyck gave Gerard money to go to Italy, where painters were honored like princes, and Gerard decided to marry Margaret Brandt at once. Although he got a certificate from the priest at Sevenbergen, the ceremony was never completed, for the burgomaster had the youth seized. Gerard escaped from the prison, bade farewell to Margaret, and set off for Italy, carrying with him written proof, which he had found in the burgomaster's prison, of the fraud against the Brandts.

On the road a gay soldier, Denys, making his way home to Burgundy, insisted on accompanying Gerard. In several adventures the two rescued each other, and after they parted Denys took a message back to Margaret, who was now in Rotterdam.

This brought a reconciliation between her and Gerard's parents, who now decided to summon him home. But Ghysbrecht was anxious that he stay away, and with the aid of Cornelis and Sybrandt concocted a letter with the forged signature of Margaret Van Eyck, in which Gerard was told that his wife was dead.

Meanwhile Gerard had reached Rome. The ship in which he had sailed from Venice was wrecked north of Naples, and he and a Dominican friar, clinging to a mast, managed to reach the shore. When Gerard arrived at the Eternal City he was no longer a boy, but a man learned in human ways, who had shed blood in self-defense and had grazed the grave by land and sea.

Gerard worked hard, and put by all the money he earned in Rome for his illuminations. Then came the forged letter. Gerard's senses failed him; he ran about the streets, then fell ill of a fever. When he recovered, his friend, Fra Jerome, who had been in the wreck with him, exhorted him to consecrate his gifts to the Church.

"Malediction on the Church!" cried Gerard, blaming it for all his woes. He rushed fiercely into pleasure and vice, the large sums he had set aside for Margaret affording him ample means for debauchery. He no longer had patience for his art. Then he flung himself into the river, but was rescued by a professional assassin and was carried unconscious to the Dominican convent.

Finding Father Jerome at his bedside when he woke, Gerard learned that he had been saved "by the hand of Heaven." He tried to pray, but found that he could only utter prayers. Then he wept, saying that "the Church is peace of mind," and confessed his sins. Now Gerard begged to remain in the convent. He passed his novitiate in prayer and mortification, and upon a shorter probation than usual became a friar.

Here Gerard became Brother Clement. His zeal and accomplishments, especially his rare mastery of language, soon became known, and he was sent with Jerome to travel and preach in England. More than a year had passed when they set out. But at Rotterdam, impatient because his companion lingered on the way, Jerome took ship alone for England and advised Clement to preach awhile to his own countrymen.

Shocked and mortified at this desertion, Clement promised to sleep at the convent and preach whenever the prior should appoint. One day he saw Margaret in the church at Rotterdam, and soon learned from the sexton, who had been in Ghysbrecht's service, of the trick that had been played upon him.

That night a Dominican friar burst in upon Elias and Catherine as they sat at supper, cursed Cornelis and Sybrandt, and flung down before his father the forged letter. Then, in a moment, he was gone, crying: "On earth ye will never see me more!" Elias drove his false sons out at the point of a sword.

Clement lay at full length on the floor of the convent church, abasing himself for his intemperate rage, while feeling gleams of joy that Margaret was alive. Then he remembered that he had neglected a dying man, and went instantly to the deathbed of Ghysbrecht, who did not recognize his old enemy Gerard. Ghysbrecht promised to make full restitution to Margaret for withholding her property.

With Margaret a rich woman, Friar Clement disappeared to the cell among the rocks which the recently dead hermit of Gouda had occupied. He did not hear that he had been made vicar of Gouda.

Margaret sought him out, and begged him to come to the vicarage.

"My beloved, I am a monk, and though my heart break I must be firm," he told her. " 'Tis best we part."

But Margaret returned and, in Clement's absence, left their child in his cell. Thinking it a deserted infant, he set to work to comfort it, crooning a lullaby, and sighing to think of what might have been.

That night Margaret returned and told him the boy was his. He was surprised; they talked long, and Clement promised to go to the manse of Gouda. Margaret stayed away, though she left their child, little Gerard, with him.

Then one day Clement came to her and said: "My sweet Margaret! We have been waiting and waiting for you every day," and he took her to the vicarage. Next day Clement preached more powerfully than ever before, and his mother and Margaret listened with streaming eyes.

Margaret vowed never by word or deed to let her love come between this young saint and heaven.

Little Gerard was already winning a famous name at school when Margaret was stricken with the plague and died. A fortnight later Clement entered the Dominican convent, and a few days later he, too, was dead. Their son lived to become the great Erasmus.

The Story of an African Farm

By OLIVE SCHREINER

THE DAUGHTER *of a simple German missionary-shoemaker and an Englishwoman, Olive Schreiner was born in Basutoland, South Africa, in 1862. She wrote her first book while working as a governess in Boer families, and in 1882 took it to England, where George Meredith saw the manuscript and helped her to get it published under the pen name of* Ralph Iron. *None of her later books measured up to this novel. In 1894 she married S. C. Cronwright, a member of the South African Parliament, who changed his name to Cronwright-Schreiner. In later years she worked for the emancipation of women. Death came to her on Dec. 12, 1920, at Cape Town.*

THE FULL AFRICAN MOON poured down its light on the lonely, sandy plain; on the small kopje, a heap of round ironstones, and on the homestead, a group of sheep kraals and Kaffir huts, with a square red-brick thatched dwelling house and an open wagon house from which jutted several outbuildings.

Sleep ruled. In the farmhouse the huge Boer-woman, Tant' Sannie, had bad dreams, but not of her dead second husband, the consumptive Englishman, nor the first, the young Boer. In the next room lay yellow-haired Em, a plain child, the Englishman's daughter, and Lyndall, a girl of elfin-like beauty, Em's orphaned cousin. Em's father had married Tant' Sannie so that she would take care of the girls.

Otto, the religious German overseer, slept soundly in one of the outbuildings, but his curly-haired son Waldo lay awake thinking of his father's readings from the Bible about the many who go through the wide gate that leads to destruction. He wept at the picture, and cried: "O God! save only a few!"

By daylight the farm and Boer-woman were ugly, Em's freckles were more apparent, and Otto was a huge childish man who preached at the Kaffir boys without seeing how slowly they worked.

Waldo, tending his herd of ewes and lambs, put his dinner meat on a stone at midday, and prayed to God to "send fire down from heaven to burn it." Nothing happened, and Waldo told himself: "God cannot lie. I had faith. No fire came. God hates me."

It was two years later that Waldo sat on the kopje one night and dared to look at a secret he had carried in his heart for a year. "I hate God!" he said; "I love Jesus Christ, but I hate God." He was lost now; he did not care. But oh, the loneliness. The barb in childhood's suffering is its intense loneliness, its intense ignorance.

At last came the summer of the great drought of 1862. On a hot afternoon the girls, still mere children of twelve, sat in their ugly dresses on the kopje. Lyndall declared her intention of going to school; "nothing helps in this world but to be very wise, and to be clever." Em was to have the farm at seventeen. She did not care for school, and Lyndall's talk of silk and diamonds was beyond Em's imagining.

Waldo, now a heavy, slouching youth of fourteen who had outgrown his religious agonies, appeared and mentioned that an Englishman who called himself Bonaparte Blenkins had come on foot that day.

Blenkins, the newcomer, had a long red nose, and battered clothes. Otto fed him, gave him a suit, and believed his story about having lost his money in a stream. In Otto's suit Blenkins impressed Tant' Sannie when he spoke at their Sunday prayer and, though the Kaffir maid had to interpret between his English and her Dutch, she hired him as school-master for the girls.

Lyndall refused to attend Blenkins' classes after he told her that Copernicus was a Roman emperor, but the Englishman's flattery of the Boer-woman made his position secure. He no longer visited Otto, he ate well, he announced that his absent wife had died.

Some sheep were missing. Bonaparte convinced Tant' Sannie that they had been lost by Otto, not stolen by the Kaffir herdsman. Waldo was sent to the mill with the wagon, and in his absence Otto was ordered to leave. The girls were locked in their room, and Otto meekly prepared to depart, empty-handed after years of service. But the old man's heart was weak, and in the morning they found him peaceful in death.

Otto was buried before Waldo returned; the weather was very hot. The triumphant Blenkins, now overseer, and marriage with Tant' Sannie next in his schemes, searched Otto's poor belongings for anything of value. Waldo, sullen and silent, was told to obey Blenkins.

Then Blenkins crushed a model of a sheep-shearing machine on which Waldo had worked nine months, and burned a book on political economy which Em had given to Waldo. One night, with no effort to move silently, the boy climbed onto the roof of the house to get some more books from the loft. Bonaparte heard him, and next day accused Waldo of stealing dried peaches, fastened him to a pole in the fuel house, whipped him and locked him in. Waldo only looked at Blenkins with a wild, fitful terror that frightened him.

Blenkins could not marry Tant' Sannie until Em was sixteen, or she would lose the sheep Em's father had left. The Boer-woman's wealthy niece came for a visit, and Bonaparte started to make love to her in the sitting-room. Tant' Sannie was in the loft above, watching through a trap-door. She emptied a barrel of salt-mutton on Blenkins. He fled outside, then vanished from the farm forever after begging food, money and a hat from the silent Waldo.

Three years passed. Waldo, awakened from his youthful dreaminess, studied and worked hard, and found the world as wonderful as it was when he had looked at it mystically instead of with scientific understanding. Em, grown fat at sixteen, was excited about Gregory Rose, the brown-haired young Englishman to whom the Boer-woman had leased half the farm.

One day a well-dressed stranger stopped to rest for an hour, and admired a post which Waldo was carving for his father's grave. The stranger told Waldo an allegory about the search for truth, and drew out of the overgrown boy his thoughts about life. Then, bidding Waldo to stay on the farm if he sought happiness, the stranger rode away. Waldo gave him the post.

Gregory, full of moonings about his own fine nature, soon fell in love with Em and won her consent to marry him, though she said humbly that she didn't seem to be able to love him as much as he loved her.

Lyndall had been away at school; now she returned, looking like a princess, fashionably dressed, having learned much—and contemptuous of boarding-schools, more humble about what she did not know, as gentle as ever toward Em and Waldo. And she was full of thoughts about women's rights and handicaps, conscious of her beauty and unwilling to make use of it. With a weary look, she spoke of love for its own sake, and not as a means of making bread. All this she talked of to Waldo.

'Tant' Sannie married Little Piet Vander Walt, a well-to-do widower, while Waldo planned to go and see the world when Gregory should become master of the farm. But Gregory began paying more attention to Lyndall than to Em, and Em called off their engagement. Waldo departed anyway, leaving his dog for Lyndall.

Then Lyndall surprised Gregory by saying that she would marry him—but only for the use of his name. A tall, slight stranger came to see Lyndall, and she placed him secretly in the unused outbuilding. He pleaded with her to marry him, and she refused, "because Gregory is a fool; you are not. I can shake him off when it suits me; once you have me, you would hold me fast." Then she offered to go away with the stranger to the Transvaal, and when they did not love any more, they could say good-by. Otherwise she would marry Gregory. The man agreed, and Lyndall slipped away in the night, saying farewell to old Otto's grave and feeling very much alone.

Six months later Gregory set out in search of Lyndall, packing in his saddlebags a dress and cap which had belonged to Em's mother. It was another seven months before Waldo returned to the farm. He sat down to write a letter to Lyndall, about how he had worked as a clerk and a teamster, but had made no money and had found no one to whom he could talk. "If the world were all children, I could like it. I was not meant to live among people," he wrote. Then Em interrupted. "It is no use writing," she said. "Lyndall is dead."

Gregory arrived and told his story. He had followed Lyndall's trail to where her path had parted from the Englishman's. Gregory found her lying ill in an inn in a little town. She had come there alone six months before, and eight days later a baby was born; it was buried in the graveyard. Lyndall visited the infant's grave on a drizzly day. Since then she had not left her bed.

Gregory shaved his beard and dressed himself in an old-fashioned gown and a frilled cap. Then he returned to the hotel and announced himself as a nurse seeking employment. He was hired for Lyndall.

Gregory's heart bled when he saw a little white, white face, transparent as an angel's, on the bed cushion. "Never get up again, the doctor says," whispered the landlady. He helped Lyndall to turn. "Thank you. Other people hurt me when they touch me," she said. Four days after, the doctor said of Gregory: "She is the most experienced nurse I ever saw."

Day after day Lyndall lay gazing into space. She never complained, but one night he heard her cry: "I do not ask for wisdom, not love; only one little hour without pain." Then suddenly she ordered her oxen; she would go to the Cape Colony. She had Gregory dress her, but could not stand up. A letter came from the Englishman, again urging her to marry him; she wrote another refusal.

There was a look of despair on her face when they started off in the ox-wagon; the doctor had told Gregory that the end was close. It was night when Lyndall looked into her mirror for the last time. In death her face was beautiful and tranquil.

In a dream Waldo saw Lyndall again, then felt a very real pain in his heart. He was in agony until at last he found peace in contemplation that "it is but the individual that perishes, the whole remains."

Gregory and Em were to be married. One pleasant day Em found Waldo sitting in the sun, his forehead on his knees, the timid little chickens climbing about him. She left a cup of milk for him, saying: "He will wake soon." But the chickens were wiser.

Ivanhoe

By SIR WALTER SCOTT

WALTER SCOTT, *born at Edinburgh on Aug. 15, 1771, was educated for his father's profession, the law, and practiced it with success, occupying his leisure time with writing literature. His first work was published in 1796, and his novels began pouring forth in a steady stream in 1814, anonymously at first. In 1820 he was made a baronet. Six years later he entered upon a publishing venture which left him bankrupt. He sat down to repay his debts with his pen, and in two years had realized £40,000 for his creditors. The effort exhausted him, and he was stricken with paralysis, dying Sept. 21, 1832, at Abbotsford.*

IN THE REIGN OF RICHARD I, when the wounds left by the Norman conquest were still unhealed, Cedric the Saxon sat at table in the hall of Rotherwood and waited for his evening meal. He was melancholy with thoughts of his son, Wilfred of Ivanhoe, disinherited for serving a Norman king.

The blast of a horn announced the arrival of the Prior Aymer and Brian de Bois-Guilbert, commander of the Order of Knights Templars, on their way to a tournament at Ashby-de-la-Zouche. Grudgingly the Saxon granted hospitality to the Normans. As the guests were seated, the Lady Rowena, Cedric's ward and niece, entered, and all rose for her. The Knight Templar's eyes bent on her rare beauty with such ardor that she drew the veil around her face.

A dispute arose over who had best borne arms for the Cross in Palestine, and the Templar, who was upholding his Order, was challenged by a pilgrim at the foot of the table who said that King Richard and five of his knights had bested the Templars in a tournament at Acre. De Bois-Guilbert agreed that the youngest of the six, the Knight of Ivanhoe, had bested him, but declared that he feared not to face him again.

That night the pilgrim helped a Jew, Isaac of York, to flee from a plot against him at Cedric's home, and the discerning Isaac gave the pilgrim an order for a horse and armor.

Prince John himself was present for the passage of arms at Ashby. First the five challengers, all Normans, headed by Brian de Bois-Guilbert, took the field against all comers. Four parties of knights went down before them, then there entered a new champion in steel armor which bore the motto "Desdichado," Spanish for "disinherited."

The Disinherited Knight boldly defied Brian to combat, and they closed with the shock of a thunderbolt. The Templar's spear shivered on the center of his foe's shield, and the Disinherited Knight reeled in his saddle. But his lance had hit the Norman on the visor, the point kept hold of the bars, and the Templar fell, his saddle girths bursting. Then the new knight defeated each of the four other Normans in turn.

The victor had the privilege of naming the Queen of Honor and of Love to preside over the next day's festival; the Disinherited Knight, receiving a coronet of green satin from Prince John, presented it to the Lady Rowena, then rode off without revealing his identity.

Next day two bands of fifty knights each were to fight it out in the general tournament, under the rival leaderships of the Disinherited one and the Templar. When the field had thinned, the Disinherited Knight was set upon by three rivals. Then a knight in black armor with no device, who had abstained from the thicker combat, rode to his rescue and beat off two of the attackers. The Templar, the last of the three, fell easily because his horse had bled much.

The knight of the black armor having vanished, the Disinherited Knight was named the champion of the day. His helmet being removed, he bowed before Rowena, who uttered a faint shriek when she recognized him as Ivanhoe. Then the knight fell prostrate, having been wounded in the side.

After the tournament Cedric, Rowena, and Athelstane, a Saxon lord, were waylaid by Bois-Guilbert and carried off to Torquilstone, the castle of Front-de-Boeuf. These Norman nobles intended to hold the men for ransom, and to win Rowena as a bride. Also prisoners, unknown to the others, were the wounded Ivanhoe and the beautiful Rebecca, daughter of Isaac.

But Gurth, Cedric's swineherd, rallied the Saxon yeomen and outlaws, including Robin Hood and his band, and stormed Torquilstone under the leadership of the Black Knight. The castle was in flames, but the knight carried Ivanhoe to safety and Rowena was rescued along with all the other prisoners except Rebecca, who remained in the Normans' hands.

The flames were resisted by the thick stone walls, and the besiegers pursued the defenders from chamber to chamber, giving no quarter in their desire for vengeance against the tyrant Front-de-Boeuf. The last remnant of the defenders fought in the courtyard, the Templar in their midst. Athelstane snatched up a mace and battled to Bois-Guilbert's side, but was felled by a sword blow, and the Templar escaped with his followers.

Cedric entreated the Black Knight to go with him to Rotherwood "as a son or brother," and the knight warned that "when I come, I will ask such a boon as will put even thy generosity to the test."

A funeral banquet for Athelstane was going on at his castle of Coningsburgh when the Black Knight entered, accompanied by Ivanhoe, whose face was muffled. He boldly told Cedric that it seemed to him fit that "certain prejudices and hasty opinions" be abandoned. When the Saxon objected that a stranger should not interfere in a family matter, the Black Knight said:

"Know me now as Richard Plantagenet, King of England. I

require of thee, as a man of thy word, to forgive the good Knight, Wilfred of Ivanhoe."

Ivanhoe prostrated himself, and Cedric granted his forgiveness. Then he told Ivanhoe that two years of mourning for Athelstane, to whom Rowena was betrothed, must pass before his son could hope for her hand.

Suddenly the door flew open and Athelstane stood there in the garments of the grave, pale and haggard. He revealed that he had been stunned by the flat of the Templar's sword, but was unwounded. He recovered his senses only when he found himself in an open coffin in an altar in church. Then the abbot had kept him a prisoner three days on bread and water.

Athelstane, a wiser man than before, admitted that Rowena loved Wilfred of Ivanhoe far more than she loved him. He was about to present her hand to Ivanhoe, when he found that the knight and King Richard had disappeared.

A secret message had called Ivanhoe again to fight Brian de Bois-Guilbert. Infatuated with Rebecca and spurned by her, the Templar had saved himself from condemnation by the Grand Master of his order, only by accusing her of sorcery, and challenging to mortal combat all who dared to champion her.

As he closed with Ivanhoe, Bois-Guilbert fell dead, a victim to the violence of his own contending passions. Then Richard, who had followed Ivanhoe, proclaimed himself King again, having routed the conspirators who had grown up in his absence in Palestine.

Now Cedric gave his consent to the marriage of his son and Rowena, with the King himself attending the nuptials. The presence of high-born Normans, as well as Saxons, marked the marriage as a pledge of the future peace and harmony betwixt the races.

Kenilworth

By SIR WALTER SCOTT

IT WAS in the eighteenth year of Queen Elizabeth's reign that a traveler was ushered, late in the evening, into the large public chamber in the inn of Giles Gosling at the village of Cumnor, a few miles from Oxford. The host soon recognized with no pleasure his graceless nephew, Michael Lambourne, who had not been heard of for many years. But Gosling invited all who would to join them at supper, and soon Lambourne and many of the others had passed the limits of temperance.

Michael learned that many of his old friends had come to sad ends, but that one, Tony Foster, had married and become a good Protestant, and now scorned his old companions. Foster now dwelt at Cumnor Place, an old mansion house, and his aloofness was not entirely from pride; it was said there was a fair lady in the case.

At this point a guest named Tressilian, who had sat aside, intervened in the conversation and was told that Foster had a beautiful lady at Cumnor Place, and would scarcely let her see the light of day. Michael at once wagered he would force Foster to introduce him to his guest, and Tressilian asked permission to go along. When they arrived next morning, Foster turned to the obviously well-bred Tressilian for an explanation, but it was Michael who answered and was led to another room by Foster, who plainly did not want to renew their old acquaintance.

Soon a beautiful and richly clad young lady of eighteen entered the room where Tressilian had been left alone. She was the object of his search, Amy Robsart, his promised bride. He greeted her, and called her dwelling "a prison, guarded by the most sordid of men, but not a greater wretch than his employer." Then he told her that her father was ill, perhaps dying, and had sent Tressilian for her.

"I dare not leave this place!" she said. "Tell my father I come as sure as there is light in heaven—that is, when I obtain permission."

"Permission from whom?" he repeated, and advanced toward her. She screamed, Lambourne and Foster appeared, and Tressilian angrily departed.

At the gate he met a muffled cavalier whom he recognized as Richard Varney, the scheming master of horse to the Earl of Leicester. Tressilian drew his sword, though Varney swore that Amy had no injury from him. Forced to defend himself, Varney was swiftly overcome and was saved only by the arrival of Lambourne.

Tressilian resolved to obtain the Queen's intervention for Amy's freedom from Varney, not knowing that Leicester himself had secretly married her. On his way to Sir Hugh Robsart, the knight had his horse shod by a mysterious farrier named Wayland Smith, who proved to be an alchemist, and was persuaded to enter Tressilian's employ.

The knight and Wayland won Lord Sussex' intervention with the Queen, and went to the court at Greenwich with him. There they saw Sir Walter Raleigh first win favor by spreading his cloak for the Queen to walk on. And when Sussex told the Queen about Amy, she summoned Varney and Leicester. Varney quickly said that Amy was his wife, and Elizabeth ordered him to appear with Amy at the forthcoming festivities at Kenilworth, Leicester's estate.

Now the Earl and Varney faced a dilemma, for Amy was tiring of seclusion and insisted on appearing as Leicester's wife, though he had told her that secrecy was necessary to preserve his court favor. Indeed, she was resolved to see her husband at Kenilworth. Varney employed an alchemist, Demetrius, to drug Amy so that she could not depart, but Wayland fed her an antidote and helped her along the road to Kenilworth.

A tremendous and colorful carnival had been prepared for the Queen. Adorned with jewels, she witnessed pageantry and fireworks, and found a throne waiting for her in the gorgeously tapestried great hall of the castle.

Amy, who had accompanied some strolling players, found herself lodged by chance in the same room as had been assigned to Tressilian. She gave Wayland a letter to deliver to Leicester, but it was stolen from him. Meanwhile Tressilian had found Amy in his room and was bound to silence by her.

The Queen soon asked for Varney's wife, and when Varney declared his lady was indisposed, Tressilian madly cried out a refutation, then stammered so that the Queen ordered Raleigh to place him under restraint. Amy, though she had no answer to her note, kept out of the way of the Queen. And after the great banquet that night, Varney assured Leicester that the stars promised his marriage to the Queen.

The next morning the Earl escorted Elizabeth to the castle garden and there spoke of love to her. The Queen answered: "Were I, as others, free to seek my own happiness, then indeed— but it cannot be. Leave me." The Queen turned into a grotto where Amy lay concealed. The unfortunate Countess begged protection from Varney and declared that she was not his wife. But, desiring to protect her husband, she explained only by saying: "The Earl of Leicester knows it all!"

Mystified and angry, the Queen took Amy to where the Earl stood in the midst of a group of lords and ladies. There Amy's speech became so distraught that the Queen believed her mad and placed her in custody.

That night the Earl asked Amy to let herself be known as Varney's wife. She scornfully refused, and called upon Leicester as a man to acknowledge her as his Countess before Elizabeth. The Earl was about to yield, when Varney poisoned his mind by declaring she was in love with Tressilian. Thus the Earl was silent when the Queen placed Amy in the hands of Varney, who took her to Cumnor with the object of killing her.

Leicester's mind finally was made clear after a duel in which he nearly killed Tressilian. Interrupted by the belated delivery of the letter stolen from Wayland Smith, the Earl realized that Amy was true to him. He acknowledged the marriage to the Queen, and in her rage she declared that it had "cost me a husband, and England a king." Then she ordered Tressilian and Raleigh to fetch Amy from Cumnor, and to seize Varney, alive or dead.

Varney had confined Amy in the bedchamber of his henchman Foster at Cumnor Place. Part of the wooden gallery immediately outside her door was really a trapdoor, and beneath it was an abyss. Varney withdrew the supports, so that one step outside the room would send her to her death. But Foster was so moved by Amy's mildness and patience that he warned her to stay within the chamber until Leicester should come.

The bait that lured Amy outside was Varney's imitation of the whistle which was the Earl's usual signal. The next instant the door to the Countess' room opened, and in the same moment the trapdoor gave way. A rushing sound—a heavy fall—a faint groan, and all was over.

A moment later Tressilian and Raleigh broke in on them. Foster escaped all search; years later his skeleton was found in a secret chamber where he hid his gold. Varney was captured, but killed himself.

Leicester retired from court for a season, but the Queen recalled him to favor, and the rest of his career is well-known to history. Tressilian at length embarked with Raleigh for Virginia, and died there before his day.

The Heart of Midlothian

By SIR WALTER SCOTT

THE HEART OF MIDLOTHIAN was the name which the populace had given to the Tolbooth, an ancient, gloomy prison which harbored the malefactors of old Edinburgh. At one time it housed two prisoners who could look forward to nothing but death. These were Captain John Porteous, the erstwhile captain of the guard who was to die for having fired on the mob during a previous execution, and beautiful Effie Deans, accused of the murder of her illegitimate child.

Porteous was hated by the populace and when on the very day he was to die a temporary reprieve from the Crown arrived, there were angry murmurs and threats from the downtrodden of the city. That night a vengeance-bent mob stormed the Heart of Midlothian and carried off the terrified prisoner. The leader of the mob, George Robertson, an outlaw, was disguised in woman's clothes and was recognized at the prison by one Ratcliffe, a thief, who informed in order to save himself. This Robertson had incited the mob to break open the prison gates, not to seize Porteous, as he avowed, but really in an effort to rescue Effie Deans whose lover he was. The attempt failed and the unfortunate girl remained in peril of her life. John Porteous was dragged to the Grass-market, the public place of execution, and was there hanged by the infuriated populace. An unwilling witness to this murder was Reuben Butler, a young minister whom the mob had forced to attend upon Porteous in his last moments.

Reuben Butler was devoted to the Deans family, with whom he had grown to manhood. The Butlers and the Deans had been fellow-tenants on the land of the Laird of Dumbiedikes. It was with the advice and help of David Deans and his elder daughter, Jeannie, that Reuben had been able to go to the University and study for the ministry. Jeannie was a sturdy, hard-working girl, deeply religious and dedicated to piety and the dictates of her stern Presbyterian conscience. She and the frail young Butler had always been friends, and Reuben hoped one day to make Jeannie his wife. Jeannie's half-sister, David Deans' child by his second marriage, was the gentle and lovely Effie, now in such hopeless case through her passion for the outlaw Robertson. David Deans, now a widower for the second time, had at last achieved some small degree of prosperity, but he was a stricken man, bowed by the grief brought him by his younger daughter.

Reuben Butler carried a message to Jeannie which a stranger had given him for her. The message bade her to a tryst at moonrise with Robertson. Robertson told Jeannie that if she would swear in court that Effie had confessed her condition before the birth of the child, the young girl could thus be cleared of the suspicion of infanticide. But Effie had at no time given any indication to her sister that she was about to be a mother, and Jeannie's stern conscience would not allow her to perjure herself even to save her sister's life. Meanwhile neither the child nor its body had been found and, except by a miracle, Effie must surely die.

On the evening before Effie's trial, Jeannie was conducted to the Heart of Midlothian and allowed to see and speak with her unfortunate sister. Effie refused to give evidence against her lover, even to save herself from execution; she was overjoyed to hear of Robertson's efforts to save her, for she had feared that he had abandoned her. But on learning that no trace of her babe had been found she fell into a swoon. Effie reaffirmed to Jeannie her love for Robertson and asked Jeannie if she would not say the false word that would save her, but Jeannie replied that she could not.

At the trial next day, although Effie called upon her to spare her life and old David Deans fell unconscious to the floor, Jeannie would not bear false witness. Effie, despite the sorrow of all, was condemned.

All abandoned hope but Jeannie. She heard that pardon to a condemned criminal could be granted by the King at London and to him she decided to go. Leaving her ailing old father in the house of a sympathetic cousin, she hastened to the prison to tell Effie of her resolve. Effie forgave her her silence at the trial and with prayers and tears bade her godspeed. Ratcliffe, the informer, was so impressed at the girl's courage that he advised her as to the proper course to take on her mission and gave her a note which should serve as passport if she fell among thieves.

At last Jeannie said good-by to Reuben Butler. This young man, never strong, was quite ill from anxiety and his recent difficult experiences. Nevertheless he pleaded with Jeannie to marry him so that he might protect her on her difficult mission. She refused him until their present worries should be over and left him with love and anxiety, commending her father to his care. Reuben at parting gave her a letter to the powerful Duke of Argyle, whose grandfather had been under some great obligation to Reuben's own.

Jeannie, lacking other conveyance, was determined to walk to London. She walked the weary Scottish miles barefoot. Once in England the stares of the populace induced her to purchase a pair of shoes. Nearing London she was often helped to a ride in some conveyance.

Finally Jeannie reached London. Reuben's letter brought her an audience with the Duke of Argyle, who immediately set about to use his not inconsiderable influence in her behalf. He arranged an interview with Queen Caroline, who, at first doubtful of extending a favor to the rebellious Scots, was soon won over by Jeannie's courage and high moral purpose. A few days later Jeannie learned that the King had granted Effie a pardon but had stipulated in it a fourteen-year banishment from Scotland.

The Duke of Argyle sent Jeannie forth from London in his own carriage. Jeannie's destination was the Isle of Roseneath and there she found her father waiting for her. She learned that Effie had been released from prison and had fled to the arms of her outlaw lover. The father had then banished the wayward girl from his heart forever.

Reuben Butler was soon able to marry Jeannie, for he had been given a parish at Roseneath by the Duke of Argyle. Jeannie learned that Effie had married Robertson and that he had reformed from his outlaw life. Effie's love child was lost forever, stolen by gypsies. Later Effie's husband, under the name of Sir George Staunten, achieved recognition and respectability and the two sisters were restored to one another.

Frankenstein

By MARY SHELLEY

MARY WOLLSTONECRAFT SHELLEY *was born in London on August 30, 1797, the only daughter of William Godwin, famous editor, and Mary Wollstonecraft, author of* The Rights of Women. *Percy Bysshe Shelley, the poet, separated from his first wife, met Mary at her father's home and induced her to elope to Europe with him in July, 1814. When the first Mrs. Shelley died, the poet married Mary on Dec. 30, 1816. After Shelley's death in 1822, his widow obtained a pension from his family. On this she lived while she edited his works. Mary Shelley died on Feb. 21, 1851.*

RESCUED from the frozen seas north of Archangel as he pursued a strange giant of a man across the ice, Victor Frankenstein told this story to the British explorer who had saved him:

Frankenstein was the first child of an honored Geneva public servant who had married late in life. After a happy childhood in which he read deeply in the works of Cornelius Agrippa and other alchemists, Victor went, at the age of 17, to the University of Ingolstadt. His mother had died shortly before that time, and on her deathbed had pledged him to marry Elizabeth Lavenza, fair-haired orphan who had been reared by the Frankensteins after the loss of her father, a Milanese nobleman.

From his childhood studies Victor had become enamored with the thought of discovering the elixir of life, but at Ingolstadt the old alchemists were banished from his mind by the study of the modern sciences of natural philosophy and chemistry under the guidance of gruff Professor Krempe and gentle Professor Waldman. Guided by this pair, in two years he made such rapid progress that they could teach him no more. He thought of returning to Geneva, but then he made a remarkable discovery— brilliant, yet so simple that he was surprised to be the first to find it.

Spending days and nights in charnel houses observing the natural decay of the human body, he had asked whence the principle of life proceeded. Then—and this was not the vision of a madman—he found the cause of generation and life; nay, more, he became capable of animating lifeless matter.

He plunged into the task of constructing a man, for his imagination could conceive of nothing less. He planned a being eight feet in height, and grew pale and emaciated as for several months he collected his materials, dabbling by moonlight among the unhallowed damps of the grave, or gathering parts from the dissecting room and slaughterhouse, or torturing living animals in order to animate the lifeless clay. In his first enthusiasm he thought of himself as the creator of a happy new species.

A summer passed, and another came as Frankenstein labored in his workshop of filthy creation, a cell at the top of his house. He neglected his correspondence with his family and, though his work went well, his anxiety caused him to shun his fellow-creatures as if he had been guilty of a crime.

It was on a dreary November night that Frankenstein, almost in agony, infused the spark of being into his lifeless thing. The rain pattered dismally outside when he saw the creature's dull yellow eye open. Breathless horror filled Frankenstein's heart. The wretch's giant limbs were in proportion, and his lustrous black hair and pearly teeth had been selected as beautiful, but they only formed a horrid contrast with the shriveled yellow skin, the watery eyes and the straight black lips.

Frankenstein rushed away to his bedroom and at length fell into a troubled sleep which was broken when the monster made his way to the bedroom. He muttered and grinned, and Frankenstein fled outside. No mortal could support the horror of that countenance, worse than a mummy endued with animation.

The monster was gone when the young scientest returned with Henry Clerval, a childhood friend who had just arrived at the university. Frankenstein, pale and excited, at first was wild with joy, and then fell ill of a nervous fever which possessed him for several months while he raved incessantly about the monster. Another summer and winter passed before Frankenstein had recovered, now with a violent antipathy to even the name of natural philosophy.

In May, as Frankenstein prepared to return to Geneva, word came that his young brother William had been found strangled after he had strayed away at play. Near the end of his hasty journey home, Frankenstein saw, on a mountainside near Geneva, the giant figure of the monster and knew that he must be the murderer. Distraught, he saw the court convict Justine Moritz, a gentle orphan whom the Frankensteins had adopted, of the crime. All of the pleadings of Victor and Elizabeth could not save her from the scaffold after a miniature which William had worn was found in Justine's pocket, and after Justine, harried by her confessor, falsely admitted her guilt. Victor did not dare to tell the story of the monster, for he would only be thought mad.

Bowed down by the deaths of William and Justine, the first

hapless victims of his unhallowed arts, Frankenstein refused to be consoled by Elizabeth. Instead he sought to forget his sorrows in the Alps. Then, on the glacier below Mont Blanc, he was horrified to meet the monster, who bounded across the ice with superhuman strength and speed. Unable to escape, Victor consented to hear the creature's story after the monster said:

"I am miserable beyond all living things. Even you, my creator, detest me. I was benevolent and good; misery made me a fiend. If mankind knew of my existence, they would arm themselves for my destruction. I will keep no terms with my enemies. On you it rests whether I lead a harmless life."

Then, in a mountain hut, the monster told how he had wandered off, had found that humans fled from the sight of him, and at last had stayed for a winter in a hovel which adjoined a cottage where lived a blind man and his children Agatha and Felix. Observing them through a crack in the wall, he learned to speak and developed an affection for these gentle and poverty-stricken people who, he learned, were exiles from France. The monster, who disliked meat and lived on berries, gathered wood secretly to make Felix' tasks lighter. Learning to read, he devoured "Paradise Lost," Plutarch's "Lives," and the "Sorrows of Werther," books which he had found. Then, when he sought to discover himself to the benefactors who, unknowingly, had taught him about the world, he was driven off with the same horror that he had met before.

The embittered monster had carried off Frankenstein's journal when he first fled, so that he knew the story of his creation. Now he set out for Geneva. Encountering William in the woods, he killed him and put the miniature in the pocket of Justine, whom he found sleeping in a barn.

His tale completed, the monster made his demand. He must have a female in his own image. Frankenstein did not want to consent, then did so reluctantly when the monster promised to go off to South America's jungles with his mate.

On a remote island in the Orkneys, Frankenstein set up his new laboratory. Then, near the completion of his reluctant and horrible labors, the monster appeared. Frankenstein gazed upon his devilish face and, feeling mad for having promised to make another like him, destroyed his handiwork. The monster vowed revenge in these words: "Your hours will pass in dread and misery. Remember, I shall be with you on your wedding night."

The monster's next victim was Henry Clerval, strangled under such circumstances that Frankenstein was arrested and could not prove his innocence for three months. On his release, he returned to Geneva and resolved to marry Elizabeth at once, for it was clear that this would make her and his father happy, while the murder of Clerval showed that the monster knew no truce.

Nevertheless it was with foreboding that Victor spoke his marriage vows and set off with Elizabeth for Evian, where they were to spend their wedding night. At the inn Elizabeth retired first. Suddenly a scream interrupted Frankenstein's inspection of the house by which he had hoped to spy out his enemy. He rushed to the room and found Elizabeth across the bed, lifeless and with distorted features. At the window stood the grinning monster. He pointed toward the corpse with a fiendish finger, then leaped down and plunged into the lake as Victor drew his pistol.

The sad news soon killed the elder Frankenstein, and his son for a time lost his mind and was confined in a solitary cell. When he was released, Frankenstein found that he could win no credence for his story from the authorities. If he was to destroy his evil creation, he must do it himself.

Finding the monster's trail, Frankenstein pursued him across France and the Mediterranean, the Black Sea, and the wilds of Tartary and Russia. Sometimes the monster left marks behind, carved on trees and stones, such as: "Follow me; I seek the everlasting ices of the north." At length they reached the northern ocean, and Frankenstein pursued his prey across the ice by dog sledge.

Picked up by an explorer, Frankenstein, already weak, sickened and died. The monster came aboard the explorer's ship for a last look at his creator, then leaped to an ice floe and was borne away by the waves.

Dr. Jekyll and Mr. Hyde

By ROBERT LOUIS STEVENSON

BORN *in Edinburgh, Nov. 13, 1850, Robert Louis Stevenson early acquired a liking for literature. To please his father he studied civil engineering and read law, but he abandoned both for writing. From the time of his birth he was sickly. He went to France, California, the Adirondacks, and the South Seas to improve his health. His wife was a source of strength and inspiration to him, though he suffered mental anguish because of isolation from his friends. Much of his literary output was produced while he was confined in bed. On Dec. 3, 1894, he died at Samoa.*

MR. UTTERSON, a lawyer, and Richard Enfield, his distant kinsman, on one of their Sunday walks about London came upon a sinister, windowless, two-story wing of a house on a by-street.

Enfield recalled a horrible sight near the house. He said that early one morning a man who was hurrying down the street collided with a little girl, knocked her flat and calmly trampled over her body. "I took to my heels," he said, "collared my gentleman and brought him back."

The ugly-looking fellow offered to pay damages to the child's family, went into the sinister house and came back with ten pounds in gold and a check bearing the genuine signature of a most respected citizen, Enfield said.

"I want to ask the name of that man who walked over the child," said the lawyer.

Hesitating, Enfield answered, "It was a man by the name of Hyde."

"If I do not ask you the name of the other, it is because I know it already," said Utterson.

That night Utterson re-examined the will of Dr. Henry Jekyll. In case of the death of Jekyll it provided that all his possessions were to pass to Edward Hyde. But it also provided that Hyde should step into Jekyll's shoes without delay in case of Jekyll's "disappearance or unexplained absence for any period exceeding three calendar months."

"I thought it was madness," said Utterson, putting the will away, "and now I begin to fear it is disgrace."

Utterson called on Dr. Lanyon, an old friend of Jekyll. He found they were no longer close. "Jekyll became too fanciful for me," said Lanyon. Hyde was unknown to Lanyon.

After persistent watching, Utterson finally intercepted a small, plainly dressed man who admitted he was Hyde at the doorway of the sinister house. The two stared at each other, and before entering the house Hyde gave the lawyer his address in Soho.

Going around the corner to Dr. Jekyll's house, Utterson was told by the butler that Jekyll was absent and it was in order for Hyde to have a key to the dissecting-room entrance.

About a year later, England was shocked by the brutal murder of the aged Sir Danvers Carew, a client of Utterson. The murderer left the cane with which he clubbed his victim to death at the scene of the outrage. Utterson recognized it as one he had given to Dr. Jekyll.

Inspection revealed that Hyde had disappeared from the Soho address, leaving nothing but a charred checkbook. And at the bank it was found that several thousand pounds in Hyde's account was unclaimed.

At the home of Jekyll, Utterson found the scientist in the

dissecting-room sitting close to the fire and looking deathly sick. He had heard the news of the horrible crime.

"You have not been mad enough to hide this murderer?" Utterson asked. Jekyll swore that he was not hiding the killer. "He will never more be heard of," he added, and showed the lawyer a letter signed "Edward Hyde" to substantiate this conviction.

Utterson was startled to learn from a handwriting expert that the letter was written in a hand identical with that of Jekyll. "What!" he shuddered. "Henry Jekyll forge for a murderer!"

Calling on Dr. Lanyon one day, Utterson found a man with death written on his face. Lanyon said he had had a shock from which he did not expect to recover. On the mention of Jekyll, Lanyon trembled and said, "Spare me any allusion to one whom I regard as dead."

In less than a fortnight Lanyon was dead. And the lawyer opened an envelope sealed and addressed to him by the hand of the dead man. Inside was another enclosure marked "Not to be opened till the death or disappearance of Henry Jekyll."

The lawyer learned from Poole, Jekyll's butler, that the doctor had grown very silent and morose. He appeared to have a burden on his mind, and he rarely left the laboratory.

On a Sunday walk with Enfield, Utterson saw Jekyll at the window with an infinite sadness of mien, like some disconsolate prisoner. Jekyll refused to join the two for a walk. Suddenly his face took an expression of such abject terror and despair that it seemed to freeze the blood of the two friends below.

Greatly agitated, Poole suddenly appeared at Utterson's home one night. He reported that his master had been shut up in his cabinet for a week. The butler was in a state of terror. He begged that the lawyer go back with him.

Utterson found the servants at Jekyll's in a state of panic. Following Poole through the surgical theater, Utterson heard a response to a knock on the cabinet door: "I cannot see anyone." They retraced their steps to the kitchen.

"Sir," said Poole, "was that my master's voice?"

"It seems much changed," replied the lawyer.

Poole confessed he believed his master had been murdered, but he could not explain why the killer stayed.

"Whoever it is that lives in that cabinet has been crying night and day for some sort of medicine and cannot get it to his mind," said Poole. He showed Utterson one of the papers which had been thrown out of the cabinet. It was an agonized plea for a special kind of salt which the occupant had used and wanted again. The order was in the name of Jekyll and in handwriting like his.

"I've seen him," said Poole. "That thing was not my master. He is tall, a fine build of a man; and this was more of a dwarf."

They threatened to smash the door down with an axe.

"Utterson," said the voice inside, "for God's sake, have mercy!"

"Ah, that's not Jekyll's voice—it's Hyde's!" cried Utterson. "Down with the door, Poole!"

The axe crashed against the door. A dismal screech, as of mere animal terror, rang from the cabinet. The door fell. There lay a body of a man sorely contorted and still twitching. An empty vial lay next to him. They turned the body over. It was the corpse of Edward Hyde, dressed in the clothes of Dr. Jekyll. Nowhere was there any trace of the scientist, dead or alive.

They found a confession addressed to Utterson, and a will drawn in his favor. The lawyer opened the missive given him by Dr. Lanyon. The mystery was solved by that letter.

One night Hyde, dressed in grotesquely large clothes, had appeared at Lanyon's office very ill. He had come for some powders which Jekyll had left there for him some time previously. He had eagerly seized them and mixed a liquid which turned quickly from purple to green.

He drank it at one gulp. A cry followed; he reeled, he stared, he seemed to change—to swell—to go black in the face. His features melted and altered. Terrified, Lanyon leaped back, because before him stood Dr. Jekyll.

In a "Full Statement of the Case," Dr. Jekyll said he had in-

vented a salt which would completely change him from the
highly respected, kindly, amiable man of science to the diabolical
fiend, Mr. Hyde. As the use of the salts continued, the Hyde
personality became the natural one. After a time he was unable
to obtain the salts which would temporarily cause him to be
Jekyll, so suicide was the only way out.

Gulliver's Travels

By JONATHAN SWIFT

BORN *in Dublin on Nov. 30, 1667, of English ancestry, Jonathan
Swift was educated at Trinity College, then served 10 years, until
the age of 32, as private secretary to Sir William Temple. Ordained in the Church of England, he expected a bishopric because of his services to the Government, but was made dean of
St. Patrick's, Dublin, the office he held until his death on Oct.
19, 1745. Perhaps the most brilliant political pamphleteer of all
time, he was a member of the unofficial cabinet of Queen Anne.
Biographers have puzzled over his long love affairs with "Stella"
and "Vanessa."*

LEMUEL GULLIVER, a Nottinghamshire man, studied at Cambridge,
then became apprenticed to an eminent surgeon of London, after
which he studied navigation, then went to Leyden to study
physic. He took several voyages as ship's surgeon, then married
and settled in London. His ventures in medicine on land being
a failure, he at length accepted an offer to be surgeon on the
Antelope.

Driven by a violent storm to the northwest of Van Diemen's

Land in the South Seas, the ship was driven on a rock, and only Gulliver escaped. Almost exhausted by swimming, he reached shore and fell into a sound sleep. When he awoke at daylight, he found himself strongly fastened to the ground, unable to move arms, legs or head.

He found that he had been captured by human creatures not six inches high; and a shower of poisoned arrows decided him against attempting to free himself. Transported to the capital, he was housed in an old temple and, by the Emperor's order, taught the language of the strange country of Lilliput.

The ruler found Gulliver's watch and pistols as interesting as the surgeon did the Lilliputians' horses, which he could take up in his hand, and their geese, which he could eat at a mouthful. Soon Gulliver was granted his liberty, with an allowance of food sufficient for 1,728 of their people, and 600 servants.

The Lilliputians were divided into factions which favored low and high heels, and had exiled those who opened their eggs at the big end, instead of the small, as the Emperor had ordered. Favor was won at court by skill at performing on the high rope.

Gulliver saved Lilliput by capturing the fleet of the neighboring kingdom of Blefuscu, but incurred the Emperor's anger by asking mercy toward the conquered. Secretly informed of a court decision to put out his eyes and starve him to death, the expense of his maintenance being a serious drain upon the kingdom, Gulliver determined to pay a visit to Blefuscu.

Soon Gulliver was enabled to make his escape by a ship's boat which had washed ashore. Picked up by an English captain, he returned home with a number of live cattle and sheep from the tiny kingdoms. His family being well provided for by an inheritance, Gulliver's insatiable desire of seeing foreign countries caused him to sign up within two months for a voyage on the merchant-ship *Adventure*.

A great wind blew the vessel hundreds of leagues to the east of Molucca Islands. They put in for water at a strange island, and Gulliver was left behind when a huge creature forced his companions to flee. Hiding in a field, he was captured by a man who seemed as tall as a church steeple. He was put in the hands of the man's nine-year-old daughter, forty feet high, whom Gulliver called Glumdalclitch and who taught him the language of Brobdingnag. He found these great people as coarse as those of Lilliput seemed delicate, but soon decided it was a matter of size alone.

Exhausted by being forced to perform in public, Gulliver was glad to be sold to the Queen and to be treated as a pet at court. A quilted box was made for him to live in, with furnishings in proportion. He found that the King laughed at the wars, religious disputes and political disputes of Europe, which he questioned Gulliver about, and indeed the men of Brobdingnag seemed to be as large in mind as in body, holding, for example, that it was tyranny for a government to dictate its people's opinions. Of England, the King said: "I cannot but conclude your natives to be the most pernicious race of little odious vermin that nature ever suffered to crawl upon the face of the earth."

Even the court had dangers for Gulliver. The dwarf, only 30 feet tall, was jealous of him and tormented him, and there were wasps as large as partridges, as well as a dog and a monkey. He learned that the country was 6,000 miles long and up to 5,000 in breadth; the King's palace was seven miles round, with ceilings 240 feet high, and the chief temple was 3,000 feet in height.

Having been two years in this country, Gulliver yet had hope of recovering his liberty, and with it his dignity. Going with the King and Queen to a town on the south coast, he was left in the care of a pageboy, who put his box down on the shore. The box was carried off by a great bird, which dropped it into the sea, whence by good fortune Gulliver was rescued by an English ship and once more reached home.

Winning his wife's consent, Gulliver soon set forth again. This time his ship was taken by pirates, and he was set adrift in a canoe in the seas east of Japan. He came to an island called Balnibarbi, which was governed from another island called

Laputa, which floated in the air above it, being sustained by an enormous loadstone.

The Laputans were deeply versed in mathematics, but despised making practical use of it, so that their houses were all a-kilter. Music was their other chief interest. The King kept the people below in submission by using the island to shut off the sun and rain from recalcitrants.

Visiting Lagado, capital of Balnibarbi, he found it in control of an Academy of Projectors, where he found a man who had been working eight years to extract sunbeams from cucumbers, another who was trying to reduce human ordure to its original food, an architect who proposed to build houses from the roof down, and a professor who sought to compose books by spinning blocks of wood on which words were written.

Next Gulliver went to Glubbdubdrib, the Island of Sorcerers, where he spoke with great men of ancient and modern times, and found the modern men much overrated.

On the Island of Luggnagg he discovered there were a people called the Struldbrugs, who were born occasionally among them, and who never died. Gulliver decided that these must be the world's wisest men. He found instead that they grew senile and cantankerous, and weak in their memories, until other men would have nothing to do with them, so that there was no fear of death in that kingdom.

Gulliver went back to England by way of Japan, then accepted an offer to be captain of a ship. The crew mutinied, and he was set down on a strange island ruled by horses, the Houyhnhnms, who had as field-servants a degraded race called the Yahoos who, disgusting as they were, looked so much like humans that Gulliver was taken for one of them.

Here Gulliver had to live on milk, oat-cakes, herbs, and an occasional rabbit, but he found his health improved thereby. He found these intelligent horses to be simple in their lives, incapable of lying, and without words for such matters as government, law, lust, punishment, war, or envy. Nor could they conceive of any disease except the infirmities of age.

Among the Houyhnhnms the chief virtues were friendship and benevolence, and death was taken as a natural thing, not to be mourned.

Gulliver was treated with kindness by the Houyhnhnms who found him, but the others feared that he might become the leader of a Yahoo revolt, so he was permitted to build a large canoe of Yahoo skins and sail away. Although he found his way home again, a long time passed before he was able to suffer willingly the presence of other men, having found the company of horses so superior.

Vanity Fair

By WILLIAM MAKEPEACE THACKERAY

Son *of a British civil servant, William Makepeace Thackeray was born July 18, 1811, in Calcutta. Versatile and light-hearted, he went gaily through Cambridge, Paris art school and London law school, living on inherited wealth. He tried journalism, drew caricatures, did a variety of writing, and delivered lectures when money ran short. Sorrow came into his life in his later years when his wife lost her mind. He died Dec. 24, 1863, in London.*

The family coach called at Miss Pinkerton's school for Miss Amelia Sedley, who after six years of studying music, orthography, embroidery and moral principles was ready to take her place in the refined circle of her father, a well-to-do London merchant. Kind and gentle, she had won the hearts of servants, teachers and fellow students. There was not so much to-do about the departure of Miss Rebecca Sharp, an articled pupil who was to visit Amelia before starting her career as a governess. In fact Becky, orphaned daughter of a penniless artist and a French opera girl, insulted Miss Pinkerton, who had given her a scanty living and education in exchange for speaking French to the young ladies. Becky was small and slight, sandy-haired, but with eyes that were large, odd and unusually attractive. Reared in Bohemian poverty, Becky said she had been a woman since she was eight.

At the Sedley home Becky set her cap for Amelia's brother Joseph, a large, fat man, overdressed and lazy, who was enjoying London's dissipations after years in India. Becky was getting on well until George Osborne, an old friend of Amelia, shamed Joseph into staying away after Joseph had made a spectacle of himself on punch.

Becky went on to be governess in the home of Sir Pitt Crawley, Baronet, at Queen's Crawley, Hampshire; the master was miserly and unkempt, and Becky called the place Humdrum Hall. The dullness of country life was broken by a visit from Sir Pitt's wealthy spinster sister, Matilda Crawley, and the baronet's second son, Capt. Rawdon Crawley, a London dandy who was her favorite. Both took a great liking to Becky.

Meantime George Osborne had become engaged to Amelia Sedley, although his sisters were sure he was throwing himself away on this wax doll. All the battles of Napoleon meant nothing to her except as they might affect Lieut. George, but he, often away on duty and enjoying a good time, at times neglected her and was angry when his awkward friend, Capt. William Dobbin, let the Horse Guards regiment know that George was engaged. And all the while the fortunes of Amelia's father, a stockbroker, were failing.

Miss Crawley, taken ill at Sir Pitt's house, took Becky back to London as a companion, and Rawdon took to seeing Becky often. Miss Crawley recovered but the baronet's insignificant wife, stricken at the same time, died. Sir Pitt went to London and asked Becky to return to his home—"as Lady Crawley, if you like." Becky, a picture of consternation, wept some of her most genuine tears, and cried:

"Oh, sir—I—I'm married already."

When it came out that the husband was Rawdon Crawley, Miss Crawley had hysterics and Sir Pitt raved like a madman. But the captain did not worry. "You can do anything," he told his bride, and they went out to dine.

Old John Sedley went into bankruptcy, so George Osborne's father forebade him to see Amelia again. Defying his father's pocketbook, George immediately married Amelia, with Dobbin egging him on, and the couple went off to Brighton on their honeymoon. There they fell in with the Rawdon Crawleys and compared notes; two couples who had defied the husbands' families to wed. Miss Crawley had not yet forgiven her nephew, and Becky had to manage their establishment and social position on nothing a year, wheedling and staving off creditors.

Then Napoleon escaped from Elba, and both the young husbands were called to Brussels for the final battle. George, cut off with two thousand pounds, did his best to dissipate it and, though only six weeks wed, became infatuated with Becky. But the Battle of Waterloo interrupted all this, and when it was over Amelia was a widow.

But Rawdon Crawley was promoted to colonel for gallantry, and he and Becky spent a resplendent winter in Paris. Rawdon did well at cards, dice and billiards, until people tired of losing to him. But when word of all this, and of the birth of a son to Becky, reached London, Miss Crawley promptly named Rawdon's brother Pitt as her heir.

Amelia, too, was the mother of a son, whom she named George, but otherwise her life was sad. She lived with her penniless parents; and her father-in-law refused to see her.

After a couple of years in Paris, Becky bought off Rawdon's English debts at a shilling on the pound, and they returned to

London to live in the same nothing-a-year style. Young Mrs. Crawley neglected her son, but kept a smile always ready for the men, all the while doing her dull-witted husband's thinking for him. When the old baronet died, Pitt surprisingly made friendly overtures to Rawdon, and Becky plotted to win lucrative positions for her husband. Becky could flatter Pitt into attendance on her, but his purse strings did not loosen so easily.

Becky actually rose so high as to be presented at court—and to be invited to dine at the home of wealthy, elderly Lord Steyne, whose interest was not entirely altruistic.

Meantime, poverty having prostrated the Sedley family, Amelia, with many tears, at last consented to let her son go to her father-in-law so that she and her parents might have food and pay their rent.

Becky, flying high in society and waited on by Lord Steyne, paid little attention to Rawdon, who felt more and more estranged from his wife, particularly after their son was sent off to school. Then one night Rawdon was seized for debt, was set free earlier than Becky had expected, and returned home to find her with Lord Steyne. Crawley knocked down the nobleman, carried off the gifts she had accepted, and left his wife amid the ruin of all her schemes.

Ten years had passed since Joseph Sedley and William Dobbin had gone out to India after Waterloo. Now they returned home, to find old Mrs. Sedley dead and Amelia's son a little pampered tyrant in the home of old Mr. Osborne. Though Amelia never had reciprocated, all William's thoughts had been of her throughout the years. Now a Major, Dobbin found her still faithful to a dead husband when he visited her after wealthy Jos set up a home in St. Martin's Lane and took his sister and soon-to-die father there. Dobbin's guidance, too, made little George more of a man, and the boy was made rich by old Mr. Osborne's death.

On a tour of the Continent, Jos, Amelia, William and little George met Becky Sharp in Germany. Rebecca had sunk low. Lonely after her disgrace, she had wandered about Europe, careless of her reputation, fleeing creditors, supported by various admirers, gambling away the little pension paid her by her husband, now Governor of far-away Coventry Island.

Amelia immediately wanted to give a home to Becky—who had told a pitiful tale of having been wronged—and William went off angry when Amelia refused to listen to his warnings against her old schoolmate. Jos rediscovered his old attachment for Becky. When that lady learned that Amelia had rejected Dobbin's hand out of memory of George, she showed Amelia a note George had written the night before Waterloo, asking Becky to elope with him. At once Amelia sent for William, and his long quest was over; they married and settled in the country.

Becky made Joseph her slave; they traveled about together, and he insured his life heavily in her favor. Soon after that he died, as did Rawdon on his tropical island, and Becky went to live at Bath and Cheltenham, where she busied herself with charities. Her son, now Sir Rawdon Crawley, Bart., made her an allowance but refused to see her.

Ah! Vanitas Vanitatum! Come, children, let us shut up the box and the puppets, for our play is played out.

Henry Esmond

By WILLIAM MAKEPEACE THACKERAY

IN THE DAYS when the last Stuart king was losing the English crown, a precocious boy with a dark, sallow face was growing up, half-neglected, in Castlewood House, of which he knew every secret chamber and hidden passageway. The boy was Henry Esmond, reputedly the illegitimate son of Thomas, Viscount Castlewood, whose wife years before had been a great beauty and a court favorite. Lady Castlewood, her beauty gone, now tried to replace it with paint and powder. In her entourage she kept a Jesuit, Father Holt, who trained little Harry at both Latin and swordplay.

But King James was deposed, and Thomas of Castlewood died in his service in Ireland, while King William's men took his lady prisoner in her bed. Henry Esmond was left in Castlewood House while it was in possession of a company of soldiers, among whose number was Corporal Steele, known as Dick the scholar, who in later years was to edit the Spectator with his friend Joe Addison. Then another Esmond, named Francis, came to take over as Viscount Castlewood, and Henry Esmond met Rachel, the new Lady Castlewood, a pretty girl much younger than her husband.

That was the beginning of Harry's lifetime devotion to Rachel and her children Beatrix and Frank. The Lady worshiped Viscount Frank, and as was natural, this devotion cloyed on him. He deserted her to make love to London ladies when smallpox took the bloom off her beauty for a time, although he was passionately jealous when Lord Mohun made love to her. This jealousy led to the Viscount's death in a duel with Mohun—a duel which Harry, who was present and sober, tried to take upon himself instead. In a deathbed confession Viscount Castlewood disclosed that Henry Esmond should have held his title— that Harry was the legitimate son of Viscount Thomas, and the true head of the house of Castlewood. But Henry burned this paper, vowing that Lady Rachel should not know sorrow through him, and that Little Frank should become the Viscount.

Distraught by her grief, Rachel denounced Henry when she visited him in prison, where he lay wounded and locked up for his part in the duel. Choosing to think that he could have prevented the Viscount's death, she forbade him the house and her friendship. Henry would have been destitute if his father's widow had not summoned him to her new house in Chelsey. Something about his manner as he kissed her hand told her that this boy whom once she had ordered about knew that he was his father's rightful son and heir. Thereafter she called him "Son

Esmond," and her influence at court enabled Harry to obtain an ensign's commission.

Esmond, serving with valor and distinction in the campaigns of Marlborough, was wounded at Blenheim. He obtained successive advancements to the rank of colonel, although as aide to General Webb he learned to think little of the Duke who was his commander-in-chief. By chance he met Father Holt in the Low Countries, and the priest told him the story of how his father had preserved the honor of his mother, a poor weaver's daughter, and then had deserted her. She died in a convent, and Henry had been taken into his father's house.

One happiness came back to Esmond. He had met his Lady Rachel in the Cathedral of Winchester, and as soon as their eyes made contact, their estrangement was past. Rachel was some years older than Harry, but his heart was hers—until he saw Beatrix, Rachel's daughter, now a sixteen-year-old maid of honor at court. With her dark curls and snowy complexion, she was as beautiful a girl as lived in England. Esmond's heart went out to her, and for ten years he wooed her in vain, while she spurned him as a fortuneless and nameless soldier who was too serious for her taste.

Young Viscount Frank was another charming youngster. Handsome, gay, already a sportsman and swordsman at fifteen, Frank was irresistible. He went abroad to the campaigns with Harry, and at his majority married a Dutch noblewoman older than he, who wooed the young lord back to the Papist faith from which Harry and his family had departed.

While Harry, back in England, occupied himself with literary work—he began by helping Addison with his famous poem about the Blenheim campaign—Beatrix went on about her gay career of breaking hearts. But she remained unwed, while less spectacular beauties found husbands with solid fortunes. Beatrix became engaged to more than one fine catch, but always something intervened, while always Esmond remained quietly faithful.

At length the Duke of Hamilton, a widower of the highest

station, sued for Beatrix's hand, and she accepted, though the Duke was twice her age. Esmond submitted to fate. For a wedding present he gave her a handsome necklace of diamonds, an inheritance from his father's wife, who had died, leaving her moderate property to Harry.

The bridegroom protested that Beatrix should not accept gifts from men who had no right to the names they bore. Then the angry Rachel replied:

"Henry Esmond is his father's lawful son and true heir. We are the recipients of his bounty, and he is the head of a house as old as Your Grace's."

Then milady explained that the old Viscountess had told her the true story before her death. Beatrix, to whom this was a revelation, kissed Harry and whispered, "Oh, why didn't I know you before?"

But on the eve of the wedding the Duke of Hamilton was killed in a duel by Lord Mohun, whose murderous career was ended in that same encounter. Beatrix mourned him honestly, but Esmond hoped she might yet have him.

Young Frank had served the exiled Stuart pretender in France. Now they came together to Lady Castlewood's London house, the Prince impersonating the Viscount. Harry Esmond had never given up his loyalty to the old royal family, and now he hoped to please Rachel and Beatrix by managing an attempt to win back the throne.

The maid of honor contrived an interview between the Prince and Queen Anne, his sister, whose health was failing. All hoped she would name him her successor. Then Beatrix' friends began to worry about her, for the Prince, who was no respecter of women, was infatuated with her and she listened to him. Against her will she was sent to Castlewood.

Suddenly the Queen was reported dying and the Prince could not be found. Henry and Frank rode to Castlewood, where they found the pretender with Beatrix. Esmond's old infatuation was ended. Taking out the papers which proved his birth, Esmond burned them before the King's eyes, and broke his sword, renouncing Stuart. Frank followed him.

As they rode back to London, the heralds proclaimed George of Hanover as King of England. Queen Anne had died that night.

The Stuart chevalier escaped to France, where he was joined by Beatrix. And Esmond married Rachel, and they sailed to America, where they built a Castlewood in Virginia, and lived happily the rest of their days.

Barchester Towers

By ANTHONY TROLLOPE

ANTHONY TROLLOPE *was born April 24, 1815, at London. He had his education at Harrow and Winchester. In 1841 he became a clerk to the Post-Office Surveyor in Ireland. Thereafter he held various positions in the Post Office which provided him with leisure enough to write a long series of novels. Later in his life his government work took him to the West Indies, Egypt, and the United States. On Dec. 6, 1882, he died in London.*

ONE SUMMER in the year 185–, the clergy of the old English cathedral town of Barchester were agitated by one question: Who would be selected as the Bishop of Barchester? The hopes of the high-church faction of Barchester were centered on the local Archdeacon, Dr. Grantly. When the powers that be in the government chose an outsider, Dr. Proudie, the dismay of Dr. Grantly and his followers was equaled only by the indignation which the views of the new bishop's chaplain aroused.

Dr. Proudie's own views were not alarming to Dr. Grantly,

but when it was discovered that he was completely submissive to the will of his domineering wife and counted on the low-church Mr. Slope to represent him in his official life, the lines of battle were drawn. The immediate occasion was a sermon preached by Mr. Slope, which not only offended the theological sentiments of Dr. Grantly but also aspersed the traditional church ceremonies of Barchester.

Another point of issue between the old and new clerical factions was the vacant wardenship of Hiram's Hospital, a charitable institution under the control of the diocese. Old Mr. Harding, choirmaster in the cathedral and former warden, was the candidate of Dr. Grantly, and almost everyone assumed that Mr. Harding would be renominated for the post. Dr. Grantly's wife was the eldest daughter of Mr. Harding.

But Mr. Slope saw in the disposition of the wardenship a chance to impose some of his own ideas on the clergy of Barchester. When he tendered the offer of the wardenship to Mr. Harding, he attached, without Dr. Proudie's knowledge, such conditions to the acceptance that Mr. Harding—though neither a proud nor a forceful man—could not feel it within his dignity to accept. Mr. Slope had merely proved to Mr. Harding what Dr. Grantly had maintained all along—Mr. Slope was not a gentleman.

But Mr. Slope had his supporters, of whom Mrs. Proudie was the most important. The women of the congregation were generally enthusiastic about him and his sermons.

Mrs. Proudie's first reception in the bishop's palace was not an unqualified success. The Rev. Vesey Stanhope, long absent in Italy from his livings, had returned to Barchester with his wife and children under pressure from the new bishop. The impression two of his children made on the Proudies at the reception was, to say the least, painful. La Signora Neroni, as she styled herself, was Dr. Stanhope's younger daughter; she had been deserted some years ago by her Italian husband, and had returned to the shelter of her father's home, badly crippled through some mysterious accident. Borne in by four men to a sofa that had been arranged by Mr. Slope, her fascinating manners and beauty drew the attention of the men to her. To her disgust, Mrs. Proudie noticed Mr. Slope in close attendance on the Signora all evening. Her younger brother, Bertie Stanhope, an amiable ne'er-do-well, with neither income nor vocation, made himself particularly disagreeable to Dr. Proudie by his unorthodox comments on religious questions.

Mr. Slope soon discovered that the best catch for a clergyman in Barchester was Mr. Harding's widowed daughter, Eleanore Bold, who had £1,200 a year. When he had got to know Eleanore better, he began to feel that he had been hasty with Mr. Harding. In the meantime, Mrs. Proudie had promised the wardenship to Mr. Quiverful, a poor clergyman in a rural living, who was trying to bring up a family of fourteen on £400 a year. But Mr. Slope was more than a match for Mr. Quiverful, and slyly got from him a refusal of the wardenship.

When Mrs. Proudie heard of this, she marched into her husband's study. But for once the Bishop and Mr. Slope were able to resist her unitedly. Mr. Slope did not leave the room, and Mrs. Proudie was forced to retire to tell the tearful Mrs. Quiverful that she had not given up yet.

Somehow Dr. Grantly got it into his head that Eleanore regarded Mr. Slope with some favor. Mrs. Grantly decided to ask her to visit awhile at their home at Plumstead. There Eleanore met Mr. Arabin, the new minister of a near-by parish; he was one of Dr. Grantly's favorites, a doctrinal opponent of Mr. Slope, and a man who had seen very little of the world. Thus it was that he did not quite know how to talk to Eleanore Bold once he had begun to feel that he was in love with her.

When Eleanore received a letter by messenger from Mr. Slope, the atmosphere at Plumstead became quite tense. Everyone— even her father—was sure that Eleanore had made up her mind to marry Mr. Slope. When she found out what they were thinking, she decided to return to Barchester at once, but only after she made the mistake of believing that Mr. Arabin was the one who had imputed to her a desire to marry Mr. Slope.

Back in Barchester, Mr. Slope was bewitched by La Signora Neroni. But he was still determined to ask Eleanore for her hand. Nor was he much troubled by the fact that his one-time patroness, Mrs. Proudie, was now furious with him for his attentions to Madame Neroni, and his interview with Mr. Quiverful.

Not until he met Eleanore at a party given by the local squire, Mr. Thorne, did Mr. Slope have a chance to propose to Eleanore. Her refusal was peremptory. At the same party Eleanore turned down another offer of matrimony from an unexpected quarter. Bertie Stanhope lamely offered himself, urged on by the promptings of his sisters that he should take this way of mending his broken fortunes. An unhappy day ended for Eleanore with a view of Mr. Arabin in rapt attendance on La Signora.

And now the news came that the old dean of Barchester, Mr. Trefoil, was dying. That meant a new vacancy to be filled. Mr. Slope fancied himself as a likely candidate, and lost no time seeing the Bishop and writing to his friends in the government.

But he had not reckoned on Mrs. Proudie. She had replaced him once and for all as the power behind the Bishop's throne. The deanery was offered to Mr. Harding; and Mr. Slope was shortly ousted from his chaplainship. Not before, however, he had been angrily spurned by Signora Neroni. She also took it upon herself to inform Eleanore that Mr. Arabin was deeply in love with Eleanore, but lacked the ability to express himself to her.

So Mr. Quiverful became the new warden, Mr. Arabin won Eleanore, and when Mr. Harding refused the appointment to the deanery, Mr. Arabin was nominated in his place. Dr. Grantly was on good terms with his Bishop, and peace had come to Barchester.

The War of the Worlds

By H. G. WELLS

HERBERT GEORGE WELLS *was born on September 21, 1866, at Bromley, Kent, the son of a professional cricketer. The lower-middle-class vicissitudes of his youth were followed by a scholarship to the Royal College of Science, after which he graduated from London University in 1888. He became a science instructor, then began doing some journalistic writing. Following the publication of his first book in 1895, he wrote scores of novels, histories, philosophical books, and popularized scientific works. Wells lives in England today.*

WHEN my friend Ogilvy the astronomer let me look through his telescope at one of the mysterious jets of flame that had been seen on Mars, we had no idea that for ten consecutive nights missiles were being fired at us by the Martians. And the England of the last years of the nineteenth century went about its petty concerns without suspecting that the red planet was the home of vast intelligences far superior to man's.

The first "falling star" dug itself one midnight into Horsell Common, near Woking and my home on Maybary Hill. Ogilvy went to look at it at dawn, and found that it was a metal cylinder thirty yards in diameter—with an end that was slowly unscrewing. At once Ogilvy linked it with the flashes from Mars, and decided there must be men inside who needed help. But it was not until sunset that the lid disengaged itself. Then there were shrieks of horror from the crowd that had gathered, for it was no man who emerged.

I was among those who saw the grayish, rounded bulk, the size of a bear, pull itself painfully out into the air with its tentacles that were bunched under its grotesque "face." It had two large dark-colored eyes and a quivering lipless V-shaped mouth with no chin. The oily skin glistened like wet leather, and the creature breathed tumultuously in the strange atmosphere.

It was dusk when Ogilvy and a few others, carrying a white flag, approached to show the Martians we were intelligent, friendly creatures. Suddenly there was a flash of light and a puff of green smoke, and a metallic shape rose from the pit. A droning noise was heard, and the ghost of a beam of light swung about in a semi-circle. Flames sprang from the delegation—the first killed by the Martian heat ray—and trees and houses caught fire in a huge arc. I ran home in panic.

At midnight the second cylinder fell a few miles to the northwest. The next day I took my wife to her cousins at Leatherhead, 12 miles away, for our house was in range of the deadly ray. When I returned that night with the borrowed horse and dogcart, it was to a scene of desolation. And it was then that I saw my first Martian walking-machines. They were monstrous tripods, higher than a house, and they reeled along like animated milking stools. Long, flexible, glittering tentacles swung from them, and they emitted a deafening howl—"Aloo! aloo!"

I had underestimated the Martians. Seeing their sluggishness on our heavier planet, I had not reckoned with their having machines that would serve as bodies for them. The newspapers and authorities had the same reaction, and even after the initial massacre had assumed that the visitors were immobile and could easily be dealt with.

Two companies of troops had been sent to the scene. A fleeing soldier told me how they had been wiped out, after which the machines had smashed Woking. Now the Martians were leisurely consolidating their forces. The third cylinder fell that night, and seven more were to arrive.

I started back toward Leatherhead at dawn, keeping to cover

in the desolate countryside from which a few last refugees were fleeing. Guns had been emplaced along the way—bows and arrows against the lightning. It was at the junction of the Wey and the Thames, where an excited crowd of fugitives waited to cross, that five of the Martians caught up with me. I took to the water as our artillery opened fire, and saw one of the machines hurtle into the Thames when a shell killed the Martian inside the control hood. His infuriated companions destroyed the soldiers, the crowd, and Weybridge and Shepperton. I escaped only by a miracle.

Joined by a hysterical curate, that afternoon I saw the Martians at a distance firing canisters which broke and released clouds of heavy smoke which clung to the ground. We were to learn that this inky vapor killed everything that breathed; the only ones to escape were those who climbed trees or church steeples. We could see the Martians advancing methodically on London as resistance collapsed.

Meantime my brother in London had seen the slow realization of the danger that threatened, had joined the evacuation to the north that quickly degenerated into a panicky rout as the government fell apart. On the Essex coast he got aboard one of the last ships that was able to flee to France, and saw a warship sacrifice itself to destroy two of the Martian monsters that had waded into the sea. But those who did not flee from London were killed by the black smoke.

The curate and I hid in a house near Halliford, saw the smoke eddy near us, and then moved on after a Martian laid the stuff with a jet of superheated steam. It was outside the town of Sheen that we broke into a house to obtain food. Suddenly a loud explosion knocked us headlong. We found that the fifth Martian cylinder had fallen alongside the house, and that we were completely buried by the splash of earth. For a fortnight I was to be trapped in the two rooms that remained uncrushed. A small crevice opened into the new Martian pit and thus I became one of the few who lived to tell of seeing the visitors at close hand.

The Martians had handling machines so complex that they seemed alive. And another machine turned out heaps of aluminum bars from clay. But the horrible discovery was the way the Martians fed. I was to learn later that their internal anatomy was very simple—an enormous brain, with lungs, a heart and no digestive system. They did not eat; instead they injected the fresh, living blood of other creatures into their veins. That was why they had no interest in killing humans once they had destroyed our resistance. They wanted us as food. I saw the end of one of their captives, a stout, well-dressed man, and for hours I did no more peeping out the crevice. These Martians seemed totally unemotional—they even reproduced by a sexless budding process. I am convinced they communicated with each other by telepathy.

It was soon apparent that the curate was losing his reason. He would not restrain his hunger for our limited rations, and our sixth to ninth days in the house were a continual struggle for me to quiet his loud rantings, which I feared would attract the Martians' attention. At length I had to knock him unconscious with a meat-chopper. Suddenly a Martian discovered our crevice, and the tentacle of a handling machine groped inside. From the coal cellar I saw the curate dragged away, and the thing almost caught me. There was no food left now; only water.

It was on my fifteenth day in the house that I looked outside. The pit was empty, and I crawled to the surface to find a deserted earth overgrown with the red weed whose spores apparently had been carried from Mars. I pushed on into London, meeting no Martians, no men—nothing but a few dogs and crows. Even food was hard to find. At length I encountered a soldier who had been living in the sewers, and had made his plans to exist like a rabbit.

Then suddenly the Martian menace passed, as quickly as it had come. The invaders had not provided against bacteria. Coming from a planet they had made germ-free, they became easy victims of disease. The dogs found them first, and only one un-eaten Martian was preserved complete for science.

As for me, I had despairingly made my way back to my home, and found my wife searching for me there. We had counted each other as dead.

The Picture of Dorian Gray

By OSCAR WILDE

OSCAR O'FLAHERTIE WILLS WILDE, *the son of a famous surgeon and a woman poet, was born in Dublin on Oct. 15, 1856. He won distinction in the classics and poetry at Trinity College and Oxford, but achieved far greater fame as the leader of the aesthetic movement of the Nineties in London. Famed as a wit, poet, novelist, and dramatist, his social position collapsed when he was sentenced in 1895 to two years at hard labor for violating the morals laws. He died in Paris on Nov. 30, 1900.*

THE STUDIO was filled with the rich odor of roses, and from the corner of the divan on which he was lying, Lord Henry Wotton could just catch the gleam of the honey-colored blossoms of a laburnum in the garden. The sullen murmur of the bees seemed to make the stillness more oppressive.

In the center of the room stood the full-length portrait of a young man of extraordinary personal beauty, in front of which sat the artist, Basil Hallward, whose sudden disappearance some years ago gave rise to so many strange conjectures. "It is your best work," said Lord Henry. "You must send it to the Grosvenor." "I won't send it anywhere," said Hallward. "I have put too much of myself into it."

The artist let slip that the subject's name was Dorian Gray, and explained that the youth's personality was so fascinating that it dominated him, his mere presence showing Hallward the way to a new mode of expressing himself artistically. But sometimes, he added, "I feel that I have given my whole soul to someone who treats it as if it were a flower to put in his coat." Then, just as Hallward entreated the cynical Lord Henry not to spoil his friend's simple and beautiful nature, Dorian Gray was announced.

Lord Henry observed Dorian's scarlet lips, frank blue eyes, and crisp gold hair, and decided that here was a candid, passionately pure youth. As the artist painted, Dorian chatted with Lord Henry, entranced by such remarks as: "The only way to get rid of a temptation is to yield to it," which touched some secret chord within him. Lord Henry told him to make the most of the beauty of youth while he had it.

Then Hallward cried that the portrait was finished, and the three examined the magnificent work. "How sad!" murmured Dorian. "I shall grow old and horrible, but this picture never will be older. If it were I who was to be always young, and the picture that was to grow old! I would give my soul for that!"

Lord Henry learned that Dorian was the heir to great wealth, the son of a beautiful woman of good family who had run away with a subaltern, only to have her husband killed in a duel and to follow him promptly in death. The older man cultivated the youth, going with him to the opera and to dinners, and shrugged his shoulders when he learned that Dorian had fallen in love with Sibyl Vane, seventeen-year-old actress in a little theater.

Engaged to be married to this girl who knew him only as "Prince Charming," Dorian took his friends to see her act—and for the first time saw her perform badly. When she told him that the stage no longer meant reality to her, he cried, "You have killed my love," and left her despite her tears. When he arrived home, he saw a touch of cruelty about the mouth of his portrait; the mirror showed him that his own features were unchanged.

With a shock he remembered his wish, but told himself that he had not been cruel; it was Sibyl's fault.

Next afternoon he wrote a letter begging the girl's forgiveness, but Lord Henry called to tell him that Sibyl had killed herself by poison. His friend said it was as well; Sibyl would have bored him, and Dorian found himself agreeing. In the end he concluded that it was a marvelous experience to have had a part in this stage-like tragedy. Smiling, he placed a screen before the portrait which would serve as a mirror for his soul.

The next morning Dorian was blasé when Basil Hallward called to commiserate with him. He refused to let the artist look at the portrait, but drew from him the story of how he had idolized Dorian, though the confession failed to win Dorian's promise to sit for him again. When he left, the youth moved the portrait to the disused upstairs schoolroom in his home, where it could be kept behind a locked door.

Now Lord Henry sent Dorian a strange novel about a Parisian who had spent his life trying to realize all the passions and modes of thought of previous centuries, both the virtues and the sins. It was a poisonous book, and it fascinated Dorian. For years it influenced him; it seemed the story of his own life, written before he had lived it.

Dorian's wonderful beauty and purity of face seemed never to leave him, though evil stories and strange rumors about him crept through London. He would return home from a mysterious and prolonged absence and stand with a mirror in his hand in front of the portrait. His sense of pleasure was quickened by the sharp contrast between the evil and aging face on the canvas, and the fair young face in the glass. The portrait's mouth was heavy and sensual, there were hideous lines in the forehead, the body was misshapen.

He frequented in disguise an ill-famed tavern near the Docks, and his mad hungers grew more ravenous as he fed them. Yet he gave dinners and musicals for society, seeking to become more than a leading dandy—to be the elaborator of a new scheme of life in which the senses would be the elements of a new spirituality dominated by a fine instinct for beauty.

Dorian was stirred by the Roman Catholic ritual; he studied perfumes and devoted himself to music; he collected and studied jewels and embroideries. But he found himself more and more fascinated by his picture, so that he could not bear to be away from London. And now a few gentlemen began to slight him, and after his 25th year stories became current about his consorting with low characters, though such scandals only increased his charms for many.

On the eve of Dorian's 38th birthday, Basil Hallward called on him late at night before leaving secretly to work in Paris. The artist began to lecture Dorian on his reputation, and in anger Dorian took him to look at the portrait, now horrible and loathsome. Basil shuddered and urged Dorian to pray; instead, overcome by a mad passion, Dorian stabbed him to death.

No one knew they had met; Dorian summoned Alan Campbell, a man whose life he had helped to ruin. Campbell was a student of chemistry, and Dorian forced him to destroy the body. Then Dorian went to dinner at Lady Narborough's, where the conversation, aided by Lord Henry, was witty.

But Dorian still felt nervous, with a sense of terror. That night he made his way to an opium den, where a sailor overheard a woman call him Prince Charming. The sailor was Jim Vane, brother of Sibyl; he almost killed Dorian, who escaped by virtue of his youthful face. A week later, at a country house, he saw Vane watching him, and felt that nemesis was near. Vane took employment as a beater, however, and was killed by a hunter's accidental shot.

Some weeks later Dorian told Lord Henry that he was beginning his good actions now; he started by not seducing a pretty country girl. His friend laughed, and chatted about Basil Hallward's disappearance and his own wife's elopement with a man who played Chopin. Hallward had lost his skill anyway, Lord Henry said. They said goodnight, and Dorian strolled home.

He felt a wild longing for the unstained purity of his childhood; he knew that he had tarnished himself, but was it all
irretrievable? The portrait was the cause of his failure. He could
alter his future; Alan Campbell had killed himself, and Dorian
was perfectly safe. He wondered if the portrait had begun to
change for the better. He looked at it, and a cry of pain burst
from him. A look of cunning and of the hypocrite had been
added, and there was a stain of blood on the hand.

He seized a knife and stabbed the picture. There was a cry, and
a crash. The servants forced the schoolroom door. They found
hanging upon the wall a splendid portrait of their master as they
had last seen him, in all the wonder of his exquisite youth and
beauty. On the floor was a dead man, a knife in his heart. He
was withered, wrinkled, and loathsome of visage. It was not
until they had examined the rings that they recognized who it
was.

American Novels

Little Women

By LOUISA MAY ALCOTT

LOUISA MAY ALCOTT *was born in Germantown, Pennsylvania, on November 29, 1832, the eldest daughter of Amos Bronson Alcott, a man of intellectual abilities but little talent for supporting a family. At sixteen Louisa was the mainstay of the family; she was seamstress, a school-teacher, and even did domestic work in Concord, Massachusetts, where they had made their home. Her literary career started when, out of financial necessity, she wrote pot-boilers for periodicals. In 1862 she went to Washington as a war nurse; her health was seriously impaired, and in 1866 she took a trip to Europe. On her return in 1867 she wrote* Little Women, *a fictionized biography of her sisters and herself. She continued to support her family and never married, devoting her entire life to her father and her orphaned niece and nephew. On March 6, 1888, she died in Boston of a fever brought on by the strain of nursing her father through his last illness.*

THE MARCHES were a happy family. Poverty, hard work, and even the fact that Father March was away with the Union armies could not down the spirits of Meg, Jo, Beth, Amy, and Marmee, as the March girls affectionately called their mother. Now it was

Christmas. Though the girls sacrificed their own gifts, each brought a token to Marmee. And to a neighboring family dreadfully in want, the girls brought their own holiday breakfast. But virtue had a speedy reward in the form of a surprise Christmas feast sent over by old Mr. Laurence, a wealthy neighbor. Mr. Laurence lived with his young grandson, Laurie, and the boy's tutor, John Brooke. Laurie seemed lonely, and friendly Jo would have made his acquaintance had not her more proper sisters restrained her.

The March sisters, despite their efforts to be good, had their share of faults. Pretty Meg was apt to become discontented with the schoolchildren she taught; boyish Jo lost her temper easily, particularly when she thought of old Aunt March, whose companion she was; golden-haired schoolgirl Amy was inclined toward affectation; but Beth, who kept the house, was loving and gentle always.

A party was an event to the Marches, and when Mrs. Gardiner invited the two eldest to her home there was much excitement in the little March cottage. At the party Jo found that their neighbor, young Laurie, was as shy as she, and the two became fast friends. When Laurie was ill, Jo unconventionally arrived at his big home as an amusement committee. Even crusty old Mr. Laurence was completely won over to the Marches. His special favorite was gentle Beth, and when he learned from Jo how dearly the little girl loved music he sent Beth a piano of her very own. Tutor John Brooke preferred pretty Meg of all the sisters, and Laurie soon scented romance between the two.

The happy days passed and darkness came when a telegram arrived for Mrs. March. "Your husband is very ill," it said, "come at once." The girls tried to be as brave as their mother, who planned to go immediately to Mr. March. Each looked for some method to help Marmee, and Jo found the most practical way; she sold for twenty-five badly needed dollars her one beauty, her long chestnut hair. Mrs. March left for the front under the escort of John Brooke and the girls could only wait and pray. But little

Beth, on a mission of mercy to a sick neighbor, contracted scarlet fever. The little girl became very ill indeed and finally, despairing of her life, the doctor summoned Mrs. March. But Beth miraculously passed the crisis safely and by the time Marmee arrived her little daughter was on the mend. By the next Christmas Beth was, if not her old rosy self, at least no longer an invalid. And a happy surprise was in store for the March family —Father March came home from the front and at that jolly Christmas dinner they were once more all together with their friends, the Laurences and Mr. Brooke.

It soon became clear that John Brooke's suit of Meg was serious, and when Aunt March threatened Meg with disinheritance if she married John, the young girl accepted her suitor. The Marches consented to the match although they stipulated that the wedding not take place for three years.

Three years later the March girls were grown to young womanhood. Meg became Mrs. Brooke, and after a few domestic crises adjusted happily to her new state. Jo had found a source of pleasure, even of income, in her literary efforts. Amy was grown into an elegant young lady with a talent for sketching and an even greater one for society. But Beth had never fully regained her health, and her family, feeling they were not to keep her long, watched her with love and anxiety.

The greatest disappointment of Jo's young life came when a connection of the Marches, deciding she wanted a companion on a European trip, asked, instead of stormy Jo, poised and lady-like Amy. But Jo bore the blow bravely and remained at home with Marmee and Beth while Miss Amy broke hearts in Europe.

Jo grew restless in the little March home. She knew that Laurie had loved her for a long time and would soon speak to her of marriage; she knew too that she could never regard him as anything but a brother. So Jo, with wise Marmee's permission, went to New York to "try her wings." She found a place as a governess with Mrs. Kirke, who ran a large boarding house. At first

Jo, despite her pride in her own independence, missed her family sorely, but soon her literary efforts and her friendship with Professor Friedrich Bhaer, an odd and lovable German tutor, chased thoughts of homesickness out of her head.

Then, too, Jo had the satisfaction of seeing her work in print, for some of her lively tales soon found a publisher. But the time came for Jo to return home and she regretfully said good-by to Professor Bhaer.

Jo found Laurie awaiting her homecoming eagerly; the lad proposed and Jo refused him, since she knew she didn't love him as he would wish. But her own heart was sore when she watched his suffering; Laurie went to Europe with his grandfather in an effort to forget his disappointment and while he was there saw much of Amy.

But at home the bitterest blow was yet to fall. Beth had known for some time that she hadn't much longer to be with her family, and in the springtime she died.

News came from Europe that Laurie, recovered from his heartbreak, had proposed to Amy and the two planned soon to be married.

Now Jo, despite her ever more successful writing, found herself very lonely, and when Professor Bhaer came to see her she realized that it was he whom she wanted. They were married, and soon afterwards founded a school for boys.

And so the little women had reached maturity, surrounded by their children and the children for whom they were caring, and reaping the harvest of love and goodness that they had all their lives been sowing.

Looking Backward

By EDWARD BELLAMY

EDWARD BELLAMY, *the son of a Baptist clergyman, the grandson of two others, was born in Chicopee Falls, Massachusetts, in 1850. He attended Union College, Schenectady, where he studied law, although he never practiced it. He took up journalism, then fiction, dealing with subjects of social reform. Influenced by Karl Marx, Bellamy reproduced his views with considerable accuracy in novel form, in his best-known book,* Looking Backward. *Written in 1887,* Looking Backward *anticipated and described such modern inventions as radio in the home. Bellamy was shy and avoided capitalizing on his literary reputation. Contracting tuberculosis, he died in his old home in 1898.*

JULIAN WEST, handsome, wealthy young Bostonian, finally fell asleep in a specially constructed underground chamber on May 30, 1887. A sufferer from insomnia, he left his beautiful fiancée, Edith Barlett, and subjected himself to the ministration of his private mesmerist, his final recourse in inducing sleep. He awoke to hear a girl say:

"Promise me, then, that you will not tell him!"

With the girl were her parents, all three simply but oddly garbed. Julian was given restoratives and regained consciousness in strange surroundings. He learned he was still in Boston, but that it was September 30th. . . . September 30th in the year 2000 A.D.! His hosts were Dr. and Mrs. Leete, and their charming daughter, Edith.

West learned his house had burned the night he retired. He

was believed to be dead but, hypnotized, he had slept until excavators had uncovered his chamber. The Boston he now beheld was a magnificent city, without squalor, without chimneys or smoke.

Dr. Leete was curious as to whether men of the 19th century had not been aware of great impending social changes. Julian replied no, and inquired in his turn if there were now strikes. The doctor answered that strikes had been defensive actions of workmen against concentrated capital; since capital no longer existed in that form, there were no strikes. Business had merged into great combinations, so that after 1925 there was comparatively little small business left. Evolution was completed when all capital was placed in governmental hands. Julian was shocked by this extension of power, deeming it the sole prerogative of government to keep the peace and defend against enemies. Dr. Leete replied that countries such as France, England and Germany were no longer enemies; the enemies of mankind were hunger, cold, and nakedness. In Julian's day, governments sent hundreds of thousands to their death over incidents to profit the wealthy, but without motive to the people. No government in 2000 had the power to wage war.

Julian asked about corruption of public figures, and was answered that not human nature, but conditions of life had changed; there was no longer incentive to misuse power.

Today, all began work at the age of 24, terminating labor at 45, when they retired. Each worked according to education and capabilities, each determined his own calling. All citizens were familiar with industry, agriculture, science, and the arts. If enrollment in a pursuit drew too many or too few, hours of labor were adjusted to make the endeavor more or less attractive. Common labor was engaged in by all during the first three years of working service. During this period aptitude decided whether one would study further, or go directly to work. A final change and choice could be made up to the 30th year.

Reaction to the terrific change affected Julian, but in Edith, to whom he was strangely drawn, he found solace. Again in command of himself, he went on to discover:

There were no more stores, but sample rooms in each locality, where all commodities were found. Orders were taken there, and purchases sent by pneumatic tubes directly from a central warehouse, delivery being accomplished in a matter of minutes from time of purchase. This, like all services, was paid for by a credit card issued to every person yearly, more than ample for the needs of anyone. Money was not used. Education and medical care were provided for by the state. Ambition was instilled not by the accretion of money and power, but by rank and honor according to service rendered the community.

Julian was shown the Leetes' music room, which proved bare save for easy chairs, and two knobs on a wall panel. He was amazed to find he could select programs at all hours, and control their volume.

Asking about inheritance, he found people could will personal possessions freely; but since all were amply supplied most such chattels were burdensome, rather than valued as in the 19th century. Hence most reverted to the state. Housework was now entirely mechanical; there were public kitchens which supplied public and private dining rooms. For such things as a new house, labor and materials were charged against the purchaser's credit card. Doctors were selected individually, but were paid by the state. Charity was obsolete and the concept of "self-support" had vanished, inasmuch as no man was, or had been for centuries, really self-sustaining. He lived by and in a co-operative society. Thus all sick and chronic invalids were cared for by the entire human family, even as of old a private family would provide for an ailing relative.

International trade was accomplished by bookkeeping, with balances settled every few years. Usually nations balanced fairly evenly. Emigation worked upon the same general principle, people being free to select and change nationality. Travel was accomplished by the credit card, the card from any nation being good the world over. . . . It rained, and Julian discovered all the sidewalks mechanically covered during the storm. It was characteristic that there were no longer "private umbrellas."

No censorship existed. The state was in duty bound to publish any work, the author paying for first printing, and this anyone could now afford. As to periodicals, the staff was supported from subscriptions. Julian learned his place could be that of university lecturer on the 19th century, when he felt ready. Edith asked him about his friends of the past. Julian told her of the Edith of a bygone day, and the girl was profoundly moved.

Dr. Leete showed Julian schools of higher education, available to all, conducted as were public schools of the past. Physical and mental development were carefully watched with a resultant more attractive and healthier generation.

How, asked Julian, had the vast increase in national wealth which made all these things possible, been accomplished? Dr. Leete explained elimination of national, state, county, and municipal debts and service thereon. He remarked on abolishing tax assessors, clerks, collectors, police, sheriffs, and a criminal group supported in jails. There was less loss through physical disability. There were no people involved in financial operations, lawyers, no duplication of stores, laundries, kitchens, factories; no competing vast distributive systems, salesmen, advertising agents, jobbers, wholesalers, middlemen. There were no competition between businesses, no duplication, no waste of idle capital or labor, no cyclical crises. Finally there was no waste from over-production; no throat-cutting, but universal co-operation. And there was no confusion from a credit situation in which credit is a symbol for a symbol, in itself an explosive binding together the economic fabric.

Examining the status of women, Julian found all fields open to them according to their physical ability. There no longer was any dependency on men, and they did not leave jobs when they married. Ambition and opportunity equaled that of men, so girls no longer wished they were born boys. Relationship with men was more frank and open, so that in proposal and marriage natural selectivity operated freely, continually improving the race.

Julian sat up in bed. He was back in the 19th century. He went out, seeing for the first time the squalor and barbarity of the age. He preached his dream and was shunned, finally ousted from the home of his fiancée. Then he awoke to find he had been dreaming.

Now he told his love to Edith Leete, and found rapturously that she loved him too. She then explained the phrase "Promise me then, that you will not tell him," which he heard on first coming to, had to do with the fact they had discovered who he was, and that Edith Leete was the great-granddaughter of Edith Barlett. Edith had waited fourteen years after his supposed death, and finally married. Julian West had found both new life, and reincarnated love!

The Good Earth

By PEARL S. BUCK

PEARL S. BUCK, *born in West Virginia in 1892, was taken at the age of four months to Chinkiang. She attended school in China, and received degrees from Randolph-Macon and Cornell in America. Returning to China as a missionary, she taught English literature and married Professor J. Lossing Buck of the University of Nanking. They and their children had a narrow escape from rioters in 1927. Mrs. Buck returned to America. The Good Earth, her best-known work, was published in 1931 depicting life in China prior to the Japanese aggression.*

IT WAS Wang Lung's marriage day. His father had arranged the marriage, procuring a slave from the great House of Hwang as wife to his son: "Not too young or pretty, but one to tend house, bear children, work the field." Wang Lung replied, "At least not pock-marked nor with split lip."

O-lan, his bride, was square, tall, clothed in blue coat and trousers. Her face was short, honest, with a broad nose, her eyes black. Her parents had sold her when she was ten, in a year of famine.

Wang Lung took her silently to the farm, where she prepared the wedding feast. The guests were his uncle, sly, jovial, worthless; his uncle's son, fifteen and impudent; Ching, a neighbor, and other farmers. O-lan handed the food from the kitchen, for it was not meet that other men see her before consummation of marriage. When the last guest departed, Wang Lung said, "There is this woman of mine. The thing is to be done." He undressed doggedly, she crept silently to him. He gave a hoarse laugh, and seized her.

Morning, and she brought steaming water to him and the Old One. He arose, went to the field. When he returned food was prepared. Fuel there was, gleaned leaf and stick at a time. Afternoons she took basket and hoe to the main road, collecting droppings of horses and mules for fertilizer.

One day she appeared in the field with a hoe. "No household tasks 'til nightfall," she said, and swung into rhythm in the furrow beside him. The sun set; he straightened up and looked at his woman, wet with sweat, streaked with earth, brown as the soil itself. In her plain way she said, "I am with child."

They were also in the field when she said, "It is come. Bring me a newly peeled reed, slit, that I may cut the child's life from mine." When he returned to the house she had prepared food. Through the partly open door to their room he handed her the reed. He heard her panting, there was the smell of hot blood. Then, a thin fierce cry. "Is it a man?" cried Wang Lung, and faintly as an echo O-lan replied, "A man!"

Next day O-lan arose, prepared food, and a few days later she took her place in the field.

Came the New Year, and they proudly called on the House of Hwang. There squandering and decadence had taken toll. Land was for sale and Wang Lung bought a piece.

By spring O-lan was again with child and in autumn she laid down her hoe and crept into the house. Before the day was out she was back again, saying calmly, "Another male." Wang Lung bought more land from the House of Hwang.

Ten moons passed. Wang Lung's shiftless uncle borrowed silver from him. O-lan bore a daughter. Across the oyster-colored sky flew a flock of crows. The omens were bad.

Crops failed from dryness, O-lan was once again with child. Again his uncle came to borrow, and Wang Lung divided with him his shrinking store of beans and rice. And again he returned, but Wang Lung had nothing. The uncle aroused the neighbors, saying Wang Lung had hidden grain. Even Ching helped to invade his house with the recklessness of the hungry. Again a child was born, but when Wang Lung came in there lay on the earthen floor an emaciated, dead body.

Sacrificing their furniture, they struggled to the fire-wagon. It bore them from Anhwei to Kiangsu, where Wang Lung pulled a jinriksha, and O-lan and the children begged. His eldest learned to steal, and was soundly cuffed. Others, such as Wang Lung, were impressed for far-away wars. He hid in terror, working nights now pulling freight vans.

The murmurings of the poor increased, while the rich sealed within high walls lived fabulously. As by magic, crowds formed and attacked the houses of the rich. Wang Lung, swept along, found before him a fat, cowering man. In terror he offered Wang Lung gold in return for the promise that Wang Lung would not molest him.

With gold they returned to the land. One night Wang Lung felt something hidden between the breasts of O-lan. It was a bag containing jewels. These she had found behind a loose brick in the Kiangsu raid. Wang took them, save two pearls for which she mutely pleaded. Through Cuckoo, shrewd, last remaining slave of the Old Lord of the House of Hwang, he bought the lands of Hwang.

With much land, Ching, now a widower, came to him as overseer. O-lan gave birth to twins, a boy and a girl. And now they found that the oldest girl, from privation, was a smiling speechless idiot, Wang Lung's "poor fool."

Five years passed. Wang Lung was rich. Handicapped by lack of learning, he sent the oldest boys to school. Two years more, and came the floods; but they weathered the storm. While water covered his lands, Wang Lung encountered Cuckoo, now a procuress, and through her met and loved Lotus. She was delicate, beautiful, but no longer young, though Wang Lung did not at first realize this. He perfumed himself and cut his queue. Then he beheld O-lan anew, seeing how homely she was, how large her feet and stomach. He was angry that he could not love her who had been so faithful. And he took from her the two pearls, giving them to Lotus.

Wang's uncle returned, and because one must do thus, Wang Lung suffered him to stay, and bring his lazy lustful son and fat termagant wife. This last perceived Wang's infatuation and arranged that Lotus be brought to the house. With the concubine came Cuckoo as her slave; and O-lan's heart was heavy. Despite Wang's riches, she worked in house and field, while Wang dallied with Lotus in her court. O-lan hated Cuckoo, who had beaten her in the House of Hwang, even more than she hated Lotus. Wang's father awoke from senile musing to shriek, "Harlot!" The younger children plagued Lotus.

The floods receded, Wang went back to the fields and was refreshed from the good earth. Then he arranged for the marriage of his eldest son with the daughter of the grain merchant, Liu.

Tiring of the parasitic family of his uncle, he would have driven them forth, but discovered his uncle to be a bandit leader. In fear he suffered them to stay. Then came the locusts, and were fought with fire and moat.

The eldest desired to go south to school, but Wang Lung

denied him. Then he caught the lad with Lotus, beat him cruelly and sent him south. The second boy he apprenticed to Liu, the merchant, and likewise arranged that his youngest daughter, the twin, should some day marry Liu's ten-year-old son.

Now he began to think of O-lan, but even as he pondered she fell ill. In the spring she caused him to send for his eldest, and his daughter-to-be. And thus marriage came about with feasting; then O-lan died, and Wang wished he had not taken away her two pearls. Wang's father died, also, and he and O-lan rested on a hill, in the good earth.

Then was there flood and famine such as none had ever seen. Wang Lung overheard his uncle and his wife plotting against him. His eldest counseled giving opium to render the couple ineffectual. There remained their son, before whom their women were afraid, even his cousin, the girl who was a twin.

The floods receded, many sold their daughters. Wang bought five slaves. One, Pear Blossom, he gave to Lotus. Then because his eldest was still fearful of his uncle's son, he bought and rehabilitated the House of Hwang, where once he had gone timorously seeking a wife. When there his second son came unto him desiring a practical wife. Wang Lung was astonished at the boy's shrewdness, and in his displeasure with his extravagant brother. The eldest sought position, while the younger was afraid that his inheritance would be dissipated before it was divided. Wang's uncle's son demanded silver, and went forth to the distant wars.

Wang's first grandson, born to the eldest came amid turmoil. Wang thought of O-lan when her time had come. Ching labored too hard for his age, and died, and Wang sorrowed mightily.

Wang smoked his water-pipe, but still there was no peace. The third son, an intended farmer, rebelled and was given a tutor. In five years came four grandsons, three granddaughters and in them Wang found some consolation. Then his uncle died, and the widow came with her opium to the town house to die later.

Soldiers appeared, among them his uncle's son. They lodged

in and desecrated the courts, frightened the women. The uncle's son demanded Pear Blossom, now grown, and Wang's third son also desired her. Wang refused his nephew, to Lotus' displeasure, and denied his son. When the soldiers had gone, his last passion flamed with senile gentleness, and though Pear Blossom was eighteen and he seventy, she came willingly to him. The third son, with no word, went to the revolution.

Though his sons did him honor he was alone now with Pear Blossom and his poor fool. They returned to the old house, and Pear Blossom promised she would guard the poor smiling fool when Wang Lung should die.

Old Wang Lung stumbled silently through the furrows he loved. His sons, planning on his death to sell the land, did not hear him. Wang Lung, recalling the decay of the House of Hwang when severed from the land, cried out in trembling anger. The brothers assured him they would never sell. But over the old man's head they looked at each other and smiled.

The Prince and the Pauper

By SAMUEL LANGHORNE CLEMENS

SAMUEL LANGHORNE CLEMENS, *famous under the pen name of Mark Twain, was born in Florida, Missouri, on November 30, 1835. The family shortly removed to Hannibal, Missouri, where Samuel grew up, receiving little formal schooling. He became a journeyman printer and then the pilot of a river-boat. In 1861 he went to Nevada, where he wrote for the Virginia City Enterprise. Then he went to San Francisco, where he achieved quick success as a humorist. In 1870 he married Olivia Langdon. A business failure forced him into a world lecture tour to pay off his debts.*

much as Scott wrote novels in a similar situation. Clemens died at "Stormfield," his country home in Connecticut, in 1910.

ONE AUTUMN DAY in the seventeenth century two little boys were born. One was born in a palace. His name was Edward Tudor, and his long-hoped-for arrival brought rejoicing throughout the land. The other was born in a crowded verminous slum called Offal Court. His name was Tom Canty, and his birth meant one more mouth to feed.

The two babies grew to boyhood, the little Prince of Wales cherished, protected, carefully trained in the usages of royalty. The pauper lad survived somehow. His father and grandmother, brutal and drunken, were beggars by profession and trained Tom to help them eke out a sordid existence.

The Canty clan—father, mother, grandam, Tom, and Nan and Bet, Tom's two sisters—all lived in one dark, dirty room. Blows and curses were the boy's portion, and, although his mother and sisters loved him, his father assuredly did not. An old priest, disinherited by Henry VIII's conversion of the Church, taught Tom his letters and some Latin. The imaginative boy read what he could and dreamed great dreams of—being a prince. Thoughts of royalty so filled his mind that when he was not begging or fighting, he conjured up a royal dream-world for himself.

One day Tom, after a begging tour, wandered to the great gates of Westminster Palace and stood there staring with admiration at Edward, the boy prince. A sentinel cuffed him away but the kindhearted young prince indignantly rebuked his servant and bade the guards open the gate and admit the beggar boy.

Edward took Tom to a private room in the palace and there asked the pauper all about his life and family. The two boys had plenty to tell each other, and soon Edward found himself envying Tom's freedom as Tom envied Edward his wealth and high estate. The two boys changed clothes, and, to the surprise of both, discovered that they bore an amazing resemblance to each other. When Tom told Edward that a guard had struck him, the young prince sped away, still in his pauper disguise, to discipline his man-at-arms. But the soldiers at the gate mistook him for the pauper and turned him out with blows. When he declared that he was the Prince of Wales, the mocking crowd hurried him off from the palace gate and pursued him through the town.

Tom Canty, left alone in the palace, enjoyed the beauty and splendor about him until he became alarmed at Edward's delay in returning. As the hours passed he grew more and more frightened, particularly as the servants and even the court nobles persisted in treating him as though he were the true Prince of Wales. He steadfastly denied that he was Prince Edward and declared himself to be Tom Canty of Offal Court. But the nobles and even King Henry treated him as though he were suffering from a temporary madness which would pass. Gradually, out of necessity, he adapted himself to the life at court. As time went by, although convinced of his madness, the court was impressed by his gentleness to malefactors and the interest he took in the poor and criminal classes. He soon learned even court etiquette. The only mystery that he was unable to solve was the whereabouts of the Great Seal, which King Henry had confided to the care of the true Prince of Wales. The King asked the boy to return the seal, since it was needed, and took it as another proof of the poor Prince's madness when the lad obviously did not even know what the seal was.

Meanwhile the real Prince, in Tom's rags, was suffering poverty and privation. Having no place else to go, he sought out the hovel in Offal Court and was greeted with a beating from Canty and the grandmother. He stoutly maintained throughout that he was the Prince. Canty declared him mad, but Tom's mother, noting the absence of a familiar gesture, suspected that this was not her lad.

John Canty soon fell afoul of the law by murdering the kindly priest in a brawl, and the family fled for its life. Edward managed to escape. But, hearing that the "Prince" was being feted at the Guildhall, Edward declared that he was the true prince and that the other was an impostor. The mob grew angry, and had not a champion come to Edward's aid he would have been killed. This champion was Miles Hendon, stout of arm and of heart, who admired Edward's pluck although he doubted his sanity. Hendon took Edward to his lodgings, fed and cared for him. In return Edward knighted him and gave him the privilege of sitting in the royal presence—for Henry VIII had died and Edward was now King.

But John Canty soon learned of Edward's whereabouts and decoyed him away to join a gang of ruffians. Edward escaped them and fell into the hands of a mad hermit who believed the boy's story of being King, but tried to murder him in revenge for a wrong he had suffered at the hands of King Henry. John Canty found Edward before he was harmed and set the boy to stealing. The boy was apprehended as a thief, but by this time Miles Hendon had arrived and by persuading the magistrate and threatening the constable he got Edward off.

Hendon took the boy with him to his ancestral home, but there a bitter disappointment awaited them. Miles' father and older brother were dead and an evil younger brother, Hugh, had usurped the titles and estates and had even connived a marriage with Edith, Miles' sweetheart. Hugh professed to doubt Miles' identity and forced his unhappy wife to agree that Miles was an impostor. Miles was flogged and driven out of the town. The two homeless friends turned toward London.

They reached the city just in time for the coronation, but in the crowd they were separated. Edward set out for Westminster Abbey, where the ceremony was to take place.

As Tom Canty rode to the Abbey gorgeously appareled he saw his mother's face in the crowd, and although he had to ignore her he wished sorely that he was not the King.

Just as the crown was about to be lowered onto Tom's head, a ragged little figure stepped forward and cried, "I am the King!" Guards rushed forward to seize him but Tom Canty upheld Edward, declared that Edward was indeed the King, and fell on his knees before him.

The Lord Protector and the courtiers asked many questions of Edward, but he finally proved his identity by describing, first incorrectly but then correctly, the whereabouts of the Great Seal.

The rightful King was restored to his throne. Tom Canty lived happily with his mother and sisters as the ward of the King. To Sir Miles Hendon were restored his rights and his love, Edith— and his privilege of sitting in the royal presence was confirmed. Edward himself, having lived and suffered as his meanest subject, ruled well and mercifully throughout his short life.

A Connecticut Yankee in King Arthur's Court

By SAMUEL LANGHORNE CLEMENS

AN OLD MAN haunted the environs of Warwick Castle. He was a strange old fellow with almost an archaic charm of manner and a familiarity with ancient armor. In his chamber a pipe and a glass of liquor induced him to tell a curious story. Weariness overcame him, but in a manuscript was written the unbelievable tale of his adventure in time.

Hank Morgan was a Connecticut Yankee with a genius for putting things together and making them run. He wasn't a very poetic soul—he liked hard work, a good scrap, and a pretty little telephone operator in West Hartford. Her name was Puss Flanagan, and when he lifted the receiver and said, "Hello, Central," it was her voice that answered. Hank came to grief in a fight with another workman. A clout on the head precipitated him into swift oblivion.

The Connecticut Yankee returned to consciousness in a green meadow. Regarding him with the greatest astonishment was a personage on a horse, both man and beast clad in complete armor. The knight extended an invitation to joust. When it was declined he decided to joust anyway, and Hank deemed it expedient to retire up a tree. The gentleman in armor took the New Englander prisoner.

It was a great shock when Hank first realized that he was not in an asylum. From a pretty youth clad in shrimp-colored tights he learned that the date was the nineteenth of June in the year 528. Before he had fully digested this piece of information, he was haled into the banquet hall of the King, who turned out to be King Arthur. The King, Queen Guinevere, and Sir Launcelot and the other courtiers were frightened by the Yankee clothes, so he was divested of them on the spot. He was then haled off to a dungeon under sentence of death.

The Yankee found this a rather discouraging reception. From conversation with the shrimp-tighted page—whom he dubbed Clarence—he learned that the people of the time were in deadly fear of magic; indeed, that, next to the King, Merlin the Magician was the most powerful man in England.

The Yankee immediately announced that he, too, was a magician, and the open-mouthed Clarence immediately conveyed the news to the King. Wise Merlin demanded proof of Hank's magicianship; the American recalled from his reading that an eclipse of the sun had taken place at noon on the twenty-first of June, 528, which was the moment set for his execution. Hank threatened to steep the world in darkness. Through over-zeal on the part of Clarence, who wanted to get his new friend out of jail as quickly as possible, the execution was set ahead a day and Hank abandoned himself as lost. But the feather-brained Clarence had made a mistake and just as the lighted fagot was about to be applied the sky started to darken. The

Yankee made a good thing of the eclipse, and when he was released from the stake he was the first magician of the country.

To satisfy further miracle-seekers, the Yankee promised to blast Merlin's tower with lightning. With dynamite and lightning rods, he frightened half the population of England.

Hank soon became King Arthur's right-hand man. He received the title of the Boss, and was surrounded by sixth-century luxury. But he didn't like it very well. He missed modern conveniences, and the simplicity of the people and barbarity of the rule appalled him. Quietly he set about reform, introduced inventions which weren't to come along for thirteen hundred years, and tried his best to educate the people. Since it was impossible to teach anything to the stupid nobility, he concentrated on the populace, whom he found groaning under the taxation and cruelties of the King, the nobles, and especially the Church.

King Arthur expressed a wish that Sir Boss should distinguish himself in knight errantry as did the other knights who sporadically trotted off in search of the Holy Grail. When a damsel yclept Alisande la Carteloise came to court with the story of forty-five beautiful demoiselles kept captive by three one-eyed, four-handed monsters, the Yankee was sent out to rescue them. Alisande—the Yankee soon named her Sandy—jumped up on the American's horse and prepared to lead the way to the enchanted castle. Sandy turned out to be very charming, although she talked constantly, prattling the most outrageous lies in her pretty, archaic manner.

En route the Boss and Sandy stopped at the castle of the wicked and beautiful Queen Morgan le Fay and emptied her dungeons of the prisoners she had enslaved. Sandy finally found her enchanted maidens, who turned out to be hogs which the Boss paid for and finally got rid of. The Yankee's next miracle was an especially fancy one; he mended a leak in a holy well to the accompaniment of many fireworks and even fixed things so that the monks could bathe in the water.

The Boss decided to make an incognito trip through the

country to familiarize himself with peasant life, and King Arthur insisted on accompanying him. The two saw indescribable horrors implicit in the system of feudalism but it was not until the King himself, with the Boss, was taken into slavery by a nobleman that Arthur realized what his subjects had to endure. Unable to convince anyone of his kingship, Arthur was greatly annoyed when he brought only seven dollars in the slave mart. When the two were condemned to death in a slave uprising, the Boss was really worried; he telegraphed to Clarence for help, but he was sure the rescuers would come too late. At the last moment, however, Sir Launcelot and five hundred picked knights came pedaling on bicycles, and saved them.

The Yankee's last hurdle was a duel with Sir Sagramor, whom he had offended. The Boss prevailed against the knight's armor with a lasso, but at the last minute, when confronted with treachery, was obliged to use a pistol.

Now his power was supreme. He established schools, curbed the power of the Church, introduced modern conveniences and in general introduced the nineteenth century thirteen hundred years ahead of time. Sandy, who had declared him her knight, followed him wherever he went, so he decided he'd better marry her. She proved a wonderful wife, and they were very happy together.

The whole thing fell apart when the Boss and Sandy went on a cruise for the sake of the baby's health—Sandy had named it Hello Central after a name that her husband kept repeating in his sleep. Launcelot, it seemed, had cornered the stock market, and Sir Modred in revenge had informed the King of the Launcelot-Guinevere affair. Guinevere had been condemned to death, and although her lover rescued her at the stake, the kingdom had fallen apart. The Church, which hated the Boss, now ruled.

After making a last stand against the nobility, the Yankee was finally betrayed by Merlin who, in the disguise of an old woman, cast a spell on him. The faithful Clarence, who wrote the last part of the manuscript, watched the Boss fall into an enchanted sleep and left his body in a remote cave where it might not be found.

The Yankee could not forget his years spent in King Arthur's court. When he died, a queer old man, the names of Sandy and the King were the last on his lips.

The Last of the Mohicans

By JAMES FENIMORE COOPER

JAMES FENIMORE COOPER, *born in New Jersey on Sept. 15, 1789, was reared in his Quaker father's almost feudal domain at Cooperstown, N.Y. His early experiences at sea gave him an interest in naval history, and his violent expressions of his views gave him as far-flung a set of enemies as any writer who ever lived. He was said to have written his first novel at 30 to show that he could turn out a tale as interesting as one he had just read. Death came to Cooper at his family home Sept. 14, 1851.*

IN THE third year of the war between France and England in North America, word was received at Fort Edward, where General Webb lay with 5,000 men, that the Frenchman Montcalm was moving up Lake Champlain with a numerous army to attack the forest fastness of Fort William Henry.

This fort was held by a small force under the veteran Scotchman, Munro; and General Webb sent only a handful to help him. Captain Duncan Heyward was detached to escort Munro's daughters Alice and Cora safely to Fort William Henry. They engaged as their guide a famous Indian runner named Magua, known as Le Renard Subtil.

The girls were fearful when Magua led them down a narrow, dark forest path which he said was a shorter way. Soon they heard a horse behind them, and they were joined by a singular-looking emaciated person who said his name was David Gamut, declared he also was bound for Fort William Henry, and began singing New England hymns until warned to be silent because of the danger from Indian allies of Montcalm.

A savage painted face peered out exultantly as the cavalcade walked unconsciously toward the trap Magua had prepared.

In the same forest a magnificent Indian named Chingachgook, with a terrific emblem of death painted on his chest, stood talking with a white hunter whom he called Hawkeye. "We Mohicans," said the Indian, "drove the Maquas into the woods; then came the Dutch with fire-water, and my people parted with their land. Now I, a chief and a Sagamore, have never visited the graves of my fathers. Uncas, my son, is the last of the Mohicans." Uncas appeared and said that the hated Maquas, spies of Montcalm, were hiding in the forest.

Presently the cavalcade from Fort Edward appeared, and Heyward told Hawkeye they were lost. "An Indian lost in the woods?" exclaimed the scout. He crept into the thicket and quickly returned with the word that they had been led into a trap. Hawkeye and the Mohicans were unable, however, to prevent Magua from escaping. As the party lay in a cave that night, the Maquas attacked and the whites ran out of ammunition.

Hawkeye and the Mohicans set out to get help from Munro, but in the night the others were captured. Magua announced the prisoners' fate; Cora was to become his squaw, Alice would be set free. Rebuffed, he tied the four whites to trees, and stakes of glowing wood were prepared for their torture. Again offered dishonor or death, Cora was strengthened by Alice's cry: "Better we die together." The Maquas' knives and tomahawks were raised when Hawkeye and the Mohicans appeared and routed the torturers. Only Magua escaped alive.

The party reached Fort William Henry, but, outnumbered

twenty to one by Montcalm, the defenders were forced to accept his offer to let them return honorably to Fort Edward. The troops marched out and into a narrow defile. The civilians followed. Cora and Alice, with David Gamut, saw Magua addressing the Indians and soon one of the savages seized a baby and dashed its brains out on the ground. It was the signal for a massacre, and while two thousand savages fell on their victims, Magua bore off Alice and Cora, permitting David to follow.

Three days later Hawkeye, the Mohicans, Munro and Heyward, unable to find the girls' bodies, knew that they had been carried off. Hawkeye and the Indians followed Magua's trail, and found David in war paint near a Huron encampment. His captors had tolerated him because they believed him insane. The girls were near at hand, so Duncan entered the camp in the disguise of a medicine man. As he arrived Magua appeared, with Uncas as a prisoner. The chief asked him to cure a sick woman, and led him to a cave which had a bear tethered at its entrance. The Indians left Duncan with the woman, and he quickly made two discoveries; the bear was Hawkeye in disguise, and Alice was a prisoner in another part of the cave.

Magua discovered Duncan and Alice together, and was about to order them tortured when Hawkeye overpowered him. Thinking that the bearskin concealed one of their own wizards, the other Indians allowed Duncan and Hawkeye to leave the cave with Alice, who was in the sick woman's clothes. Their trick was not discovered until they had escaped after releasing Uncas. David, whom the Indians would not harm, was left behind. The others' rifles discouraged their pursuers.

Learning that Magua had left Cora with the neighboring tribe of Tortoise Delawares, the scout and his companions went in search of her. But Magua followed. Though Uncas displayed a tattooed symbol which showed that he was a long-lost scion of the Delawares, the laws of Indian hospitality forced the tribe to let Magua depart with his prisoner of war without pursuit until sunset.

At the moment the sun dipped below the horizon, the Tortoises and the others rushed down the trail after the Hurons. They fought a desperate and bloody battle, and their enemies fell until only Magua and two companions were left. Then, with a yell, Magua rushed off with Cora up a steep defile toward the mountains. When she refused to move onward on the side of the precipice, Magua cried:

"Woman! Choose—the wigwam or the knife of Le Subtil?"

Just then a piercing cry was heard on high, and Uncas leaped down from a fearful height upon the ledge. He fell prostrate, and Magua plunged the knife into his back. At the same moment one of Magua's companions stretched Cora lifeless. With his last strength, Uncas hurled Cora's murderer into the abyss. But his power had deserted him, and Magua seized his arm and killed him with several thrusts of his dagger.

Now Heyward cried from above: "Give mercy and thou shalt receive it!"

Magua's answer was a shout of triumph. He leaped a wide fissure and made for the summit of the mountain, until a single bound would carry him to the brow of the precipice and safety. Before taking the leap he shook his hand defiantly at Hawkeye, who waited with raised rifle, and shouted:

"The palefaces are dogs! The Delawares women! Magua leaves them on the rocks for the crows!"

Making a desperate jump and falling short of the mark, Magua saved himself by grasping some shrubs on the verge of the precipice. With an effort he pulled himself up. Hawkeye, whose rifle shook with concealed excitement, watched him closely, and as Magua drew his body together, the scout raised the weapon to his shoulder and fired.

The Huron's arms relaxed and his body fell back a little, but his knees retained their position. Turning a relentless look on his enemy, he shook his hand in grim defiance. But his hold loosened, and his dark person was seen cutting the air, with its head downward, until it glided past a fringe of shrubbery in its rapid flight to destruction.

The Red Badge of Courage

By STEPHEN CRANE

BORN *in Newark, N.J., on Nov. 1, 1871, the last of 14 children of a minister, Stephen Crane was raised by a literary mother who instilled in him a code of stoicism in the face of troubles. As a boy he was interested in books and baseball, which he played at Lafayette College and Syracuse University. Entering newspaper work, he drifted to New York, and began to do serious writing, publishing his first book at his own expense. He became a war correspondent, and once was shipwrecked off Cuba, reaching Florida in an open boat. Later he married and lived in England, making many friends among the great literary figures. Always sickly, he died June 5, 1900, at Badenweiler, Germany, while trying to regain his health.*

THE COLD passed reluctantly from the earth, and the retiring fogs revealed an army stretched out on the hills, resting. Across the river at night one could see the red, eyelike gleam of hostile campfires.

A certain tall soldier went to a brook to wash a shirt, and came flying back with a tale that "we're goin' t' move t'morrah." There was much disbelieving comment, to which a youthful private listened with eager ears. He had dreamed of battles, but had regarded them as crimson blotches on the pages of the past.

From his home he had looked upon the war in his own country

as some sort of play affair, but had burned to enlist. Against his mother's discouragement, he finally accepted a blue uniform, and was disappointed when she told him only: "You watch out, Henry, an' take care of yourself in this fighting business. Choose your comp'ny, and yeh must never do no shirking, child, on my account." Still, he had seen her weeping when he looked back.

Then had come months of monotonous camp life, when his thoughts turned to whether he would run from a battle. Today he felt reassured when the tall soldier admitted that "it might get too hot for Jim Conklin," but when Jim's report proved false, Henry's doubts returned.

One morning, however, the youth found himself on the move with his regiment, and two nights later they crossed the river by a roundabout route.

Presently the army again sat down to think, but one gray dawn the youth found himself running down a wood road in the midst of the others, while a spattering of firing came from the distance. The time had come; it occurred to the youth that they were taking him out to be slaughtered.

Twice, three times, they halted, dug little barricades, then were moved on. A once-loud neighbor gave him a little packet to hold, quavering: "It's my first and last battle." Held in reserve, the regiment heard the firing eddy about them. Suddenly running men emerged from the smoke, and it was seen that the command was fleeing, heedless of the officers' exasperated shouts.

Someone cried, "Here they come!" and a gray swarm of yelling men came running across the fields. "You've got to hold 'em," shouted a hatless general. Suddenly the youth began to fire along with his regiment, like a carpenter, a man with a task. A red rage overcame him. Men fell about him, awkwardly and crying out, until at last an exultant yell went up. The charge had been repulsed.

Suddenly the charge began again, with shells bursting near the youth. His ecstasy of self-satisfaction was blotted out. The enemy seemed like redoubtable dragons. He saw a few companions run, and he dropped his gun and joined them in great leaps toward the rear, blundering into trees like a blind man. It was a race from death. He pitied the men of a still-firing battery as methodical idiots.

The youth came up to an excited general who was joyfully roaring, "They've held 'em," and suddenly he cringed as if discovered in a crime. Then he felt anger at his comrades who had withstood the blows, and began to pity himself with thoughts of his reception when he returned to camp. The youth wandered through woods and swamp until he approached the battle line again and joined a column of wounded. He flushed when one asked him: "Where yeh hit, ol' boy?"

Then he met the tall soldier, whose face was gray as he walked forward swiftly with his wounds. The youth gazed helplessly as Jim struggled for breath, stiffened and fell over dead. Presently a fresh column of infantry appeared, moving swiftly toward the battlefield. Their haste seemed heroic to the young man. He started to turn back toward the battle, but shame stopped him. He wished he was dead.

Overwhelmed by a new rush of retreating soldiers, Henry Fleming was clubbed on the head by a man he tried to stop. Dazed, he stumbled along until a friendly man led him to his regiment. He staggered to the campfire with a story of having been shot; he was greeted and treated with tender respect, and went to sleep on a comrade's blanket.

In the morning all was friendship; it was assumed that Henry had been fighting with another regiment. As they waited for the order to go into battle, with shame his loud friend retrieved his letters.

The youth's regiment took over some damp trenches along the line of woods, facing a level stretch peopled with stumps. Then they were ordered to retreat, and the youth heard himself say: "Don't we do all that men can?" with no one questioning his right to say it. The enemy's infantry pursued until battle was joined again in a clearing where the men had stopped and grumbled for a long time. The youth wanted rest, but the enemy seemed relentless.

The youth fired with savage fury as the smoke of battle settled down again. Protected by a little tree, he shot again and again until the rifle barrel seared his hands. He was so engrossed that his comrades had to stop him when there was a lull. They looked on him with awe; he relaxed, realizing he was a hero. Overhearing a general again, he learned that his regiment was to lead a charge from which few were expected to get back.

The youth ran forward desperately when the order came, unconsciously in the lead. Winded, the men slackened, ceased their yelling and realized that some had been shot. Their lieutenant urged them on. They began to move forward again awkwardly, until the enemy's fire stopped them at an open space. Goaded by the lieutenant, the youth took the lead in another charge, running like a madman toward the opposite woods, wrenching the flag from the fallen color sergeant.

He looked back to find the crumbled remnant of the regiment in retreat. Dejectedly they fell back to the woods, pelted by the enemy's bullets. The youth walked in shame; he harangued his fellows, but they had lost heart. The army was a discouraged mob. The officers tried to rally them, then suddenly the pursuing enemy crept up on them.

The blue regiment fired in angry defense, and when the smoke rose the attackers had vanished. Enthusiasm returned, and the men perceived that they were back in the blue lines. They were mocked by the soldiers there, but restrained their anger. Bewildered, they learned that they had been reproached for failing of their objective by 100 feet, and angrily they defended themselves.

Some of his comrades told Henry the colonel had seen him in the battle and had said: "A very good man to have." The youth was very happy.

The enemy poured forth again, and the youth watched the battle for a while. Then his regiment was in the fight again.

Still the color-bearer, the youth watched his comrades' fire weaken as their ranks were again depleted. He heard the officers call for a charge, and was surprised to see the soldiers willing. The men leaped forward, the flag at their front, and the youth saw that many of the men in gray fled. Their color-bearer fell, and the regiment was victorious, with four prisoners.

Marching back, the youth said, "Well, it's all over." He thought back on his achievements, and sweated with shame at his flight. But at last he found that his earlier bombast had been replaced by manhood. He smiled as he trudged through the mud in the rain, for he saw that the world was a world for him.

An American Tragedy

By THEODORE DREISER

THEODORE DREISER *was born in Terre Haute, Indiana, on August 27, 1871. He attended Indiana University for a year, but lack of money forced him to leave. For a while he worked as a clerk, until in 1892 he was hired as a reporter on the Chicago* Globe; *thereafter he became a writer for and later editor of various American newspapers and magazines. He was one of the first of the modern American realistic novelists. Dreiser is now living in California.*

THE EARLIEST MEMORIES of Clyde Griffiths centered around the dingy missions which his evangelist parents ran, poorly attended street meetings in which as a tiny child he was forced to participate; the sordid atmosphere of unpleasant rooms, and worry over food, shelter and the wherewithal to maintain the various derelicts whose souls were being wrested from drink and the devil.

The education that Clyde and his four brothers and sisters received was meager. His mother and father, well-meaning moralists, had neither the strength nor the wisdom to bring up their family properly. Hester, the oldest girl, who led the music at the street meetings, ran off with an actor who soon deserted her. Clyde, horribly ashamed of his parents, his ugly clothes, his squalid surroundings, dreamed only of the day when somehow he would find his way into the kind of life of which he had caught glimpses in the dress and manner of some passing "swell."

Clyde reached boyhood in Kansas City. He was behind in school, partly due to the wanderings of his family and partly to his own vacillating character. He gladly stopped his education to become the assistant to a soda-dispenser; when he became a bellhop in the Green-Davidson Hotel he abruptly found himself in possession of what seemed an immense sum of money.

He lied to his gullible mother about his earnings, and proceeded to spend most of the money that the well-to-do patrons tipped him on clothes and luxuries for himself. His fellow bellhops soon introduced him to liquor and a brothel, although his religious upbringing conflicted with his sensual nature and kept him from excess. He soon became enamored of a cheap and pretty flirt, Hortense Briggs, who realized that she could get many expensive presents from him without giving more than promises in return. But when one of his companions killed a little girl in a stolen car which was carrying Clyde and other youngsters, the boy grew panic-stricken and fled.

Clyde changed his name temporarily. Finally he drifted to Chicago, where he found a place at the Union League Club. Here he encountered his wealthy uncle, Samuel Griffiths, a collar manufacturer of Lycurgus, New York, who was favorably impressed with the young nephew who presented himself with a good deal of diffidence.

Griffiths offered Clyde a place—very lowly to begin—at his

plant in Lycurgus, and the boy accepted. On the whole Clyde made a good start in Lycurgus. Gilbert Griffiths, his cousin and an official in the mill, resented and disliked him, but the older man was fair and kindly toward his young relative. Clyde started off in the shrinking room of the factory. He earned fifteen dollars a week. He was very lonely, but although the middle-class people in the town were eager to be friendly—so impressed were they by the magic Griffiths name—Clyde dreamed only of becoming one of the gay social set that the wealthy young persons of the town comprised. One night he was asked to dinner at the Griffiths home, and there he caught a glimpse of wealthy, spoiled, beautiful Sondra Finchley. She filled his thoughts for days.

Clyde was elevated to the managership of a small department at the mill. Under his supervision were twenty-five mill-hands, all young girls who were greatly impressed by his authority and dark good looks. Clyde was troubled greatly by secret sexual desires, but he had been warned to have nothing to do with any of the factory girls. Furthermore he determined to conduct himself circumspectly and sometime get for himself the glamorous future which he imagined.

But when he saw Roberta Alden his good intentions vanished. She was rather better than the average mill-hand in his charge—pretty, fairly intelligent, highly moral and religious, and sprung of poor but sturdy American farmer stock.

Roberta was as young, ardent and lonely as he. She romanticized his good looks, his family connection, his superiority. She consented to secret meetings. When her scruples kept her from becoming his mistress he became angry and, fearing to lose him, Roberta allowed herself to be seduced.

For a while Clyde was very happy. But one day Sondra Finchley, mistaking him for his cousin Gilbert, whom he greatly resembled, offered him a lift in her car. She found herself intrigued by him, and arranged to have him invited to some of the most exclusive parties in town. Clyde's early dreams started to come true. He soon became part of the smart young social set that he yearned toward. Their hospitality was lavish and they were well aware of his poverty, although his meager salary went into clothes.

Gradually Sondra Finchley became interested in Clyde more than superficially and, intoxicated by her beauty, wealth and social position, Clyde was soon insane about her. He dreamed that Sondra, despite the protests that he knew he could expect from her family, might marry him. Then the world would be his—money, social position, a beautiful wife. His castles abruptly tumbled when Roberta, whom he had been neglecting, told him she was pregnant.

It had been understood, although without a definite promise, that in the event of Roberta's becoming pregnant they would marry. But now Clyde saw marriage to Roberta as the end to all his dreams. He looked frantically for a way out. Medication failed and he was unable to find a doctor who would perform an abortion. Meanwhile precious months passed while Clyde procrastinated with Roberta and continued his suit of Sondra. Sondra, by this time, was completely his; she promised that when she came of age—in a few months' time—she would elope with him. Clyde felt he could not lose this, his big chance at happiness.

But Roberta was panic-stricken and demanded that he marry her or she would make the whole thing public. Clyde could find no way out. But he saw a newspaper item describing a young couple who had gone out rowing and not returned. The girl's body had been found; the man's had not.

Clyde was horrified at his own thoughts. But time pressed. Soon he must lose everything which he considered important. And surely Roberta was unfair in trying to force him into marriage. Hadn't it been her fault, too? Her pitiful letters having failed to move Clyde, she decided to force the issue. And Clyde decided on murder.

He promised the girl marriage, lured her out into a boat and became overcome with fear and remorse before he could carry through his plan. But by mistake the boat tipped over, and, disregarding her cries for help, he swam off and watched her drown.

Clyde was soon apprehended. The plans he had made to murder the girl were soon discovered, and he was sentenced to death. An appeal was not granted and his mother pleaded in vain with the Governor to revoke the sentence. Clyde was electrocuted. He had been comforted at the end by the presence of his mother and Duncan McMillan, a preacher who pitied the boy though he realized his guilt.

Clyde's mother returned to her street evangelism. Clyde's place was taken by little Russell, Hester Griffiths' illegitimate son, who was destined to grow up in the same sordid hopelessness that his uncle had.

The Scarlet Letter

By NATHANIEL HAWTHORNE

NATHANIEL HAWTHORNE, *born July 4, 1804, at Salem, Mass., spent a lonely country boyhood with his mother, widow of a mariner. After attending Bowdoin College, he attempted unsuccessfully to support himself by writing and had to take a post in the customs service. Except for an interlude at Brook Farm, this was his life until he finally won literary fame in 1850. Later he lived in Concord, Mass., and visited Europe. He died May 19, 1864.*

A CROWD stood before the jail in seventeenth-century Boston, their eyes fastened on the iron-clamped door from which there presently emerged a young woman who bore a three-month-old baby. Hester Prynne was tall, and her beauty was set off by her serene dignity, but all eyes were drawn to the breast of her gown, where there appeared a letter A, cut from fine red cloth and surrounded with elaborate embroidery and gold thread.

Hester walked on to the scaffold where the pillory was set up in the market place. On the outskirts of the crowd stood an elderly man, short but intelligent of features, who put his hands to his lips when Hester looked at him and seemed to recognize him. Then the man asked another man who she was.

The Bostonian explained that Mistress Prynne had raised a great scandal, of which the penalty was death, but that the magistrates instead had doomed her to stand three hours on the pillory, then wear a mark of shame the rest of her life.

At the pillory the Rev. Arthur Dimmesdale, the eloquent young minister of Hester's church, exhorted her: "Speak out the name of thy fellow-sinner and fellow-sufferer. Better were it so for him than to hide a guilty heart through life." Hester only shook her head.

That night in jail the child was in pain, and the jailer brought in a physician, the man who had asked about her in the crowd. Announced as Roger Chillingworth, he asked Hester, when they were alone, not to reveal that he was her husband who was to have joined her in America when she left England two years before. "I shall seek this man whose name thou wilt not reveal," he told her.

When Hester left prison she established herself with her child in a tiny, lonesome cottage on the outskirts of the town. Without an admitted friend, she supported herself by needlework, gave any surplus money to those more poverty-stricken than herself, and won a certain regard by never complaining against bad usage.

Her baby she named Pearl, as being of great price, and the child grew into a strange, lovely creature, sometimes seeming to be more a sprite than a human child. Pearl never played with other children, but was her mother's constant companion.

Once an effort was made to take the child from Hester, and

she pleaded her case at the governor's mansion before a group which included the Rev. Arthur Dimmesdale and Roger Chillingworth, now the town's leading physician. "God gave me the child!" she cried. "Ye shall not take her! I will die first!" And she asked Dimmesdale, as her former pastor, to speak for her. He defended Hester, saying that Pearl might be able to bring her mother to heaven. The governor decided in Hester's favor.

Now young Dimmesdale, overworked in the performance of his duties, began to fail in health, and was sent to Chillingworth. The physician determined to know the minister, delving into his life and principles, before attempting to heal him. Finally it was arranged for the two to live in the same house so that the doctor might better observe his patient.

Roger Chillingworth found that Dimmesdale concealed a strong animal nature beneath his pure exterior, and in his cold search for truth the physician tried to become a chief actor in the minister's inner world. But Dimmesdale was not so ill as to become a helpless tool; instead he resisted, and developed an unspoken hatred and horror for the doctor.

More than once Dimmesdale went into the pulpit determined not to leave until he had told the truth about himself, but each time he weakened and spoke only in general terms about his own sinfulness. Tortured by his troubles, one night in May he went to the scaffold where Hester Prynne had stood, and was found there by Hester, who was returning from a deathbed. As they stood together, Roger Chillingworth approached and the minister told her of his horror of the physician. Bound by her promise, she was silent, and Chillingworth led Dimmesdale home.

Hester soon after told Chillingworth that she was going to tell Dimmesdale about him. She said the minister's fate was in the physician's hands, but that it was better for him to know the truth, regardless of consequences, rather than go on "living a life of ghastly emptiness." She told Chillingworth she pitied him "for the hatred that has transformed a wise and just man to a fiend." But the doctor refused to forgive.

A week later Hester met the clergyman in the woods. He gazed at her and said: "Hester, hast thou found peace?" and admitted that he had found nothing but despair. Then she told him who Roger Chillingworth was, and they agreed to seek a new life together in England.

A new governor's election was to be celebrated, and Dimmesdale was to preach the sermon. Meanwhile Hester obtained passage in a ship that was about to sail. Then, on the day of holiday, she learned that Roger Chillingworth had taken a berth on the same vessel.

Dimmesdale delivered a brilliant sermon, and then, while the multitude praised him and Hester pondered what to do about the latest turn of affairs, walked to the scaffold in the market place. Suddenly he called Hester and Pearl to him and, shaking off the restraining hand of Roger Chillingworth, ascended the steps. "I am a dying man," he murmured to Hester. Then the Rev. Arthur Dimmesdale spoke to the people again:

"At last I stand where seven years since I should have stood. Lo, the scarlet letter which Hester wears! Ye have all shuddered at it! But there stood one in the midst of you at whose brand of sin and infamy ye have not shuddered! Stand any here that question God's judgment on a sinner? Behold a dreadful witness of it!"

And he tore his minister's gown from his breast, while the multitude gazed in horror. Then he sank down on the scaffold, his head against Hester's bosom. "Thou hast escaped me!" Roger Chillingworth said, as the minister told him: "May God forgive thee!"

Dying, Dimmesdale bade Hester farewell and kissed Pearl. The multitude, silent until then, broke out in a strange, deep voice of awe and wonder.

Afterward, though most of the spectators testified to having seen a SCARLET LETTER imprinted in the flesh of the minister—whether by his own hand or by other means—some denied that there was any mark there, and declared that his dying words admitted no guilt, but were intended as a parable to show that we are all sinners alike.

Within the year old Roger Chillingworth was dead, bequeathing his considerable property to Pearl. Mother and daughter went to England, but years later Hester returned alone. She was seen working on infant garments, by which it was supposed that Pearl had found a husband in England. And Hester voluntarily wore her symbol, living out her days in helping others.

The House of the Seven Gables

By NATHANIEL HAWTHORNE

HALFWAY DOWN A BY-STREET of a New England town stands a rusty wooden house, with seven acutely peaked gables, and a huge clustered chimney in the midst. The street is Pyncheon Street; the house is the old Pyncheon House.

Once this was a cow-path called Maule's Lane, from the name of Matthew Maule, who had a humble cottage there. In the growth of the town the site became more valuable, until Colonel Pyncheon, a man of iron energy, claimed it on the strength of a grant from the Legislature. Maule was stubborn in his resistance, and the dispute came to a close only when the Colonel raised a cry of witchcraft and old Maule was executed.

On the scaffold the condemned man pointed his finger at his enemy and said: "God will give him blood to drink!"

But the Puritan soldier and magistrate did not fear curses, and he built his mansion on the spot where Matthew Maule had had his home. And the head carpenter was no other than Thomas Maule, son of the dead man. The Colonel invited all the town when the house was finished, but his guests found him dead in his study, with blood on his cuff and beard. The coroner's jury returned a verdict of "Sudden Death."

The son and heir came into a considerable estate, but papers were missing that would prove a claim to a large tract of Maine land. Still the Pyncheons cherished a delusion of family importance because of this claim, and for two centuries they clung to the ancestral house.

Some thirty years earlier the chief member of the Pyncheon family, a wealthy bachelor, had died a violent death, and a nephew, Clifford, was sentenced to perpetual imprisonment as the murderer. Another nephew, Jaffrey, became the heir, and was now a judge. The only other known living members of the family were Clifford's sister, Hepzibah, who lived in extreme poverty in the House of the Seven Gables; the Judge's son, now traveling in Europe; and a little country girl of 17, Phoebe Pyncheon, daughter of a now-dead cousin of the judge.

Hepzibah, now 60, was reduced to setting up a little shop in the house. Her first customer was a daguerreotypist named Holgrave to whom she had let rooms. She wept when he spoke kindly to her, and would not take money for her biscuits; indeed, she committed so many errors that her first day's proceeds were only a few coppers.

That night Phoebe arrived for a visit, and comforted her cousin by saying that she intended to earn her bread and try to bring some cheer into the house. Hepzibah revealed that Clifford was coming home from prison: "He has had but little sunshine in his life," she said.

As Phoebe saw him, Clifford was an elderly man, with gray hair of an unusual length. His expression seemed to waver, glimmer, and nearly die away, then feebly to recover itself again. It was hard for him to understand who Phoebe was, but when food was placed before him his vague smile was replaced by a coarser expression, and he ate with voracity and asked for "more—more!"

Phoebe was attending to the shop when a man of portly figure, deep voice and high respectability entered. He learned who she was, introduced himself as Judge Pyncheon, and began to bestow a kiss upon her. But she found something repulsive in his demonstration. She drew back, and was startled to see his face turn cold and hard, so that he looked exactly like the Colonel of 200 years before.

But an expression of benevolence returned to the Judge's face. He began asking about Clifford, and was about to step inside when Hepzibah appeared and forbade him to talk to her brother. The Judge's voice rose in warning, and then Clifford was heard wailing in alarm lest his cousin enter. The Judge left, and Hepzibah, deathly white, murmured: "That man has been the horror of my life. Shall I never have courage to tell him what he is?"

The shop thrived with Phoebe managing it, and so did her friendship with Mr. Holgrave, an attraction that ripened so gently and sweetly that they were hardly aware that it had turned into love.

Then Phoebe was called away on a visit to her mother, and the old house, which had been brightened by her presence, was once more dark and gloomy. And once again Judge Pyncheon, with his most benevolent smile, asked to see Clifford.

"You cannot," said Hepzibah. "Clifford has kept his bed since yesterday." The Judge, startled, said, "Then I must and will see him!" "Give over this loathsome pretense of affection for your victim," Hepzibah cried. "You let him go to prison under false accusation. You hate him! Say so, like a man!"

At last the Judge explained that he believed Clifford could give him a clue to the dead uncle's wealth, of which not more than a third was apparent when he died. "And what if he refuse?" asked Hepzibah.

"My dear cousin," smiled the Judge, "the alternative is his confinement for the remainder of his life in a public asylum for the insane."

Defeated, Hepzibah went in search of her brother, and the Judge flung himself down in an old chair in the parlor. Clifford did not answer when she knocked, and Hepzibah could not find him upstairs. She ran to the parlor, asking Judge Pyncheon to help in the search, but the Judge did not move, and Clifford appeared at the parlor door. Pointing at his enemy and laughing with strange excitement, he said:

"Hepzibah, we can dance now! The weight is gone, and we may be as light-hearted as little Phoebe! What an absurd figure the old fellow cuts now!" And the brother and sister departed hastily from the house.

Phoebe found the shop closed when she returned that day, but Holgrave admitted her through the garden door. He told her that the Judge had died as did his ancestor "to whom God had given blood to drink." He convinced her that both these men— and the uncle for whose supposed murder Clifford had suffered— had been carried off by strokes.

And then, in that hour so full of doubt and awe, Phoebe and Holgrave paused to confess their love for each other, and in this old house with its dead tenant they were conscious of nothing sad.

Now they heard the voices of Hepzibah and Clifford, who had returned, with the brother looking the stronger of the two. Clifford smiled and murmured that the flower of Eden had bloomed in that house at last.

A week later came news of the death of the Judge's son, and so Hepzibah became rich, and so did Clifford, and so did Phoebe and, through her, Holgrave. It was far too late for the formal vindication of Clifford to be worth the trouble involved. For the truth was that the Judge had let suspicion fall on his cousin because he himself had been busy among the uncle's papers, destroying a will which favored Clifford, and had wanted to divert the blame from himself.

The heirs decided to live at the Judge's country place. As they were leaving, Clifford remembered that when he was a boy he had discovered the secret spring which caused the Colonel's portrait to swing forward and disclose a recess in which were important papers. But he had forgotten the secret. Then Holgrave touched the spring, and there were revealed deeds to vast Indian lands.

"And now, my dearest Phoebe," said Holgrave, "how will it please you to assume the name of Maule? In this long drama of wrong and retribution I represent the old wizard, and am probably as much of a wizard as ever my ancestor was. This secret is the only inheritance that came down to me from Thomas Maule."

Phoebe's smile forgave him, and as their carriage rolled away, the old House of the Seven Gables, its curse wafted away, smiled after them brightly.

The Marble Faun

By NATHANIEL HAWTHORNE

Two young women and a young man were merrily comparing a second young man to a statue. The young man that they were discussing was a handsome and lively Italian, Donatello by name; the statue was the famous "Faun" of Praxiteles. And truly the similarity in feature and spirit between the marble faun and the laughing young man was amazing. Donatello—the Count de Monte Beni, to give him his true title—combined physical beauty with an almost animalistic simplicity. Untutored, concerned only with the joy of living, and utterly unconscious of soul or spirit, he was vastly different from his companions. The other three members of the quartet were artists who were studying and working in Rome and finding in each other rich companionship and community of interest. Kenyon, the other young man of the party, was a sculptor who had come from America to perfect his art and, finding Italy to his taste, had remained.

The two young women were in sharp contrast to each other. Frail, pretty Hilda was a New England girl who reflected her strict upbringing by her high moral sense. She was not aware that her own purity often made her intolerant and lacking in understanding; gentle and affectionate, she was known as "The Dove," not only because in the high tower where she lived she kept an altar-light afire and tended a flock of doves, but because of her character as well.

The fourth member of the party was the most striking. This was Miriam. Possessed of an amazing dark, oriental beauty, her origin was shrouded in mystery, and Kenyon often thought that some dark secret clouded her life. The two girls were fast friends. Miriam was a painter and Hilda a copyist, and they admired each other's work greatly. Hilda and Miriam felt only friendship for the two young men, but Donatello's passion for Miriam was simple and avowed; and Kenyon, in his more reserved way, loved the little Puritan, Hilda.

The badinage concerning Donatello's resemblance to the faun continued until Miriam playfully demanded to see his ears, declaring that she knew they would be pointed and furry. Donatello refused, and, not wishing to anger the simple boy, the friends dropped the discussion. The four descended into the catacombs. Poor Donatello distrusted the dark passages for he loved sunlight and nature, but the winding, mysterious ways suited Miriam's somber soul. However the three remaining members of the party grew alarmed when Miriam wandered away and could not be found. She reappeared soon, but with a strange guide—a shaggy, gloomy, ill-kempt man who announced to her that he would never leave her but would follow her always. Kenyon thought that the man was a model finding employment in a novel and spectacular way, but it seemed to the more sensitive Hilda that Miriam seemed shocked and distraught at the man's appearance.

Miriam's follower continued his pursuit and soon became known as her shadow in the bohemian part of Rome that the four friends inhabited. Miriam daily grew stranger and, it seemed to Hilda, more unhappy. One day Miriam climbed to Hilda's studio with a package which she begged the New England girl to hold for her—if she, Miriam, did not claim the package at the end of four months it was to be delivered to a Signor Barboni.

Hilda accepted the commission, although not without misgiving. What could be bothering her beautiful friend? Could it be Donatello? Hilda thought not, for, despite the young Italian's devotion and sweetness, he was more faun than man, lacking soul, perception, and intellectually far below his mysterious beloved.

Meanwhile Donatello was suffering intensely. Dedicated only to joy as he was, he could not but see that the man who dogged Miriam's footsteps had brought into her life a shadow she could not escape. He became obsessed with the idea of releasing her from her pursuer. And one frightful night Donatello's endurance reached its limit. As he and Miriam stood on the edge of a precipice which some said was the site of Traitor's Leap, the ancient Roman spot of execution, the shadow of Miriam's persecutor fell upon them. Donatello seized his enemy. He looked once into Miriam's anguished eyes, in them read consent, and hurled the pursuer to his death on the stones below.

The enormity of the deed struck the two immediately. Miriam knew that the fault was hers since she was the instigator. Feelings of love and protection for the young instrument of her crime filled her and she knew that their destinies were bound together.

Miriam soon found herself an outcast. Hilda had, inadvertently, seen the deed, and blamed Miriam rather than Donatello. Hard in her own virtue, she bade Miriam leave her. Donatello was haunted by remorse. When wandering into a chapel they chanced upon the body of the pursuer laid out for burial and found that their victim had been a Capuchin monk, Donatello's sufferings drove him nearly mad. He shrank from the woman he had so passionately loved and seeking a refuge, returned to his ancestral home of Monte Beni.

Kenyon visited Donatello in his mountain home and found that, through suffering, the faun was slowly changing into a human soul. It seemed as though spirit and intellect had entered into Donatello in exchange for the innocent wild joy he had lost.

Unaware of the true story, Kenyon yet knew that Miriam was somehow concerned with Donatello's bitter unhappiness; when the young woman came to him and begged for his help, Kenyon took Donatello on a trip and then arranged that he and Miriam should meet. When Donatello again saw his love he realized that their sin had been mutual and that they must sustain and uphold each other.

Kenyon returned to Rome and while wandering in St. Paul's chanced upon Hilda making confession to a Catholic priest. Shocked at the Puritan girl, Kenyon remonstrated with her, and she told him that she had been so troubled by a secret she possessed that she had been unable to rest until she confided it. This secret was of course the story of the murder. The Catholic priest, since Hilda was not Catholic, told her he was not bound to the secrecy of the Confessional.

Hilda bethought herself of the packet that she had promised Miriam she would deliver at the end of four months and went off on her promised errand without telling Kenyon. For days the girl did not reappear, the lamp at the shrine she tended went out, and Kenyon was sick with anxiety.

But he received a message bidding him to an assignation and there he encountered Donatello and Miriam disguised as peasants. They bade him be patient. It was Carnival time in Rome, and Kenyon wandered distractedly among the revellers searching for his love. Finally she reappeared and Donatello and Miriam bade him good-by forever.

The mystery was not fully solved. Hilda had been detained by the authorities and Donatello had turned himself over to the police. But what was the secret of Miriam's past? Kenyon never knew. He learned that she was of a wealthy family, that misfortune had dogged her steps, that she had been accused and cleared of a dreadful crime, and that the monk who pursued her had been mad. The rest—mystery.

Kenyon won Hilda's love and the two were married. Donatello remained in prison while Miriam waited and prayed.

A Farewell to Arms

By ERNEST HEMINGWAY

ERNEST HEMINGWAY *was born on July 21, 1898, at Oak Park, Illinois. He started his writing career as a Kansas reporter. During the first World War he served as an ambulance driver in the French army and later in the Italian army. After the war he reported battles in the East for the Toronto* Star. *He settled in Paris as a member of the American expatriate group. In 1927* A Farewell to Arms *was published and was immediately hailed as a masterpiece. In 1937 and 1938 he covered the Spanish Civil War as a correspondent. He married Martha Gellhorn, newspaperwoman and writer, in 1941.*

WHEN Frederic Henry came back to Gorizia after his leave, the Austrians had started their spring offensive. By this time the Italians were sick of the war, even the officers. Henry was a lieutenant in the Italian ambulance corps. He was an American.

When the Austrians weren't attacking there wasn't much to do in Gorizia. There was an English base hospital in the town, and English nurses, and a bawdy house, a special one for officers.

Henry liked the Italians, especially Rinaldi who shared his quarters, and a brown-faced priest from Abruzzi whom the mess deviled for his devoutness. Rinaldi was a surgeon, clever, warmhearted, a drunkard, partial to whores; he called Henry "baby"; in emotional moments he tried to kiss him but this Henry usually managed to avoid.

At the moment Rinaldi was in love with an English nurse

called Catherine Barkley. Rinaldi wanted Henry to see her. She turned out to be very beautiful, tall, with golden hair and gray eyes. She was Scottish, a V.A.D. Henry saw her several times at the hospital. He continued to think her very beautiful; he also thought she was a little crazy. When she asked him if he loved her, he said he did although they both knew he was lying.

News came that there was to be an attack above Plava. When Henry said good-by to Catherine she gave him a St. Anthony medal to wear for luck. Henry and his drivers moved up the line. While they were stopped for supper a shell hit their dug-out. When Henry came back to consciousness he found out that his knee wasn't where it ought to be.

At the field hospital Rinaldi came and brought him cognac, and the priest from Abruzzi came and brought him vermouth. Soon he was moved to Milan because his legs needed X-ray and therapy. Rinaldi told him that Catherine Barkley had been transferred to Milan. When Henry got there she hadn't arrived. The next morning she came. When he saw her, he was in love with her.

All that summer Henry lived in the hospital convalescing. Catherine asked for night duty, and when the hospital was quiet and safe she came and stayed with him. Later Henry was able to get about on crutches, and they went to the races and drank wine and rode in open carriages through the old city. It was a beautiful summer. They didn't marry because if they did Catherine would be sent away. They were happy and together; only, one night it rained and Catherine wept because she saw herself or him dead in the rain.

One day in September Catherine told Henry she was going to have a baby. At first he felt frightened and trapped, but in a moment everything was as it had been.

They were going to Pallanza for the two weeks' leave that Henry had been granted after his convalescence. But they didn't go because Henry got jaundice. Miss Van Campen, the superintendent of the hospital, discovered the empty liquor bottles that

Henry had smuggled in, and reported him. She had never liked him. His leave was canceled.

The night Henry left for the front it rained. They went to a hotel with plush curtains and a cut-glass chandelier. They said good-by in the rain.

In Gorizia the summer had been very bad. The war had gone on too long. The priest from Abruzzi looked worn, and the officers didn't bother to bait him any longer. He had hoped for victory but now he told Henry he did not care. Rinaldi was afraid he had contracted syphilis. Henry tried not to think about Catherine all the time.

Henry took his ambulance up the Bainsizza. Almost immediately the retreat began. The Germans and Austrians broke through in the north and the Italian troops marched back through Gorizia in the rain. Soon the whole country was in retreat, not just the army. The rain continued.

The Italians were in great confusion. Some of the men had shot their officers. Henry saw a Lieutenant-Colonel shot for having become separated from his troops. The men who had shot him were young officers; they were reorganizing the army and saving Italy. They didn't like Henry. He spoke Italian with a foreign accent. Since he didn't want to be shot he made a break and escaped by swimming the icy river.

Henry jumped a freight train carrying ammunition. He lay under the canvas with the clean-smelling guns and thought of Catherine and how hungry he was. When the train slowed at Milan he dropped off it.

Catherine wasn't at the hospital; she had gone to Stresa. Henry went after her. When he reached Stresa and found Catherine again, he was happy.

They stayed at Stresa only a little while. One stormy night the barman warned them that Henry was going to be arrested for desertion. They escaped to Switzerland in a small boat. Henry rowed all night and by morning they were across the lake. They had a fine breakfast; after breakfast they were arrested and sent to Locarno. Since they had money there was no trouble. They went to Montreux.

Snow came late that year. Henry wanted to get married, but Catherine wouldn't because her pregnancy was now so obvious. They lived in a brown house in the pines on the side of the mountain. They walked in the woods, and the air was clear and cold. Henry grew a beard. They were happy and the war seemed far away. But all along Henry waited and knew that if life cannot break you it will kill you.

When the spring started to come they moved down into Lausanne. They felt that they hadn't much time now.

Catherine went to the hospital at three o'clock one morning. Near the hospital was a café. Henry had his breakfast there. By noon Catherine was in great pain and the doctor had to give her gas frequently. Henry had his lunch at two o'clock in the little café. Later in the afternoon the doctor told Henry that a Caesarean operation was necessary. When Henry saw Catherine she was hysterical and gray with pain.

After the operation Henry saw his son and then Catherine. She was very weak. Soon they told him that the child was dead, but it didn't seem to matter. He knew that Catherine would die too. He walked through the rain to the little café and ate his supper.

When he got back to the hospital they told him that Catherine had had a hemorrhage. He saw that she knew she was dying. They made him leave but soon the nurse called him back. Catherine was unconscious and very soon she died. He made them all go out of the room and leave him alone with her for a little while. Then he walked back to his hotel in the rain.

The Rise of Silas Lapham

By WILLIAM DEAN HOWELLS

WILLIAM DEAN HOWELLS was born on March 1, 1837, at Martin's Ferry, Ohio. When he was nine, he started to work in his father's printing office. He educated himself through his own reading and continued working on several newspapers in Ohio until 1860 when he took a trip to Boston. In 1865 he began a career of editorial work at Boston; later he edited some of the leading magazines of the day. Besides his novels, he wrote much criticism, a series of short plays, and travel sketches. He died in Boston, May 11, 1920.

AT 55, SILAS LAPHAM was regarded in Boston as an example of the successful, self-made business man. In his earlier years he had seen the potential value of a large deposit of mineral paint in his father's farm, and had scraped up enough cash to begin operations. Now the name of his paint was advertised along every main road in New England on rock, rail, and board.

Silas gave a lot of credit for his success to his wife, an untiring, devoted and sensible woman. He was well aware that she had some misgivings about his treatment of an early partner. Milton K. Rogers had invested some money in the business at a time when Silas sorely needed capital. Later Silas had bought him out, thus keeping him from sharing in the profits of a prospering business.

At present the Laphams were thinking about the future of their two girls, Penelope and Irene. The younger, Irene, was a real beauty, but Penelope had a ready wit and an ability to converse which Irene wholly lacked. Silas and his wife decided that it would be a social advantage to the girls to build a new house on some land he had acquired on Beacon Hill.

As the building of the house got under way, the Laphams eagerly watched its progress. Outside the new house one day they met Tom Corey, a young acquaintance, whom the parents vaguely suspected of being interested in Irene.

Tom Corey belonged to an old Boston family. He had not yet settled down since his graduation from Harvard, and at the moment was looking for a business connection. Bromfield Corey, his father, had chosen to live on his inherited wealth; Tom might have done likewise. But the secluded, dilettantish life of his father held no appeal for him, and the demands of his mother and two unmarried sisters on the family income made it desirable for him to find a career.

To his father's astonishment, Tom decided on the mineral-paint business and went to see Silas Lapham. Silas was secretly delighted and took Tom at once, though he held out no prospects of a future partnership. Mrs. Lapham was puzzled because she did not yet know what Tom's intentions were toward Irene.

In the following summer Tom spent many week-ends with the Laphams at Nantasket. His mother and sisters returned from Maine in the fall, resigned to the unpleasant prospect of an even closer attachment to the Laphams than Tom's present one. One afternoon Mrs. Corey called on the Laphams; only Mrs. Lapham and Penelope were at home. Penelope took an immediate dislike to Mrs. Corey, because she sensed what her real attitude to the family was. The same evening an invitation to dinner from the Coreys arrived, and Penelope at once announced her intention to stay at home.

Preparations for the dinner agitated the Laphams for a week. Silas was not sure of the correct dress. When the three arrived at the Coreys, there was an awkward moment when the embarrassed Mrs. Lapham had to offer their excuses for Penelope. Mrs. Corey's other guests monopolized conversation at dinner, but Silas unfortunately drank too much wine, and after dinner launched into a long, personal discourse in which he did more than his usual amount of bragging.

The next day he felt so ashamed that he summoned Tom into his office and tried to apologize. Tom showed that he understood how poorly Silas had acted, but tried to reassure him that all had thought the wine responsible.

That evening Tom went to the Laphams to see Silas again. Only Penelope was at home. Then he told her why he had come to see her father—he wanted to ask for her hand. Penelope was shocked by the proposal, since, though she half suspected that he had been coming to see her, she knew that Irene believed he had been coming to see her. She told him he must not come back, and he promised to respect her wishes.

The next morning Penelope told her mother about Tom's call, and she in turn told Silas the same afternoon. Yet they could not decide what to do. In desperation they sought the advice of a minister, Mr. Sewell. And his opinion agreed with their better judgment; it would be better for Penelope to accept Tom rather than for her to make a futile sacrifice for her sister.

Mrs. Lapham then broke the news to Irene. She took it well, and the next day left for a brief stay at the Lapham farm. Several days later, Tom called on Penelope again and heard the whole story, but she was not yet ready to accept him.

In the meantime Silas found himself in the most desperate situation of his career. Some time before, Milton K. Rogers had turned up in Boston. To ease his own conscience and to please his wife, Silas had loaned him $20,000. When Rogers' venture proved highly speculative, Silas had thrown good money after bad, and now the only security he had for the loans to Rogers was some milling property out west. On top of this, a company in West Virginia had found a cheap source of fuel for baking its mineral paint, and Silas' selling price was being undercut by more than 50 per cent.

When Tom Corey heard about the crisis in Silas' affairs, he

offered to invest $30,000 of his own in the business. But Silas told him there was more reason for not taking him into the business than before.

Grimly Silas resolved to attempt to retrieve his failing fortunes. But he refused to consider an assignment as a way out of his difficulties, although that was suggested by James Bellingham, a prominent business man, and Tom's uncle. Then one night the still unfinished house on Beacon Hill burned to the ground, a week after the insurance on it had expired.

With his assets considerably diminished, Silas entered upon negotiations with the West Virginia paint men. Their best offer was a merger of the two companies, for which Silas was to supply a large amount of capital. After many efforts—when he was still far short of the sum he needed—Rogers came to him again with an offer from some Englishmen to buy the milling property. Silas at once detected the shady nature of their proposition; he also had to consider the prior rights of another potential purchaser. He had to decide between financial ruin and the subtly dishonest deal with Rogers.

He spent a long night deciding; the following morning, he gave Rogers the answer—No. Soon the Laphams went back to the farm, where Silas continued his business in a small way. They were both glad to see Tom Corey marry Penelope, and when Tom entered the West Virginia paint company, Silas knew that he would not have to worry about the future of his holdings. But, as he told his wife, he had learned his lesson, and he had no regrets for what he had done.

The Legend of Sleepy Hollow

By WASHINGTON IRVING

BORN *on April 3, 1783, in New York, N.Y., Washington Irving was trained for the law, but his health and a lack of interest in his profession turned him to writing, which supported him after he had lost his money in business ventures. Living in Europe from 1815 to 1832, he returned to the United States with a literary reputation. Later he served as Minister to Spain. Irving died on Nov. 28, 1859, at his home, Sunnyside, at Tarrytown on the Hudson.*

IN A COVE on the eastern shore of the Hudson lies a small market-town known as Tarry Town, and perhaps two miles from this village there is a little valley among high hills which is known as Sleepy Hollow and is one of the quietest places in the world. Its inhabitants are descendants of the original Dutch settlers, and are given to trances and visions, and tales of haunts.

The dominant spirit of the region is the apparition of a figure on horseback without a head, said to be the ghost of a Hessian trooper whose head had been carried away by a cannon-ball, and said to ride forth nightly in search of it, returning with the speed of the wind to the church-yard where he is buried.

Soon after the end of the Revolutionary War, there abode in Sleepy Hollow a worthy wight named Ichabod Crane, who instructed the children of the vicinity. A native of Connecticut, he was tall and exceedingly lank, with feet that might have served for shovels, a small head flat at the top, huge ears, large green glassy eyes, and a long snipe nose.

In his one-room log schoolhouse he administered the birch rod with discrimination, saving his severest chastisements for the tougher little Dutch urchins. Especially he kept on good terms with pupils whose mothers kept good cupboards, for he boarded a week at a time with each of the farmers, and his huge appetite could not otherwise have been satisfied from the school's small revenue.

Ichabod made himself useful by helping the farmers with their chores, by carrying gossip to their wives, and by acting as neighborhood singing-master. He was a master of Cotton Mather's history of New England witchcraft, in which he firmly believed, and in fact had swallowed every tale which the old Dutch wives told in the long winter evenings. When he walked home at night, every shrub seemed a sheeted spectre.

Now Ichabod Crane found Katrina Van Tassel, only child of Baltus Van Tassel, a tempting morsel. A blooming, plump and rosy-cheeked coquette of 18, her father's farm was the picture of abundance, and the pedagogue in his mind's eye devoured roasting pigs, pigeon pies, fat geese and ducks, and juicy hams. From the time Ichabod laid eyes on Van Tassel's comfortable farmhouse, his only study was how to gain the affections of the farmer's peerless daughter.

The most formidable of the rustic rivals for Katrina's hand was burly Abraham Van Brunt, a herculean youth who had more mischief than ill-will in him, and was foremost in all the frolics and feats of strength in the Hollow. Nicknamed Brom Bones, he had singled out Katrina for the object of his gallantries, and she did not altogether discourage him.

Ichabod was not mad enough to take the field openly against such a rival, but saw Katrina often as singing-master, and soon Bones was seldom a caller at the Van Tassels'. Ichabod was too wary to give Brom an opportunity for single combat, but he found himself the victim of innumerable practical jokes at his school-house and singing classes.

One fine autumnal afternoon Ichabod was summoned to a

quilting frolic that evening at Mynheer Van Tassel's. The gallant schoolmaster spent an extra half-hour brushing up his only suit of rusty black, and borrowed a horse named Gunpowder from Hans Van Ripper, the choleric old farmer with whom he was domiciled. Gunpowder was a gaunt, broken-down plow-horse that had outlived almost everything but his viciousness. His arms flapping like a pair of wings, the skirts of his coat fluttering almost to the horse's tail, Ichabod was a rare daylight apparition as he rode along, his thoughts all of Katrina.

Heer Van Tassel's castle was thronged with the pride of the countryside, including Brom Bones, who had come on his mettle-some steed Daredevil. A world of charms burst on the enraptured gaze of Ichabod in the parlor: Platters of cakes, pies, meats and fowl, and preserves. As he ate he chuckled to think that he might one day be lord of all this splendor.

And now the sound of music came, and Ichabod danced with Katrina, not a fibre about him idle, like St. Vitus in person. Then Ichabod joined a knot of the older folks for stories about the war and the Hollow's ghosts, including the great tree where Major André was taken, and of course the headless horseman, who had been heard several times of late.

Soon the frolic broke up, Ichabod lingering to have a word with the heiress, from which he sallied forth desolate and chop-fallen. Could she have been encouraging the pedagogue only to conquer his rival? Heaven only knows, but Ichabod strode straight to the stable and roused his steed with several hearty cuffs and kicks.

It was the very witching time of night that Ichabod approached Major André's tree, where so many of the ghost story scenes had been laid. He thought he heard a groan, and saw something white, but passed safely by. But two hundred yards ahead a few rough logs served for a bridge over a creek in a glen known as Wiley's swamp, and here a group of oaks and chestnuts threw a cavernous gloom over the road.

Ichabod's horse perversely balked at crossing the bridge, and just then Ichabod spied something huge, misshapen, black and towering in the shadow of the grove. The terrified pedagogue demanded in stammering accents: "Who are you?" Unanswered, he broke forth into a psalm tune and the unknown took the center of the road. He appeared to be a horseman of large dimensions, on a powerful black horse. Keeping silent, he jogged along on one side of the road, on the blind side of Gunpowder, who had gotten over his fright.

Ichabod quickened his steed, and the stranger kept up; he fell into a walk, and the other did the same. His heart sank, and he could not utter another word of his psalm tune. Then, on a rising ground, the gigantic figure of his fellow-traveler was brought in relief against the sky. Ichabod was horror-struck to perceive that he was headless!—but his horror was increased on observing that the head was carried before him on the pommel of the saddle.

Raining kicks upon Gunpowder, Ichabod started off full jump, the spectre with him. They raced up and down hill toward the famous church-yard. Ichabod's saddle girths suddenly gave way, and he jounced along clinging to Gunpowder's neck. "If I can just reach the bridge before the church," thought Ichabod, "I am safe." He thundered across and cast a look behind, and just then he saw the goblin rising in his stirrups and hurling his head at him.

Ichabod endeavored to dodge, but too late. The horrible missile encountered his cranium with a tremendous crash, he was tumbled headlong into the dust, and Gunpowder, the black steed and the goblin rider passed like a whirlwind.

Next morning the old horse was found, but Ichabod did not appear. The saddle was found trampled in the dirt, and beyond the bridge were discovered Ichabod's hat and close beside it a shattered pumpkin.

No body was found in the brook, and the countryside came to the conclusion that Ichabod had been carried off by the galloping Hessian. But an old farmer, who had been down to New York, learned that Ichabod was still alive, had studied law. and was now a justice of the Ten Pound Court. Brom Bones, who had conducted Katrina to the altar, was observed to look knowing whenever the story was related, and always laughed heartily at mention of the pumpkin. But the old country wives still maintain that Ichabod was spirited away supernaturally.

Ramona

By HELEN HUNT JACKSON

HELEN HUNT JACKSON *was born Helen Maria Fiske on October 18, 1831, at Amherst, Mass. At the age of twenty-one she married Capt. Edward Hunt, and lived the wandering life of an army wife until her husband's death in 1863. It was then that she began writing, at first only as an avocation. Her work was very prolific from 1867 until her death; at first she employed the initials "H. H." as a pen-name. After her marriage to W. S. Jackson, a banker of Colorado Springs, she became very much interested in the plight of the American Indian, who had lost his lands and possessions. Mrs. Jackson agitated for the righting of the Indian's wrongs. Her greatest plea was her novel Ramona, which was published in 1884 just a year before her death in San Francisco on August 12, 1885.*

SHEEP-SHEARING TIME at the ranch of Señora Moreno was the busiest season of the year. True, there was less fine pasture land than there had been in the days before the bloody Mexican War and the cession of Southern California to the United States, but the widowed Señora had preserved much of the Moreno wealth. Her resolute fight to keep the family lands was not for her own sake, but for that of her adored son. Felipe was a charming, handsome young man; if he was under his mother's thumb, nobody who knew the strong-minded Señora could blame him.

But now Felipe was ill of a fever and the sheep-shearing must be postponed until he had recovered. Gradually the young man mended under the care of his mother and his foster-sister, Ramona. Beautiful nineteen-year-old Ramona had been the Señora's ward for nearly sixteen years, and had grown to be a gay, gentle, devout young woman. The facts of the girl's origin were a sore point with the proud and conventional Señora. Ramona's father, Angus Phail, a Scotsman, had been jilted long ago by the Señora's older sister; mad with pain and anger, he had drifted into drink and disreputable living and had finally married an Indian squaw. The child of this union, Ramona, he had taken to his old love and the once gay and heartless Señorita, now crushed by a wretched and childless marriage, had adopted the little girl. The child had been adopted by Señora Moreno upon her sister's death. Now Ramona was grown, dark as her Indian mother had been, but blue-eyed like her father and as completely oblivious of her beauty as she was of the fact that young Felipe loved her. But if she was not aware of Felipe's love she knew well enough that the Señora loved her not; provide for, protect and educate the girl, the Señora could and did— love her she could not.

At last Señora Moreno pronounced her son well enough to take charge of the sheep-shearing. The ranch staff and the band of Indians, who, led by Alessandro, the handsome son of their chief, had come to help with the shearing, began the work. But Felipe, overcome by heat and fatigue, fell victim to a relapse of his fever and the household waited anxiously while the young man lay near death. Finally he passed the crisis and started toward recovery. But many weeks went by before he ceased to be an invalid, and meanwhile Alessandro, surprising and charming all by his intelligence and courtesy, directed the sheep-shearing.

The inevitable happened. Alessandro fell madly in love with Ramona and the girl gradually came to return his passion. Finally the young Indian could conceal his emotion no longer and declared his love to Ramona. The girl consented to be his wife and the lovers embraced—only to be surprised by the Señora! Furiously the proud Mexican tore the girl from Alessandro's arms and next morning coldly demanded an explanation. Her pride of race revolted by Ramona's decision to marry an Indian, Señora Moreno divulged the whole of the girl's origin, and Ramona first became aware of the fact that she was part Indian. Despite the Señora's threat to withhold her inheritance, Ramona held firm to her decision to marry Alessandro; patiently she awaited the return of her Indian lover, who had gone to his home to inform the chief of his betrothal.

But the days passed and Alessandro did not come. Certain that he was dead, Ramona drooped with grief and loneliness. One evening, somehow convinced that her sweetheart was near, she wandered down to their old meeting place. And there, hoping to catch a farewell glimpse of her, was Alessandro—but an Alessandro so changed, so wasted by sorrow and privation that she scarcely knew him! Ramona finally drew the story from him. American settlers had driven the Indians out of their village, stolen their horses and cattle, pillaged their homes—and all in the name of the law! Alessandro, once a chieftain, was now landless and penniless. How could he take for his bride a gently bred and inexperienced young girl? But Ramona was not to be swayed, and finally, moved by her threat to enter a convent, Alessandro consented to take her with him.

At San Diego the lovers were married, Ramona using the pet name that Alessandro had given her—Majella. No trace was left of the old life as in the little town of San Pasquale Ramona and Alessandro started the new. At first the pair prospered. Alessandro built up a fine little ranch and when a little blue-eyed girl was born to them Ramona felt herself to be indeed blessed. But their happiness was short-lived. The Americans came on and

Alessandro was forced to sell his home and lands. Once again the Indians were exiles.

Now Alessandro's one idea was to find some place where he would be safe from the ruthless American settlers. Scorning Ramona's plea that they settle in a town where he might find steady employment as a laborer, Alessandro turned his face toward the San Jacinto Mountains. But the journey there was long and cold and, caught in a fierce storm, Ramona, Alessandro and their baby nearly perished, saved only by the kindness of a traveling American family.

For a few months the sun shone again and the Indian family started to make another home in the little Saboba village. But the worst tragedy was yet to come. The baby, ailing all summer and treated with neglect and indifference by the American Indian-agency doctor, died. Alessandro and Ramona could endure no more. Into the mountains they went to live in solitude. In time another daughter was born to them, and this time the little girl was named for Ramona.

But Alessandro's reason had been undermined by his wrongs, and in a moment of irresponsibility he took the horse of an American settler. The white man cold-bloodedly shot down the Indian. Alessandro had endured his last injustice.

Widowed, without will to live, Ramona sank into a fever. But by this time the faithful Felipe had found her and, since the Señora was dead, he took Ramona and her child back to the ranch. In gratitude and affection Ramona eventually became his wife and they removed to Mexico. Their union was blessed with many children, but the best beloved was the eldest one, Ramona, daughter of Alessandro the Indian.

The Portrait of a Lady

By HENRY JAMES

BORN *in New York City on April 15, 1843, Henry James was taken abroad by his parents when he was two years old, and most of his early schooling took place in various parts of Europe. In 1862 he entered the Harvard Law School, but an interest in letters pulled him away rapidly from a legal career. In 1869 he went to Europe once more; with the exception of a few sojourns in America, he spent the rest of his life abroad, making his home in England after 1880, writing short stories and novels and criticism. In 1915 he became a British citizen, and shortly thereafter, on February 28, 1916, he died in England.*

ONE AFTERNOON IN SPRING three men were sitting on the lawn of an old English country house called Gardencourt, discussing the expected coming of a young American girl, Isabel Archer. One of them was her uncle, Mr. Touchett, also an American, owner of Gardencourt; failing in health, he spent his days in a wheel chair. The other men present were his son, Ralph Touchett, a semi-invalid, and their neighbor, Lord Warburton.

Isabel soon arrived, escorted by her aunt, the bustling and energetic Mrs. Touchett. Though the visit to Europe—which meant to Isabel a by no means unpleasant detachment from a respectable family living in straitened circumstances and the sincere, but unimaginative attentions of a man named Caspar Goodwood—was Isabel's first real experience of the world, she already had a desire for knowledge and an eagerness for the opportunities to live which her aunt's interest in her had provided.

Her beauty, her independence of mind, and her freedom from the usual feminine artifices charmed both her cousin and Lord Warburton. As the days passed, both of them sensed that a brilliant future lay ahead of Isabel, and Lord Warburton soon brought it within her reach by a proposal of marriage. When she refused him, Ralph Touchett began to see that Isabel wanted more than anything else a fuller view of European society and a larger knowledge of its cultivated past. To make that possible she would need money; so Ralph persuaded his father to remake his will, leaving the greater part of his own share to Isabel.

In the meantime a Madame Merle had arrived at Gardencourt to visit her old friend, Mrs. Touchett. In Madame Merle, Isabel found a woman who knew well the world into which she wished to venture. When Mr. Touchett died, Isabel was wealthy. Her opportunity had arrived. With Mrs. Touchett she set out on a tour of Europe. At Florence they met Madame Merle, who introduced Isabel to Gilbert Osmond, an American long in residence there; according to Madame Merle, a clever man, but lacking any desire to make use of his talents.

For Osmond, as Madame Merle hinted to him, Isabel, with her intelligence and her wealth, would be an ideal match. After many meetings, including one with Osmond's young daughter Pansy, Isabel became deeply interested in him and at last received from him a proposal of marriage. She decided, however, to delay a decision and continued to travel with Madame Merle.

When they returned to Florence after several months, she accepted Gilbert Osmond. Now she heard that her old suitor, Caspar Goodwood, had come to Europe; and it was her painful duty to tell him of her engagement. To her dismay, Isabel then learned from Ralph of the shock and the hurt which the news had brought him. His feelings about Osmond were hard to disguise. Though he had small hope for himself, he betrayed to Isabel this time something of his feeling, but what disturbed her most was his opinion that Osmond was no more than a "sterile dilettante."

Three years passed. Isabel lived now in Rome, and at the moment was concerned with the future of her step-daughter Pansy, who had taken a fancy to a poor young man, Ned Rosier, with nothing more to recommend himself than an interest in book-collecting.

Lord Warburton and Ralph Touchett, in the meantime, had arrived in Rome. Ralph had come there ostensibly for the sake of his health, but both he and Warburton were still deeply interested in Isabel and wanted to discover, if possible, whether she was happy.

When Lord Warburton showed that his old affection for Isabel extended to Pansy, Madame Merle sensed the possibility of snaring a highly acceptable husband for Osmond's daughter. Osmond agreed with her, and made the successful execution of the plan entirely the responsibility of Isabel. This act of his brought their relationship to a crisis. Isabel had to review for herself the reasons for the gulf that had widened between them since their marriage.

Osmond had not been able to change her ideas about life— indeed, what he resented was her right to hold *her* ideas and reject his. He hated her, she felt, because her mind remained independent; he had never been able to subordinate her mind to his. Yet she had tried to please Osmond—even in the present situation she desired to follow his wishes, though she knew perfectly well that Lord Warburton was still in love with her.

The next time she saw Lord Warburton she rebuked him for paying his attentions to Pansy and delaying speaking to Osmond. The effect of this upon Lord Warburton was the announcement shortly thereafter of his return to England. Osmond blamed Isabel for the collapse of the plan, and in doing so demonstrated the meanness, the narrowness and essential cruelty of his nature.

Madame Merle also upbraided Isabel for her failure to keep Lord Warburton at Rome, and Isabel now saw clearly what she had sensed for a long time—that Madame Merle's interest in Pansy was identical with Osmond's.

Faced with this revelation, Isabel received a telegram from Mrs. Touchett informing her that Ralph, back in England, was dying, and that he wished to see her. Osmond forbade her to go, and Isabel could not decide what to do. The Countess Gemini, Osmond's sister, finding her distraught, told her the whole story about Osmond; Pansy was the child of Madame Merle. One more encounter with Madame Merle was yet to come.

Isabel met her again at the convent where she had gone to say good-by to Pansy. At this meeting Madame Merle placed all the blame for what had happened to Isabel upon Ralph and his kindness. Isabel was stunned by this attack on Ralph, but she realized at last how much she had meant to Ralph all along.

She went to Gardencourt at once. At his bedside she waited a long time until he was strong enough to speak. For the last time they were able to consider what their true relations to each other had been. Her consciousness of Ralph's love would prove to be one source of strength in her uncertain future.

What should she do? She had promised Pansy not to desert her, yet . . . One day Caspar Goodwood appeared at Gardencourt, eager to take her back to America. But once more she refused him, though this time reluctantly. She had decided that it was wrong for her to seek an escape from her life with Osmond. Whatever the consequences, she could not retrace her steps. With that conviction in her heart, she returned to Rome.

Arrowsmith

By SINCLAIR LEWIS

SINCLAIR LEWIS *was born February 7, 1885, a native of Sauk Center, Minnesota, son of a doctor. His education at Yale, where he took his A.B. in 1907, was interrupted by work which he did at Upton*

Sinclair's socialist experiment, Helicon Home Colony. The next years were spent in travel and reporting and editing for various newspapers and publishing houses. In 1928 Lewis married Dorothy Thompson. In 1930 he received the Nobel Prize for Literature. Lately Lewis has turned to the theater and has become an actor and director. He was offered and declined the Pulitzer Prize, and is a member of the American Academy of Arts and Letters.

MARTIN ARROWSMITH'S ODYSSEY began in a shabby office in a little midwestern town. Dr. Vickerson was dirty and a drunk but in his frowsy front room were such magic keys to adventure as a torn copy of Gray's *Anatomy* and a skeleton with a gold tooth. Fourteen-year-old Martin constituted himself the Doc's assistant; in return for sporadic cleanups and post-binge nursing duties the boy received such instruction as the doctor's foggy mind could administer.

Martin's parents were dead. The legacy they left saw the boy through the University of Winnemac and then, less grandly, through medical school. Martin succumbed to a medical fraternity and promptly regretted it. To young Arrowsmith, hot-tempered, incautious, stubborn and often wrong-headed, yet completely and idealistically in earnest about medicine, the commercial attitude of the "brothers" to their profession was blasphemy. And Martin alienated many of his professors by questioning the medical dogma they preached. His only friend was Professor Gottlieb, a German Jew, an emigré, himself skeptical and an iconoclast, dedicated to pure science. Gottlieb it was who saw that Martin's field was research, that the boy possessed a scientific curiosity amounting to genius. Martin soon discovered his milieu —bacteriology.

Martin met Madeline Fox. Madeline was high-spirited, handsome, and utterly unable to understand the young medical student whose vocation was sacred to him. All through Martin's junior year Madeline tried to make him over into the kind of husband she planned to have. Except for a lucky accident she might have succeeded.

One day on an errand for Dr. Gottlieb to Zenith General Hospital Martin inquired a direction of a student nurse. The little probationer looked up from her work—she had been set to floor-scrubbing as a disciplinary measure—and answered the young man very rudely indeed. This was Leora Tozer. Leora was from Dakota. She was little, pretty, unworldly, unclever, provincial, slangy and unfailingly warm. A few weeks later Martin found himself engaged to two girls at the same time. Panic-stricken, he arranged a meeting of the two at lunch. Horrified Madeline, when she learned of the situation, stalked off, but Leora stood her ground.

The next year was hell for Martin. Leora was called home to Wheatsylvania, and Martin, lonely, overworked, sleeping too little, drinking too much, soon alienated even his champion, Gottlieb. He left school. For a while he drifted aimlessly about the country, then he set out to Leora.

Leora's people were suspicious and possession-ridden. When Martin and Leora ran off and got married they were horrified. They bullied Leora into staying with them when Martin returned to finish his last year at medical school. Finally, torn by his need of her, Martin demanded that Leora's people send her to him.

Martin first hung out his shingle in Wheatsylvania. Leora's people grudgingly backed him. He set up shop in a shack. The villagers grew fond of him, laughed at him, took his advice sometimes, more often didn't. He became known as an alarmist. After he'd been in Wheatsylvania a little over a year he found a case of smallpox and, fearing an epidemic, he tried to bully the population into being vaccinated. The epidemic didn't materialize, and he rode out of Wheatsylvania on great tides of laughter.

On a trip to Minneapolis, Martin found a new hero—Gustaf Sondelius, a merry Swedish giant, noted for his love of liquor, humanity, and fighting epidemics. Meanwhile Martin's old idol, Gottlieb, had known disgrace and terror. He sought to bring about scientific reform in the University of Winnemac; he lost his chair. Frantic and penniless, he looked hopelessly for work, finding it finally in a patent medicine company. But when the company tried to sell commercially an anti-toxin that he had discovered after twelve years of research, the old man knew he would have to move on. Prepared for poverty and obscurity, Gottlieb was saved at the eleventh hour by an invitation from the McGurk Institute of Biology in New York.

Next stop for the young Arrowsmiths was Nautilus. Nautilus was a midwestern town, prosperous, thriving and brisk almost beyond endurance. Martin was assistant to Dr. Almus Pickerbaugh, Director of the Department of Public Health. Dr. Pickerbaugh carried on his campaign for health as if it were a political drive; he made speeches, composed slogans, wrote little health songs, and never stepped on important toes. He was immensely popular.

When Dr. Pickerbaugh went to Congress, Martin became director. He made no speeches; he went after rats, fleas, and tenement owners. The town officials forced him to resign by lowering his salary below subsistence level.

At Rouncefield Clinic, a shining, successful hospital for the rich, Martin's research was discouraged. When Martin had been at Rouncefield a year he felt that he was through as a scientist and a doctor. Only Leora, shabby and loyal, upheld him. Escape came when old Gottlieb wrote and told Martin that there was a place for him at the McGurk Institute. Leora said she thought she would love New York.

McGurk Institute was paradise. The equipment was magnificent and Martin was able to work independently. That many of the staff were merely society doctors, Martin neither knew nor cared. Gottlieb was there and Martin soon found a kindred spirit in another of the men on the staff, pugnacious, red-headed Terry Wickett, who loved science and hated hokum.

Then, after many months of research, quite by accident Martin stumbled on something. He noticed that a bacterial culture had died for no apparent reason. Hectic weeks of overwork and consequent nervous reaction followed, but Martin finally found that he had discovered a principle—he called it phage—deadly to growing bacteria.

The Institute was jubilant at the prestige this unsocial young medic would bring them. When bubonic plague broke out on St. Hubert's Island, Martin and his phage were dispatched there to check the epidemic and experiment with the new principle. His old friend Gustaf Sondelius accompanied him and at the last minute Leora went along, too. Gottlieb and Terry Wickett warned Martin against sentimentality—part of the population must be kept without the phage as a control.

At St. Hubert's the plague was running wild, and the panic-stricken natives were dying like flies. Nor were the Americans safe. After a valiant fight against the epidemic Sondelius died in Martin's arms. And one day, while Martin was far away talking with beautiful Joyce Lanyon, a rich American woman, Leora was stricken and died quite alone.

For weeks Martin worked in a frenzy of pain, living on liquor and his nerves. But somehow the epidemic was halted, somehow the phage was proved, and Martin returned to America, famous—and lonely.

When he married Joyce Lanyon he had not forgotten Leora; but Joyce was beautiful and desirable. For a little while Martin was content to be part of his wife's society, but soon he was restless and unhappy; even the birth of his son gave him no new interest.

So at last he went back to his first love—research. He and Terry Wickett built their own laboratory in a forest shack. The place was bare and cold, but Martin was at last contented with the silence of the wilderness, his test tubes, and his own inspired curiosity.

Moby Dick

By HERMAN MELVILLE

The son of an importer, Herman Melville was born August 1, 1819, in New York. His father died a bankrupt when he was 13, and Herman worked as clerk, teacher, and seaman before, in 1841, he joined the crew of a whaler. In the Marquesas he jumped ship, stayed with the cannibal natives for four months, then worked his way home on other whalers and on a U.S. Navy frigate. With nothing else to do, he wrote a story of his adventures which launched him on writing as a career. But success deserted him in his middle years, and he spent 20 of the last years of his life as a customs inspector in New York, where he died on Sept. 28, 1891.

CALL ME ISHMAEL. Having little money in my purse, I thought I would sail about a little. Like Narcissus, all of us see in the ocean the ungraspable image of life. It was the overwhelming idea of the great whale, and my everlasting itch for things remote, that put a whaling voyage in my head. And so, on a December night, I found myself in the Spouter Inn at New Bedford, awaiting the packet to Nantucket.

I had to share my bed with a brawny harpooner, a tattooed South Sea islander named Queequeg, who proved not very talkative, but civil enough. Together, at the Whaleman's Chapel, we heard the famous Father Mapple preach on Jonah: "Delight is to him whom all the waves can never shake from this Keel of the Ages." That afternoon Queequeg and I smoked his tomahawk pipe together; he gave me half his money, and I helped him worship his idol.

Crossing to Nantucket, Queequeg and I signed aboard the *Pequod,* a rare old craft, seasoned in four oceans and fitted out with whale ivory. We did not see Captain Ahab, the master, but were told that last voyage he had lost one leg—"devoured by a monstrous parmacetty," and that "ever since he's been desperate moody, and savage sometimes." Soon we sailed, ignoring a warning from a strange sailor. We could see nothing of four or five men we had spied going toward the ship in the morning mist.

The chief mate of the *Pequod* was Starbuck, Nantucket native and a Quaker by descent. His flesh was as hard as twice-baked biscuit; uncommonly conscientious, the welded iron of his soul was tempered by prudence. Stubb, the second mate, a Cape-Cod-man, was happy-go-lucky, neither craven nor valiant. The third mate, little Flask, from Martha's Vineyard, an ignorantly fearless and ruddy young fellow, had no reverence for the whale; to him it was but a species of magnified mouse. These three commanded the *Pequod's* boats, and their whaling spears were as lances to the harpooners' javelins.

Queequeg was Starbuck's harpooner. Stubb had chosen Tashtego, an Indian from Gay Head, lithe and brawny. And the third harpooner was Daggoo, a gigantic coal-black Negro savage, six feet five in his socks. As for the residue of the crew, they were nearly all islanders, not half of them Americans.

Several days out of Nantucket, Captain Ahab first appeared. He looked like a man cut away from the stake, when the fire has wasted all the limbs, without taking away one particle of their aged robustness. He stood on a barbaric white leg, fashioned at sea from a sperm whale's jaw bone, and auger holes were bored into the quarter-deck to steady it. He walked the deck daily with moody, silent dignity.

One night, finding no pleasure in his pipe, Ahab soliloquized: "This is meant for sereneness, not to send up mild white vapors among torn iron-gray locks like mine," and he tossed the pipe into the sea. He was as grim at table in his cabin, where the mates ate with him in awful silence.

Then, not a great while after, Ahab ordered everybody aft one evening, and ordered the lookouts down. Then he held up a broad bright coin, and nailed it to the mainmast, crying:

"Whoever of ye raises me a white-headed whale with a wrinkled brow and a crooked jaw, with three holes punctured in his starboard fluke, he shall have this Spanish ounce of gold!"

The seamen cried, "Huzza!" and the three harpooners asked if Ahab meant the whale that was called Moby Dick. "Ay," cried Ahab, "it was that accursed white whale that dismasted me, and I'll chase him round perdition's flames before I give him up." All shouted agreement but Starbuck, who told Ahab: "I am game, but I came here to hunt whales, not my commander's vengeance," and added that it was madness to seek revenge on a dumb brute.

"In each event," answered Ahab, "some unknown but still reasoning thing puts forth the moulding of its features from behind the unreasoning mask. That unscrutable thing is chiefly what I hate; and be the white whale agent, or be he principal, I will wreak that hate upon him."

The steward drew the grog, and the harpooners drank a fiery toast from the sockets of their harpoons. Even Starbuck was conquered, if not convinced. Ahab told himself: "What I've dared, I've willed; and what I've willed, I'll do. They think me mad; but I'm demoniac, I am madness maddened."

It was a cloudy, sultry afternoon when we sighted our first school of whales; for Ahab had the wisdom to continue true to the nominal purpose of the *Pequod's* voyage. At the cry to lower the boats, five men appeared whom no one had seen before—a crew for his own boat whom Ahab had taken aboard secretly. Their leader was Fedallah, a tall, swart man in Chinese dress with long white hair wound about his head like a turban, and the others were aborigines from the Manillas. I was in Starbuck's boat, which was half-swamped by a whale, and we sat drenched all night in a storm before the ship found us. Learning that such matters were of common occurrence in this kind of life, I made my will. We had killed no whales.

We rounded the Cape of Good Hope. When we met another whaler, Ahab would stop only to ask if they had seen the white whale. Then we continued along the currents followed by the sperm whales, ignoring right whales we sighted in the Indian Ocean, making our way from one feeding ground to another. It was in this ocean that Stubb killed our first whale and we stopped to fill our first barrels with oil and spermaceti. And there we met the whaler *Jereboam,* whose mate had been killed by Moby Dick.

We passed into the China seas and the Pacific through the Straits of Sunda, where we became entangled in an immense herd of sperm whales making the same passage, and ended by killing only one of them. It was a few days later that poor little Pip, the Negro ship's boy, jumped overboard from a boat that was being pulled by a whale and was not rescued from the sea until hours later. But Pip's mind was gone.

Hailing the *Samuel Enderby,* an English ship, Ahab met her captain, who wore an arm of whale ivory that was a match for Ahab's leg. Captain Boomer, too, had met the white whale. Returning from the *Enderby,* Ahab broke his ivory leg and had to have another fashioned. It was at this time that Queequeg caught a near-fatal fever and had his coffin made, keeping it as a sea chest when he recovered.

One day Ahab himself helped forge a harpoon for the white whale, with the barbs made from his razors and tempered in the blood of the pagan harpooners. And on a night when Ahab's boat was staying beside a whale it had killed, Ahab heard this prophecy from Fedallah: Ere Ahab could die, he must see two hearses on the sea, one not made by mortal hands, the other made of wood grown in America. Further, Fedallah would die before Ahab, and only hemp could kill the captain.

At last the day came to turn toward the Equator; and on that day Ahab trampled on his quadrant and declared he would guide the ship by the compass and dead reckoning. The same evening an electrical storm enveloped the ship, the next day it was found that the compasses had been reversed. And when the log was heaved, its rotted line parted. Then the first man who mounted the masthead in Moby Dick's own favorite seas was lost overboard. The dried-out lifebuoy sank when it was dropped after him, and Queequeg gave his coffin as a substitute.

Now the *Pequod* met the *Rachel,* captained by a Nantucket man. The captain's own son had been lost the day before—after chasing Moby Dick. Ahab refused to help search for the lost boat, but set out on the warm trail of the white whale. Now Ahab did not leave the decks; and when three or four days passed without any sign of a spout, Ahab had himself lifted aloft. Another ship, the *Delight,* was described; her captain was preparing to bury one of five seamen who had been killed in an encounter with Moby Dick the previous night. It was a clear day, and Ahab spoke to Starbuck of his forty years at sea. Starbuck pleaded with him, but could not turn Ahab from his unnatural quest.

And then came another dawn, and it was Ahab who cried: "There she blows! A hump like a snowhill! It is Moby Dick!"

All the boats gave chase. Moby Dick sounded, and came up, as if with malicious intelligence, under Ahab's boat. Lying on its back, in the manner of a biting shark, the whale took the boat's bows full within its mouth and shook it as a cat shakes a mouse. Ahab fell into the sea, and the ship sailed upon the wreckage to drive off the whale. The other boats were unable to catch up with Moby Dick, and returned to the ship.

The second morning Moby Dick breached early, and the boats were launched again, Ahab taking the spare boat. The whale bore down on them, ignoring the irons darted at him, trying to destroy the men who eluded him. Ahab cut his tangled lines in time, but Stubb's and Flask's boats were destroyed by the whale's flukes. Then Moby Dick rose again and dashed his broad forehead against Ahab's boat. But the whale swam off again, and the ship picked up the men—all but Fedallah. And Ahab's harpoon was gone.

It was afternoon before the whale was sighted on the third

day. All of Starbuck's reasoning had been futile; Ahab would not give up the chase. New boats were lowered. When Moby Dick rose he seemed possessed by a devil; once again he swamped the mates' boats. Then a cry went up, for the body of Fedallah was seen, entangled in the harpoon ropes that clung to the whale. Ahab had seen one hearse. The others returned to the ship; Ahab pursued the tiring whale and sank his iron into Moby Dick. Angry, the whale turned, then caught sight of the ship and charged it. Water poured into the gap in the *Pequod's* side, and Ahab saw his second hearse—the ship herself. As the ship went down, Ahab hurled a harpoon into the whale, with a cry of: "For hate's sake I spit my last breath at thee." The line fouled, and the flying turn caught him around the neck. He was shot out of the boat, and then the vortex of the sinking *Pequod* drew down with it Ahab's craft and its crew.

The great shroud of the sea rolled on.

Only I survived, and two days later I was picked up by the *Rachel*.

Uncle Tom's Cabin

By HARRIET BEECHER STOWE

HARRIET BEECHER *was born in Litchfield, Connecticut, on June 14, 1811. She was educated at her sister Catherine's school at Hartford, and also taught there. In 1832 the Beechers moved to Cincinnati, and in 1836 Harriet Beecher married Calvin Ellis Stowe, a professor in Lane Theological Seminary. Mrs. Stowe began publishing fiction in 1843, and in subsequent years contributed many things to the anti-slavery press. Her writing continued after the Civil War; toward the end of her career she gave public readings. She died in her Hartford home, July 1, 1896.*

In his part of kentucky, Mr. George Shelby was reputed liberal and humane in his treatment of the slaves on his plantation. Nevertheless, when he found that a slave-trader named Haley had got hold of one of his mortgages, he was willing to submit to the man's terms. In settlement of the claim, Haley asked for Uncle Tom, a middle-aged Negro, noted for his piety and his devotion to the Shelby family, and a five-year-old Negro boy, the only son of Mrs. Shelby's personal servant, Eliza.

In spite of his wife's protestations, Shelby yielded to Haley's terms. In the meantime, Eliza's husband, George Harris, a talented young man whose father was white, had rebelled against the cruel mistreatment which his master had dealt him, and he was planning to cross the Ohio River and escape to Canada.

By eavesdropping Eliza learned that Mr. Shelby had sold her son, and at once she began preparations for flight. The next morning Haley discovered that they had fled, and immediately called for horses. One of the slaves accompanying him was able to warn Eliza when they reached the house where she was hiding. Holding her boy, she ran to the river and jumped on to the moving ice floes one step ahead of her pursuer. Miraculously, she got across the river and found refuge some time later in a Quaker settlement in Ohio before a new searching party was organized.

There was deep sorrow in Uncle Tom's small cabin when his wife and children learned the dread news. Tom submitted willingly to his master's decision; the comfort the Bible gave him in adversity he tried to communicate to his wife. The next day Haley put him into a wagon, clamped on the leg irons, and started the journey toward the Mississippi. Young George Shelby, outraged by what his father had done, tearfully promised Tom that he would some day try to buy him back. Further along in their trip Haley bought several more slaves, including a woman and her ten-month-old child. Before they boarded the boat for New Orleans, Haley sold the child. The first night on the river, the woman threw herself overboard. Haley took this bad luck philosophically; it was one of the incidents of his trade.

Among the passengers on the boat was a gentleman of New Orleans, Augustine St. Clare, traveling homeward with his six-year-old daughter Eva, and his cousin Ophelia, a native of Vermont. Eva's childish beauty and ethereality were noticed by Tom, and through small tokens of friendliness he attracted her attention. He jumped overboard to rescue Eva who had fallen into the river, and after that it was not hard for the child to persuade her father to buy Tom from Haley.

Augustine St. Clare had married a woman of New Orleans society who shared none of his views and who thought herself much abused by her husband. Marie lived as a semi-invalid, affecting an illness the better to impose her desires on those around her; she was selfish, arrogant, and cruel to her servants. St. Clare, deploring the viciousness of slavery, and the horrible results of the slave trade, tried to placate his own conscience by his unusual humanity toward his own slaves.

Uncle Tom, because of little Eva's liking for him, had nothing externally to complain of. He was now master of the stables, and lived more comfortably than he ever had before. Eva often read to him from the Bible, and she even tried to help him learn to write so that he could let his wife know of his whereabouts.

In the meantime, George Harris had joined his wife in the Quaker settlement. A man named Marks had organized a posse and had planned to seize all the fugitive slaves he could find, under the powers granted by the recently passed Fugitive Slave Law, and claim them as his own and sell them. Aided by two able-bodied Quakers, Eliza and George and several Negroes set out for Canada. Overtaken by Marks and his gang, they took refuge behind some rocks, and George shot and wounded one of the pursuers. At this, Marks departed, and the company made its way to Canada in safety.

Several years passed. The things she had seen in New Orleans had increased Miss Ophelia's hatred of the institution of slavery, yet she still found it difficult to treat the Negroes as she would other human beings. One day St. Clare brought home a little orphan named Topsy, who had been beaten and maltreated all her life, and made her Ophelia's particular charge. Topsy's pranks and mischief enlivened the household, and when she was punished, she insisted that she was wicked and even invited Miss Ophelia to chastise her. Only when Eva showed true kindness and love to her was Topsy's heart touched, and then she said that no one had ever loved her. This gave Ophelia something to think about, but she still disliked the child.

The only shadow in the household was the illness of Eva. When she began to lose strength, her father became alarmed, but new doctors could do little for her. That summer they spent as usual on the shores of a lake in the country. Eva became more compassionate; she spoke more often about the slaves, and urged her father to grant Uncle Tom his freedom. One day she asked Ophelia to cut some of her curls to give away to her friends. Later she told Uncle Tom that she had heard the voices of the angels. Soon after she passed away.

After his daughter's death, St. Clare thought more and more about her wishes, and took the first steps toward securing Uncle Tom's freedom. He began to take Uncle Tom into his confidence, and Uncle Tom was moved to attempt to dispel some of his doubts about God and his ways. St. Clare wanted to believe, but the skepticism engendered by a long distrust of humanity held him back. One day St. Clare was fatally stabbed while trying to separate two drunken brawlers.

Marie decided to go back to her family's estates with her own slaves. Disregarding the wishes of her husband, and the intercessions of Ophelia for Tom and the other slaves, she callously turned them over to her lawyer, and he consigned them to a slave market.

Uncle Tom went under the hammer at New Orleans and was sold, along with a beautiful 15-year-old girl named Emmeline, to a brutal plantation owner, Simon Legree. His estate was in an isolated section along the Red River, where his word was the law, and that law was enforced by his fists, whips, boot, and dogs. He was his own overseer, and his helpers were two Negroes whom he had brutalized and set against the others. His plan was to make Tom his assistant.

Tom found that Legree's slaves lived in filth and poverty. They were completely broken and helpless; most of them had no knowledge of the Bible. Tom's kindness and his piety ill-fitted him for the role in which Legree had cast him. Legree's only enemy was a mulatto woman named Cassy who lived with him in his house. She managed to protect Emmeline from Legree; after a terrible beating of Tom, she bathed his wounds and talked to him.

Working on Legree's superstitions, Cassy planned to escape with Emmeline. Her ruse was successful, but Legree blamed Tom for the escape. Though he had no part in Cassy's plot, he aroused Legree's anger to its highest pitch. Tom knew that he would not recover from the beating he received, but in these last few days Tom had been uplifted by the hope of his salvation. Triumphantly he told Legree that he could not touch his soul.

Long before this young George Shelby had set out to find Uncle Tom to take him back to Kentucky. When at last he arrived at Legree's plantation, he found Uncle Tom dying, happy in his deep conviction that his earthly suffering was finally to give way to a better life.

Simon Legree, half-crazed, failed to find Cassy and Emmeline. The two fugitives eventually reached Canada, where there was a joyful reunion between Cassy and her long-lost brother, who turned out to be George Harris.

Ben-Hur

By LEW WALLACE

LEWIS WALLACE *was born in Brookville, Indiana, on the tenth of April, 1827. His study of law was interrupted by the outbreak of the Mexican War, in which he enlisted as a second lieutenant. After the war he resumed his career and became successful in politics, serving four years in the State Senate. At the beginning of the Civil War, Wallace was made an adjutant-general, and he emerged from the war a major-general with a reputation for heroism. In 1865 he returned to his law practice, then served as the governor of New Mexico from 1878 to 1881 and spent the years from 1881 to 1885 in Turkey as United States Minister. Writing was Wallace's avocation only; in 1880* Ben-Hur *appeared. Its worldwide success was instantaneous. Wallace died in Crawfordsville, Ind., on February 15, 1905.*

WHEN the star in the east first appeared to the three wise men, the entire civilized world was greatly in need of the King who was promised. At that time the Kingdom of Judæa was under Roman rule, as, indeed, were almost all nations.

About twenty years after the birth of Christ had been prophesied to the wise men, a young Jew of wealth and noble house, Judah Ben-Hur by name, broke off his dearest boyhood friendship. The object of this friendship was the Roman, Messala, with whom Ben-Hur had passed many years of a happy childhood. But now the lads were grown, and Messala had come back from schooling in his country's capital full of Roman cynicism and Roman arrogance which made friendship between him and the young Jew no longer possible. The young men parted with bitterness, and that very day Messala had his revenge. While Ben-Hur was watching from his window the triumphant approach of the new Roman Procurator of Judæa, the hated Valerius Gratus, a tile became dislodged beneath his hand and fell on Gratus, wounding him severely. Ben-Hur was seized immediately. Messala refused to help his erstwhile friend. The Jew's explanations were unheeded and he found himself sentenced to the galleys for life, his lands confiscated, his widowed mother and little sister, Tirzah, torn from him and taken he knew not where.

For three years, while Ben-Hur toiled as a galley slave, Gratus and Messala fattened on the fortune they had seized. Ben-Hur, instead of succumbing to the degradation of galley life and sinking beneath his miseries, grew strong and awaited the day when he might find his mother and sister or else avenge them.

Finally the young Jew found a friend. Quintus Arrius, a Roman tribune, became impressed with the strength and nobility that he so surprisingly found in a galley slave. When the vessel was attacked by pirates, Ben-Hur saved Arrius from drowning at the risk of his own life and the grateful tribune adopted him as his son. On the Roman estates of Arrius, Ben-Hur was educated in the skills of a Roman warrior and absorbed all that he found best in the Roman culture. But when the death of his benefactor left him free, he returned to Jerusalem to seek vengeance on those who had betrayed him.

In Judæa Ben-Hur could find no trace of his mother and sister, whom, indeed, he had been seeking since his release from the galleys. But he did discover that, while his family estates had been confiscated by Gratus and Messala, the actual moneys of the family were in the hands of one Simonides, a Hebrew bond slave of his father, who had resisted torture in order to retain them. Simonides had by skillful trading increased the fortune of Ben-Hur until it was a fabulous amount. Simonides at first pretended to doubt the young man's claim, but in reality he wished only to test Ben-Hur and see what manner of man he was before entrusting him with so large a fortune. Simonides' daughter, beautiful and virtuous Esther, loved Ben-Hur from the moment she first saw him and prevailed upon her father to grant immediately to the young Jew that which was rightfully his.

Meanwhile Ben-Hur had once more encountered his old enemy, Messala. The Roman had great athletic prowess and planned to drive his own horses in the chariot race which was soon to be held in the arena. The Jew saw in this circumstance the possibility of vengeance. Hearing that the Arabian Sheikh, Ilderim, was looking for a driver for his magnificent quartet of bays, Ben-Hur offered his services. The Sheikh was a friend of Simonides, and had heard much of the young man; he granted the request. Another friend of the Sheikh was Balthasar, one of the three kings who had seen the star in the east so many years before and who was even now awaiting the King whose coming had been promised.

The chariot race was a triumph for Ben-Hur. Although Messala attempted foul play, the young Jew not only emerged victorious but also saw his enemy ruined financially and crippled for life beneath the wheels of his own chariot.

But Messala sent assassins after the young man, and Ben-Hur in order to escape let it be thought that he was dead. Stories of the Messiah who was to come and who might restore the glory of Judæa stirred the Jewish youth and he resolved to put the whole of his immense fortune at the disposal of this King when he should come.

Ben-Hur secretly reopened the home of his forefathers, for he wished to dwell in Judæa. Meanwhile Valerius Gratus was removed, and Pontius Pilate was sent as the new Procurator. And all through the country were heard whispers of a Nazarene who called himself King of the Jews and was said to have raised the dead. Ben-Hur waited for the time when his help should be needed.

When the prisons of Valerius Gratus were cleared the guards found in a dungeon, whose existence they had not been aware of, two women who, once beautiful, were now haggard and wasted and afflicted with leprosy. These women were the mother and the sister of Ben-Hur. The two were released but sent forth in exile lest they afflict others with their disease. They did not communicate with Ben-Hur, deeming it better that he should think them dead.

Now the opposition against the Nazarene reached its height, and influential persons, Romans and Jews alike, demanded his death. While he was passing to his judgment the Nazarene met two leper women who begged that He cleanse them. Thus were the mother and sister of Ben-Hur healed of leprosy.

The crucifixion of Christ followed. Ben-Hur begged the Nazarene to allow him to try to save Him, but Jesus made it plain to the young man that God willed He should die.

But Ben-Hur was convinced that this Man was indeed the Messiah. He embraced Christianity, as did Esther who became his wife. When the Roman persecutions of the Christians began, Ben-Hur lent his strength and wealth toward building catacombs where his fellow Nazarenes might find a haven.

Ethan Frome

By EDITH WHARTON

EDITH NEWBOLD JONES *was born in 1862 of an old New York family. She was carefully educated at home and in foreign travel. She began writing early; at fifteen her verses were recommended to the* Atlantic *by Longfellow. Around 1890, shortly after her marriage to Edward Wharton, she began to publish short stories in the magazines, and by 1899 her short stories and novels were appearing in book form. She lived abroad most of the time after 1900, chiefly in France, from 1907 to her death in 1937.*

THE village of Starkfield, Massachusetts, lay under two feet of snow as young Ethan Frome walked at a quick pace along the deserted streets. Outside the church he paused and listened in the shadow to the sounds of laughter and music within. Frome's heart was beating fast.

A year before, Mattie Silver had come to live with Ethan and his wife, Zeena. Mattie was Zeena's cousin; she had had no place to go after her father's death, and Zeena, looking around for someone to help her with the housework, had decided that she could give Mattie a home and save the expense of a hired girl. On rare occasions Mattie came into Starkfield for an evening's pleasure with the young people of the church. On this evening, as on others, Ethan had come in to walk back the two miles to the farm with Mattie.

With a twinge of jealousy Ethan watched Mattie dance the last reel with a lively young Irishman. When the party broke up, Ethan waited outside in the shadow. Mattie refused the invitation of the young man to drive her home in his sleigh, and came back to meet Ethan.

Walking home through the snow, Ethan thrilled to the pressure of her arm. There had grown up between them a silent bond of understanding, and yet they avoided any word or gesture which might express the feelings that lay below the surface. At these moments the thought of Zeena rose up in their minds.

Tonight, on the way home, when Ethan awkwardly mentioned that Mattie might some day be leaving them, she asked him if Zeena was not suited with her any more. But Ethan had been thinking only that such a lovely young girl might want to get married. When they reached the farm, they could not find the key that Zeena usually put under the mat. She came down to let them in, complaining more than usual about her aches and pains. As they went to bed, it occurred to Ethan that his wife had lately been a little more grim and querulous than usual.

When he came in for dinner the next day, Zeena was dressed in her best outfit, and she announced that she was going to go that afternoon to Bettsbridge to consult a new doctor. Because of the weather and the train trip, she would not return until the following day. In order to get back to the house early, he offered an excuse for not driving her to the junction and got his hired man to take her.

That evening, for the first time since Mattie had been living with the Fromes, she and Ethan were alone together. The room was warm and cheery; Ethan's supper was already on the table when he came in. He noticed that his favorite pickles were on the table in a dish of gay red glass. During the meal Ethan was unable to voice any of the thoughts he had had in the afternoon in anticipation of this moment.

Unobserved, the cat had jumped to the table, and suddenly it overturned the pickle dish on the floor. In a panic Mattie picked up the pieces. The dish was Zeena's most treasured object; it was a wedding gift from her aunt and had never been taken from its place at the top of the china closet. Ethan tried to calm Mattie. He put the pieces together and returned it to the shelf. Tomorrow he would get some glue and mend it. The rest of the evening was pleasant. Ethan sat before the fire and watched Mattie at her sewing. But again the thought of Zeena returned and acted as a restraint on his feelings.

When Ethan came in the next afternoon from his work, Mattie told him that Zeena had returned and had gone directly to her room. She did not come down at supper time, so Ethan went upstairs. Zeena was sitting stiffly by the window; she had not taken off her good dress. She began by telling him that the new doctor had warned her that she might have "complications," and ended up by informing him that she had hired a new girl to do all the housework and that she was coming tomorrow. Slowly Ethan came to a realization of what she wanted: Mattie was to leave at once, the new girl taking her place. The scene that followed was the worst of their seven years of marriage. After supper the tension was increased when Zeena discovered the broken pickle dish.

Ethan had to tell the news to Mattie. Thus far he had been

powerless to resist Zeena. That night he retired to a small room downstairs which he had once fixed up as a study, and tried to think out what he should do. He began a letter to Zeena in which he told her that he and Mattie were going west to start over . . . but where would he get the money?

Ethan spent the next morning in town—it was to be Mattie's last day at the farm—trying to think of some way to raise enough money to leave with her. When he returned home late in the afternoon, he had to admit that he was beaten. Though Zeena had arranged for Mattie to be driven to the station by the hired man, Ethan told her that he would do it.

At about four o'clock they set out in the sleigh. Ethan took a roundabout way, revisiting the spots that were familiar to them. Where would she go? What would she do? he asked her. She did not know exactly. But she finally told him how long she had loved him, and as six o'clock drew close, they found it harder and harder to part. At the top of the local coasting hill, Ethan stopped the sleigh. In the distance they could see the huge elm tree which the coasters had to swerve by at the foot of the hill. Suddenly Mattie asked him to coast with her down the hill. Ethan found a sled among the trees, and after the first ride, Mattie begged him for one more, and this time she asked him not to miss the elm tree.

Down they went for the last ride. As they neared the bottom, Mattie urged him once more. The tree loomed before him; Ethan twisted the runners—there was a sickening crash. . . .

Twenty years later a stranger, who had learned something of the story of Ethan Frome, was forced in a heavy snowstorm to ask Ethan for overnight shelter at the Frome farm. In the kitchen of the house he saw a tall, angular woman who waited on Ethan's needs; sitting in a chair was a younger woman, badly crippled, with feverishly bright eyes. She could move her head, and that was all. The stranger knew that Ethan Frome had lived thus with Zeena and Mattie Silver for twenty years. The people of Starkfield were loath to discuss the tragedy, but it was the opinion of many that Ethan had suffered the most.

French Novels

Père Goriot

By HONORÉ DE BALZAC

HONORÉ DE BALZAC, *born May 20, 1799, at Tours, France, knew little but hard work and poverty until he won notice in 1829 for his realistic writings. A prodigious eater, drinker, and worker, he labored hard to meet a great volume of debts, eventually producing 96 novels. Attempting various business schemes, he collected only new debts. After a long affair with the Polish Countess Eveline Hanska, he at last married her only a few months before he died in Paris on Aug. 18, 1850, worn out from having produced enough literature to have kept five men busy for a lifetime.*

MADAME VAUQUER for forty years has kept a middle-class boarding house in the Rue Neuve Sainte-Geneviève, between the Latin Quarter and the Faubourg Saint Marcel in Paris. Scandal has never attacked the establishment's moral principles. For more than thirty years no young woman has been seen in the house, but in 1819, when this drama begins, a poor young girl was living there.

The ground floor of the Maison Vauquer consists of a depressing parlor which has a boarding-house odor, yet is elegant compared with the dining room which adjoins. In this room Madame

283

Vauquer appears at seven each morning, a front of false hair hanging under her tulle cap, her hand small and fat, her bust too full and tremulous.

At this date there were seven boarders in the house. On the first floor lived Madame Vauquer, and Madame Couture, widow of an army paymaster who had with her a very young girl named Victorine Taillefer. Her simple dress betrayed her youthful form; she was happy, and might have been beautiful if love had given sparkle to her eyes. Her father doubted her paternity, and had cut her off with 600 francs a year, making his only son the heir to his millions. Madame Couture, a distant relative, had brought up Victorine as her daughter.

On the second floor lived an old gentleman named Poiret, a pensioned government functionary, and a man about forty who wore a black wig, dyed his whiskers, and said that he was a retired merchant named Monsieur Vautrin. On the third story, with its four single rooms, were: an old maid, Mademoiselle Michonneau; an aged former manufacturer of vermicelli, who allowed himself to be called Old Goriot; a medical student known as Bianchon; and a law student named Eugène de Rastignac.

De Rastignac, eldest son of a poor southern baron, had black hair, blue eyes, and a manner and figure that displayed his aristocratic education. Vautrin, despite his invariable breezy cheerfulness, at times had a steely expression which inspired fear; no one could divine his real business.

In this house, as in the world at large, there was a patient butt for mocking pleasantries. This was Goriot. Six years before, retired from business, he had come to live there, dressed handsomely and flourishing a gold watch. Among his articles were a silver dish and porringer which, he explained, "my wife gave to me on the first anniversary of our wedding day. I would rather scratch the ground with my nails for a living than part with that porringer. But I have on the shelf, as the saying is, plenty of baked bread for a long time to come."

After a year Goriot began to practice little economies, and after two years he removed to the second floor and did without a fire, although his name was on the list of state funds for an income of over 8,000 francs. When two young ladies in the most fashionable attire visited him in a semi-stealthy manner, the boarders were sure he was a libertine. Challenged on this, Goriot meekly declared they were his daughters, though he never disclosed that they visited him only to wheedle money from him.

The years passed, and with the gentle docility of a broken spirit Goriot moved to the third floor, curtailed his expenditures, grew thin and gaunt, and at the end of the fourth year was a worn-out septuagenarian, stupid and vacillating, his clothing shabby, his gold and jewels vanished.

Eugène de Rastignac wanted to enter the aristocratic society of Paris. He obtained an introduction to the Vicomtesse de Beauséant, relative of an aunt of his, and was invited to a ball. Deserted by her lover, the vicomtesse became interested in him and stood sponsor for him in society. Eugène met the Duchesse de Langeais, who told him the history of Père Goriot.

Goriot was a flour and vermicelli merchant during the Revolution, and made a fortune by selling his goods for 10 times what they cost him. His only passion was his daughters; by giving each a dowry of 800,000 francs, he married the elder, Anastasie, to the Count de Restaud, and the younger, Delphine, to the Baron de Nucingen, a German financier. Then the old man saw that his children were ashamed of him, and he made the sacrifice of banishing himself from their homes.

The duchesse did not reveal that Anastasie had a dissolute lover, and had induced Père Goriot to give her 200,000 francs, almost all he had left, to pay her lover's gambling debts.

Returning from a ball, Eugène saw Goriot twisting his silver dish and porringer into a lump, and next morning they were sold so that Anastasie could redeem a note. "Old Goriot is sublime," Eugène muttered when he heard of this.

Delphine also had an admirer by whom she expected to be introduced into the exclusive society which barred her German husband; she visited the gambling dens to seek the money which her father could no longer supply.

Meantime Eugène's family stripped itself so that he might have 1,200 francs to keep up his position in society. One day Vautrin saw the student with Victorine, and later took him aside. He told Eugène that he would help him get Victorine as a bride, with a dowry of a million francs, if Eugène was willing to pay 200,000 francs. This he would do by having a friend, an army colonel, pick a quarrel with her brother Frederic, the heir, and kill him in a duel. Eugène indignantly refused.

A few days later it was learned that the police suspected Vautrin to be a dangerous escaped convict named Trompe-le-Mort. Given a drug by trickery, the boarder was exposed and arrested, just as word came that Frederic had been killed in a duel anyway, and that Victorine was the sole heir to her father's millions.

Instead of marrying her now, Rastignac began an intrigue with Delphine; and Père Goriot encouraged them, spending his last 10,000 francs to furnish an apartment for them, so that he could see his daughter daily.

The vicomtesse, Eugène's first patroness, gave a ball to celebrate the marriage of a lover; and Anastasie, among those invited, sent to her father for money to redeem the Restaud family diamonds, which she had pawned. Goriot rose from a sickbed to sell his last forks and spoons, and pledge his annuity for a loan. Delphine also received an invitation, through Rastignac.

As they danced, Père Goriot was sick unto death in his cold garret. A messenger was sent to the ball, to tell the sisters that their father wanted "to kiss them before I die." "To die is not to see them there, where I am going," the old man told Eugène. The messenger returned with word that the daughters refused to come; Delphine was too tired and sleepy; Anastasie was busy quarreling with her husband.

In a semi-delirium, Goriot alternately blamed his daughters and pardoned their behavior: "My daughters were my vice—my mistresses. I am justly punished; I have spoiled them. Are they coming? Am I to die like a dog? They are wicked; they are criminal." Then, saying: "Ah, my angels!" he sank back on the pillow and breathed his last.

Anastasie did come, but too late. She kissed her father's hand and said, "Forgive me."

Goriot had a pauper's funeral; the aristocratic sons-in-law refused to pay the expenses. The law student and the medical student scraped together the money, but only Eugène and a servant mourned at the burial. A short prayer was all that Eugène could pay for.

Eugène went to a high place and surveyed the part of the city where lives the world of fashion. "Now there is relentless war between us," he muttered bitterly, and went off to dine with Delphine.

Eugénie Grandet

By HONORÉ DE BALZAC

IN THE OLD-FASHIONED TOWN OF SAUMUR, whose prosperity depends on the vineyards of its district, lived M. Grandet, whose large house once was the residence of nobility. A master cooper in 1789, and a good man of business, M. Grandet prospered in the Revolution, bought up confiscated church lands, married the daughter of a wealthy timber merchant, and became mayor under the Consulate and Monsieur Grandet under the Empire. And every year he grew wealthier and more miserly.

In 1817 M. Grandet was 68, his wife 47, and their only child, Eugénie, was 21. He cultivated 100 acres of vineyard, owned 13 farms and an old abbey, and had 127 acres of grazing land. The town estimated his income at five or six million francs, but the only people in a position to guess accurately were M. Cruchot, the notary, and M. des Grassins, the banker.

There was rivalry between these two families for the hand of Eugénie. The Cruchot hopes were centered on the notary's nephew, M. Cruchot de Bonfons, a rising lawyer who at 33 was a president of the court of first instance. Mme. des Grassins was equally hopeful on behalf of her son Adolphe. The whole town watched the struggle between these two families, though some declared M. Grandet was rich enough to marry his daughter to a peer.

With all his wealth, M. Grandet lived as meanly as he could. His house was cold, his table was supplied with poultry, butter and corn by his tenants, and he never had guests for dinner. One strong servant, Nanon, who had worked 28 years for the Gran-dets, did all the work of the house and watched her master's interests with fidelity. In the evening she joined the family in the sitting-room, where only a single candle was allowed. Every morning M. Grandet doled out the bread, sugar and other pro-visions for the day.

As for Mme. Grandet, her gentleness was no match for her husband. Although she had brought more than 300,000 francs as her dowry, she had only an occasional six francs for pocket money, and the four or five louis which M. Grandet collected above the regular price from the Belgian merchants who bought his wine. Too mild to revolt, Mme. Grandet was too proud to ask an extra sou from her husband. As a result she hardly left the house except to go to church, and always wore the same dress. But M. Grandet never considered that his wife might suffer; it was satis-factory to him that no one tried to cross him.

Eugénie, whose company was her mother's only solace besides religion, had five francs a month for a dress allowance. On her birthday and her saint's day her father would give Eugénie a gold piece, but they were to be kept, not spent.

On Eugénie's twenty-third birthday, in November, 1819, the Cruchots and des Grassins paid their respects to the heiress. The

Cruchots brought flowers, but the des Grassins eclipsed them with a showy workbox. M. Grandet understood that both families were after Eugénie's fortune, and made up his mind that neither should have her.

Suddenly a heavy knock was heard at the front door. A good-looking, fashionably-dressed young man was admitted. He was Charles Grandet, the son of M. Grandet's brother, a merchant in Paris. Charles brought a great number of trunks, and a letter for his uncle.

Charles' father had sent him to visit in Saumur. A dandy who already had had an affair with a great lady he called Annette, he was a vain, selfish youth who was contemptuous of these provincials. But Eugénie thought him a perfect gentleman, and did all she could to make him comfortable.

The next day the young Parisian, reared in luxury, learned that the letter he had delivered told of his father's business failure. Victor Grandet had written to his brother that the default of his broker and notary had left him owing nearly four million francs, against assets of only a quarter of that sum. "You can be a father to my unhappy child," the brother had written. Without glossing the facts, M. Grandet showed Charles a paragraph in the papers referring to the ruin and suicide of his father.

Charles had had no inkling of the truth. For the moment his penniless state was nothing to the youth; the loss of his father was his only grief. In a day or two, Charles had strength to face the situation. The Grandet women were full of sympathy, and Eugénie fell in love with him. One day Eugénie saw a letter from Charles to Annette in which he said that he needed money. She gave him her whole stock of gold coins, worth six thousand francs, and in return he gave her a small leather box containing portraits of his parents, set in gold.

Selling his finery, Charles waited at Saumur for the sailing of a ship which would take him from Nantes to the Indies, where he intended to seek his fortune. In those weeks came Eugénie's springtime of love, while Charles became aware of her purity and kindness. One morning they met at the foot of the staircase, and Eugénie told Charles she loved him and would wait for him. He kissed her, and said: "A cousin is better than a brother; he can marry you."

The house seemed empty to Eugénie when Charles was gone.

M. Grandet saved his brother's estate from bankruptcy, but refused to make up the deficit—still 1,200,000 francs after five years. M. des Grassins and his son Adolphe went to Paris to handle the negotiations, and stayed there, both gaining unpleasant reputations for their love affairs.

Meantime old Grandet had discovered that Eugénie's gold was gone, and when she refused any explanation, merely saying, "The money was mine," he made her a prisoner in her own room. This lasted six months, and Mme. Grandet, whose character had grown stronger, supported her daughter. But the mother was ill and grew weaker. Finally M. Grandet, fearing that his daughter would demand her mother's share of the estate if Mme. Grandet died, decided to attempt a reconciliation. He burst into the room where the women were, then caught sight of the portrait case. About to wrench off the gold, he was not deterred when Eugénie cried: "It is a sacred trust!" But when she threatened to stab herself with a knife, he was frightened, tried to make it up with his wife, and even promised Eugénie that she could marry her cousin.

Mme. Grandet died in October, and Eugénie renounced her mother's share of the family fortune in exchange for 100 francs a month while her father lived. He survived seven more years, and on his deathbed his eyes kindled at the sight of the priest's sacred vessels of silver. His brother's creditors were still unpaid.

Eugénie learned that she had 17,000,000 francs. Her heart was still faithful to her cousin, who had never written to her. The poor heiress was very lonely, and paid no attention to Magistrate Cruchot, who still hoped to marry her. She gave away enormous sums in charity; her only treasure was the portrait box.

Meantime Charles, who had become known as Carl Shepherd,

had become wealthy. An active slave trader, he soon forgot his love for Eugénie, who became merely a person to whom he owed 6,000 francs. Returning to Paris in 1827 with a fortune of 1,900,000 francs, he decided to marry Mlle. d'Aubrion, daughter of an impoverished aristocratic family, with the expectation that he could thereby obtain a title for himself.

Des Grassins, anxious to collect something for all his troubles, asked Charles for 300,000 francs to pay the last of his father's debts. When Charles coolly refused, des Grassins wrote to his wife that he would yet make the dead Grandet a bankrupt, and thereby stop the marriage. Eugénie saw the letter, but she had already heard from Charles. He had sent her 8,000 francs, asked for the portrait case, and casually mentioned his forthcoming marriage. This was the shipwreck of all Eugénie's hopes.

Eugénie told M. Cruchot de Bonfons, the magistrate, that she would marry him if he would claim none of the rights of marriage, and would pay all of her uncle's creditors in full. Only too glad, the magistrate set out for Paris with Eugénie's check for 1,500,000 francs. Charles was astonished to hear of the forthcoming marriage, and dumfounded to hear that Eugénie had 17,000,000 francs.

But the payment of the debts removed an impediment to Charles' marriage.

Now the magistrate, who had changed his name to M. de Bonfons, married Eugénie and shortly afterward was made councillor to the Court Royal at Angers. He dreamed of higher honors, perhaps a peerage, but within three years he died.

Mme. de Bonfons lived on, a pale and beautiful woman, in the cold old house. Spending little on herself, she gave large sums to the needy. But she remained very lonely. She dwelled in the world, but was not of it.

Sapho

By ALPHONSE DAUDET

ALPHONSE DAUDET *was born in Nimes, France, on May 13, 1840, the son of a silk manufacturer. He was educated at the Lyons Lycée, and from the first his interest lay in literature and the arts. He became estranged from his family in early youth and, after supporting himself as a tutor at Alais, emigrated to Paris in 1857. He gained some success as a versifier and managed to make a living by journalism and through the production of several plays. But his real success was as a novelist and with the appearance of* Sapho *in 1884 he found his true place in French letters. His marriage to Julia Allard was a very happy one. He died in Paris on December 16, 1897.*

IT WAS at a masquerade party in the bohemian Paris atmosphere of the demi-monde that young Jean Gaussin first met Fanny Legrand. No two people could have been more unlike in temperament and background than these two, and yet from the first there was strange fascination between them. Jean, scion of an upright bourgeois family, the Gaussins d'Armandy, had left his family estates to study for the consular service in Paris; Fanny, nearly twenty years the boy's senior, a courtesan by profession, a dilettante by avocation, could trace her career to the fact that she was born illegitimate and poor. Her beauty and wit had opened the doors of the unconventional literati to her. She counted her past lovers by the score.

It was the woman who, attracted by Jean's youth and good looks, made the first advances. After the masquerade Fanny accompanied Jean to his apartments. She remained with him two days, and when she had departed the young man returned to his studies with little more than an exciting memory of the short liaison. But Fanny soon returned to him, and their assignations became more and more frequent. Finally Fanny persuaded Jean to pass a night at her apartment. The next day the young man was appalled to overhear a violent scene between Fanny and her former lover, whose money still provided for her. The cast-off lover pleaded piteously for his mistress' return, but by now Fanny was hopelessly infatuated with Jean. Jean was revolted by the thought that another man was supporting his beloved, and Fanny immediately gave up her luxuriant little home and turned to Jean for maintenance.

Jean allowed himself to be convinced by Fanny that they two should set up a home together. At first the young man found the ménage quite pleasant—after spending the day with his consular duties and studies he would return to a charming dinner for two prepared by his beautiful mistress.

But Fanny's past commenced to haunt Jean. And one day he was present at a meeting between two artists high in Parisian intellectual circles, and their conversation was a discussion of Fanny's career as a kept woman. Unaware of Jean's relationship to Fanny, these two men of the world were only too willing to boast that Fanny had been mistress to each of them. With relish and in great detail they described Fanny Legrand's past amours. One of her affairs had been a cause célèbre in Parisian society—an engraver, Flamant by name, had loved Fanny madly and, fearing to lose her because of his poverty, he had counterfeited banknotes. His detection and arrest were almost immediate and he was sentenced to ten years' penal servitude. Fanny stuck loyally by her lover and, although her innocence of any complicity was established, she received a sentence of six months at a house of correction.

Jean was sick and horrified at this recital. When it was divulged to him that Fanny had sat for the famous nude statue, Sapho, and indeed was known as Sapho in the circles of the intelligentsia, his revulsion was complete. Mad with jealousy, Jean confronted Fanny with his new knowledge; she placated him by destroying every souvenir of her former liaisons. The affair continued but now Jean felt only a sick fascination for the woman whose love, he felt, degraded him.

It was the desire to end the affair as well as genuine homesickness that sent Jean back to his father's estates. But even the home he loved could not cleanse his mind; his former joys, even his love for a favorite aunt, became tainted and evil; his every action mirrored the life that Fanny represented. Finally a sudden decline in the family fortunes gave him the opportunity he had long sought. He informed Fanny by letter that all must be over between them, since he could no longer afford to maintain her.

Four or five days of silence passed and then came "Sapho's" answer. Instead of preparing to leave Jean consequent to the financial reverse, she wrote, she had given up their home and found employment as the manager of a lodging-house. She would have Sundays to herself and she would see Jean then.

Jean accepted her decision as the middle course which would lead to the eventual rupture, and returned to Paris and his mistress.

From the very first the new situation was a source of unhappiness. They had little time together; then, too, Fanny's employer was a former courtesan, and Jean could not control his jealous fear that Fanny might return to her former associates. So Jean finally suggested that they once more set up an establishment together. Fanny joyously assented, and they found a cottage in the country.

Their new tranquillity was short-lived. Jean's old jealousy and inward contempt for himself and his mistress returned. Fanny adopted a little boy, Josaph, a wild and untractable lad whom Jean suspected of being Fanny's child by a former liaison. Quarrels between Jean and Fanny became more frequent, and only the fear of Fanny's harming herself should he abandon her kept Jean from breaking off the affair.

But the final straw was not long in appearing. Jean fell madly in love with Irene Bouchereau, a well-born and innocent young girl, and it soon became obvious not only that Irene returned his passion, but also that her family approved the match. The young man finally told Fanny that their affair was ended and that he must leave her.

After the first outburst Fanny was reconciled to Jean's departure, and for some weeks the young man heard nothing of his former mistress outside of the piteous letters she sent him. But Jean soon learned that Fanny's old love, the forger Flamant, had been released from prison and had gone immediately to Fanny's home. Mad with jealousy, Jean went to Fanny. Upon hearing his wild outburst, the woman knew that he was once more hers.

Jean now realized that he could never be free of Fanny. Released from his engagement, disowned by his family, he prepared to lead an exile's life with his mistress in the consular service at a far-off colony. But at the last minute his release was effected by the woman herself—instead of appearing on board the ship, Fanny sent her lover a note to inform him that all was ended between them, that she had decided to stay and become the wife of her former lover, Flamant.

The Three Musketeers

By ALEXANDRE DUMAS

ALEXANDRE DUMAS *was born in Aisne, France, of octoroon parentage, on July 24, 1802. The early part of his life was spent in modest circumstances. Then he found success as a writer, producing great numbers of books and soon amassing a huge fortune upon which he lived extravagantly until it was dissipated. He legitimized the son of a liaison with Marie Catherine Labay and named the boy for himself. Dumas founded the Théatre Historique. He was of marked republican tendencies. On December 5, 1870, he died.*

WHEN D'Artagnan, a very young Gascon gentleman, set out for Paris his possessions numbered only the recipe for a miraculous wound-salve, an ancient horse, and a letter of recommendation from his father to M. de Treville, captain of the King's Musketeers. By the time D'Artagnan reached Paris he had sold the horse and lost the letter in a brawl. Nevertheless M. de Treville recalled D'Artagnan the elder, and was kind to the son for the sake of the father.

To D'Artagnan's disappointment, he learned that he could not immediately become a member of the famous and privileged regiment known as the King's Musketeers. While waiting on M. de Treville, D'Artagnan tactlessly insulted three musketeers, who challenged him to duel the next day at the hours of twelve, one, and two, respectively.

Resigned to the expectancy of death at the hands of his third antagonist if he should be so fortunate as to survive the first two engagements, D'Artagnan arrived at the appointed place and was surprised to find that his two later antagonists were present as seconds to the first gentleman who had challenged him. The three musketeers were greatly impressed by the young Gascon's courage. The gentlemen prepared for the first engagement, but were interrupted by a party of the Cardinal's Guards who warned them of a recent edict against dueling. The three musketeers drew on the company of guards and D'Artagnan joined them. The four were easily triumphant and after mutual felicitations, Athos, Porthos and Aramis—for as such were the three musketeers known—accepted D'Artagnan into their ranks.

The names these gentlemen called themselves were obviously pseudonyms, and although D'Artagnan soon became inseparable friends with them it was a long time before the Gascon youth learned the secrets of melancholy misanthropic Athos, lusty, boastful Porthos, or Aramis, who was of a religious turn of mind, but was nevertheless the lover of a lady very high in the nobility.

D'Artagnan found place in a lesser regiment and set up a small apartment in the establishment of M. Bonacieux, a rich and elderly retired mercer, whose young and beautiful wife, Constance, was a member of the Queen's household. Since all three of his friends had valets (each chose his man to match his own personality— hence Athos kept silent Grimaud; Porthos, handsome Mousqueton; Aramis, religious Bazin), D'Artagnan too employed a servant, the shrewd and plucky Planchet.

It was not long before D'Artagnan found that the rivalry between the King's Musketeers and the Cardinal's Guard reflected the feeling between the masters of both. Cardinal Richelieu was the strongest man in the kingdom and Louis XIII hated him, feared him, and was completely under his influence. And Richelieu was an enemy of the Queen, beautiful Anne of Austria, whom the cardinal could never forgive for not returning the passion she inspired in him. It was known in court circles that the Duke of Buckingham, an Englishman and favorite of the English King Charles I, loved the Queen also and that, though faithful to her duty to the King she detested, Anne of Austria was not entirely cold to the handsome Duke.

One day D'Artagnan, alone at his home, was attracted by cries for help from the apartment above; seizing his sword, he ran to the rescue and was able to save from abduction Constance Bonacieux, the lovely young wife of his aged landlord. D'Artagnan's capitulation to the lady's charms was immediate. Aware that she was involved in some dangerous intrigue, he constituted himself her protector and became party to a rendezvous between the Duke of Buckingham and the Queen. At this tryst Anne of Austria presented to the Duke a casket containing twelve diamond studs which the Duke carried home with him to his castle in England. But Richelieu, well informed of all that had passed, prevailed upon the King to hold a fete and ask the Queen to be present wearing her diamond studs!

With the fete little more than a week away, the Queen felt that she was lost. But Constance Bonacieux sent D'Artagnan to England with a message for the Duke. The three musketeers accompanied their friend, and though many attacks were made on the group and Athos, Porthos, and Aramis were one by one downed, D'Artagnan was able to reach England and return with the diamond studs in time to save the Queen's honor. His rewards were a diamond ring from the Queen and the promise of a rendezvous from his beloved Constance. But when he reached the appointed trysting place, what was D'Artagnan's horror to find that his mistress had been kidnaped!

One of the most dangerous of the Cardinal's spies was a beautiful blonde woman known as Milady, sister-in-law to a British noble, Lord de Winter. D'Artagnan, convinced that this woman knew of Constance's whereabouts, set about to pay court to her. Such were Milady's charms that the young man became infatuated with her. But he soon realized her depravity. By a ring she had given D'Artagnan, who dishonorably entered her bedroom in the guise of her lover, Athos recognized Milady as the woman who had ruined his life—a woman who had been his wife until he discovered that she was a prostitute and a criminal. Just now Milady was in the employ of the Cardinal and was plotting to assassinate the Duke of Buckingham.

Although Buckingham was an Englishman and an enemy, the three musketeers and D'Artagnan were determined to save him. A message from them reached Lord de Winter and he held his wicked sister-in-law captive till she might be deported. But the woman seduced her young jailer, Lieutenant Felton, and persuaded him to attack the Duke. Buckingham soon died of the wounds he sustained, and although Felton was apprehended Milady escaped to France. The musketeers pursued and finally caught her—but not before she had reached the convent where Constance had found refuge. She filled the young woman's glass with poison, and D'Artagnan arrived only in time to kiss his dying mistress good-by. The musketeers and de Winter held their own court. Milady was declared guilty and was executed. The musketeers returned to Paris, where D'Artagnan received an officer's commission and the feud between King and Cardinal was resumed.

The Count of Monte Cristo

By ALEXANDRE DUMAS

ON THE 28TH OF FEBRUARY, 1815, the three-master *Pharaon* put into Marseilles under command of Edmond Dantes, her 19-year-old first mate. When M. Morrel, the owner, heard that the old captain had died at sea, he promised the post to Edmond, who went off gaily to see his father and his beloved, the Catalan girl Mercedes. Meantime Danglars, the supercargo, an offensive man of 26 who disliked Dantes, was informing M. Morrel that Edmond had stopped at the Isle of Elba on the voyage. The shipowner learned from Edmond that Captain Leclere had given him a packet to be delivered to Marshal Bertrand of Napoleon's staff. But Edmond said nothing of a letter which the marshal had given him to carry to Paris.

Edmond found that his father had lived on almost nothing for three months, having paid the tailor Caderousse some money which Dantes owed. The youth then hurried to the beautiful Mercedes, whom he found with her cousin Fernand Mondego, a 21-year-old fisherman. Fernand also loved the girl, and he glowered angrily at Edmond.

While Edmond and Mercedes made hurried preparations for their marriage, Fernand and Danglars plotted together. They wrote an anonymous letter to Gerard de Villefort, the deputy procureur de roi, saying that Dantes was carrying a letter from Napoleon to the Bonapartists in Paris. The drunken Caderousse watched uncomprehending as the letter was written. Thus it was that Dantes was arrested at his wedding-feast and, though he knew nothing of politics or of the contents of the letter with which he had been entrusted, was thrown into the island prison of the Château d'If, in the harbor of Marseilles. Dantes was amazed at Villefort's change of heart, for the procureur had seemed sympathetic until he learned that the letter was addressed to one M. Noirtier in Paris. In fact, the addressee was Villefort's father and the letter spoke of Napoleon's plan to escape from Elba. Thus Villefort protected his family by having Dantes imprisoned as rapidly as possible, and built his own fortunes by hurrying to Paris to warn Louis XVIII.

Hurled into a dungeon as a political prisoner without trial, cut off from his beloved, his father and his friends, who did not know whither he had been sent, Dantes fell into deep despair. Even during the Hundred Days, Villefort had managed to keep his secret, and with the restoration Dantes' last chance was gone. He became merely "No. 34." He prayed, he raged, and after he had been four years in his dark, solitary cell he began to starve himself.

Then one day Dantes heard a scratching in the wall. It was another prisoner, the Italian Abbé Faria, No. 27, who had dug for two years to make a fifty-foot tunnel, but had miscalculated so that he emerged in Edmond's cell instead of the outer wall. Edmond found a new father in this elderly man, who had made himself tools from the furniture of his cell, who had transformed a shirt and fish-bones into writing material, and who was tremendously learned.

The Abbé, more wise than Edmond in worldly matters, heard his story and quickly divined the plot which had mystified the youth. Now Dantes had a motive for life—vengeance. He resolved to win his freedom, and to seek out Danglars, Fernand and Villefort. While he and the Abbé planned a new tunnel, Edmond learned German, Spanish, Italian, English. history, chemistry, mathematics—all the varied knowledge that his scholarly fellow-prisoner could impart.

Years passed, and they were ready to attempt their escape, when the Abbé was seized with a fit that paralyzed one side. Edmond vowed not to leave him, and in return the Abbé revealed his great secret, which had made his jailers think him mad when he offered tremendous bribes. As secretary to Cardinal Spada, Faria had discovered the secret of the tremendous fortune which an earlier cardinal of the same name had hidden when invited to dine with the Borgias. The Abbé had never had an opportunity to go to the rocky little island of Monte Cristo where the thirteen million livres of gold and jewels were buried.

A new attack killed the Abbé. Dantes removed his body from the burial sack and put himself in its place. Dantes was prepared to dig his way out of a grave—but the Château d'If's cemetery was the sea. Edmond cut himself free with his knife and swam to a near-by island. The next day he was picked up by a smugglers' boat bound for Leghorn. It was 1829, fourteen years to the day since Edmond's arrest. He had gone into prison a light-hearted boy; he emerged a man of 33, strong of body, pallid of face, deeply learned, and with an implacable vengeance to exact.

Dantes found his treasure in the grottos of Monte Cristo, then went on to Marseilles. Unrecognized, he learned that his father had died of hunger soon after he was taken away. Mercedes had disappeared. Calling himself the Abbé Busoni, Dantes sought out Caderousse and learned that his dear patron, M. Morrel, was near bankruptcy. But Danglars had made a fortune in the French war with Spain, had married a rich wife and then one high in society, and now was a millionaire banker in Paris with the title of baron. He had one daughter, Eugénie. Fernand, the Catalan, had won honors as a soldier in the same war, then served with the Greeks in their war of independence, and returned to Paris with a fortune as the Comte de Morcerf. Eighteen months after Dantes' arrest, Mercedes had married Fernand. They had a son, known as the Vicomte Albert. As for Villefort, he was now procureur de roi in

Paris, in as high a station as the other two. By his first wife he had a daughter Valentine.

Then Dantes, in the guise of a clerk of the English banking house of Thomson and French, bought up all the securities outstanding against M. Morrel. The good merchant had had word of the loss of his last ship, the *Pharaon*. September fifth was near, the day on which he must pay his bills; Danglars, the last resource, had refused a loan to his old employer. Morrel's children, Maximilian and Julie, feared that he would kill himself. But at the last moment a receipted bill for his debts was delivered to Morrel. And a new *Pharaon,* loaded with a rich cargo, sailed into the harbor with M. Morrel's name on it.

Dantes had rewarded his friend, but it was not until 1838 that he set about his revenge. Now known as the Count of Monte Cristo, he befriended Albert de Morcerf during the Carnival at Rome. The Count lived in magnificence and mystery; none knew from what country came this dark-bearded, grim man who seemed familiar with all lands. In his entourage were a beautiful Greek girl known as Haydee, and a giant mute Nubian called Ali, who owed his life to the Count. The smugglers of the Mediterranean and the bandits of Rome were at the service of Monte Cristo; indeed, it was through the rescue of Albert after the bandit Luigi Vampa had kidnaped him that the Count won his introduction to Paris society three months later.

When the Count reached Paris, Albert's father was negotiating for his marriage to Eugénie Danglars. Albert introduced the Count to Morcerf and Mercedes, who voiced their thanks for the rescue of their son. But Mercedes seemed greatly shaken by the meeting, and had to retire. The ex-Fernand, now active in politics, offered to show the Count the Paris world of government.

Next the Count visited Danglars, who was still tremendously wealthy and whom he astounded by opening an unlimited credit and talking of a million livres as pocket money. Monte Cristo immediately put the Baroness Danglars under obligation to him by buying her spirited horses from the banker at a fantastic price, then returning them as a gift. The Count followed this by having Ali rescue Villefort's second wife and little son when these same horses ran away with their carriage—and thus he became a benefactor to the Villeforts, too. By skillful manipulation, Villefort had made his magistracy into a place of power.

These feats made Monte Cristo the most-talked-about man in Paris, and his magnificent style of living added to the wonder with which he was greeted. He had found his three enemies holding high positions. M. Morrel's children—their father was dead—also were in Paris, and by contrast lived in comfortable simplicity. Maximilian was in love with Valentine de Villefort; Julie was happily married. Valentine was the gentle nurse of her grandfather, M. Noirtier de Villefort, who was now a helpless paralytic.

Haydee was the daughter of Ali Pacha, the leader of the Albanian troops against the Turks. At the opera one night she saw Morcerf, and revealed to Monte Cristo that Fernand, who boasted of having served the Pacha, was the man who had betrayed her father to the Turks at a price, and then sold her into slavery—for it was thus that Fernand had made his fortune.

Now Monte Cristo began his campaign. First he cost Danglars seven hundred thousand livres by tampering with the semaphore telegraph signals from Spain. Then he shook Villefort and Mme. Danglars by taking them to a house in whose yard the procureur once had buried the illegitimate child she had borne to him. Then a correspondent of Danglars disappeared owing him a million livres, through the Count's contrivance. Meantime Villefort, disturbed by Monte Cristo's knowledge of an affair which he had thought secret, investigated but could learn nothing about the Count.

The Count aimed his first blow at Morcerf by letting his son Albert hear the story of the Pacha's betrayal from Haydee's lips, and then arranging to have the treachery hinted at in the journal of Albert's friend Beauchamp—in both cases without any definite mention of names. It was with difficulty that Albert was restrained from challenging the editor to a duel.

The first of his enemies to die was a minor one, Caderousse. Dantes actually had helped the tailor anonymously, but each time cupidity and drunkenness had dragged him down again. Now, not realizing who the Count was, Caderousse tried to rob his house and was killed outside by one Benedetto, a former galley-companion whom the tailor had been blackmailing. Caderousse had been able to do this because the Count had hired Benedetto to pose as a wealthy young Italian nobleman named Prince Cavalcanti. Eager for Eugénie Danglars' rich dowry, Benedetto had been glad to pay court to her and win her hand from Danglars—who was just as eager to wed his daughter to a rich Italian instead of to Albert, whose father's origin was well-known to Danglars.

Meantime Beauchamp had investigated the story about Morcerf and found it to be true; but he suppressed it from friendship for Albert. Soon, however, another paper printed the story, this time naming the Comte. The honor of the Chamber of Peers was at stake; an examination was proposed, and Morcerf had to agree to submit to it. Haydee appeared as witness against him, and the verdict was: "Convicted of felony, treason and outrage." Albert guessed who it was who had exposed his father's disgrace; he challenged the Count to a duel. And that same night Mercedes, the only one who had penetrated Monte Cristo's disguise, went to him, called him "Edmond," and won his promise to spare her son's life. Prepared to die himself, Dantes went to the dueling ground—and received Albert's apology! Mercedes had told her son the story of Edmond. Then Mercedes and her son went away, taking not a franc with them, to begin life anew. Morcerf, going to challenge the Count himself, learned that he was Edmond Dantes and staggered home to kill himself.

Danglars' fortune was vanishing. But his hope of retrieving it by Eugénie's marriage was dashed when Benedetto was revealed as the killer of Caderousse.

Meantime, in the home of Villefort there had been three deaths by poison. Valentine was suspected, then herself was stricken after learning that it was her young stepmother who was trying to kill all who stood between her son and the inheritance of the fortune that Valentine was to inherit. Villefort was crushed between his love of his daughter, his suspicion of his wife, and the ignominy of four deaths by poison in the home of the procureur de roi. Valentine was buried, and the Count was able to save Morrel from suicide only by revealing himself again as Dantes.

Villefort, having warned his wife that he would have her arrested unless she took poison herself, went to court for the examination of Benedetto. The assassin revealed himself to be that illegitimate child whom Villefort and Mme. Danglars had believed dead! Dantes had placed the proofs in Benedetto's hands. The haughty procureur, now totally broken in spirit, staggered home to forgive his wife and to flee. He found wife and son dead of poison. Distraught, he was confronted by Dantes, who revealed his identity yet again. The strain was too much; Villefort uttered a burst of laughter as his reason collapsed. And Edmond began to wonder whether he had the right to exact such vengeance.

Danglars, unable to meet his bills, had fled to Rome with five millions belonging to Paris' hospitals. There Luigi Vampa kidnaped him, and soon the Baron's embezzlements vanished. For in the bandit's caves a meal cost 100,000 livres, and a bottle of wine cost 25,000. But this enemy Dantes forgave. He disclosed his name for the last time, and let Danglars go, now white-haired, with 50,000 livres.

There remained Maximilian Morrel. Monte Cristo restored Valentine to him, for he had drugged her into a condition resembling death, then spirited her away from the grave. Then the Count sailed away with Haydee, with whom he had found the love that long years before had been denied to Edmond Dantes.

Camille

By ALEXANDRE DUMAS, FILS

ALEXANDRE DUMAS, FILS, *was born in Paris on the twenty-seventh of July, 1824, the natural son of Alexandre Dumas the elder and Marie Labay, a hardworking seamstress. He was later acknowledged by his distinguished sire, although the stigma of illegitimacy made his life at school unhappy. The father and son were the best of companions, but since they both lived prodigally the young man soon found himself in debt to the tune of $10,000. He turned to writing as a way out of his financial difficulties and in 1848 produced* Camille, *which later he dramatized. The younger Dumas achieved great wealth and the high respect of his literary compeers. He loved and protected his erratic father till the latter's death. Dumas fils was elected to the French Academy in 1874. He died November 27, 1895.*

THE SALE OF THE FURNITURE and personal effects of a notorious courtesan who had died wretchedly and in debt was the occasion for the gathering, in a certain house in the Rue d'Antin, of most of the scandal-mongers of fashionable Paris. But in the crowd of sensation-seekers there was one man at least whose presence could not be ascribed to such base motives. This was a literary gentleman who not only had a taste in curiosities, of which the late Mlle. Marguerite Gauthier had many, but who had also taken a sympathetic interest in the youth and beauty of this sad young woman whom he had seen only from afar. This gentleman purchased at the auction a copy of *Manon Lescaut.* When he opened the book he found that it was inscribed as follows:

Manon to Marguerite—Humility. It was signed Armand Duval.

The interest that this strange inscription aroused was further piqued a few days later when this gentleman received a visit from M. Armand Duval, a stranger to him. M. Duval was a young handsome gentleman whose courteous manner could not conceal the anxiety and grief that consumed him. His errand was the recovery of the volume of *Manon Lescaut*. Unnerved by the sympathy of his vis-à-vis who returned the book without question, the young man confided brokenly his love for the dead courtesan and his sorrow not only at her death but at the fact that he had not been at her side during her last hours. He produced a letter which Mlle. Gauthier had written him near the end of her life. In it she reaffirmed her love for him and expressed a wish that she might live only long enough to see him once more. But the hope was vain—she expired before he could reach her. Young M. Duval, overcome anew, took a rapid departure, leaving his sympathetic host wondering what the whole story of the young man's life with Mlle. Gauthier had been.

This literary gentleman continued to hear of the deceased Marguerite from acquaintances of his, several of whom had been her lovers. He learned that the girl had been superior to most women of her sort, intelligent, honest in her dealings, and possessed of none of the blatant vulgarity which characterized most of the Parisian courtesans. Curious as to the strength and sincerity of young Duval's grief, the gentleman paid a visit to Marguerite's grave in Montmartre Cemetery. He found her grave lovingly kept and covered with camellias—Marguerite's favorite flower. Haunted by the story the gentleman determined to learn the truth, and left a card at M. Duval's establishment. The young man replied that he was ill and invited a call. He was willing, eager, to speak of his loss. He was like a man crazed, and begged the interested gentleman to accompany him to the cemetery where he planned to disinter his erstwhile beloved before her reinterment in a different grave. Only thus, he declared, could he convince himself that Marguerite was dead. What he wished was done, but upon seeing the face of his mistress decaying and horrible, the young man sank into a brain fever. It was during his convalescence and gradual return to sanity that his new friend heard the sad story.

Armand had first seen Marguerite some years before. This tall very slender black-haired beauty, attired in white, and carrying a bouquet of her favorite camellias, stepped from her carriage into a shop. The impressionable young man saw her for but an instant, but her beauty burned itself on his brain forever and his every effort was bent toward gaining her acquaintance. Finally while attending a theater with a fashionable friend he caught sight of her in a box, and was able to secure an introduction. Her manner to him was indifferent, then amused and capricious and the young man retired in confusion with her laughter pursuing him. Not long after he learned that a complete breakdown in her health—she was dangerously consumptive—had forced her to retire to Bagneres for some months. While there an aged nobleman, a Duke, had been so struck by her resemblance to his daughter who had recently died that he, despite her notoriety, offered to maintain her in luxury.

Armand's passion did not abate. He followed and worshipped from a distance this beautiful creature; when she was ill he inquired daily for her at her home, although he did not again try to press his acquaintance on her. Finally he met her again through a friend of his who had taken him to the house of one Prudence Duvernoy, a courtesan-turned-milliner who despite the onslaught of middle age still occasionally reverted to her former calling. Marguerite called upon Prudence, her neighbor, to rescue her from the attentions of one Comte de N., an admirer who bored her. Her reception of the handsome Armand was this time kinder. Gaiety and wine induced one of Marguerite's consumptive attacks; the rest of the company ignored the episode but Armand begged the frail woman to take better care of herself. Strangely moved by this young man's sincerity, Marguerite responded to his kisses and tears by promising to be his mistress. But he must obey her implicitly and must make no demands on her.

The next night and the one following Armand spent in Marguerite's arms. Warring with his almost insane joy was the jealousy which attacked him when he saw her in her theater box with the Comte de G., one of her protectors. When the following night she pleaded illness, he knew that she was with her lover. His jealousy was boundless and he wrote her a bitter note and prepared to leave Paris. She replied; and, frantic, he wrote a penitent letter to her. She came to his apartments, and their reconciliation was complete.

Months of bliss followed. A day in the country convinced Marguerite that there they must live. She rented a house and soon she and her lover abandoned all discretion and lived openly together. The elderly Duke, incensed, withdrew his support, and secretly, for want of funds, Marguerite commenced to sell and pawn her possessions. When he discovered this, Armand was horrified and set about making over his small private fortune to her.

But the elder Duval learned of his son's liaison; first asked and then commanded him to break it off. Armand refused, but one day he returned from Paris and found his mistress gone. His distress when he received a letter from her saying she had gone to the rich Comte de N. was awful. After months of near-madness he returned to Paris, took himself another mistress, the beautiful and vulgar Olympe, and publicly insulted and flaunted the helpless and ill Marguerite. One night she came to beg him to cease his persecution and, the old passion reasserting itself, remained in his arms. But when he called the next day he learned that she was with Comte de N. Mad with jealousy, Armand sent Marguerite a five-hundred franc note with these words: "Here is the price of your night." Then he left the country.

It was at Alexandria that Armand learned that Marguerite was ill. He wrote, received her loving letter, and started at once for Paris. But it was too late. She, by the time he reached home, was at last free of the pain and loneliness of her last hours.

Marguerite had left a journal for Armand, that he might know

that her dying thoughts were of him. It was by reading this journal that Armand learned that his mistress had left him on the plea
of the elder Duval and for the young man's own sake. She died
in the church, comforted by her penitence and the memory of
having truly loved.

Madame Bovary

By GUSTAVE FLAUBERT

GUSTAVE FLAUBERT, *born in Rouen on Dec. 12, 1821, was the son of
a surgeon and grandson of a veterinary. A handsome boy, he decided early to be a writer, and devoted himself so completely to
his pen and to his widowed mother that he never married. Even
his mistress, Louise Colet, could not woo him from his hermit-
like existence at Croisset, near Rouen, where he settled down after
a few years in Paris. He died in 1880, weakened by overwork and
overindulgence in food and drink.*

CHARLES BOVARY, son of a retired officer and a merchant's daughter,
stumbled through school after a late start, and eventually won a
medical degree. A simple, bovine, good-natured man, he did not
protest when his mother married him off to a widow and sent him
off to practice at the village of Tostes.

The widow turned out to be ill-tempered, but Charles found
another interest when he was called to treat the broken leg of a
farmer named Rouault. Curing the leg was easy, but Rouault's
daughter Emma caught Charles' eye. Without consciousness of
wrong-doing, he was attracted by her black hair, brown eyes, her
full lips, her refined manner. Rouault had sent her to a convent
for her education.

Charles' problem was solved when his wife died shortly after a notary decamped with her money. In a few months Charles had proposed, and he married Emma as soon as he was out of mourning.

Charles was supremely happy with Emma at Tostes, finding pleasure in the merest glance at his bride. But she felt that marriage had not brought the rapture that she found described in books. She was a good housewife and helped manage Charles' affairs, but found him dull. Even the interruption of a visit to the château of the Marquis d'Andervilliers, who gave a ball to further his political ambitions, did not relieve her ennui, but merely increased her irritation at the cloddish Charles.

She became moody, careless and capricious, and developed a nervous illness. Charles decided on a change of air, and arranged to move his practice to the market town of Yonville-l'Abbaye, near Rouen. They left in the spring, with Emma pregnant.

At Yonville the Bovarys met Homais, the town chemist who read and philosophized a great deal, and had got into trouble for practicing medicine illegally. Homais had a roomer, Leon Dupuis, the notary's clerk, who found promptly that he and Emma had a common interest in music, poetry, and discussions of the dullness of small towns.

Emma soon was delivered of a girl whom she named Berthe, for whom she was somewhat lacking in affection, and whom she promptly put to nurse with the carpenter's wife. On one visit to the child she became weary from walking, and Leon helped her home. They became good friends, but the clerk's youth made him fearful of making advances, and both did much moping without overcoming their mutual diffidence.

Finally Leon went to Paris to complete his law studies, and Emma returned to her fretting. She went extravagantly into debt with Lheureux, the Yonville storekeeper, did some reading, quarreled with Charles' mother, toyed with religion.

Then Monsieur Rodolphe Boulanger, a dissipated, well-to-do bachelor, bought La Huchette, an estate near the town. Intelligent, cynical, and of brutal temperament, he resolved to have this doctor's wife as a diversion. He made love to her as they listened to the speeches at a Yonville agricultural show, was not seriously rebuffed, and followed up a few weeks later by winning Charles' consent to take Emma horseback riding for her health.

On that first ride into the woods Rodolphe played his hand cleverly, and a few minutes after he and Emma had dismounted to walk for a bit she had given herself up to him. He found her charming; she felt triumphant, without remorse. Thereafter they met daily and wrote to each other every evening.

Soon Emma was making frequent early morning visits to La Huchette, but she became more cautious when the tax collector surprised her as she was crossing the fields. Thereafter Emma and Rodolphe met late at night in the arbor at the foot of the garden, or in Charles' consulting room on rainy nights.

Against Rodolphe's worldliness, Charles seemed more stupid than ever, but Emma had a fit of remorse. When, at Homais' suggestion, Charles attempted an operation on the clubfoot of the town cripple, Emma decided perhaps he would at last make her proud of him. But the operation failed and Emma turned back to Rodolphe with renewed infatuation, all the while going deeper into secret debt for clothes for herself and gifts for Rodolphe.

Now she wanted to run away with Monsieur Boulanger; he agreed but put off the day. Finally he fled alone, not wanting to be encumbered with this woman of whom he was wearying. He sent her a farewell letter instead, and Emma fell into a long illness during which Charles went deeply into debt so that she might have everything. He had suspected nothing.

At last Emma recovered, and Charles took her to the opera at Rouen to give her a change of scene. There they met Leon, now in a law office after three years of study. The ex-clerk induced Bovary to let Emma stay over for another night of opera. Next day Emma and Leon talked long and ecstatically at her hotel room, and made an assignation for the following morning.

They met at the cathedral, got in a cab together—"It is done in Paris," Leon said—and rode about for hours with the blinds drawn. Emma missed the Yonville coach that evening, took a cab to catch up with it, and arrived home to learn that Charles' father had died, leaving some small property. At Lheureux' suggestion, Emma got Charles to agree to give her a power of attorney in his business matters, and she won consent to spend three days at Rouen to get Leon's advice.

Those three days were a honeymoon for Leon and Emma, but the separation that followed was intolerable to them. Then Emma decided to study music again, and induced Charles to let her go to Rouen once a week for lessons. She met Leon at a hotel, acted the aggressor in their affair, and charmed Leon by her beauty and her knowledge of the art of love.

But several times she was almost caught in the structure of lies she had built, and Lheureux, who had spied out her affair, forced her to sell the senior Bovary's farm and sign new notes for the money she had borrowed to finance her affair. The growing financial worries made Emma distraught, and Leon's love was running down as the novelty lessened. Emma found again in adultery all the platitudes which she had found in marriage. And Leon resolved to break off with her.

Finally the blow fell; a judgment was executed on one of her notes, and a bailiff was installed in the Bovary home, though she kept him away from Charles. Over the week end she tried to raise money, but Leon and the Rouen money-lenders could do nothing for her. She returned to Yonville to find her furniture listed publicly for sale.

Avoiding Charles, she took her appeal for a loan to the notary, and then to Rodolphe, who had returned to Yonville. The old love was gone; he refused her. In despair she staggered to Homais' shop, and seized and ate a handful of arsenic.

Charles, uncomprehending and overwhelmed by the sudden

crash of his fortunes, was unable to save her. She died in agony, and he was prostrated. Little by little Charles learned of her affairs. He became a recluse, and soon died in poverty.

Mademoiselle de Maupin

By THÉOPHILE GAUTIER

BORN *at Tarbes, France, on Aug. 31, 1811, Théophile Gautier com-pleted his education at the Collège Charlemagne and the artists' studios in Paris. He soon turned from art to write poetry, and became a leader in the Romantic movement of his youth. Also a novelist and dramatist, Gautier depended for his income largely on journalistic work, chiefly art criticism. He traveled widely to get material for his writings. Gautier died in Paris on Dec. 23, 1872.*

THE CHEVALIER D'ALBERT, a poet of 22 years, found life very monotonous. Though he had a hunger for adventure, he had never made a journey beyond his own town, and though he had conceived for himself an ideal of womanhood, he had never been in love.

Wanting a mistress, he feared that familiarity would bring boredom. Having had experience, he did not want to teach some little simpleton the alphabet of love; nor did he want a married woman with whom he would have to yield the first place to another.

His ideal would be 26 years old, plump and firm of figure, of medium height, a blonde with dark eyes, her walk undulating like a snake standing on its tail. She must be dressed in velvet or brocade, and she must have a good income.

Not finding this ideal, he made a liaison with a lady whom he called Rosette, an animated woman of perhaps 25, with blue-black hair, a well-formed but small figure, and a sensual mouth and white arms. This practical and witty woman, skilled in love and agreeable to the poet's wishes, was his nightly—and daily—companion for five months. Though d'Albert never felt himself truly in love with her, she was so skillful in acceding to his desires that his pleasure in her did not begin to recede until nearly the end of this period.

He suspected that Rosette divined the change in his feelings and was seeking a way to break off their affair painlessly, when she took him to her Arcadian country mansion. He had told himself that his attitude was ridiculous, that Rosette's beauty fell not far short of the perfection he demanded, but reason could not penetrate the wall about his soul.

Of the guests at the mansion, the most pleasing was a young cavalier, not very tall, but with a good figure, though he seemed to be too delicate and beautiful for a man. This witty and pleasant-voiced beardless youth had with him a pretty page boy whom he treated tenderly.

Rosette entered the room of Théodore de Sérannes, the new arrival, and their conversation revealed that she knew him and was in love with him, though the youth confessed that "there is an insurmountable obstacle between us which I cannot explain to you." Rosette, speaking of d'Albert, showed that she understood him thoroughly, and was preparing to break off with him in such a manner that he should blame her; such was her tenderness toward her lover.

Going hunting, with Théodore displaying remarkable horsemanship, the page, known as Isnabel, had an accident, and Rosette went to his rescue and discovered that this pretty boy was actually a girl, though she kept her knowledge to herself.

Now d'Albert, somewhat to his own horror, discovered that he had fallen in love with the young man Théodore, with his soft skin, long eyelashes, and lustrous hair, and perfectly formed

hands. Though he said to himself, "It is a woman," and philosophized on the desire of women to be known as men, he feared
that his own judgment was deceiving him and that he was the
victim of an unnatural attraction.

If he could have seen a letter from Théodore to his friend
Graciosa, he would have been reassured. The cavalier was in
truth Madelaine de Maupin, a girl of 20 who had a desire to
"study man thoroughly, to anatomize him with inexorable scalpel
fibre by fibre." To this end she had trained herself in horsemanship and swordplay, and had set out in men's clothes to learn what
she could. After a night at an inn in which she had to share a
bed with a drunken man to whom she had an almost unconquer-
able desire to reveal herself, she joined a company of well-to-do
youths.

Meantime d'Albert prepared to present *As You Like It* at
the mansion, and since Rosette objected to appearing in man's
attire, Théodore agreed to play the part of Rosalind. From the
moment the youth appeared in woman's clothing, the poet lost
his last doubt that the cavalier was indeed a girl. This graceful,
beautiful creature could not be a man; and since d'Albert could
not summon the courage to declare his love in person, he wrote a
letter in which he announced his discovery and declared that
"Théodore" was his ideal.

Continuing her letters, Mademoiselle de Maupin told how she
had made up for the effeminacy of her appearance by her skill on
horseback and with the sword, so that Alcibiades, one of her
companions, had invited her to visit his widowed sister, the same
Rosette. Playing the man, Théodore unintentionally won the heart
of Rosette, who believed her a timid youth afraid to proclaim his
love. Twice rescued from embarrassing positions, in one of which
she was forced to wound the brother in a duel rather than marry
the well-to-do Rosette, Théodore at last fled from Rosette's home.
Unwilling to end her deception so soon, Mademoiselle de Maupin
had been hard put to explain her coldness.

The mademoiselle had planned to search among men until she

found one whose appearance pleased her, and whose feelings and thoughts were such as she wished to live with. Having found such a man, she intended to win his heart in woman's garb, being willing to live with him as mistress without feeling dishonor. But none she met could overcome her contempt, particularly for their treatment of women, and she found herself becoming accustomed to her masculine attire and speech.

Indeed, she rescued a girl named Ninon from a coarse suitor, and dressed her as a page boy, not letting her suspect the true sex of her benefactor. "I took a malicious joy in thus depriving men's rapacity of such a treasure," Mademoiselle de Maupin told her friend. Now she declared that her beloved "would have to be both sexes in turn in order to satisfy me; for my lovers I should keep all the cat-like and woman-like elements; with my mistresses I should be enterprising, bold, impassioned."

Fully aware of d'Albert's thoughts about her, Mademoiselle had given him a little assistance in divining her sex—he was the first to penetrate her masquerade—but let his letter go unanswered for more than a fortnight in which he was torn by doubts. She did not love him, she said, but had an inclination for him, finding him less brutal and more appreciative of beauty than other men.

One evening d'Albert was moodily contemplating suicide, when he felt a gentle hand on his shoulder, and turned to find Mademoiselle de Maupin before him in her Rosalind costume, with a panting, white bosom so revealed as to leave no doubt of her sex. She threw her beautiful arms round his neck, and he kissed her effusively. She confessed her virginity, but few more words were necessary.

Delicately d'Albert unlaced her dress and lightly pressed with his mouth the two beautiful roses of paradise thus revealed. Her hair became loosened and her gown fell to her feet. The dazzled d'Albert gazed with rapture. Everything of which he had dreamed was united in this beautiful form—delicacy and strength, grace and color.

He took up the fair one in his arms and bore her to the couch. Madly inflamed, all their kisses became one.

All night they made love, and when toward morning d'Albert fell asleep, his mistress slipped away to Rosette's room. What she there said has not been ascertained, but a maid found two pearls that Théodore had worn in the guise of Rosalind. Théodore rode off with his page.

A letter for d'Albert arrived in a week, explaining that Mademoiselle de Maupin had decided never to give herself to another, and had feared to go on with him because one or the other would cease to love. She urged him to comfort Rosette, and told them to love each other in memory of her.

Les Misérables

By VICTOR HUGO

VICTOR MARIE HUGO *was born on Feb. 26, 1802, at Besançon, France, the son of a distinguished peasant-descended soldier of Napoleon. Given a good education, he began writing verses and plays in childhood, but found it difficult at first to live by the pen when thrown on his own resources. Soon, however, he attained the preeminent position which he retained the rest of his life. From 1852 to 1870 he was exiled from France for his political activities. More than a million people lined the streets of Paris at his funeral; he died May 22, 1885.*

AN HOUR BEFORE SUNSET, on a day in October, 1815, a man about 46 entered the little town of D—— on foot. Of middle height, he was stout and hardy, but his beard was long and he was dusty and shabby. Though he offered money, neither inn would give him food or shelter, for he was an ex-convict. Driven from every place, he lay down on a stone bench.

Then an old woman told him to knock on the door of M. Myriel, the Bishop. When admitted he said loudly:

"My name is Jean Valjean. I have been 19 years in the galleys. Four days ago I was set free." And he said that because of his yellow passport he had been turned away everywhere.

"Put on another plate," the Bishop told his elderly sister. And the bewildered Valjean, believing his host to be a poor priest, ate his supper off silver plates and went off to a real bed.

In the middle of the night Valjean awoke. He had been a pruner in his youth. One cold winter night, he had broken a baker's window to get a loaf of bread for his sister and her seven starving children. For this the prison term was five years, and repeated efforts to escape had raised it to 19 years of misery in chains. He had gone into prison sobbing and shuddering; he emerged full of hatred toward man.

Still unable to understand kindness, Jean left his bed, gathered up the Bishop's silver, and fled. He was captured, and in the morning the gendarmes took him before his host.

"I gave you the candlesticks also," said the Bishop, and told the officers to release Valjean, adding: "Never forget that you have promised me to use this silver to become an honest man." Dazed, Valjean walked out into a new world, then sat down at the roadside to think.

A boy passed by and dropped a forty-sou piece. Jean put his foot on it, and drove the child away. Then he woke from his reverie, and called after the boy, but no answer came. "What a wretch I am," Valjean exclaimed, and he burst into tears for the first time in 19 years.

Two months later a stranger rescued the children of the captain of gendarmes from the burning town hall in the town of M——, and as a result no one asked for his passport. The man settled there, and became known as Father Madeleine. From a tiny capital, he had become wealthy by simplifying the manufacture of the black glass trinkets made there, and at the same time brought prosperity to the entire town.

By unanimous request, Madeleine was made mayor in 1820. He employed everyone who came to him, demanding only honesty from them, and good morals from the women. He had given a million francs to the city and the poor, but he lived simply, avoided society, and refused honors, giving up his leisure time to reading. It was also noted that he was tremendously strong.

Only one man in M—— failed to venerate Father Madeleine. That was Javert, inspector of police, born in prison, an implacable enemy of all lawbreakers, merciless in pursuit of duty, the personification of the spy and informer. He had been stationed in the galleys, and was sure he had seen the Mayor elsewhere.

One day in 1823 the Mayor saved from prison a poor woman named Fantine who had been dismissed from his factory without his knowledge. She was dying, and left her little girl Cosette in Madeleine's care.

And at this time Javert went to the Mayor and asked to be dismissed, saying that he had denounced him as Jean Valjean, wanted for robbing a boy, and that an old man arrested at Arras had been identified as the ex-convict.

After a night of anguish, the Mayor went to the Arras court and proved that he was Valjean. Then he returned home, arranged his affairs, withdrew his fortune and buried it, and was sent for life to the galleys at Toulon, where in November, 1823, a newspaper reported that a convict named Jean Valjean had drowned after rescuing a sailor.

At Christmas that year an old, poorly dressed man called at the inn at the village of Montfermeil, paid 1,500 francs to Thénardier, the landlord, and carried off to Paris little eight-year-old Cosette, now an ill-treated servant there.

Jean Valjean had never loved anything before, but he found himself strangely moved by this child with whom he lived in a large old garret. And Cosette, who did not remember her mother, found a father in this 55-year-old man. Happy with her,

Valjean never went abroad by day, but became known for his gifts to the poor. He usually dropped a coin in the hand of a beggar who sat by some church steps. One day the mendicant looked up, and Valjean recognized the face of Javert.

Soon Valjean found that Javert had taken lodgings in his house. He at once set out to seek new quarters, but found that four men were following him. Trapped in a cul-de-sac, he climbed a wall at the end of the street and lifted Cosette over by a rope. They descended into a convent garden, leaving a baffled Javert behind; he could not conceive that an old man and a child could scale a fourteen-foot wall.

Valjean discovered that the convent gardener was an old man whose life he had saved at M——. He told the nuns Valjean was his brother, and they educated Cosette. For six years they stayed there, Valjean working in the peaceful garden and seeing Cosette daily.

Then the old gardener died and Jean Valjean, now bearing the name of Fauchelevent, moved with Cosette to a house in the Rue Plumet, since he no longer feared recognition. But he rented other rooms in Paris in case of an emergency.

Cosette was growing up into a good-looking young woman, and Valjean was distraught at the thought of losing her when he learned that she was secretly in love with Marius, the son of Baron Pontmercy.

In June, 1832, the revolutionaries of Paris took to the barricades, at one of which Marius was in command. Javert was captured as a spy, and Jean Valjean asked the privilege of executing his old enemy. He led Javert into a side lane, cut the ropes, and let Javert go free, telling him his new name and address. "I would rather you killed me!" said Javert, but he accepted his liberty.

Soon the soldiers destroyed the barricade, and Marius lay wounded. There was only one chance for life. Valjean tore open a grating and disappeared into the sewers with Marius on his shoulders. Through darkness and quicksand, pursued by soldiers in boats, Valjean carried his unconscious burden through a maze of horrors. At last he emerged at the bank of the river, only to find Javert waiting for him.

Valjean obtained the inspector's aid in taking the youth home, saying: "Then do with me what you please." But the officer, torn between duty to the government which paid him, and imprisoning the man who had saved his life, returned to the police station and then solved his dilemma by plunging into the Seine.

When Marius recovered he married Cosette, and Jean Valjean lived by himself. He told Marius who he was, but it was not until Valjean was near death that Marius learned the whole story of the old man's heroism.

Marius hurried with Cosette to Valjean's room, and found him breathing his last. "Come nearer, my children. I am happy in dying," he told them. And Jean Valjean was dead.

The Hunchback of Notre Dame

By VICTOR HUGO

ALL PARIS was celebrating the double festival of Epiphany and the Feast of Fools on January 6, 1482. The Lord of Misrule was to be chosen, and all the competitors in turn made grimaces at a broken window in the great hall of the Palace of Justice. The populace was unanimous that the victor, the one with the ugliest face, was the hunchback of Notre Dame. The square nose, the horseshoe-shaped mouth, the one eye overhung by a bushy red brow, the forked chin, the strange expression of amazement, malice, and melancholy—who had seen such a grimace?

In fact, all of Quasimodo, the bell-ringer of Notre Dame, was a grimace. Humpbacked, with enormous head, feet and hands, and crooked legs, nevertheless he had wonderful vigor, agility and courage. He was a giant broken to pieces and badly mended.

With a pasteboard tiara and imitation robes, Quasimodo was

borne away at the head of a procession of the vagrants and rascals of Paris. For the first time in his life he felt a thrill of vanity; though deaf, he enjoyed the plaudits of the mob.

Suddenly a man in priest's robes darted out and snatched the gilded crosier from the mock pope. Instead of tearing him limb from limb, Quasimodo fell on his knees before the priest, then saved him from the angry fraternity of fools, and meekly followed him away.

The priest was Claude Frollo, the Archdeacon of Paris, the one human being Quasimodo loved. Frollo had found the deserted child in a sack at the entrance to Notre Dame, and had adopted him, teaching him to speak, read and write, and making him Notre Dame's bell-ringer. Reared in the cathedral, he had been made deaf by the bells, and could understand only Claude Frollo's signs. In 1482 Quasimodo was about 20, Frollo 36.

That same day Esmeralda, a young gypsy girl, graceful and beautiful, danced before a great bonfire in Paris. Among the crowd that watched was Archdeacon Frollo, his deep-set eyes youthful in their absorption in spite of his graying hair. But when the girl's goat, Djali, performed tricks, Frollo cried: "Sorcery!" Later, when darkness had fallen, Quasimodo seized the girl as she walked back toward her lodgings.

She screamed, and a horseman, Captain Phoebus de Chateaupers of the King's Archers, dashed forward and placed the girl on his saddle while a squadron of royal watchmen seized the surprised Quasimodo. The girl slipped away, but Quasimodo was taken to court the next day and sentenced to two hours on the pillory.

Beaten and bound on the horizontal wheel of oak on top of a cube of masonry, Quasimodo was stoned by the crowd. Frollo approached, seated on a mule; the hunchback smiled. Then the priest saw who it was on the pillory. He hastened off, while Quasimodo's smile became profoundly sad.

An hour and a half later, wounded and nearly dead, Quasimodo hoarsely cried: "Water!" The mob only sneered. At his third cry, he caught sight of the gypsy girl. She climbed to the platform while he looked at her with rage in his eye; but a tear rolled down when she lifted a gourd to his jagged mouth. The mood of the crowd changed at this sight. Soon the hunchback was released, and crept back to the cathedral.

Claude Frollo's life was austere, but his silent secretiveness caused him to be suspected of magic. Now he found that some burning passion possessed him whenever he saw Esmeralda. But he could not approach her, and fuel was added to the flames when he learned that she was in love with Captain Phoebus. He was ready to give up all for the dancing girl, and to destroy her with a charge of sorcery if he could not have her.

One night Frollo stabbed the captain when he was with Esmeralda; and the girl was accused. The priest was in court every day of the trial of the girl and her goat for witchcraft. She denied everything, and the president of the court ordered her put on the rack. At the first turn of the screw, she agreed to confess everything. The sentence was hanging on the city gibbet, along with her goat.

Bewildered Esmeralda still would have nothing to do with Claude Frollo when he visited her cell, though he promised her liberty if she would love him. He told her Phoebus was dead, at which she called him "assassin." The captain actually had recovered, but had ignored the gypsy girl, as he was about to be engaged to a young lady of wealth.

Just as the hangman's assistants were about to do their work, Quasimodo slid down by a rope from his gallery in Notre Dame, flung the executioners to the carth, and seized up the girl as if she were a doll. Shouting "Sanctuary!" he held her above his head and ran with her to the church, while the mob shouted approval.

Quasimodo put the girl in a cell built over the aisles in Notre Dame. He untied her, and brought her a basket of provisions. But the girl could not utter a word of thanks, so frightful was he to look at. He warned her to stay in the cell in the daytime, and never to leave the church at any time.

"Don't be frightened," he said. "I am your friend. I seem to you like some awful beast, eh? And you—you are a sunbeam!"

Two forces were at work to remove Esmeralda from Notre Dame. The priest, who had left the city to avoid witnessing her execution, returned and resolved to give her up to justice if she still refused him. And Esmeralda's friends, six thousand gypsies, vagabonds and thieves, resolved to rescue her forcibly lest some evil overtake her.

At midnight the ragged army moved on the cathedral, and attacked the great west doors. Quasimodo hurled a great beam of wood on them, and then stones and other missiles. Finally a tall ladder, crowded with men, was raised to the first gallery. Quasimodo, by the force of his arms alone, pushed it away until it fell back. The battle ended only with the arrival of a large company of King's Archers.

While the battle raged, the cloaked Frollo persuaded Esmeralda to leave with him by a secret door at the back of the cathedral. They escaped by the river, and she did not recognize the priest until they stood at the foot of the gallows in the city.

"I have saved you," he said. "Choose between me and the gibbet!"

She was silent. Then she said: "The gibbet is less horrible to me than you are."

He poured out his soul, but the girl was unmoved. It was dawn when he said, "For the last time, will you be mine?" Again she answered: "No!"

Frollo called out loudly. Soon the public hangman was aroused, and the interrupted execution was carried out.

Meantime Quasimodo, the battle over, discovered that Esmeralda was gone. He searched every cranny of Notre Dame, then sat for an hour in despair, convulsed by sobs. Suddenly he remembered that Claude Frollo had a secret key. At that very moment the priest returned to the cathedral. Quasimodo followed him to the top of the tower, and saw the priest gaze across the

city at the gallows. The hunchback followed his glance, and saw
the hangman doing his work.

A demoniac laugh burst from the priest's livid lips. Quasimodo
rushed furiously on the archdeacon, and with his great fists hurled
Frollo into the abyss. The priest caught at a gutter, hung for a
few minutes, then fell two hundred feet.

Quasimodo looked at the gypsy's body on the gibbet, and at the
shapeless mass on the pavement. "And these were all I have ever
loved!" he sobbed.

The hunchback was never again seen in Notre Dame, but two
years later the deformed skeleton of a man was found in close
embrace with the skeleton of a woman in the vault where Esmeralda's body had been deposited.

The Man Who Laughs

By VICTOR HUGO

ON A BITTER JANUARY NIGHT in the late seventeenth century a ten-
year-old boy stood on the bleak English coast near Weymouth
and watched a small ship recede from sight. The boy was quite
alone. He knew no one else in the world save the people who
had abandoned him. Although they had never been kind to him,
he had nowhere else to turn for shelter or sustenance. The boy
watched the ship out of sight, then turned away and set out to
find some place of refuge from the dreadful cold.

The ship he watched never reached her destination. She foun-
dered off the coast of France and went down with all hands. But
one of the passengers, knowing his death was upon him, consigned to the sea a bottle which contained a message concerning
the child left on the English coast.

The boy himself wandered toward the town, hoping that
someone would take him in. In the dark and cold he heard a

woman moaning, and discovered in the snow a frozen form. The body proved to be that of a woman from whom all life had fled. As the lad started to move on he heard a tiny cry—a baby who still lived lay in the dead woman's arms. Finding a creature as wretched and abandoned as himself, the boy felt an immediate bond between himself and the small unfortunate. Wrapping the baby as warmly as he could in his own coat, the waif pressed on, nearly frozen.

The doors in the town remained closed to his knock. Nearly in despair the boy finally heard a sound of life—the growl of some fierce animal. Since he could be in no worse case than he was at present, the boy moved toward, rather than away from, the sound. He soon saw a small van on wheels that seemed to be lighted from within. A gruff voice asked the lad what he wanted, and although the voice bade him ungraciously to begone, the door opened and an old man took the boy and the baby girl in.

The boy had found refuge with Ursus the Philosopher. Ursus was a mountebank, magician, doctor, and student. He distrusted man and loved only his wolf, Homo, who had been his sole companion for many years.

Ursus fed the boy and the baby girl and then set out into the night to see if he could find any trace of the hapless mother. He returned at dawn and in the early light caught his first glimpse of the boy's face. The old man recoiled in horror. The little lad's face had been fixed into a horrible grin; no matter what his feelings, it always looked as though the boy were laughing! This was the work of Comprachicos, a gang whose dreadful practice it was to mutilate children in face or form so that they could be sold as freaks.

Ursus and Homo adopted the two orphans. The boy—Gwynplaine, he said his name was—grew to be a young man normal in every respect save his grotesque countenance. The infant, whom Ursus christened Dea, developed into a beautiful young girl—sweet, affectionate and intelligent. The four were a happy household and the two young people were deeply in love with one another. Dea was spared the sight of her lover's mutilation because, from earliest babyhood, she had been blind!

From Ursus, Gwynplaine learned the profession of mountebank. He was very successful because people would come from miles around to laugh irresistibly at his ridiculous visage. Gwynplaine was really of a melancholy temperament, frequently depressed by his own wrongs and the wrongs of the world. But Dea, Ursus and Homo were dear to his heart and while they were all together, his life was worth living.

Gwynplaine became famous as "The Man Who Laughs" and his history—what Ursus knew of it—was familiar to the world.

One day, in Southwark, misfortune overtook the little caravan. Gwynplaine was summoned to Southwark Prison, why he knew not, and was conducted, wondering and fearful, to a secret torture-chamber. Manacled to the floor lay one Hardquanonne, a man who seemed to know Gwynplaine well. Gwynplaine identified him as a man for whom the authorities were seeking. Hardquanonne was the Comprachico who had altered the face of Gwynplaine and he confessed under torture that the mutilated mountebank was none other than Lord Clancharlie, a Peer of the House of Lords.

Gwynplaine shortly learned his own history. His father, the elder Lord Clancharlie, had incurred the enmity of King James II because of his attachment to the Puritan cause of Oliver Cromwell. At the death of Gwynplaine's father in exile, the lad had been spirited away to the Comprachicos by royal decree and his estates confiscated. The bottle containing Gwynplaine's secret had been found after these many years. Queen Anne and the Lord Chancellor believed that the wrong must be righted; the Queen also wanted to use Gwynplaine as vengeance against one Duchess Josiana, whom she did not like and who was destined to marry Lord Clancharlie—the present incumbent of the title could easily be removed.

Gwynplaine was told that his investiture in the House of Lords was to take place on the morrow. He thought of his old friends and his beloved Dea, but they seemed far away and he determined to be useful and help other unfortunates in his new estate.

Meanwhile Ursus and Dea had been convinced by the Southwark officials that Gwynplaine was dead, and had been told that they were henceforth exiled. Dea fell ill of a brain fever and Ursus feared that she would not long be with him.

When Gwynplaine first entered the House of Lords, the other Peers could not clearly see his face. But when he stood up to make a speech the horrid countenance appeared to them. He begged them not to be amused by his laughing face and tried to preach to them against the evil system of government which they upheld and which allowed poverty, crime, and the misuse of privilege. But the House rocked with laughter at his grinning mouth and listened to not a word. Crushed and disillusioned, unable to find his old friends, he nearly flung himself into the sea. But Homo discovered him and brought him to where Dea lay dying, tended by Ursus.

The girl, revived by joy, lived long enough to declare again her love for Gwynplaine. Just before she expired her eyes opened and she saw light. Then she died.

Gwynplaine took the dead girl into his arms and walked to the edge of the water. Smiling, he passed across the bulwarks, and the sea took to her bosom the two waifs who had found happiness only together.

Gil Blas

By RENÉ LE SAGE

ALAIN RENÉ LE SAGE *was born on May 3, 1668, at Sarzeau, Brittany, the son of the novelist Claude Le Sage. Educated by the Jesuits at Vannes, he studied law later at Paris. But his guardians had dissipated his father's wealth, so he turned to writing for the stage to support his wife. Between his plays and his novels, he became widely known in France, and made a moderately comfortable income. Writing until he was more than 70 years old, he died on Nov. 17, 1747, at Boulogne.*

GIL BLAS, only son of an old soldier, was taught a little Latin, Greek and logic by his uncle, a priest at Oviedo, and then was sent off at the age of 17 to study divinity at the University of Salamanca. He was promptly captured by brigands, who took the 40 ducats and the mule his uncle had given him. Among his fellow-prisoners was a wealthy lady, Dona Mencia of Burgos, and when he helped her escape she rewarded him with a diamond ring and a thousand ducats.

He promptly changed his plan of life, deciding to seek his fortune in this world at Madrid, rather than in the next world at school. Buying a pretentious outfit, he engaged a man named Lamela as his servant. In two days they arrived at Valladolid, where one Dona Camilla introduced herself as a cousin of Dona Mencia and invited Gil Blas to her great house. He was feasted and called handsome, and Camilla exchanged her ruby ring for his diamond ring.

But in the morning he found himself alone in the house, and his baggage, mules and money were gone. Lamela and his fellow rogues had hired the house for a week to cheat our hero; even the ruby ring was false. As he walked along the street disconsolate, he met an old Oviedo schoolfellow, Fabricio, who found a place for him as secretary to the famous Doctor Sangrado, who taught Gil Blas his science of treating people by blood-lettings and draughts of warm water. One of his patients was Camilla, from whom he took his diamond ring and all her other jewels by dressing six of his friends as police officers and pretending to arrest her.

Another patient of Gil Blas died, and the youth had to flee to

Madrid to escape from her betrothed. He took various positions as valet, after spending all his money with a wild company of actors and actresses, and at length humbly accepted work as a lackey in the house of a rich old libertine, Don Vincent de Guzman, who had a lovely only daughter, Aurora. Don Guzman soon died.

Gil Blas fancied that Aurora was in love with him, but her heart was fastened on a young nobleman, Don Luis Pacheco, who was unaware of her passion. Aurora resolved to follow him to Salamanca, where he was studying, and took Gil Blas and her maid along. At Salamanca she set up two establishments, dressing in men's clothes as "Don Felix" at one, and living as herself at the other.

She promptly won Don Luis' friendship as a gay fellow cavalier, and arranged for him to meet her "cousin," Aurora. Don Luis told "Don Felix" that he meant to wed Aurora, upon which "Felix" removed his wig. In a fortnight they were married and Gil Blas, who had helped arrange the meeting, was well-rewarded.

After working for two other employers in Madrid, he got in trouble over a girl and started for Toledo. On the road he fell in with a young cavalier, Don Alfonso, with whom he took shelter from the rain in a cave. There were two old hermits there who turned out to be Lamela and an accomplice in disguise. The ex-valet had no money, but they joined forces and robbed a band of brigands. Then, at the town of Xeloa, they disguised themselves as officers of the Inquisition and paid a visit to one Samuel Simon, a converted Jew and a usurer, whom they robbed on the pretense of examining his private papers.

Now having a thousand ducats each, Don Alfonso and Gil Blas went on to Toledo, where the young cavalier became reconciled with the Count of Polan, whose son he had killed in a duel. Marrying the Count's daughter Seraphina, Alfonso settled down happily. Grateful to Gil Blas for his assistance, Alfonso found the adventurer a position as secretary to his relative, the Archbishop of Granada.

The Archbishop was tremendously vain and equally fat. Gil Blas praised his sermons and got along well with him, until one day the prelate had an attack of apoplexy which disturbed his mind. His preachings became confused ravings, and Gil Blas made the error of obeying the Archbishop's command to tell him if his sermons became worse. The secretary was discharged without ceremony.

Again without money, Gil Blas posed as the brother of a dissolute actress and thus obtained appointment as secretary to a Portuguese grandee, the Marques de Marialva. But his trickery was exposed, and once more he returned to Madrid. There, after a variety of adventures, more amusing than creditable, he was made under-secretary to the Duke of Lerma, who was the King's prime minister.

In his new employment, Gil Blas found that "one makes a merit of any dirty work in the service of the great." Because of his broad experience with thieves and honest men, libertines, quacks, poets, people of the stage, adventurers and country gentlemen, his wits were sharp, and he won great influence, his bit of education also coming to his service.

Flattered, sought out and well-paid, Gil Blas grew greatly in self-esteem and greed for money. But his structure collapsed when he was arrested by the King's orders after he had been employed to procure a doubtful mistress for the heir-apparent. Thrown into the dungeon of Segovia, he was rescued with the Prince's help, but was exiled from the Castiles and all his wealth was seized.

His friend, Don Alfonso, for whom he had won the governorship of Valencia, gave him a small estate near that city. Now Gil Blas decided to visit his birthplace. He found his father dying, his mother exhausted from caring for him, and his uncle a nervous wreck. Though he gave his father an expensive funeral and provided an annuity for his mother, the people of the town were so angry at him for his long neglect of his family that he was glad to escape with his life.

At Valencia Gil Blas found that Don Alfonso had provided

at least seven servants for his new estate. Frugally dismissing most of them, he settled down happily and married Antonia, daughter of Don Basilio, his farmer. But sorrow came with the death of his wife in childbirth.

Now the Crown Prince succeeded to the throne, and offered a high position to Gil Blas, who replied that "all he wanted was a good situation where there was no inducement to violate his conscience, and where the favors of his prince were not likely to be bartered for filthy lucre." Experience had made him wiser.

His reward was appointment as confidant to the prime minister, who intrusted to our hero the rearing of his illegitimate son and heir. From this Gil Blas obtained a title, and he followed the Duke of Lerma into retirement when his patron lost the King's favor. When the Duke died, Gil Blas received a bequest of 10,000 pistoles.

He returned to his comfortable estate, married a second time, and lived out his life happy and respected, occupying his days with the education and training of his children, and with the writing of his memoirs, in which he expressed his opinions of all manner of things, as well as relating his adventures.

Une Vie

By GUY DE MAUPASSANT

HENRI RENÉ ALBERT GUY DE MAUPASSANT *was born into a well-to-do and aristocratic family of the Seine-Inférieure region in France on August 5, 1850. The novelist Flaubert, a friend of the boy's mother, was his godfather and was the literary model for De Maupassant, whose interests were literary from earliest youth. De Maupassant was employed as a clerk in the Navy Department at Paris and served during the Franco-Prussian War. Finally he*

began to publish verse and short stories which were characterized
by a deep pessimism and a lack of moral sense. In 1890 De Maupas-
sant began to show symptoms of mental derangement and two
years later became completely insane. He died in an asylum in
Paris, July 6, 1893.

WHEN Jeanne le Perthuis returned to her home in Rouen after
her convent schooling, she was a lovely, innocent girl of eighteen,
deeply sensitive to the beauties of nature, and supremely happy
to be once more with her parents. Her greatest desire was to go
back to the Poplars, the family estate on the Norman coast.

At the Poplars, a charming and free life began for Jeanne. She
wandered in solitude in the sweet freshness of the countryside
and spent long hours by the sea. The Baron, her father, visited
his peasants and took a great interest in the progress of the local
agriculture. The Baronne (Baroness), because of the condition
of her heart, limited herself to short walks near the house.
Jeanne's only friend was a peasant girl, Rosalie, of her own age,
who worked in the house, but who had been brought up in almost
sisterly relation to Jeanne.

One day the local curé, Abbé Picot, came to see the Baronne.
Though neither the Baron nor the Baronne was a strict Catholic,
they were on friendly terms with the Abbé. The following
Sunday, after mass, he introduced them to Vicomte Julien de
Lamare, a young nobleman of the neighborhood who was living
very economically on the remainder of his family's estates.

Vicomte Julien, in his manners and his family, proved acceptable to Jeanne's parents, and his handsome face and gracious
bearing soon won him a place in Jeanne's affections. Her many
happy excursions with Julien to near-by towns in her father's
boat, and evening walks near the Poplars seemed to bring into
reality her most cherished dreams about love.

When Julien asked her father for her hand, Jeanne was immensely happy. After the betrothal, the marriage date was set, and a wedding trip to Corsica was planned. At the wedding the only guest was Jeanne's maiden aunt, Lison.

But Jeanne had not been told by anyone, not even her parents, what a husband expected from his wife, and her first night with her husband was an unpleasant shock to her sensibilities. On the wedding trip she was alternately embarrassed and disgusted by his approaches. They set out on a tour of the Corsican countryside, and during the days of travel Jeanne was deeply stirred by the natural beauty of mountains and ravines. Her senses were reawakened, and once she was able to respond passionately to her husband.

But when they returned to the Poplars, Julien became strangely indifferent, and a feeling of disenchantment came over Jeanne as her illusions faded in the monotony of her daily life. Julien began to institute petty economies around the farm, to the amusement of the Baron, and sometimes to the annoyance of Jeanne. They went calling on neighbors. Toward the close of the year Jeanne's parents decided to return to Rouen.

After their departure, Jeanne was overcome with sadness. The place had changed; even Rosalie was no longer the same. She seemed sick and miserable. One night Jeanne found her in the bedroom, sprawled on the floor and groaning. She had just delivered a child. Julien was furious when he learned about the baby; he wanted to send both of them away at once. Jeanne could not persuade Rosalie to name the father of the child.

One night, many weeks later, Jeanne found out that Julien was Rosalie's lover. Completely unnerved by this discovery, she quickly dressed and ran out into the snow toward the sea. At the top of a cliff Julien found her, exhausted.

Her parents returned at the news of her illness. Since Julien denied his guilt, Jeanne decided to force the truth from Rosalie. In the presence of the Abbé, Rosalie told them that Julien had seduced her on his first visit to the Poplars. The child was his. The Baron decided to settle a farm worth 20,000 francs on

Rosalie, and the Abbé thought he could find her a husband.

At this time Jeanne learned that she was pregnant, and this helped to soothe some of her wounds. She transferred all her frustrated emotions to the unborn child, and from the day the boy was born gave all her love to him. In the meantime, their circle of friends grew, and Julien's attachment to their neighbors, the Count and Countess de Fourville, seemed to make him very happy and more considerate of Jeanne. He showed no interest, however, in his son Paul.

Early the following year Jeanne discovered that Julien and the Countess de Fourville were in love. They took daily horseback rides together into the country. Riding out one afternoon by herself, Jeanne found their horses in a secluded grove, and the lovers nowhere in sight. At this time her mother returned to the Poplars, and soon after died from a heart attack. In her grief Jeanne sought consolation by reading old letters of her mother, and to her dismay she found that her mother long ago had had as a lover the best friend of the Baron.

One day the Count de Fourville came striding up the lawn of the Poplars. From his wild expression Jeanne knew that he had at last learned the truth. Before she could even speak to him, he broke away in search of the lovers. He found the two horses tethered near a rolling house used by the shepherds in cold weather. In a fury of passion, he seized the shafts of the house and pulled it up to the top of the cliffs and plunged it over the precipice to the rocks below. When the peasants got to the wreckage, they found both Julien and the Countess dead.

From that time on Jeanne gave her whole life to the care of Paul. He was petted and spoiled by his mother; and his grandfather and his Aunt Lison were slaves to every whim of the little boy.

By the time he was fifteen, Jeanne could not bear the thought of their separation and wanted him to grow up, without formal education, as a gentleman farmer. But the Baron's view that Paul should go to the college at Havre prevailed with Jeanne.

After his second year at college, Paul's visits at the Poplars grew less frequent as he found new friends and pleasures. Before Jeanne realized the change, he seemed a grown man, and his attentions to his doting family became more and more perfunctory.

He left the college in his fourth year without notifying Jeanne. He now had a mistress, and for a period of years his only correspondence with his family consisted of intermittent requests for money. When he came of age, he went through his inheritance in six months, and after that became involved in several dubious financial ventures, from which his grandfather rescued him by mortgaging his estates. The Baron died while he was making arrangements for another payment on Paul's debts.

Jeanne aged rapidly. Her income was nearly exhausted. Her life was embittered by the hatred she felt for Paul's mistress, and she lived a secluded existence, her mind always on the past.

One day Rosalie returned to the Poplars, and Jeanne was overjoyed to see her again. Rosalie took Jeanne's finances firmly in hand and told her she must try to salvage what she could. She told her she must sell the Poplars. Unwillingly Jeanne agreed, and went to live with Rosalie in a small cottage some distance away.

Jeanne went to Paris to find Paul, but the only persons she met were his creditors. When she had finally resigned herself to not seeing Paul again, she received a telegram informing her that the woman he loved was dying after the birth of a child.

This time Rosalie went to Paris to bring back the child and to insist on the marriage of its parents. The next day word came that Paul's wife had died and that he was coming home. For the first time in many years Jeanne was happy. Rosalie said to her, "You see, life is never quite so bad or so pleasant as one imagines it is."

Swann's Way

By MARCEL PROUST

MARCEL PROUST *was born on July 10, 1871, of French and Jewish parentage. He attended the Lycée Condorcet and afterwards helped to produce the* Revue Blanche, *an intellectual periodical. In 1902 failing health compelled him to retire almost completely from salon society, in which he was a great favorite. His years as a recluse he employed in writing his great work,* Remembrance of Things Past, *of which the first book was* Swann's Way. *His work gained most of its fame after his death on November 18, 1922, in Paris.*

IN THE DIM TWILIGHT between sleeping and waking, and sometimes on midnights when sleep eluded his invalid body, the Narrator found his past brought back to him through a thousand impressions of light, shade, or position.

As a boy he had been sickly. His frailty was one of spirit as well as of body. His loves were few, but so intense that he was frequently made ill by emotion. The night at Combray, he remembered, when M. Swann had come, the little boy had been sent to bed without his mother's good-night kiss. Usually she came to him when he had gotten into bed, and the moment of joy and security when her soft cheek brushed his helped him through the frightening night. Although he knew he would be punished, he waited, trembling, until the visitor should have gone and mamma came upstairs. Then he flung himself upon her, weeping. To his surprise, instead of the punishment that was rightfully his, he received a very special dispensation—his mother stayed in his room that night.

M. Swann was a frequent visitor in the household. He was the special friend of the lad's grandfather, who had known the elder Swann. The Swann estates were on the outskirts of the town. Latterly Swann had been less friendly with the little boy's family because they could not approve of Mme. Swann. The little boy's aunts said that she was "one of those women." Swann made no attempt to introduce his wife to this family although perhaps he wished that his little girl, Gilberte, for whose sake people said he had married Mme. Swann, might have more companionship.

Swann was quiet and almost diffident with the family. Although they knew that he was a dilettante in the arts, they had known him for many years and so had no very great opinion of him. When they learned inadvertently that Swann traveled in the most exalted circles of the aristocracy, the aunts thought it bad taste that a bourgeois should aspire to associate with the nobility.

The flavor of a "petite madeleine" soaked in tea suddenly brought back to the Narrator's conscious mind all the details of his childhood in Combray, fresh and living. They lived with Aunt Leonie who, wealthy and a widow, indulged herself in invalidism and was happily confined to her bed. The routine of the house was unvarying, and Aunt Leonie from the window could watch the doings of the little town, which were just as static. A stranger in Combray was more than an event, he was an affront—Françoise, the peasant maid who ran the household, must be immediately dispatched to the grocer, who would identify the stranger as the brother of someone's gardener or another's nephew home from the university.

The cathedral at Combray was large and ugly, but the environs of the town were beautiful, and in the late spring the hawthorn bloomed, snowy or pink, along the roads. Sometimes the little boy would be lured from his books and the family would go for a long walk. On these occasions they would take either of two routes: the Guermantes way, which led near the estate of the aristocratic Duchesse de Guermantes; or the Meseglise, or Swann's way, which passed through the grounds of M. Swann. It was on a jaunt along this latter way that the little boy first encountered Mlle. Gilberte Swann, a chubby, red-haired four-year-old whom the lad immediately fell in love with because she must consort with such wonderful personages—Bergotte, the boy's favorite author, Berma, the actress, and all the artistic people whom her father knew. Soon the boy's family removed to Paris for the winter, and gradually the memory of Combray faded. "The heart changes," says the Narrator, "and that is our worst misfortune."

At Mme. Verdurin's salon only the unsuccessful were tolerated. To value Rubinstein above the hostess' pianist was heresy. Aristocracy was vulgar and the literati bores. This was the true intelligentsia and any member of the "little nucleus" who did not ascribe to this view was soon dispensed with. Swann entered this circle under the patronage of Odette de Crecy.

Swann, an inveterate and tireless lover of women in all walks of life, who could be possessed utterly but never for very long, was at first not especially attracted by Odette de Crecy. Her style of beauty was too angular, too melancholy for a man whose sexual preferences ran to a rosy vulgarity. But at their first meeting at the theater, Odette became warmly attracted to him, wrote him notes, begged him to summon her whenever he wanted. He allowed her to introduce him at the Verdurins and gradually she became more attractive to him.

He fell in love with her one night when he had expected to meet her at the Verdurins and, upon arrival, found that she had left. He pursued her all over town and finally found her. Their private idiom for love making was "doing a cattleya," after the orchids that she wore pinned to her bodice.

Gradually Swann's love for Odette grew to an unquenchable passion. Perfectly aware that she was a kept woman, realizing that she was inherently stupid, that she lied to him, that she was bourgeoise and snobbish despite her past, Swann nevertheless soon became completely possessed.

Odette's passion waned. She became evasive. Swann was soon

dropped from the Verdurin circles—they resented, secretly snobs, his aristocratic friends in the Fauborg Saint-Germain, his association with the Prince of Wales and the nobility—and De Forcheville took his place in the circle and, he suspected, in Odette's regard.

He was tortured with passion and doubt. When he heard a musical phrase which he had heard with Odette he suffered horribly. He continued to give her money but deviled her with suspicious questions. He found that not only had she been unfaithful but also that she had had relationships with women even while she had been his mistress.

Swann's whole existence was completely shadowed. Finally an incident happened which started his recovery. Mme. Cottard, a member of the Verdurin circle, mentioned to him that Odette always spoke of him with the greatest feeling and friendship. Abruptly his love lessened. In a dream his relationship with Odette was clarified, and he restored her to her stupid lover. He woke refreshed. He decided to return to Combray.

The little boy was to have gone to Florence and Venice, he remembered, but excitement had precipitated his nervous disorder, and the doctor had said he must not travel. Upon recovery, Françoise took him daily to the Champs-Élysées. Gilberte Swann played there. One day the little red-haired girl asked him to play with her and her friends. He loved her passionately. He lived only for the time when Françoise would take him to the Champs-Élysées. As he had at first loved Gilberte because of the romantic associations of her family, now he conferred godhead on her father and mother because they belonged to her. He would try to get his family to talk about the Swanns. Every day he would pray that Gilberte would write him a letter. Of course she never did. Finally she told him that she would not come to the park any more because she must shop and then there would be Christmas and maybe, after that, she would travel. This seemed almost like the end of life to the little boy. In the Bois-de-Boulogne he would watch for the chic Mme. Swann and bow his little boy's bow as she went by. When she did not come the whole avenue was altered. For, says the Narrator, "Houses, roads, avenue, are as fugitive, alas, as the years."

Jean-Christophe

By ROMAIN ROLLAND

BORN *at Clamecy, France, on Jan. 29, 1866, Romain Rolland resolved early in life to make a career in music. He attended the École Normale Supérieure, and obtained his Doctor of Letters degree by a study of early music. In 1895 he was made professor of the history of art at the École Normale Supérieure, and later he directed the study of the history of music at the Sorbonne, meantime winning honors, including the 1915 Nobel Prize, for his novels and plays. During the World War he was a pacifist and went into voluntary exile in Switzerland, where he was living when Germany conquered France in 1940.*

JEAN-CHRISTOPHE KRAFFT, offspring of the unhappy union of Melchoir, a drunken musician, and Louisa, a cook, was born in the little Rhine town where his grandfather, Jean Michel, had settled 50 years before. Very early Christophe showed an interest in music. His father forced the young child to sit at the piano and practice daily by the hour. He rebelled, but after his grandfather took him to the opera he was so enthralled that he resolved to become a composer.

One day Jean Michel wrote the score of the songs Christophe was making up and singing while at play, entitling it "The Pleasures of Childhood." Melchoir, quick to take advantage of his son's genius, arranged a concert at which the seven-and-a-half-

year-old musician played his composition to Grand Duke Leo-
pold, to whom it had been dedicated.

Christophe won court favor. He was granted a small pension
and was asked to play at the palace frequently. His grandfather,
who had aided in the support of the family, died. His father's
drunkenness increased until he lost his job in the Hof-Theatre
orchestra, and Christophe, who played first violin in the orchestra,
became the sole support of the family at 14.

Influenced by Gottfried, his mother's brother and a simple man
of the people, Christophe early formed a philosophy based on
honesty. He fell in love with a young pupil of a wealthy family.
She jilted him. Made unhappy by this and the death of his father,
Christophe adopted a Puritan creed.

He fell in love with Sabine, a young widow, but before their
love was fully developed, she died. Sorrowing, he took long
walks into the country. On one of these trips he met Ada. They
spent the night together in a hotel, and Christophe fell in love
again. He was seriously shaken when he found that Ada was
carrying on an affair with his younger brother.

Christophe threw himself into his work with new energy. But
as he matured, his sincerity, integrity and honesty caused him
to revolt against German Philistinism through his compositions
and the criticisms he wrote for a local review. After a quarrel
with the editors he transferred his column to a Socialist paper
and so enraged the Grand Duke that he lost his court support.
As he continued to fight, the persecution of the townspeople
increased and he lost all of his friends. The only person who
could understand him or his Lieder was the aged Peter Schutz,
retired professor of the history of music.

Dancing with a peasant girl he loved, Christophe became involved in a fight with some drunken soldiers at an inn. So at
20 he was forced to flee to Paris to avoid imprisonment.

In Paris he supported himself by giving music lessons. He was
taken in tow by a boyhood friend, Sylvain Kohn, who traveled in
the Parisian smart set. He soon had his fill of Parisian society; he

could not bear the emptiness of it, the idleness, the moral im-
potence, the neurasthenia, the aimless, pointless, self-devouring
hypercriticism.

Christophe refused to compromise himself to attain popularity,
and soon was so isolated that he could no longer live by teaching.
He was reduced to transposing music for a publisher.

After a serious illness in which he was nursed back to
health by a young neighbor, Sidonie, Christophe found a friend
in Olivier Jeannin, a young lecturer at the École Normale. He
discovered that Olivier was the brother of Antoinette, whom he
had met in Germany and had caused to lose her position through
no fault of his own. She had died of tuberculosis after slaving to
educate her brother.

Olivier showed Christophe that he had not yet come in contact
with the real France—the French people. The companions en-
riched each other's nature. Olivier had serenity of mind and a
sickly body. Christophe had mighty strength and a stormy soul.
They were in some sort like a blind man and a cripple.

However, they became estranged when Colette, whom Olivier
loved and Christophe formerly loved, made use of an old enemy
of Christophe, Lucien Levy-Coeur, to cause a misunderstanding.
Christophe, enraged, insulted Levy-Coeur at a party, and found
himself faced with a challenge to duel. They met, both missed,
and Christophe and Olivier were reunited.

After a period of panic caused by a threat of war between
France and Germany, Christophe flung himself into creative
work with tenfold vigor. His works were published and both
French and German orchestras played them. At the height of
success, he was called to the bedside of his dying mother in
Germany.

Olivier fell in love with and married Jacqueline Langeais, a
spoiled, fickle, pretty girl. They settled in a town in the west
of France where Olivier had gained an appointment. Later
they returned to Paris. Jacqueline tired of Olivier. A child was
born, but it failed to bring them together. Finally, after attempt-

ing to trifle with Christophe's affections, she ran off with a profligate writer.

Again Christophe and Olivier were united. In their desire to understand the people, Olivier's idealism and Christophe's feeling for humanity drew them close to the working-class movement. In a May Day demonstration a disturbance took place and Olivier was killed. Christophe became involved in a fight with the police but was saved by his friends and was sent safely over the frontier. He again became a fugitive from authority, as he had been ten years before.

He found refuge with a German friend, Dr. Braun, and his wife Anna. After a time a love affair developed between Christophe and Anna. Try as they might to break it off, they were unsuccessful. Braun was deceived and Anna suffered so greatly because of the deception that she attempted suicide. Finally Christophe tore himself away and took refuge in the Swiss mountains.

Years passed. While living in Italy, Christophe met Grazia, whom he first had met in his youth in Paris. In later years she had, through the influence of her husband, an Austrian count, promoted Christophe's music at a time when he was at odds with his public. Her husband had died in a duel and she was with child. Christophe and Grazia fell in love, but later parted. Christophe returned to Paris; and Grazia's health gave way and she died.

Christophe spent his declining years with his old friends in Paris. The delight of his old age was the marriage of Christophe Olivier Georges, son of Olivier, and Aurora, daughter of Grazia.

His principal horror at that period was the gathering clouds of a war between his two countries: Germany and France. He was sure that even if war should come it would not break the clasp of brotherhood between the two countries.

Until the end he kept within reach his music pad. And when he was dying he picked up his pen and wrote the hymn he had composed:

"Thou shalt be born again. Rest. Now all is one heart. The smile of the night and the day entwined. Harmony, the august marriage of love and hate. I will sing the God of the two mighty wings. Hosanna to life! Hosanna to death!"

Paul and Virginia

By BERNARDIN DE SAINT-PIERRE

JACQUES HENRI BERNARDIN DE SAINT-PIERRE *was born at Le Havre in 1737. An emotional dreamer, he was forever wandering about from place to place. Educated to be an engineer, he went to sea, served in the army, and was dismissed. He received an appointment at Malta; held posts at St. Petersburg, Warsaw, Dresden, Berlin and Mauritius, and was superintendent of the Jardins des Plantes at Paris. He was professor at the École Normale and was a member of the Institute. He was the first to break away from the classic French school, and led the way to the great romantic movement. Among his friends he counted the first Napoleon. Saint-Pierre died at Eragny, France, in 1814.*

IN 1726, a young Norman came to the Isle de France, bringing with him his young wife, who was of noble birth. Soon after their arrival, he was stricken with a fever and died, leaving his wife, Marguerite de la Tour, and a baby daughter.

Poor and needy, a stranger to her family, the young widow traveled to a lonely island, where she could till the soil without paying rent, and there she built a crude dwelling place for herself and her little daughter Virginia.

After a while, another woman, Marie, came to live on the island, bringing with her her small son, whom she called Paul. The two women, regardless of the fact that they came from very different stations in life, soon became fast friends, helping and comforting each other greatly.

Domingo, a powerful black man, was the servant of Marguerite. The two lonely women spent a great deal of time together, and the children, of course, were inseparable. They grew up virtually naked, and they could not read or write. They called each other brother and sister.

When Madame de la Tour saw how beautiful her daughter was becoming, she resolved to write to her aunt to bring her up in France. The aunt replied with great coldness, adding that the disgraceful marriage had brought about its proper result.

Thus, in poverty, the two children grew up, Paul becoming a planter, and Virginia tending the goats and helping around the house. While the mothers were debating the wisdom of permitting their children to marry, a letter arrived from the aunt, requesting that Virginia be sent to her in Normandy to be educated.

Virginia and Paul were alarmed at this, but, since there was a promise of Virginia's becoming the aunt's heiress, they finally consented. The governor of the tiny island urged her departure, and was supported by a missionary who added his voice to the plea. At length Virginia made up her mind to go, and prepared to sail.

The aunt in Normandy sent money for clothes and jewels, and her passage. In her new clothes, she was transformed into a goddess. As she paraded before Paul, decked in jewels and satins and silks and furs, his heart was near to breaking with his love of her. But his mother told him that Virginia was an heiress well born, whereas Paul was only the illegitimate son of a poor and ignorant peasant.

One day as Paul wandered in the forest, with his grief gnawing at his heart, Virginia quietly departed on the boat, and sailed away from her well-loved island home.

Returning to the farmhouse, Paul determined to learn to read, in order that he might know something of the country to which his love had sailed. At length a letter came from Virginia and he was able to read it himself. It was full of love for him, but she was unhappy so far from her dear island and her friends. She sent him some flower seeds, and bade him plant them near the spot where they had said good-by, which she called Farewell Rock.

After some months, the rumor came that Virginia was about to marry some rich nobleman. On hearing this, Paul's faithful heart was once more cast down to the depths of despair.

At daybreak one morning, Paul saw a white flag flying, which always announced the arrival of a ship. A little later, Madame de la Tour gave Paul a letter from Virginia, in which she told them she was coming home. Paul kissed it rapturously and thrust it into his bosom. As Madame de la Tour read the letter to the household, every heart rejoiced, and all embraced each other in their joy.

As Paul hastened to inform all the neighbors of Virginia's pending arrival, a messenger came to announce that the ship which had been sighted was foundering and signaling for help. A terrible storm was coming up, and by midnight the sea was pounding with terrific fury against the rocks. Paul was desperate as he heard the signal guns. All night long he stood and watched, unable to do anything to help.

At daybreak the governor and the islanders gathered at the shore, where they could dimly see the foundering ship. They feared a hurricane, and hoped they might help land the passengers and crew.

At nine o'clock a whirlwind swept the harbor, and the ship was seen, lying like a broken thing upon the rocks, her proud prow pointed to the sea.

A desperate cry arose, and Paul tried to throw himself into the ocean. They held him back, then tied a rope to him, so that he might be pulled out. As he swam furiously toward the ship, he saw the white figure of Virginia, her arms outstretched to shore. He never reached the ship. They pulled him out unconscious, and recovered the body of the drowned Virginia. In one hand she clasped a picture of Paul to her breast. They carried her gently to a fisherman's hut.

Paul was brought home. He regained consciousness, but his loving heart was broken.

At a touching and beautifully simple ceremony, in which all the servants of the island took part, they buried Virginia on the western side of the little island church, at a point where she had often rested on her way to mass with Paul.

And there, after a few weeks, they brought the body of Paul for burial. His heart was broken and he had died for love.

They buried him near her, so that she might rest forever at his side.

The Red and the Black

By STENDHAL

HENRI-MARIE BEYLE, *who wrote under the pseudonym of Stendhal, was born in Grenoble on January 23, 1783. He was educated at the École Centrale, where he distinguished himself scholastically. Through family influence he obtained a post in the War Office and was eventually sent to Italy, which soon became more dear to him than his native land. He served as a soldier of the Empire, then returned to Italy, from which he was exiled in 1821 for nine years under suspicion of espionage. His literary work was always an avocation; he was constantly oppressed by poverty which was especially trying to one who fancied himself a dandy and dilettante. His early death came in 1842, before he had known complete recognition of his genius.*

JULIEN SOREL was possessed of a demon. The demon's name was Ambition. The son of a poor, brutalized, and avaricious carpenter, held in contempt and hatred by his stupid brothers, Julien, from earliest days of conscious thought, was determined to get ahead in the world. His weapon was hypocrisy.

Julien was blessed with a type of melancholy good looks which women were to find irresistible; he had, too, an amazingly retentive memory and had committed to memory the whole of the Bible in Latin. Although he was secretly an unbeliever he planned to use the Church as the steppingstone of his ambition. His sympathies were Jacobin, and he had a passionate concealed admiration for Napoleon, whose shadow, despite the return of the monarchy, still covered the land. Unwilling to ally with any but a successful movement, Julien kept his true thoughts on every subject as secret as though they were crimes.

The young man's first step upward from his peasant origin came when M. de Renal, the bourgeois mayor of Verrières, in an effort to impress his social and political rivals hired Julien as tutor to his children. At the start, Julien adapted slowly to the mayor's menage. He was conscious of affronts to his dignity and secretly feared that he was classed as a servant in the house. In an effort to justify himself he started to pay assiduous court to Mme. de Renal, a good, simple, beautiful woman whose husband, although she did not guess it, bored her. As innocent as he, Mme. de Renal found Julien's sensibility, his delicacy of thought and spiritual beauty charming after the coarse brutality of the money-worshipping mayor. Julien determined upon the seduction of Mme. de Renal not out of passion; her capitulation was a victory which his tortured ego must win. Her final surrender was joyless to him—he feared that she might detect that he was not the gentleman of the world that he posed as. She did not. His youth and delicacy were enchanting to her. Gradually her ardor reassured him. By the fourth assignation he was madly in love with her.

The happiness ended when Mme. de Renal's youngest child fell ill and she conceived that this was the punishment of God for her adultery. Rumors of the liaison became rife. Mme. de Renal managed to convince her husband of her innocence. It was deemed expedient that Julien leave Verrières. His one friend, the peasant Fouqué, had offered him part of his prosperous lumbering business but Julien, unwilling to sacrifice the hope of future greatness for present comfort, preferred to accept an offer of a place in the seminary at Besançon.

Julien was monstrously unhappy at the seminary. Following his policy of succeeding through hypocrisy, he found that to his fellow seminarists, concerned with food and bourgeois comfort, his superiority of mind and reticence were insupportable. His one friend was the Director of the Seminary, the Abbé Pirard, a stern Jansenist, who was conscious of Julien's intellectual gifts. When Julien was appointed tutor and received a mysterious money gift—in reality from the Marquis de la Mole, an immensely rich admirer of the Abbé Pirard—his lot was slightly improved, but the secret insatiable ambition still surged within him. When the Abbé, upon leaving the directorship of the seminary to enter the service of the Marquis de la Mole, obtained a post as secretary to the Marquis for Julien that young man was overjoyed.

After quitting the seminary and before departing for Paris, Julien paid a clandestine visit to his erstwhile mistress, Mme. de Renal. She, influenced by fear and remorse, was at first cold to him but soon capitulated to his passion. After remaining with her a night and a day he was forced to make his escape by a window while the suspicious M. de Renal searched Mme. de Renal's bedroom.

Julien's stay in the Hôtel de la Mole was at first difficult. His manners were rustic and although he had had a fine classical training his knowledge of modern things was limited. Nevertheless, he soon remedied his lacks. He had the gift of silence and impressed the kindly Marquis with his discretion. The Marquis soon became deeply attached to the young man and gradually entrusted to him the management of many of his business affairs. Julien was soon introduced to the political life of the nobleman who was a confirmed monarchist, and the young man artfully concealed his inward hatred and resentment of the aristocracy.

Mlle. Mathilde de la Mole, the Marquis' daughter, was coldly beautiful, self-willed, and intelligent. From the first Julien was conscious of her antagonism toward him and felt repelled by her icy beauty. His indifference first piqued, then attracted her. This feeling kindled into infatuation, and when she wrote him a letter suggesting a rendezvous Julien knew she was his. Conquering his feelings of guilt toward his benefactor, the Marquis, Julien possessed himself of Mathilde. She regretted her rashness and lack of pride almost immediately. When he knew that she was not his Julien fell in love with her. A few days later she again surrendered to him, changed her mind again, and heaped upon him abuse aimed at his lowly birth.

His pride outraged, yet still madly infatuated, on a mission to Strasbourg for the Marquis, Julien told an acquaintance of his situation and received advice as to how to win back the fickle girl.

Julien pretended indifference to Mathilde and feigned a passion for one Mme. Fervaques. Mathilde soon became desperate with jealousy and abandoned all discretion. She became *enceinte*.

Mathilde confessed her condition to her father in a letter and avowed her determination to become Julien's wife. The Marquis, although enraged, conferred wealth upon Julien, gave him a commission in the Fifteenth Regiment of Hussars and changed his name to the aristocratic one of de La Vernaye. He seemed about to consent to the marriage when a letter from Mme. de Renal, prompted by her confessor, branded Julien as a fortune-hunter and seducer of women.

His ambitions blasted, Julien attempted to assassinate Mme. de Renal. In prison he learned that she had not died and he realized that it was she whom he loved. He was quite willing to die for the attempted murder and awaited his end with courage and calm.

Although Mathilde attempted bribery and used her immense

influence Julien lost his case when he spoke at the trial against the aristocracy and the bourgeoisie and in favor of the peasantry. Mme. de Renal visited him in prison and they were reconciled. At the end he abandoned all hypocrisy and faced the guillotine his true self.

The Wandering Jew

By EUGENE SUE

BORN *in France in 1804, Eugene Sue was educated to be a physician. Then he joined the French navy, in which he spent six years. In 1830 he inherited his father's rich estate and decided to try a career as a writer. His first novel was a success, and he settled down to produce fiction, histories, and unsuccessful plays. While he was gaining worldwide fame, he interested himself in the problems of laboring people. Driven into exile when Louis Napoleon became emperor, Sue died at Annecy, Savoy, on August 3, 1857.*

IN THE YEAR 1831, seven persons scattered through the world possessed bronze medals bearing these legends on reverse and obverse:

VICTIM	:	IN PARIS
of	:	Rue St. François, No. 3,
L. C. D. J.	:	In a century and a half
Pray for me!	:	you will be.
———	:	February the 13th, 1832.
PARIS	:	———
February the 13th, 1682	:	PRAY FOR ME!

The seven were descendants of Marius, Count of Rennepont, who had committed suicide in 1682 rather than serve a sentence in the galleys as a result of the machinations of the powerful Order of the Jesuits. The Jesuits had hated his family ever since his grandfather had broken with them, and now his property was confiscated for the benefit of the order. The Count had saved fifty thousand crowns and the house on the Rue St. François; these he left with Isaac Samuel, an honest friend, telling him to keep the money invested at moderate interest. The medals described above were distributed among the Count's relatives, with only the information that it would be to their descendants' interest to be at the house on the date specified. Meantime, Samuel's son and grandson continued faithfully to accumulate the Rennepont fortune, whose magnitude was suspected only by the Jesuits, who had vigilantly kept their eyes on the unknowing family of the Count. The Jesuits were determined that this fortune should be theirs, and their plots were based upon their knowledge that it would be divided among those holders of the medals who appeared in person on February 13, 1832.

The seven holders of the medals were: two twin girls, a dethroned prince, a missionary priest, a man of the middle class, a young lady of wealth, and a working man. And here is what happened to them as a result of the operations of Abbé d'Aigrigny, a former marquis who was head of the Jesuits in Paris.

The girls, Rose and Blanche Simon, gentle and innocent daughters of Napoleon's Marshal Simon, had left their mother's grave in Siberia to travel to France under charge of an old soldier named Dagobert, a faithful follower of their father. The children's mother had been separated from the Marshal before their birth; she was exiled to Siberia, while he was forced to flee to India. In Germany the girls and Dagobert were thrown into jail through the trickery of Morok, a wild beast showman who was an agent of d'Aigrigny.

Simon, in India, had trained the troops of the King of Mundi. The British overthrew the King, and his son, Prince Djalma, fled to Java with the Marshal. Through his French mother, the Prince held one of the Rennepont medals. The long arm of the Jesuits tried, but failed, to keep Djalma from taking passage to France.

The priest was Gabriel, an orphan reared by Frances Baudoin, the wife of Dagobert. Frances, a faithful Catholic, had been induced by the priests to let Gabriel be one of them. It was on him that the Jesuits' plot hinged, for as a member of their order he was required to yield all he owned to the Society. They knew of his Rennepont descent; he did not.

The middle-class heir was François Hardy, a manufacturer among whose employees were Agricola, the son of Dagobert, and Marshal Simon's elderly father, who refused to give up his employment as a mechanic. And the working-man heir was Jacques Rennepont, a gay young fellow known as Sleepinbuff. Neither had the slightest notion of his inheritance; it was easy for the Jesuits to get them out of the way on February 13—Hardy by tricking him into a trip away from Paris; Sleepinbuff by imprisonment for debt.

Two mysterious persons had watched over the Rennepont heirs. One was the legendary Wandering Jew, the shoemaker condemned to "go on" forever when he refused to allow Christ to rest under His burden of the cross. The Rennneponts were descendants of the Jew's sister. The other was Herodias, similarly punished when she demanded the head of John the Baptist. Never allowed to rest at one place, this man and this woman could not circumvent the Jesuits' plots, but they were able to rescue Gabriel from savages in America, and to inform Marshal Simon that he was a father. It was the additional horrible fate of the Wandering Jew that often cholera followed in his footsteps.

Freed from prison in Germany by the Wandering Jew, the girls and Dagobert took ship for France, and were cast on shore there by a storm which also wrecked the vessel on which Gabriel and Djalma were arriving from America and Java. This was but a few days before February 13, 1832, and the Jesuits were thrown into a flurry of activity by the unexpected appearance of so many heirs.

The seventh heir, the young lady of wealth, was the beautiful Adrienne de Cardoville, whose aunt and guardian, the Princess de Saint-Dizier, was a female Jesuit. The Princess and d'Aigrigny once were lovers; now they were co-plotters. Adrienne was an independent young woman, and she had some small idea of the need of keeping the appointment in the Rue St. François. Further, she had learned of the arrival of the Prince and the twins, and knew that they were relatives of hers.

The Jesuits acted swiftly to silence this threat; by a trick, they confined Adrienne in the lunatic asylum of Dr. Baleinier, a lay Jesuit. Then, acting through the confessor of Frances Baudoin— with whom Dagobert had left the children when he was called out of town after their arrival in Paris—the society secretly clapped the twin girls into a convent. Djalma was drugged on his way to Paris.

Thus Gabriel was the only heir to appear at the Count's house on February 13. With him were d'Aigrigny and Father Rodin, his secretary. Gabriel, still ignorant of the fortune, had heard of the Jesuits' machinations toward the twin wards of Dagobert, his foster-father. He demanded his release from the order, but first the Jesuits forced him to sign a legal disclaimer of all property he might inherit.

Then the aged David Samuel revealed the amount of the wealth of which he was guardian. The Rennepont fortune had increased to the tremendous sum of 212,175,000 francs—far beyond even the Jesuits' imaginings. Gabriel saw how he had been used to defraud the other six heirs, but all now seemed lost—until the mysterious Herodias appeared and produced a codicil to the Count's will. The day for delivery of the fortune was postponed to June 1, 1832!

Until now the heirs had no understanding of the depths of the plot against them. Suddenly all was made clear. And the Abbé d'Aigrigny dictated to M. Rodin a despairing letter to Rome. Rodin refused to send the letter. Instead he produced a document which enabled him to give orders to the Abbé. And this ascetic secretary became revealed as a man of cold and brilliant intellect whose secret ambition was no less than the papacy—a seat he hoped to attain by obtaining the Rennepont wealth for the Church. Rodin now set forth to attain this goal by playing upon the emotions and sincerity of the Rennepont heirs, instead of using the scarcely-concealed violence favored by d'Aigrigny.

First Rodin appeared in the role of friend to the heirs, seeking thereby to win their confidence. He obtained the release of the twins from their convent, and Adrienne from her cell. He helped Adrienne to establish Djalma in Oriental comfort in à Paris house. Gabriel had taken a rural pastorate, and was no longer a source of worry. The other two heirs were neglected for the moment.

By pretending to be the repentant ex-secretary of the Abbé, Rodin gained access to the innermost thoughts of the heirs. Then he began to sow doubts. By a devilish trick he disposed of one enemy, an honest hunchbacked seamstress known as Mother Bunch. This unfortunate girl, a friend of Agricola and Frances Baudoin, was not deluded by Rodin's words. She had been taken into the home of Adrienne; Rodin forced her to flee by threatening to publish a stolen diary in which the sensitive Mother Bunch had written her secret love for Agricola.

With the field comparatively clear, Rodin caused Adrienne and Djalma to meet. The beautiful girl and the handsome Prince fell in love. Then Rodin filled them with despair by telling each that the other loved another. Marshal Simon returned; Rodin destroyed his happiness by having the Marshal informed of the plight of Napoleon's son, so that he was torn between love for his children and duty to his old leader.

The destruction of the manufacturer Hardy and the workman Sleepinbuff was easily accomplished. Hardy's factory was burned by a mob incited by the Jesuits, and he was told of the disloyalty of an old friend and the flight of the woman he loved. Hardy, distraught, was led to join the religious order, and in his weakened condition he soon died. Sleepinbuff, released from debtors' prison, was pushed into a dance of dissipation which brought him, too, to the grave.

Meantime the Wandering Jew's unwilling footsteps were forced toward Paris by his guiding spirit. With him he brought cholera, and the great city was transformed into a madhouse of death. Rodin was stricken, but recovered by sheer willpower. Continuing his plotting, he tricked Marshal Simon into starting to Austria to attempt the rescue of Napoleon's son. With the Marshal away, his gentle daughters were easily induced to visit a cholera hospital in search of their stricken nurse. There they were themselves seized by the epidemic, and died in the arms of Gabriel, who was now succoring the sick in Paris. The Jesuit vengeance had cost this gentle priest his pulpit because he had buried a Protestant in hallowed ground.

Then Rodin completed his triumph. Adrienne and Djalma had discovered his trickery and had found happiness in their love for each other. The Jesuit lured Djalma to an apartment where he apparently saw his beloved in the arms of Agricola. The Hindu killed the girl and wounded the youth in a jealous rage. Then he went to Adrienne's house and took poison. Adrienne appeared, and Djalma found that he had stabbed a girl hired by the priest to impersonate his beloved. But Djalma already was dying, and Adrienne did not want to live on alone. She too drank of the poison, and they died in a loving embrace.

Rodin's triumph appeared complete. Six of the heirs were dead, and the Order of the Jesuits was assured of receiving whatever Gabriel inherited. But Rodin's ambitions had gained him powerful enemies, who believed that the order was doomed by the priest's scheme to become general of the Jesuits and use that position to attain the papacy. One of these enemies was d'Aigrigny. Rodin disposed of him by goading him into a duel with the bereaved Marshal Simon in which both men were killed.

June 1 arrived, and Rodin went to claim the Rennepont wealth. In his pocket was his appointment, which had just arrived, as general of the Jesuits. David Samuel had retrieved the bodies of

the six victims. Rodin was unmoved by this sight. But he was
horrified to see Samuel burn the papers which stood for the
. Rennepont wealth. The custodian was determined that the
Jesuits should never receive this fortune which the Count had so
carefully concealed from them. And Rodin had one last horror
coming to him. His enemies had poisoned him. He died before
the biers of those he had sent to their deaths.

Candide

By VOLTAIRE

JEAN FRANÇOIS MARIE AROUET *was born in Paris on November 21,
1694. Although trained for the legal profession, he preferred letters,
and with the production of his first play,* Oedipe, *in 1718 he
found himself the most popular literary figure of French society.
He took the name of Voltaire to distinguish himself from his
brother. Constantly in trouble because of his caustic wit and
independent spirit, he fled to England after two brief sojourns
in the Bastille. He returned to France in a few years where he
grew immensely rich through speculation. After the death of his
mistress, the Marchioness du Chatelet, in 1749, he accepted the
invitation of Frederick the Great of Prussia to live at the Prussian
court. Then Voltaire returned to France to live with his niece at
Ferney, a miserable village which, under his care, developed into
a thriving and wealthy town. He tried to return to Paris but the
effort was too great at his age, and he died on May 30, 1778.*

AS A YOUNG LAD, Candide was brought up in a noble family of
Westphalia. Though his legitimacy was suspect, he had the joy

of listening to the learned Dr. Pangloss, the tutor of the noble family's daughter, Cunegund, an appetizing, plump girl of seventeen. Miss Cunegund had already, unobserved, shown an interest in some lessons in experimental physics which Dr. Pangloss was giving to her mother's maid. And one day when she found herself behind a screen with Candide, she was only too willing to put into practice what she had observed from Dr. Pangloss' lessons to the maid.

Their summary interruption by the Baron, her father, led to Candide's ejection from the castle. Wandering alone, he was impressed into the army of the Bulgarians, who had begun a war against the Abarians.

In the course of the war the castle of the Baron was ransacked by the Bulgarians, and Candide, wandering among the corpses, came across Dr. Pangloss, who had barely saved his skin.

He reported that everyone in the castle had been killed and Cunegund had been ravished by the soldiers. They came across a charitable Anabaptist who took them with him and put Pangloss into his service. Two months later they sailed with him for Lisbon. In spite of his misfortunes, Pangloss' insistent belief that this was the best of all possible worlds was not shaken.

In a storm at sea, their friend the Anabaptist was killed by a murderous sailor, and the only survivors were the sailor, Candide, and Pangloss. No sooner had they pulled themselves out of Lisbon Bay and come into the city than the ground under their feet began to tremble. In the ensuing earthquake, thirty thousand lives were lost.

The Grand Inquisitor of Lisbon decided than an auto-da-fé should be held to prevent earthquakes, and Candide and Pangloss were singled out among other victims. Candide got off with a severe beating, but poor Pangloss was hanged.

Starving and in sore distress at the fate of his companion, Candide was approached by an old woman who told him to take courage and to follow her. She found him shelter and brought him food while his wounds healed. On the third day she conducted him to a house on the outskirts of the city where he was led into the presence of a beautiful girl. To his joy he found that it was Cunegund.

Cunegund told him that, in the sacking of the castle, one of her ravishers had been shot by a Bulgarian captain who had kept her as his mistress for two months and then had sold her to a Portuguese Jew, Don Isacchar. Threatened by the Grand Inquisitor with the auto-da-fé, Don Isacchar had agreed to yield her to him. That same night, the Jew found Candide on the divan with Cunegund, and Candide promptly ran his sword through him. To his own amazement, a short while later Candide disposed of the Grand Inquisitor in the same fashion.

The old woman advised them to flee, so the three set out for Cadiz, there hoping to find a ship going to the new world. At Cadiz, Candide's military experience came in handy, for the Jesuits put him in command of a company of infantry which they were dispatching to Paraguay. On the trip the old woman told them the story of her life—a woeful tale that all but undermined Candide's faith in Pangloss' philosophy.

The Governor of Buenos Aires immediately took a fancy to Cunegund on their arrival, and the old woman privately advised her to leave them in order to gain the favor of the Governor. Candide had acquired a valuable serving man named Cacambo, and with him sought an audience with the head of the Jesuit order in Paraguay. To his surprise he found the Jesuit was a German, and the son of that same noble family to which he had belonged, and the brother of Cunegund. When Candide mentioned his intention of marrying Cunegund, the brother flew into a fury and struck him a blow on the face. Candide immediately drew his sword and slew the Jesuit Baron. At once he and Cacambo took flight.

In the interior of the continent they came upon a marvelous land called El Dorado, where the people lived in utter contentment, in disdain of the gold and precious jewels which were everywhere. Candide and Cacambo could scarcely believe the wonders they saw. When it was time for them to go, the ruler of El Dorado gave them a hundred rare sheep all laden with diamonds and riches, but by the time they reached Cayenne all but two of the sheep had perished. Still, in spite of these losses, Candide was as wealthy as twenty monarchs.

Candide now sent Cacambo back to Buenos Aires with part of his fortune to ransom Cunegund, and resolved to take passage to Europe and meet Cacambo and Cunegund at Venice. He bargained with a Dutch skipper for the return voyage, but the Dutchman turned out to be a scoundrel, and departed before the sailing time with Candide's two sheep. Candide engaged passage on a French vessel, advertising beforehand that he desired as a companion the most unfortunate man in the province. An old scholar named Martin won the competition, and they sailed for Bordeaux.

On the voyage Candide witnessed a sea battle in which the vessel of the Dutch swindler was sunk. One of the sheep was the only living thing that was rescued; the Dutchman and his ill-gotten wealth went to the bottom of the ocean. Though Candide had no desire to linger in France, the travelers ran into a little Perigord abbé who was desirous of showing them something of French society. So they visited the theatre, heard the critics, and went to the salons of smart society, and Candide soon learned that the French people were very clever at separating a wealthy visitor from his money.

Touching briefly on the English coast in time to witness the execution of an admiral, Candide, with Martin, proceeded on to Venice. There he found no trace of Cacambo. He did meet Paquette, the maid who had caused Pangloss so many pains. In her company was an embittered monk, Brother Giroflèe. One day at a dinner where six exiled rulers were being entertained, Candide met Cacambo, who was now the slave of a deposed sultan.

Cacambo told him that he had lost all the money. After he had paid a huge ransom for Cunegund, the ship on which they were returning had been seized by pirates, and Cunegund had been sold as a slave. She was now washing dishes for a foreign sovereign, living on a pension near the Sea of Marmora.

So Candide, Martin, and Cacambo set out for Constantinople. Arriving at the Bosphorus, Candide paid Cacambo's ransom. They then made the astonishing discovery that two of the galley-slaves on their ship were Pangloss and Cunegund's brother, the Jesuit Baron. Neither of them had been killed: Pangloss had miraculously escaped from his hanging, and Candide's blade had merely wounded the Baron.

When they reached Cunegund, Candide saw that she was now as ugly as she once had been beautiful, and if it had not been for her brother's provoking insistence that he should not marry into his family, Candide would have been quite happy to do without her. However, they soon dropped the Baron into the sea. Candide's fortune was now spent, and so they all settled down on a farm near the Sea of Marmora. They passed their days arguing the wisdom of the philosophy of Pangloss—that this was still the best of all possible worlds.

Nana

By ÉMILE ZOLA

ÉMILE ÉDOUARD CHARLES ANTOINE ZOLA *was born in Paris on April 2, 1840, the son of an Italian-Greek engineer and a Frenchwoman. Reared in Aix, in 1858 he found work as a clerk in Paris, where he published his first book in 1864. By 1866 Zola had begun his career as a vigorous newspaper critic of art and literature, which he continued in more than a score of novels and other books. His J'Accuse in 1898 was instrumental in winning Capt. Dreyfus' vindication, which was achieved before Zola died on Sept. 29, 1902, asphyxiated by a defective stove in his bedroom.*

M. FAUCHERY, the journalist, introduced Hector de la Faloise, his country cousin, to Bordenave, manager of the Variety Theatre, at which "The Blonde Venus" was opening that evening. Bordenave insisted on calling the theatre "my brothel," and declared that Nana, his new star of whom all Paris was talking, couldn't sing or act and didn't need to.

There was an interesting crowd at the first night: Steiner the banker, with the husband of his mistress, Rose Mignon, Nana's co-star; Mignon managed his wife's love affairs; Daguenet, a young man who had squandered a fortune on women and was known as Nana's sweetheart; Lucy Stewart, Blanche de Sivry, Gaga, famous courtesans; Count Muffat de Beuville, court chamberlain, with his wife and father-in-law, the Marquis de Chouard; Labordette and the Count de Vandeuvres, young Paris blades.

The play was a mockery of the gods of Olympus, and the audience grew impatient for Nana's belated appearance. Very tall and very plump for her 18 years, with beautiful golden hair floating over her shoulders, Nana truly had no voice or stage skill, but suddenly a youngster exclaimed: "She is stunning!" and all the men cried: "So she is!" Every opera glass was fixed on her scanty tunic, and the applause was deafening when she finished.

But in the last act, when Nana appeared with no other veil than her locks, there was no applause. The men bent forward, their nostrils contracted, as out of this laughing girl there emerged a woman, appalling all who beheld her, displaying the hidden secrets of inordinate desire. Nana's smile now was the mocking one of a destroyer of men.

Next morning, in her apartment on the Boulevard Haussmann, Nana was besieged by men of all ages instead of the two paying gentlemen who had supported the establishment before. She pushed aside her host of debts, worried a bit over her child Louis, whom she had had when only 16, and talked with her maid Zoe, who had come with her from the house of Madame Tricon. Francis the hairdresser came, and Nana dressed and hurried off for an hour to a man from whom she got 400 francs she needed. Everyone who had been at the theatre seemed to be calling on Nana, and she had to slip out through the kitchen to get to that evening's performance.

The respectable side of this Paris world gathered at the Muffats' on Tuesday evening. Fauchery was interested in a rumor that the Countess, known as Sabine, had had a lover. The journalist was quietly inviting the men to a dinner at Nana's the next midnight, but the Count and the elderly Marquis refused.

The table in Nana's drawing room was crowded by the number of unexpected guests, and Bordenave, who had hurt his leg, took up two chairs. Young George Hugon, the schoolboy who had been the first to cry out at the theatre, was regaled by Daguenet with the histories of the women present. Steiner, a terror on the stock market, sat beside Nana securely hooked and looking quite dumfounded, waiting only for her to fix a price. And Rose Mignon, instead of worrying at losing a lover, played up to Fauchery, who could reward her only with notices in the press. The party broke up in drunkenness and quarreling at dawn.

A few weeks later Steiner bought Nana a country house at Loiret, near the home of the Hugons; and Nana soon won a vacation and went there, inviting all her friends to visit her. Meantime Count Muffat and his family became guests of Madame Hugon. The Count, in the company of an English prince, had visited Nana backstage a few days before and the sight of her awakened a belated youth in him; he would have given all he possessed to be with her one hour that night.

Nana was fascinated, like a little girl, by the beauty of her new house. George slipped over in the rain on her first day there, and she found the boy adorable. Count Muffat also called, but Nana was less willing, though his intensity frightened her. Steiner was there, but Nana pleaded sickness, and for a week stayed as faithful to George as a girl of 15 with her first love.

Nana's visitors from Paris arrived, and George went with them on a Sunday excursion and was spied by his mother in Nana's coach. George was scolded by his brother Philippe; and that night

Nana yielded to Muffat. Then she returned to Paris, where another actress had taken her part.

Three months later Count Muffat, who did not know that he had been sharing Nana with Steiner, quarreled when he found her with Fontan, the comedian of the theatre. Nana was angry with Fauchery because he had written an article, "The Golden Fly," about a tall, beautiful girl who had come from the gutters of Paris to corrupt and destroy the aristocracy. So Nana won a double revenge by telling Muffat his wife was deceiving him with Fauchery—which was true, though the Count could not prove it.

Now Nana threw herself into love for Fontan, letting him beat her and spend her money, and walking the streets to support him. Satin, an innocent-looking little prostitute, was her only friend now. But a near escape from the police led Nana to make peace with Muffat after several months of this. Part of the price was the role of a duchess in Bordenave's new play, which the Count financed. And a mansion near the Parc Monceau closed the deal; the Count was ready to give his whole fortune to have Nana all for himself. Nana was a great failure in the play, but she became the queen of her world.

Her home was furnished with the best; her bedroom was done in lace and silver, the floor covered with bearskins; there were many servants and five carriages, and expenses were 300,000 francs a year. Nana swore fidelity, and even advised Muffat on family affairs, but soon she was helping Count de Vandeuvres finish up his fortune. Next George reappeared, and Nana charmed his brother Philippe, who had been sent to rescue George from her. But with men about her all the time, Nana was bored; and with money pouring in she was always in debt. She would hurry to sickly little Louis and be motherly for a few hours. Then Nana found Satin, and installed her in the mansion. Satin became her vice, and the men found they had a competitor.

On a June Sunday the race for the Grand Prize of Paris was to be run at Longchamps. Vandeuvres' last hope of retrieving his fortune was entrusted to his horse Lusignan, a favorite, and a filly he had named after Nana, who was among the brilliant gathering. Nana held court from her carriage, dealing out champagne to the men who crowded about. Then the race began and the filly came from behind to win at long odds, while Nana heard her name shouted by the great crowd. Vandeuvres had engineered a great betting coup, but did for himself by laying money against Lusignan. The story got out at once, and the scandal ruined him. He burned his stable and died in the fire. Nana shrugged her shoulders.

A few days later Nana was seriously ill; she had had a miscarriage. On her sickbed she induced Muffat to make up with his wife; he at last had obtained proof of her indiscretions. Between them they had wasted his fortune, and in the wreck of their affairs they were reconciled. More important to Muffat, he discovered Nana in George's arms. She had become more careless in her living; the servants cheated her, she spent thousands of francs on pretty trifles which she carelessly broke; tremendous bills remained unpaid.

Then Philippe was arrested for having stolen 12,000 francs from his regiment to spend on Nana. George learned that she had been his brother's mistress, and stabbed himself in Nana's bedroom without succeeding in killing himself. Madame Hugon, stupefied, took George away to nurse him.

Now Nana made no pretense of faithfulness to Muffat. Men came to her openly at all hours, she stripped one after another of his money, and defied the Count to complain. Steiner, La Faloise, Fauchery were devoured. And Muffat, unable as ever to resist her, played dog to amuse Nana. But even for him the end came. He found his doddering father-in-law, the Marquis, with Nana. Muffat fled and sought peace in church. And George died after all, Nana learned.

Though all she touched rotted away, Nana remained as beautiful and healthy as ever. And then, as if by a wild prank, she auctioned off her home and all in it for 600,000 francs and vanished into foreign lands, whence stories of her exploits trickled back

Months later Nana heard that Louis was ill. She hurried back, caught smallpox from him, and died at the Grand Hotel. Her old rivals were with her at the end, but the men feared the disease and stayed away. Rose Mignon was the last to leave, just as a crowd swept past crying: "To Berlin!" France was at war with Prussia.

L'Assommoir

By ÉMILE ZOLA

ALL NIGHT Gervaise waited for Lantier, her lover, to come home but not until the next morning did he return to their frowsy little bedroom in the "Quartier." Then his manner was brutal, almost vicious, and he looked with contempt on Gervaise and little Claude and Etienne, the offspring of their liaison. He flung himself wearily on the soiled bed and sent Gervaise to the laundry to wash their few ragged clothes.

Gervaise was only twenty-two. She had fled their country town with Lantier when she was little more than a child; Etienne had been born when she was fourteen, Claude four years later. Gervaise's family had been cruel to her, but, until lately, Lantier had not. Now, she knew, he was under the influence of L'Assommoir, the dram shop and distillery of the neighborhood, and of Adele, a pretty prostitute. Gervaise was slim and fair; she would have been very pretty had it not been for a slight limp which became very noticeable when she was tired, and the worn air that came from toil and privation. Gervaise's dream was to have a nice home, hard work, and enough to feed herself and her children.

At the laundry where the neighborhood women did their washing, Gervaise was moved to confide the story of Lantier's brutal treatment to Mme. Boche, who had befriended her. She was interrupted by her children who came running in to tell her that Lantier had deserted them, leaving with Adele and almost all of

Gervaise's few possessions. Gervaise was overcome with fear for her children's future and was roused nearly to madness by the taunts of Virginie, Adele's strapping sister, who had come to the laundry to watch the effect of Adele's triumph on her rival. Although smaller than Virginie and very frail, Gervaise sprang upon her tormentor and the two women beat each other with fists, laundry implements and washing. Rage lent Gervaise strength and she emerged victorious. But Virginie never forgave her.

Gervaise was able to find employment with Mme. Fauconnier, a laundress, and by industry was able to provide for herself and her children. One Coupeau, a tinsmith who knew of her unhappy life with Lantier, wished her to live with him but Gervaise preferred to devote her life to providing comfort for the little boys. But overcome by emotion at Coupeau's proposing marriage, Gervaise finally consented to join her destiny to his.

The marriage started off inauspiciously enough. They were nearly penniless and Coupeau's sister and brother-in-law, the prosperous and tight-fisted Lorrileuxes, disapproved of the match. But Coupeau proved an excellent husband, and by perseverance and hard work the Coupeaus were able to save as well as maintain a decent home. Gervaise gained a reputation for excellence as a laundress and clear-starcher and her dream was to have a shop of her own one day. Four years after the marriage little Nana was born; soon after her confinement Gervaise had returned to work.

But while Nana was still a tiny girl an accident befell her father. The tinsmith was working on a roof when his little daughter diverted his attention for a second. He slipped and fell to the ground. Gervaise screamed hysterically. She did not allow him to be taken to the hospital, but insisted on caring for him at home in spite of the difficulty and costliness entailed. Coupeau survived, but recovered slowly and the months of inactivity left him a changed man. No longer was he characterized by vigor and a desire to be successful for the sake of his little family. Idleness no longer irked him and his visits to L'Assommoir were more frequent than even his indulgent wife suspected.

Gervaise prepared to sacrifice her dream of the little shop of her own. But a neighbor who secretly loved her, Goujet, the golden-bearded, innocent-hearted blacksmith, prevailed upon her to borrow five hundred francs from him and his mother. With this sum she opened a little establishment and soon had it running successfully.

But gradually Gervaise's debts increased. Coupeau continued to be idle most of the time; Mamma Coupeau, Gervaise's mother-in-law, was homeless and had to be taken in; Gervaise herself was inclined to be spendthrift and demanded the little luxuries of table that she worked so hard to earn. Goujet's five hundred francs were never returned to him and soon tradesmen's bills started to pile up. Still Gervaise was successful and respected in the neighborhood and she felt that she would be able to meet her obligations.

One day Gervaise discovered that Virginie, her old enemy, was a neighbor. The woman pretended to have forgiven the past incident, and plump, uncritical Gervaise was quite willing to be friends again.

Lantier returned. Gervaise had learned through Virginie that her old lover had deserted Adele and was back in the "Quartier." For some days she went in fear and trembling but Lantier made no move. Finally he appeared outside the shop at a birthday dinner that Gervaise was giving, and Coupeau, now almost constantly in a drunken condition, asked the man in. Lantier and Coupeau became drinking companions and in such a state of degradation was Coupeau that he did not mind the presence of his wife's former lover even in their home. When Lantier suggested that he live and board with the Coupeau family, the drunken tinsmith agreed. Soon Gervaise found that she must also support her seducer, who promised to pay for his maintenance but never did. And Lantier took over the entire household and ran it to suit himself. He had become quite the charming man of the world and was very popular with the ladies of the neighborhood.

Gervaise had degenerated completely. Disgusted with the continual state of filthy intoxication which characterized her husband, she found refuge in Lantier's embraces. Soon, through improvidence, she lost the shop to Virginie, who also inherited the love of Lantier.

When Nana, longing for luxury and bored with the trade of being a florist's apprentice, left home for the streets, Gervaise took to drink and became Coupeau's companion in L'Assommoir. Coupeau, suffering from delirium tremens, spent long periods in the hospital and soon died of alcoholism.

Gervaise, wretchedly poor and suffering from starvation, tried to take to the streets but she was old and nobody would have her. Her old friend Goujet rescued her from death by hunger once more, but it was too late. Worn out by liquor and starvation, Gervaise died wretchedly and alone.

Russian Novels

Crime and Punishment

By FYODOR DOSTOYEVSKY

FYODOR MIKHAILOVITCH DOSTOYEVSKY was born in Moscow on Oct. 20, 1821, and died there Jan. 28, 1881, after a life of defeats and triumphs. Educated in military and engineering schools, he quit the Russian army in 1844 to devote himself to literature. Joining a socialist study circle, he was arrested in the 1849 reactionary wave and was exiled to Siberia for four years. Then followed another period in the army, a number of years as a journalist, a period abroad to escape debts, and his final years in Russia as a popular liberal editor.

A HANDSOME, DARK YOUNG MAN, dressed in rags, walked muttering to himself from his little low-ceilinged room in a poor district of St. Petersburg. Nervously he strode to a huge house, climbed to the fourth floor, and pawned a watch with Alyona Ivanovna, a slovenly 60-year-old woman with whom he had had dealings before. His eyes were fastened on her as she secretively got out the money. Then he made his way to a tavern, sunk in wretched introspection over a plan that had been on his mind for a month.

At the tavern he listened to a jobless civil servant, Marmeladov, tell how his drinking had reduced his family to poverty and had forced his daughter Sonia to take out a yellow ticket. Then the young man, a student named Rodion Romanovitch Raskolnikov, familiarly called Rodya, helped Marmeladov home and returned to his own room, where he found a letter from his widowed mother.

His sister Dounia, he learned, had lost her job as governess in the family of Svidrigailov, a country landholder, and had decided to marry a middle-aged lawyer, Pyotr Luzhin. His mother had borrowed on her pension in order to set out for the capital, where Dounia's wedding was to be held. Rodya decided at once that his sister was marrying so that he might be provided for, and vowed to prevent any such sacrifice. Now he must end his long, passive suffering, and must act quickly.

The next afternoon he completed his long-thought-out preparations, wrapped a dummy package since he had no valuables left, and seized the porter's axe as he left the house. He told himself that criminals seemed to fail in will and reasoning power when they were most needed—he would not do that. He went to Alyona Ivanovna's room, where he found Alyona alone; and when she began to unwrap his package he struck her on the head three times. Rodya took the purse from around her neck, and was beginning to pocket the valuables from her strongbox, when Alyona's simple-minded sister Lizaveta entered unexpectedly. Killing her, too, he was about to flee when the doorbell rang.

It was two customers of the pawnbroker. Rodya heard them conclude that something was wrong, and when they went for the porter he fled, hiding in a vacant second-floor flat as the men returned upstairs. Staggering home, he returned the axe and collapsed on his bed after hiding the loot. Next day he woke and removed the marks of the killings from his clothing. Interrupted by a summons to the police station, he went in a mixture of bravado and fear, to learn that a judgment for overdue rent had been taken against him. Then he heard the unsolved murders being discussed. He fainted, explaining that he had been ill. This was indeed true. Rodya was barely able to take his loot—he had not examined it—to a courtyard and hide it under a stone, then pay a visit to Dmitri Razumihin, a student friend, before falling into a delirious fever which lasted four days.

When Rodya recovered he found that 35 rubles had arrived from his mother, who was on her way. As he lay in bed he learned that Nikolay, a painter who had been working in the empty flat, had been accused of the murders. Luzhin called, and Raskolnikov drove him away. Then he dressed, slipped away from Razumihin, who feared that his friend was still out of his mind, and went to a tavern. There Rodya jeered at Zametov, a police clerk who had been suspicious over the fainting.

Wandering about the streets, Raskolnikov saw Marmeladov mortally wounded by a cab. Again he took him home, and this time he met Sonia, a pale, frightened girl of 18 in the incongruous gaudy clothes of her profession. Leaving 20 rubles—nearly 10 had been spent for new clothes—he departed, feeling a sudden pride and self-confidence.

At home he found his sister and mother, worried over his absence. He was morbidly cold toward them, and finally Razumihin took them to the rooms Luzhin had rented for them, explaining Rodya's conduct by his illness.

As though drawn by compulsion, Raskolnikov went to Porfiry Petrovitch, head of the department of investigation, ostensibly to report that he had left valuables with old Alyona. Porfiry, a distant relative of Razumihin, chatted about an article in which Rodya had declared that true geniuses had the right to commit crimes forbidden to lesser men. Then, discussing the murders, he laid a little trap regarding certain details. Rodya sidestepped this, but realized he was suspected.

Then came a strange visit at Rodya's room from Svidrigailov, now a widower, who declared that his wife had left 3,000 rubles to Dounia, and that he wanted to give her another 10,000—and expected nothing in return.

Going to his mother and sister with news of the legacy, Rodya had the pleasure of seeing the miserly Luzhin dismissed. Now that they were provided for, he told them he wanted to see them no more. Razumihin, who was present, had by this time fallen in love with Dounia.

In another talk with Porfiry, Raskolnikov received a lecture on the psychology of crime; on how the intellectual turned criminal would lose his head, would be unable to run away, and would eventually confess. Rodya, at first too reticent, ended by shouting: "I see you suspect me. Arrest me!" Porfiry laughed at him, calmed him, and then they were suddenly interrupted by Nikolay, the painter, who confessed the murders!

Now Katerina, Marmeladov's consumptive widow, invited Rodya to a funeral feast which turned into a brawl. In the midst of it Luzhin appeared and accused Sonia of stealing 100 rubles from him—and was confounded when it developed that Luzhin had slipped the money into her pocket while openly giving her 10 rubles for her family. Rodya exposed the lawyer's plot to discredit him with his family by making it seem that their son was in love with a thief.

After this scene, Rodya confessed to Sonia that he was a murderer, and Svidrigailov listened at the door. Sonia forgave him, even when he told her that he considered the pawnbroker's life worthless, and that he had killed to prove to himself that he was a Napoleon, a great man who was a law unto himself. But finally he broke down and said: "I murdered myself, not her!" She urged him to give himself up, but he declared there was no evidence against him, that he would make a fight for his freedom.

Now Rodya wandered around for several days in a daze. In various lucid moments he recalled a vaguely threatening conversation in which Svidrigailov revealed what he knew; a visit in which Porfiry told him that he was guilty and advised him to confess and win lenience, and a last talk with his mother in which he broke down and wept.

Meantime Svidrigailov gave 3,000 rubles to Sonia so that she might follow Rodya to Siberia when the day came. Then he lured Dounia to his room, attempted to seduce her, let her escape when she convinced him she could never love him, and, after setting his affairs in order, walked up to a soldier and shot himself. But before he committed suicide, her former employer had told Dounia her brother was a murderer.

Raskolnikov, broken in spirit but not in his convictions, told Dounia when she went to him that he had only sought independence; he begged her forgiveness, and went to Sonia to get a cross she had promised him. Then he gave himself up after a final internal struggle, and was sentenced to prison for eight years, winning the mercy Porfiry had predicted.

Dounia married Razumihin, and shortly afterward her mother died. In prison Rodya was watched over by Sonia, and finally he found peace for his soul by accepting religion as she did, in place of his previous individualism.

The Brothers Karamazov

By FYODOR DOSTOYEVSKY

ONE MORNING on a bright day in August, an ancient hired carriage drove up to the grounds of a monastery. In the carriage rode a man of some fifty-seven years and his son, the first arrivals at an unfortunate meeting which had been planned to compose the differences between two members of the Karamazov family.

The old man was the infamous profligate and buffoon, Fyodor Pavlovitch Karamazov, and his second son Ivan rode with him. They were conducted into the presence of Father Zossima, one of the elders, famed for his piety and his knowledge of the human heart. Alyosha, old Karamazov's youngest son, was with him; he had been living there because of his great personal devotion to Father Zossima, who now was trying to show him that he should delay his novitiate.

Dmitri, the oldest son, appeared, and soon his father had insulted and enraged him. The issue between them had first been money—was Dmitri in debt to his father, or had the old man retained a part of Dmitri's inheritance? But more irritating and shameful than that was the revelation that they were both in love with the same woman; and old Karamazov was accusing his son of trying to extort money from him to bribe Grushenka for her love.

At the height of their argument, Father Zossima bowed to the ground before Dmitri and then left the company after beseeching their forgiveness. This brought all the family to their senses except old Karamazov, who gave a disgusting exhibition of buffoonery at the dinner prepared for them.

Later the same day, Dmitri intercepted Alyosha, his favorite brother, on his way from the monastery, and poured out a full account of all that had happened to him. He told of his meeting with the beautiful Katerina Ivanovna, of his opportune rescue of her peculating father, of Katerina's later humiliation of herself before him, and finally of the letter she had written to him asking him to marry her. Then, to Alyosha's consternation, he revealed that he considered their "betrothal" dissolved by his meeting with Grushenka, and moreover had written to Ivan about the whole affair with the hope that Katerina might fall in love with Ivan.

His last assertion was that he had spent on Grushenka 3,000 rubles, entrusted to him by Katerina, and now, in renouncing Katerina forever—so much finer and worthier than he—he wanted to restore the money. And now he proposed that Alyosha ask his father for the sum.

Alyosha told Dmitri what he already knew—that their father would not give Dmitri any money, especially since he hoped that he would be able to bribe Grushenka away from his son. Dmitri knew that his father had already drawn out 3,000 rubles for this purpose, a fact he had wormed out of Smerdyakov, the illegitimate son of old Fyodor and now his servant. To prevent his father from getting Grushenka, Dmitri said he would kill "the old man. I shan't kill her."

Alyosha continued on to the house where Katerina was staying. An odd testament of her character confronted him when he found her with Grushenka, and saw Katerina humiliated, through the miscarriage of her own designs, by Grushenka.

Shortly afterward Alyosha was drawn into the confidence of Ivan, and he learned more about this brother than he had ever known before. Ivan talked of many things. He admitted that his present hopes of gaining Katerina's love were slight, for, as long as she was driven by her terrible pride, her attention would be centered on Dmitri. Ivan also lifted the veil on some of his own inner discord and despair, telling him of a poem he had written, embodying his pessimism, called *The Grand Inquisitor*.

After talking with Smerdyakov and learning that Smerdyakov feared that some violence would shortly occur, Ivan left for Moscow.

In the meantime, the news of the death of Father Zossima came from the monastery. All the envy, the petty jealousies and spites of some of the monks came out when the corpse began to mortify, since tradition had it that the body of a true saint in death gave off no breath of corruption. Among those faithful to his memory stood Alyosha. His feet were already planted on the path to which the Elder had directed them. He was to go out into the world and learn there. Indeed, Alyosha had already plighted a troth with a young girl named Liza, although she was sickly and of a precariously unstable temperament.

What Dmitiri had heard from Alyosha confirmed in him the conviction that he had acted as a scoundrel to Katerina, and he resolved to return the 3,000 rubles. For several days he tried unsuccessfully to borrow the money, while all the time his fear that Grushenka might accept his father's offer grew more desperate.

One evening he failed to find Grushenka, unaware that she had decided to return to her first lover of five years before. He rushed to his father's house, certain that Grushenka had at last made her choice. He jumped over the garden fence and for a time observed his father through the window. . . .

Much later in the evening, Dmitri turned up at the village of Mokroe, where Grushenka had gone to meet her lover. Dmitri was excited, jubilant, and once more plentifully supplied with rubles. An orgy followed in which Grushenka's lover was exposed as a card cheat and a pompous fool, and Grushenka finally accepted the love of Dmitri. Toward morning a police official arrived to examine Dmitri in connection with the murder of Fyodor Karamazov the previous evening.

In a lengthy examination by the police officials, Dmitri maintained his innocence, but his responses only strengthened the case that was emerging against him. At the end of the examination, he was formally charged with the crime and sent to prison to await trial.

Meanwhile Ivan had returned from Moscow. Now that he fully recognized in his heart that he had had a desire for his father's death, his last meeting with Smerdyakov began to trouble him. He went to the hospital where Smerdyakov had been taken after a severe epileptic seizure following the murder. That interview was the beginning of the revelation of the truth to Ivan, and two more brought forth the whole story.

Smerdyakov told Ivan that he had killed old Karamazov after Dmitri left the garden that night. He did it solely because he felt that Ivan had directed him, had wanted him to do it. Smerdyakov had taken the money, and had left as damning evidence a torn envelope in which it had been kept. But the only evidence Ivan had was the notes themselves. And Smerdyakov hanged himself the night before Dmitri's trial began.

At the trial everything went well for the defense until Ivan took the stand. His guilty conscience proved too much for him. After he had presented the story of Smerdyakov—unsubstantiated except for the money, which he showed—he broke down completely. At the sight of Ivan's collapse, Katerina came forward with the accusation that Dmitri was, in contradiction to her earlier testimony, guilty. The letter she placed in evidence, written by Dmitri in a drunken frenzy, contained a promise to procure the money he owed her even if he had to kill his father to get it. Dmitri was not believed when he said he had paid for the orgy with 1,500 rubles of Katerina's which he had been saving.

In spite of a magnificent plea by his counsel to the jury, Dmitri was found guilty; the inevitable penalty would be a long sentence to Siberia. But now he had the complete loyalty of Grushenka and the promise of Katerina to assist him in an escape. Though she was still, at moments, a victim of her unhappy passion for Dmitri, there was a dim hope that she would eventually turn to Ivan.

Mother

By MAXIM GORKI

MAXIM GORKI (*Alexei Maximovich Pyeeshkoff*) *was born in Nizhni Novgorod on March 14, 1868. His father died when he was four. His schooling ended when he was nine, and for fifteen years he wandered all over Russia doing all kinds of work. At nineteen he attempted suicide. After that he began to write for provincial newspapers, writing articles about people he had met in his extensive journeys over Russia. He was imprisoned after the revolution of 1905, and after he won freedom he settled at Capri and continued to write. He returned to Russia in 1913 and, following the revolution, carried on cultural work among the Russian people. From that time until his death in 1936 many honors were bestowed upon him. His birthplace, famed Nizhni Novgorod, has been renamed Gorki.*

FOR THE MOTHER OF PAVEL VLASOV, one day was as empty and hopeless as the next. Her feelings were numb. Her husband was a

workingman in the factory. Most of the men in the village were
employed there. In the evening the factory ejected its people like
burnt-out ashes. In the evening and on holidays there was roister-
ing in the taverns.

Michael Vlasov was a gloomy, sullen man. "Dirty vermin" was
his favorite expression, and he used it on neighbors and family
alike. When he was fourteen, Pavel warned his father not to touch
him; and he held a hammer in his hand. When Michael died, he
died hard, and writhed in agony on his bed for five days and
begged his wife to give him poison.

Two weeks after his father's death, Pavel came home drunk one
day. His mother tried to comfort him, and Pavel remembered that
during his father's lifetime she had remained unnoticed in the
house. She had always lived in expectation of the blows of his
father.

His mother noticed that Pavel did not get drunk again. Often
he stayed up very late reading, and she worried about that. Finally
he explained to her that he was reading forbidden books. That
frightened her; she could not understand what was in his mind.

One evening he told her that he expected friends on Saturday.
On that day, Pavel went out for a while, and the mother was left
to meet his friends. They had come from the city—one was a man
called Andrey, from Little Russia, the other a girl named Natasha.
She had brought some books with her. The mother liked them
both, and found that Andrey was especially glad to talk to her.

The meetings went on—new people came from the city. The
little house at one edge of the village aroused attention. Her neighbors began to speak to the mother about it. Leaflets began to appear in the village and within the factory. Andrey was now living
with the Vlasovs to help Pavel with the work. By this time some
of the local workingmen had joined the meetings, and the interest
in their activities was shown by the increasing number of searches
that were taking place.

When her cottage was searched, the mother had a first taste
of the manners of the police. The studied insolence and threats of

the officer had angered her, but she was happy that Pavel had not been taken. But the Little Russian and a local comrade, Nikolay Vygesovshchikov, were arrested.

Not long after this Pavel was put into prison for leading a protest of the workingmen against a proposed deduction from their wages. With the help of the comrades from the city, leaflets were widely circulated in the village. Andrey was soon released. The mother helped to smuggle them into the factory, which was now closely guarded. The village was full of police spies.

The fact that her activity was an aid to her son pleased the mother, and she grew conscious of her usefulness in this new life—a consciousness that gave her poise and assurance. Before that she had never felt necessary to anybody.

Towards spring Pavel was released from prison, and they soon began to prepare to celebrate the First of May. Pavel and Andrey organized the demonstration. They had found in one of the peasants of the village named Rykin a man who had been thinking along the same lines as they had, and he was valuable to them because he knew the peasants and wanted to change their outlook on life.

On the First of May the factory workers heeded the call of Pavel and his comrades. A demonstration of five hundred followed the leaders in the streets. Soldiers had been ordered out. Pavel, Andrey, and a few of the most staunch held by their standard, but the intimidation of the fixed bayonet quelled the spirits of the others. The mother saw for the first time how the soldiers and their officers treated the workingmen. And she was in the center of the melée. Pavel and some of the others were arrested. Under the impact of her emotions, the mother spoke to her neighbors gathered around her. "Understand your children's hearts," she cried. "They have brought forth the truth; they perish for it. Believe them." Her old neighbors were moved—her words, followed by what they had seen that day, had aroused them.

There was nothing more for the mother to do in the village. Pavel and Andrey had already arranged for her to go to the city.

There she met some of the people who had come to the village. She told them about Rykin, and it was decided that she and another woman were to carry some literature to the place where Rykin was working, in a tar-works in the forest. There they found him; the men with him were already eager for reading matter.

She returned to the city and soon found that her regular task was the distribution of literature. Her life flowed on placidly. She met many new people; her work became a natural part of her life. The figure of her son appeared to be absorbing all the people into his own destiny. Many things happened; an old friend died, and at the funeral were many people who had known and admired him. But the police spies even watched the funerals closely.

There was trouble where Rykin was. The mother was sent to see him. She saw him taken as a common thief in a town square, beaten and abused by gendarmes and a police official. All the time he addressed the crowd of peasants who had gathered around. He was hauled into prison, but the mother's watchful eye had observed a sympathetic peasant. To him she took her leaflets, and he in turn gathered around him all those he could trust.

Back in the city, the mother and the comrades planned and carried out the escape of Rykin from prison. Here the mother had her most dangerous task, and her skillful execution of it made her a marked woman for the police from that time on.

Pavel finally was brought to trial. By a magnificent speech he turned the courtroom into a challenge to the policies of the ruling classes. He was sentenced to exile in Siberia, but the words of his speech were already being set in type by his comrades. The mother started out for the station with a bundle of Pavel's speeches in her valise to take to Moscow. At the station she knew the spies were watching her. Rather than surrender her precious valise to the police, she opened the bundle and passed the speeches to the crowd. Before the police could stop her, she had distributed all of them and had made an impassioned plea for the cause. But finally the officers laid hands on her, struck her, and at last began to choke her into silence.

Anna Karenina

By LYOF TOLSTOY

Count lyof nikolaievitch tolstoy *was born in the Tula region of Russia on September 9, 1828, the son of a wealthy and noble family of landowners. After studying law and languages at the University of Kazan he joined the army in the Caucasus as an ensign and was present at the defense of Sevastopol. A year spent in travel greatly changed Tolstoy's religious and social ideas, and he returned to his family estates where he lived most simply and founded a school for the peasantry. The school was soon closed by government opposition and Tolstoy turned to writing to further his reform ideas. His liberalism persisted despite continued opposition; in 1901 he was excommunicated by the Russian Orthodox Church. For some years before his death at Astapova on November 20, 1910, he lived as a peasant, having renounced his titles and lands.*

All was not well in the household of Stepan Arkadyevitch Oblonsky. His patient and faded wife, Darya Alexandrovna, had discovered his liaison with a young woman of the demi-monde, and had threatened to leave him. Stepan Arkadyevitch, an easy-going and usually carefree sensualist, saw his comfortable security slipping from him. But he looked forward to a visit from his sister, Anna Karenina, a great friend of his wife and a woman of the world, upon whom, he was sure, he could depend to smooth matters over. Then too, he was fond of his sister for her own sake, so it was with enthusiasm on two scores that he went to the station to meet the train from St. Petersburg.

At the station Stepan Arkadyevitch was surprised by an encounter with an aristocratic acquaintance, the handsome and popular officer, Count Vronsky, who was also awaiting the arrival of the Petersburg train, on which his mother was traveling. When the train arrived the two men found that the ladies they were meeting had become acquainted; Countess Vronskaya was charmed by Madame Karenina's friendliness and warm beauty and the two had spent the journey talking of their sons—for Anna was the mother of eight-year-old Seryozha, whom she adored. The greetings at the station were marred by the death of a workman who was crushed beneath the train, and Anna declared that the incident was an omen of ill.

Count Vronsky, from the first moment of his meeting with Anna Karenina, was strangely attracted by her. He had reason to encounter her again, since he was a welcome visitor at the home of Stepan Arkadyevitch; Anna, too, found her thoughts disturbed by this vital and strong-willed man. No thought of her husband occurred to her, for Alexey Alexandrovitch Karenin was a cold-blooded cynical man, twenty years his wife's senior, and incapable of any overt show of affection toward his prize possession, the beautiful Anna. But now that she had brought about a reconciliation between the Oblonskys, Anna's heart was turning homeward toward her beloved son. Soon she departed for St. Petersburg, Seryozha, and that eminent politician, her husband. But Anna left a broken heart behind her in Moscow. Pretty Princess Kitty Shtcherbatskaya, Madame Oblonsky's youngest sister, had become infatuated with Vronsky, and since he had shown her some attention she had refused the offer of her other suitor, solid, worthwhile Konstantin Levin, in the expectation that Vronsky would propose. But on the night of the ball at which Kitty had hoped Vronsky would declare himself, the Count was distrait and aloof, constantly following with his eyes the fascinating Madame Karenina. And when Vronsky followed Anna to St. Petersburg, it was obvious to all their social set that he was madly in love with her.

At first Anna resisted the love that she was beginning to feel for Count Vronsky, placing duty and her love for her son before

the illicit passion that haunted her. But time and Karenin's coldness and disinterest proved to be Vronsky's allies; she succumbed
to his entreaties and became his mistress. Karenin became aware
of the intrigue when Anna grew hysterical at a horse-race in which
Vronsky's life was endangered. Glad to be relieved of her guilty
secret, Anna confessed that not only was she Vronsky's mistress
but also that she soon expected to bear his child. Karenin's vanity
was wounded, although his heart was not; instead of threatening
to divorce his wife he demanded that she give up her lover and
resume the life that she loathed. But he soon decided to divorce
her and brand her publicly as an adulteress when he found that
she had again seen Vronsky.

Anna's confinement finally came, and for a while her life was
despaired of. Touched by Vronsky's grief and shaken by Anna's
remorse, Karenin forgave his wife and hoped that their unfortunate marriage might yet be mended. But Vronsky, crushed and
finding no way of happiness, attempted suicide and it was soon
obvious that Anna, though grateful to Karenin, experienced only
revulsion at his approach. Karenin offered a divorce, but Anna,
unable to bear the thought of thus losing her little boy forever,
preferred the disgrace of social ostracism. She and Vronsky, unable to live apart, went abroad together with their little daughter
Annie, and Karenin remained in St. Peterburg with Seryozha.

For a while Anna was ecstatically happy, forgetful even of her
little son, whom she loved as she could never love Vronsky's
daughter. But Vronsky was restless and without occupation. He
missed the army life and the respected position he had once held,
and the two soon returned to Russia.

Society had forgiven Vronsky but not Anna. Kitty, now married
to Konstantin Levin, had forgotten her old infatuation and was
entirely happy with her husband and little son. Vronsky's old
friends received him cordially, but Anna was accorded no recognition. The men of her acquaintance were as they had been, but
she was publicly snubbed at the opera, and no woman would
approach her, saving only faithful Madame Oblonsky. Karenin,

now under the influence of Countess Lidia Ivanovna, a moralistic hypocrite, refused to allow Madame Karenina to be with Seryozha, and only at a secret morning visit did Anna see her son.

Doubt crept into Anna's mind. Did Vronsky love her as before, or was he tied to her only by the bonds of honor and duty? Vronsky devoted his time and interest to his family estates, and there for a short time the two were once more happy. But Anna's fear and insecurity grew; a last plea to Karenin for a divorce, even at the price of never seeing Seryozha again, failed; Vronsky, although his love had not ceased, became irritable and restless because of Anna's constant suspicion; finally, tortured and desperate, Anna flung herself beneath the wheels of a train. Vronsky, hoping for a speedy death, left for the Serbian War. Their tragic romance was ended. Of all their friends, only Kitty and Konstantin Levin were able to salvage happiness by finding security and faith in their marriage.

Fathers and Sons

By IVAN TURGENEV

IVAN TURGENEV *was born in 1818 at Orel of a family of the provincial Russian gentry. Educated at the Universities of Moscow and St. Petersburg, he also studied at Berlin. Successively trying poetry and the drama, he achieved his greatest success as a writer of prose tales and novels. After 1850 he spent most of his life in Paris and was the first Russian writer to be widely read and admired in Europe. He died at Bougival, near Paris, on Sept. 4, 1883.*

ONE DAY in the spring of the year 1859, a middle-aged Russian gentleman was eagerly awaiting the arrival of his son from distant

St. Petersburg. This gentleman, Nikolai Petrovich Kirsanov, had what was considered thereabouts a fine property; however, the recent emancipation of the serfs had brought new problems of management, which Kirsanov was far from being able to solve satisfactorily. Now he was completely absorbed in thoughts of his son, who had just completed his work at the university.

When the coach arrived, the elder Kirsanov effusively welcomed Arkady, and politely greeted a close friend of the boy's, Yevgeny Bazarov, a student of the sciences, who, Arkady told him, was planning to spend some time at the farm.

On the way home, Nikolai rather shamefacedly confessed to his son that he had installed his mistress in his house, a young girl named Fenitchka, who had already borne him a son. Far from reproving him, his son seemed delighted, and in turn Arkady began to enlarge upon his merits of Bazarov, whose admirer and disciple he proudly professed to be.

The nature of Bazarov's ideas soon began to emerge. Another dweller at the farm was Arkady's uncle, Pavel Petrovich, a gentleman of about fifty, handsome, cultivated, who dressed in smart English fashions, and had all the graces of a fastidious cosmopolitan. Some years ago he had thrown up a career to pursue the eccentric and fabulous Princess R——. Upon her death, he had come to live with his brother in semi-retirement from the fashionable world. His first conversation with Bazarov made apparent the antagonisms between the two men.

Arkady at tea one day proudly asserted that Bazarov and he were "nihilists." Inquiring into the meaning of nihilism, Pavel found that Bazarov scorned the idea that men lived by principle; Bazarov denied that any of the traditional elements in Russian social relations had meaning for the present generation. With disconcerting candor, Bazarov stated that the job of the nihilist was to sweep out the stables—to destroy all existing concepts about politics, marriage, religion; for everything Pavel held dear in life he had only ridicule.

Bazarov's complete frankness in speaking of his uncle and, for that matter, his father, troubled Arkady after a little while; though he was pleased to observe how well Bazarov got along with the servants and the peasants. Fenitchka, especially, found him agreeable; she lost some of her shyness after he had treated her little Mitya during an illness.

Some time later Arkady and Bazarov decided to pay a visit to the near-by town of X——, the home of the provincial governor. Here, under the patronage of a government official who was a distant relation of the Kirsanovs, they were enabled to make some new social connections. They spent an evening with Madame Kukshina, famous for her feminist views and the champagne she passed out to youthful callers. Far more interesting was the governor's ball, where the two young men were introduced to Madame Odintsov. They impressed her so favorably that she allowed them to call at her hotel the next day; much to their surprise, an invitation to her country place followed.

Anna Sergyevna Odintsov's wealthy husband had died and left her his whole estate; now she lived a well-ordered existence in the country. Order, ease, refinement, she later confessed to Bazarov, were her requirements of life. Aside from her servants, the other residents were an ancient aunt, whose presence was largely disregarded, but whose royal connections added a touch of ceremony to the household, and her younger sister Katya, outwardly shy and dependent on her sister. Soon Bazarov was on excellent terms with Madame Odintsov; and Arkady, who had loved her from a distance since he first saw her, was compelled to spend most of his time with Katya.

In spite of his dislike of the way the household was run, and his ridicule for "aristocracy" and the social amenities, Bazarov was in no hurry to get on to his father's place. In all their lengthy conversations, Bazarov and Anna Sergyevna avoided the subject of themselves and the curious relationship developing between them. But at last no longer could he silence his passion; by a bold embrace he showed conclusively the frankness of his desire for her. After that, she was upset, but also somewhat frightened; and she no longer opposed the decision of the two young men to leave.

Their next stop was at the property of Bazarov's aged parents, where Arkady had the opportunity of observing the pathetic worship of the old people for their son. Their adoration of Bazarov, their concern for him was as obvious to Arkady as their ludicrous efforts to efface themselves in his presence. Both parents were fatuous, superstitious, and the father, once a doctor, though greatly admiring the knowledge of his son, was secretly religious. Nevertheless, Arkady was disturbed by Bazarov's curt decision, after a three-day visit, to leave his doting parents and return with him to the Kirsanovs.

On their return, they found that Arkady's father was having a hard time of it. Bazarov pitched into his scientific studies, but ten days after his arrival Arkady returned once more to the Odintsovs. Bazarov and Fenitchka renewed their friendship, and Barzarov so far forgot himself one day in the garden as to kiss her. They were interrupted in this embrace by Pavel, who had oddly discovered that Fenitchka reminded him of his old love.

He sought out Bazarov and challenged him to a duel, although the precise nature of the insult was not specified. Bazarov consented, in every way acting contrary to Pavel's expectations. They met the next morning in a grove not far away; with his first shot, which he had not even aimed, Bazarov wounded Pavel. Bazarov himself dressed the slight flesh wound—his deportment during the entire affair was impeccable, the unhappy Pavel had to admit. One objective of the duel he had naturally realized: Bazarov left the Kirsanovs for good the next day.

On his way back to his parents' home, Bazarov stopped at the Odintsov estate to inform Arkady of the duel; a more compelling reason was his suspicion that Arkady was now courting Madame Odintsov, which he freely intimated to his friend. That interview was cool and brief. Before he could leave, Bazarov was summoned to Anna Sergyevna. Strolling in the garden later, they were overheard by Arkady and Katya discussing Anna's feelings about Arkady. Upon hearing their words, Arkady was emboldened to declare openly to Katya his love for her, which he had been trying unsuccessfully to do before. To his utter delight, he was accepted, for Katya had loved him too all the while.

But the break between Arkady and Bazarov had become complete: in parting Bazarov told him precisely what his shortcomings as a nihilist are, though not denying a strong personal feeling for him. So Bazarov returned to his parents. Their rejoicing was short-lived: Bazarov received a fatal infection from a scratch while making a dissection on a peasant who had died from typhus. The next day he called an old servant to him and said, "Go to Madame Odintsov. Give her my greetings and tell her I am dying."

Anna came to him the next day—with a German doctor. To her he spoke his last deeply felt words—they were in Bazarov's usual vein, but now touched with love and remorse.

Katya and Arkady were soon married; and at the insistence of Pavel, Nikolai finally married his Fenitchka.

Novels of Various Countries

Don Quixote

By MIGUEL DE CERVANTES

MIGUEL DE CERVANTES SAAVEDRA *was born somewhere in Spain in 1547—late in the year at Alcala de Henares, it is said—the son of a traveling physician. As a youth he entered the army in Italy, was wounded in a naval battle, then was captured by pirates and held for five years in Algiers. Ransomed, he returned to Spain and tried with little success to stay out of debtors' prison by writing poems and plays. In 1604 his great book appeared, but the author remained ill and poverty-stricken until his death in Madrid on April 23, 1616.*

AT A CERTAIN VILLAGE in La Mancha, there lived one of those old-fashioned gentlemen who keep a lance in the rack, a lean horse, and a greyhound for coursing. His family consisted of a housekeeper, a niece and a serving man; the master himself was nigh 50 years of age, lean-bodied and thin-faced, and a great lover of hunting. His surname was Quixada, or Quesada.

Our gentleman read books on knight-errantry all the day and all the night, and even sold acres of land to buy them. His brain was full of nothing but enchantments, battles, challenges, amorous plaints and torments. Having lost his wits, he stumbled on the fancy to turn knight-errant and ride through the world redressing all manner of grievances.

He secured a suit of armor, decided to call his bony horse Rosinante, and arrived at Don Quixote de la Mancha as a name for himself. For his peerless lady he selected a buxom woman, Aldonza Lorenzo, known for her skill in salting pork, and spoke of her as Dulcinea del Toboso.

One July morning Don Quixote rode off and arrived at an inn which he conceived to be a castle and induced the host to dub him a knight. That night he was stoned by some carriers whom he had challenged when they disturbed his armor. On the road again, his horse stumbled when he tried to charge a company of merchants who would not admit Dulcinea's beauty, and a servant broke the knight's lance across his ribs. Too bruised to mount Rosinante, he had to ride back to his village on an ass.

Now Don Quixote persuaded an honest country laborer, Sancho Panza, to enter his service as squire, promising him the first island he should conquer; and they stole away in search of adventure.

They espied some thirty windmills in the plain, and Sancho could not convince his master that they were not giants. Don Quixote spurred his horse, ran his lance into the sail of the first mill, and was hurled down. He told Sancho some necromancer had converted those giants into mills.

Next they met a coach in which a lady was going to Seville. Don Quixote frightened away two monks who accompanied the lady, but her servants beat Sancho Panza. In their next encounter it was the knight who was wounded almost to death by some carriers, but when he told his squire that he must fight such common fellows hereafter, Sancho protested that he was a peaceful and forgiving man.

Arrived at an inn, Don Quixote fought a carrier over the maid, whom he took for the princess of the castle. Injured again, he concocted a balsam and drank it, becoming more grievously ill than before. In the morning he was recovered and refused to pay the landlord, because knights honored the house in which they lay. For this Sancho Panza was tossed in a blanket, but the Don blamed all their troubles on some cursed enchanters.

Spying a cloud of dust, Don Quixote exclaimed that a great battle was in progress ahead. It was only a huge flock of sheep, among which the knight did fearful slaughter until the herder's stones knocked him to earth with most of his teeth missing. Later they came upon a company of priests carrying a corpse through the night, and when the Don scattered them, Sancho made a meal off their provisions.

Next the knight deprived a barber of a brass basin which he was carrying on his head; Don Quixote declared it was the famous golden helmet of Mambrino and put it on his own pate. Then came an adventure in which he freed a gang of chained convicts who promptly mauled him.

It now came to Don Quixote that he must perform a penance in the mountains, and he divested himself of his armor and much of his underwear, and performed the maddest gambols and self-tortures ever witnessed under a blue sky.

Dreaming in an inn, with a blanket on his arm for a shield, the Don plunged his sword into the bodies of a number of giants, and their blood flowed forth in crimson streams. This roused the wrath of the inn-keeper, who kept his wine in goat-skin sacks with the heads left on. Soon afterward the knight's friends captured him and took him home again.

But soon Don Quixote was on the road again, accompanied by Sancho, who thought his master mad, but loved him and hoped for the governorship of his island. First they sought out Dulcinea; and the knight became convinced that an enchanter had turned her into a blubber-faced, flat-nosed country wench.

It chanced that one day the pair came upon a frolicsome duke and duchess who had heard of their adventures. The Don was invited to the duke's castle as a mighty hero, and some tricks were played on him, such as convincing him that a group of men in women's gowns were maidens who had been given beards by an enchanter, and sending him blindfolded on a journey through the air.

Here Sancho Panza was made governor of the town of Barataria on the duke's estate, being told it was an island. After receiving wise advice from his master on the subject of statecraft, Sancho was escorted to his city in a glittering cavalcade.

After giving delight by his wit and common-sense in judging certain disputes, Sancho sat down in a grand hall to a solitary banquet at which a physician ordered the dishes taken away as fast as they were set down, so that the governor would not prejudice his health. Just as he was growing angry, he received a warning from the duke that his island was in danger of attack, and that his food was being poisoned.

Famished and harassed by his problems, Sancho was ready to give up his office within a week. Then he was told that the attack had begun, and was bundled up in armor so tightly that he could not move. After a night in which his subjects trampled him in a mock battle, he was pleased to mount his faithful ass and ride off in humility.

Now Don Quixote was in the mood to embrace once more the life of the open road. Before and after he met the duke, he had many incredible adventures: with strolling actors and lions; in the deep cave of Montesinos; and on a magic bark, to name part of them.

But, laid low in an encounter with a friend of his disguised as a knight, the Don turned home, broken in spirit, to observe the conditions laid upon him of being confined to his village for a year. He was convinced that he would never see his Dulcinea while he lived, and Sancho was powerless to cheer him.

His melancholy increasing, Don Quixote was seized with a violent fever. His friends tried to divert him, believing that his illness arose from his disappointments; but one day he desired them to leave him, and he slept as though dead for six hours. Then he wakened and surprised his niece by speaking rationally. "By God's mercy," he said, "the cloud of ignorance is now re-

moved, which continuous reading of those noxious books of
knight-errantry had laid upon me."

But he was grieved that he had so little time to prepare his soul
for death. He called the notary, prepared his will, and apologized
to Sancho Panza for bringing shame upon him. When he died it
was after he had expressed, in a touching way, his horror at the
books of chivalry.

The Four Horsemen of the Apocalypse

By VICENTE BLASCO IBAÑEZ

VICENTE BLASCO IBAÑEZ *was born in January, 1867, at Valencia,
Spain. His father was a dry-goods merchant. After obtaining a law
degree, he plunged into politics in opposition to the government.
As a result, he spent long periods in exile and in prison. Ibañez
founded a republican newspaper, and started a publishing house
to bring great literature to Spaniards at popular prices. And he
won election to the Cortes as a republican leader. His novels, realistic and expressing his political views, have been read all over the
world. Ibañez died at Mentone, France, on January 28, 1928.*

JULIO DESNOYERS returned from Buenos Aires to Paris on the eve
of the Great War. To this wealthy and fashionable young man, an
Argentinian of French and Spanish parentage, the war which
seemed pending was little more than an annoyance. His mistress,
beautiful Marguerite Laurier, was greatly concerned that hostili-
ties might interrupt the round of festivities and dressmakers' fit-
tings which comprised her life. Julio and Marguerite planned to
marry when Marguerite's divorce from her husband should be

accomplished, although both were aware of the disapproval of Julio's stern father, Don Marcelo Desnoyers.

At the outbreak of the Franco-Prussian War, Marcelo Desnoyers lived in Paris and plied the trade of a wood-carver. He was a liberal-minded youth, opposed to the Empire and to the war and, after having been involved in an anti-government riot he fled the country with a little money and a stern conviction against war.

He found his way to Buenos Aires and in the course of years into the employment of Don Julio Madariaga, an expatriate Spaniard who had made a fortune in ranching. Madariaga was a temperamental tyrant but the young Frenchman regarded him with some affection and earned his regard by rescuing him from the knife of an infuriated peon seeking to avenge an insult. Marcelo soon became the manager of the old man's estates and married his elder daughter, Luisa. In time Madariaga hired a young German, Karl Hartrott, to assist him in bee-keeping and clerical work; Hartrott became the husband of Elena, the ranch-owner's younger daughter. Although Madariaga's sons-in-law came of hostile nations, the two got along amicably and their children passed their childhoods side by side. On the death of the old man it was found that little Julio, his favorite grandson, had received a separate legacy that greatly augmented the inheritance of his family. Although the Hartrotts, too, were made wealthy by the terms of Don Madariaga's will, their envy of Julio's good fortune was apparent. When Don Marcelo suggested that the families continue to live on the ranch, Karl Hartrott refused. The Hartrotts returned to Germany, the Desnoyers to France.

Don Marcelo, in contrast to the poverty of his youth, was now surrounded with great wealth. He provided his family with a town home in Paris and a beautiful chateau at Villeblanche-sur-Marne. Doña Luisa and Luisita, called Chichi by her family, were dressed luxuriantly and Julio lacked nothing that money could buy. No wonder he grew to be a spoiled young man.

Julio fancied himself a painter, and used his inexpert dabblings as an excuse for a disorderly and futile existence. Don Marcelo soon tired of his son's excesses, and the young man's supply of money was curtailed. Julio found himself a celebrity in Parisian society when the tango became the popular fad. Around this time he first met Marguerite Laurier, a chic social butterfly as useless as himself. The liaison which resulted between them was discovered by Marguerite's husband who bored her. A divorce followed and Julio decided that he wished to marry Marguerite. He proceeded to try to disentangle his private fortune and went to Buenos Aires to expedite matters.

Meanwhile conjectures about the war were on every tongue. Julio's two friends, Argensola, an artistic hanger-on and Tchernoff, a Russian Socialist, were greatly concerned with the coming conflict which Tchernoff felt was a direct result of German "Kultur." In a drunken vision the Russian mystic saw the Beast of the Apocalypse rising from the sea, preceded by the Four Horsemen —Conquest, War, Famine, and Death. When these had passed, he declared, nothing save desolation should be left. The next day France mobilized.

Gradually the war came close to the Desnoyers family. Don Marcelo tried to maintain the hatred of war that he had first learned in 1870, but stories of French heroism and the plight of evacués filled him with horror and a fear that he was shirking his responsibilities. The social prestige of Chichi's fiancé kept him from the front, but the girl was filled with doubt as to whether this was right.

Julio found Marguerite slowly slipping away from him. The struggle and suffering that came to her attention gradually changed her into a more thoughtful woman. Her interest changed from clothes and parties to nursing. When she saw Laurier, her former husband, in uniform she felt for him an emotion that she would not have believed possible. Laurier was cited for heroism; when he was gravely wounded Marguerite gave up her lover and returned to her husband's side. She did not warn Julio of what she planned to do and after seeking agonizedly for her he found her, worn and unbecomingly dressed in a nurse's costume.

tending her blind husband. Although she admitted that she still loved Julio she sent him away.

Don Marcelo, troubled by his changing views, decided to seek refuge at Villeblanche-sur-Marne. Disregarding the warnings of those who were well aware that the invading German armies were very near to the chateau, the old man reached his home after passing columns of wretched, homeless French civilians. The fears of his friends were only too well founded—the German onslaught could not be stopped and the little village was captured. Immediately German military law was put into effect. Don Marcelo learned with horror that the mayor and prominent civilians had been put to death because of the killing of four German soldiers. Burnings, lootings and atrocities followed which were accompanied by the most brutal indifference on the part of the invaders. The chateau was occupied by German officers, among them Desnoyers' own nephew, Captain Otto Hartrott.

The crowning villainy of the invaders occurred when they masked the artillery in the chateau grounds with the flag of the Red Cross. Finally the tide of battle turned and Don Marcelo returned to Paris.

To his joy his son, Julio, returned to him—dressed as a French soldier. The young man had at last found a reason for living in fighting for his father's country. Don Marcelo visited his son in the trenches and found the boy happy, although older and worn-looking.

Julio was made an officer and won the Croix de Guerre and the Legion of Honor. He was killed in battle.

As the bereaved father looked at his son's grave in a field in Champagne he realized that the Beast of the Apocalypse would never be still, that the Four Horsemen would ride again, although not in his lifetime. But Chichi, although grieving for her brother, embraced her lover and thought only of life.

Wilhelm Meister

By JOHANN WOLFGANG VON GOETHE

JOHANN WOLFGANG VON GOETHE, *poet, author, statesman and scientist, was born in 1749 at Frankfurt-on-Main, the son of an imperial councillor. He studied law and medicine at Leipzig and Strassburg, and published his first books in his early twenties. In 1775 he met Duke Karl August of Saxe-Weimar, who made Goethe his minister of state and in return saw his little Thuringian state become a center of culture. Gothe directed the ducal theater, and helped to apply scientific principles to Saxe-Weimar's farms and mines. In 1806 Goethe married Christiane Vulpius, who had been his housekeeper and mistress for 18 years. Death came to him at Weimar on March 22, 1832.*

IN SPITE OF THE GENEROUS GIFTS of the wealthy Norberg, the pretty young actress Mariana preferred Wilhelm Meister, whom her maid Barbara called "the callow merchant's son."

Against his father's disapproval, Wilhelm paid daily visits to the town's playhouse. Since he had seen a Christmas puppet show in his boyhood, the theater had fascinated him. Nor would he believe ill of Mariana, though Werner, his friend and future brother-in-law, tried to convince Wilhelm that she had another lover. But Wilhelm would listen to none of this; about to be sent on a business journey by his father, he resolved to make his way to the town where his friend Serlo managed a theater. There he would begin a stage career, and then he would marry Mariana.

All this Wilhelm wrote into a letter. Finding Mariana cool, he kept the letter in his pocket when he called on her in the afternoon, and left after snatching up one of her neckerchiefs. Walking the streets restlessly that midnight, he imagined he saw a dark figure issue from Mariana's door. Thrusting aside this vision, he took the neckerchief from his pocket when he arrived home, and was horrified to find in it a passionate note from Norberg making an appointment for that evening.

A violent fever felled the shocked Wilhelm, and on his recovery Mariana's company had left the town. He now mastered the details of the counting-house, and was sent off by his father on a business trip. At a pleasant little mountain town he stopped to rest and met two stranded actors, Laertes and the pretty Philina, with whom Wilhelm amused himself. He also rescued from a troupe of rope-dancers a handsome, moody twelve-year-old girl named Mignon, who thereupon attached herself to Wilhelm. A bearded harpist, a strange personage, also joined their company.

An actor named Melina appeared, and Wilhelm helped him finance an acting company. One of their number was an elderly man called the Pedant, who revealed to Wilhelm that he had been on the stage with Mariana, and that she was about to become a mother when she left Wilhelm's town. The Pedant told Wilhelm that Mariana had been left at a village inn, and he upbraided her as a "wanton jilt" who had sent him no word after he had helped pay the expenses of her lying-in. But Wilhelm could see Mariana only as a frail, ill-succored mother wandering helplessly about the world, perhaps with his own child.

The actors obtained a profitable engagement at the near-by castle of a Count who employed them to amuse the Prince who was his guest. The Countess showed an interest in Wilhelm, but both she and the Count were sobered by a prank which went wrong. Wilhelm had been induced to dress in the Count's clothes to confuse the Countess; the Count saw him instead, and believed he had seen a ghost. At the castle Wilhelm also met Jarno, the Prince's favorite, a brilliant, cynical man who upbraided Wilhelm for following the theater, but acquainted him with Shakespeare.

Well-paid, the actors left the castle for a distant town where

Melina hoped to establish his company. But in a forest they were attacked by bandits, and Wilhelm was wounded when he resisted. He woke to find himself deserted by all but Philina and Mignon. A party of horsemen led by a beautiful young Amazon passed by, and an older man whom the young lady called uncle treated Wilhelm. He lost consciousness again, and when he wakened the Samaritans were gone.

Wilhelm recovered slowly in a near-by village, nursed by Philina and Mignon, then went on to his friend Serlo, in whose company he had tried to arrange places for the actors who had been despoiled by the bandits. He had been able to find no trace of his Amazon.

Wilhelm agreed to act Hamlet with Serlo's company. The Ophelia was Serlo's sister Aurelia, a young widow who was morose at having lost the love of a baron whom she called Lothario. There was a pretty boy of three years in Serlo's house, and Philina declared he was Aurelia's son by another lover. Mignon and undisciplined little Felix became fast friends. Meantime Wilhelm received letters from his father and Werner, and learned that he was forgiven for his laxity in writing to his family. But another letter informed him that his father had died; and Wilhelm told Werner that he was again resolved to follow the stage and would leave the family business in the hands of Werner.

Soon after the first performance of the Hamlet there were two strange occurrences. The half-mad Harper set a fire in which Felix almost was caught, and Philina had a fair-haired visitor who she told Wilhelm was a lady in disguise. Indeed, Philina said the lady's name was Mariana, but would not let him talk to the visitor, and went off with him or her the next morning.

Now Aurelia fell mortally ill, and gave Wilhelm a letter to be delivered to Baron Lothario after her death. Moved by her sorrow, he left Mignon in the care of Frau Melina and set off for Lothario's castle.

Wilhelm delivered the letter, but found Lothario preoccupied with a duel he was to fight next morning. Wilhelm stayed at the castle and saw the baron return wounded. The surgeon who treated him carried the same pouch as was carried by his Amazon's uncle in the forest, but Wilhelm could not learn where he had obtained the pouch. In Lothario's household were Jarno, whose Prince had died, and an abbé. Also there was Lydia, Lothario's mistress, and Jarno and the abbé enlisted Wilhelm to take her to the home of Theresa, a friend of Lothario, because Lydia's passionate expressions of love were hindering the baron's recovery.

Wilhelm learned that Theresa, an extraordinary woman with a man's ability at management, had once been at the point of marrying Lothario when he learned that her mother was a woman with whom he had once had an affair of love. Instead the baron had taken into his house Lydia, a pretty girl who had been brought up with Theresa.

Returning, Wilhelm found Lothario near recovery. Having seen Theresa, he understood why Aurelia had been forsaken. He also was told by Jarno that Felix was not Aurelia's child, but had been brought to her by an old woman who said Wilhelm was the father. Wilhelm hastened back to Serlo's home and found the old woman. She was Barbara, and she told Wilhelm bitterly that Mariana was dead, and that, in spite of all appearances she had never yielded to Norberg after falling in love with Wilhelm. It was much later that Wilhelm learned that it was really a man he had seen with Philina; actually he was Friedrich, young brother of Lothario. And Mariana had left behind a letter which filled Wilhelm with belated grief and self-reproach.

Wilhelm now took Felix with him to Lothario's castle, and sent Mignon, who had been ill, to stay with Theresa, who sent the girl on to a friend who was educating some other girls.

One evening Jarno took Wilhelm to a secret part of the castle, where he was left in a tapestry-hung room. There a man made a speech to him which began: "To guard from error is not the instructor's duty, but to lead the erring pupil," after which the abbé gave Wilhelm a roll inscribed "Indenture" which said in part: "No one knows what he is doing while he acts aright; but of what is wrong we are always conscious." There was another roll entitled: "Wilhelm's Apprenticeship," on which were inscribed the events of his life, as well as like rolls for the others in the castle. Wilhelm was to learn that all this was an outgrowth of the abbé's theory that the young should not be guided, but that their teachers should learn their inclinations and assist them to realize them. Wilhelm now had decided to abandon the stage, and his preceptors hailed this decision.

Seeing little Felix grow up untamed, however, Wilhelm made a private decision of his own, and sent a letter to Theresa, asking her to be his bride and a mother to his son. Before an answer could arrive, Wilhelm was summoned to the home of Natalia, Lothario's sister. Wilhelm had learned that the Countess was also the baron's sister; now he found that he had another sister, the friend to whom Theresa had sent Mignon. Mignon's condition had grown worse, and Wilhelm was needed.

He entered Natalia's stately home, and a young lady rose and came to him. It was the Amazon! He fell on his knee and kissed her hand with unbounded rapture. Wilhelm learned that her uncle, the surgeon, was now dead, and that this had been his home. Mignon was wasting away, consumed by some secret brooding that seemed connected with the Harpist.

In a day or two a letter came from Theresa which said: "I am yours," but begged forgiveness if she should be unable to forget Lothario entirely. Natalia and Wilhelm were about to inform the baron, when Jarno appeared and told them that Theresa had been found not to be the daughter of her reputed mother, and that there was now no impediment to her marriage with Lothario.

Then Theresa arrived and the excitement proved fatal to the weakened body of Mignon. In his grief, Wilhelm avoided a decision between keeping his pledge to Theresa and voicing his love for the Amazon he had at last rediscovered.

Meantime an Italian Marchese, a friend of Lothario, arrived. Through certain signs he discovered that Mignon was his niece, stolen by the rope-walkers. The Harper was found to be Mignon's father; he had lost his reason and wandered off after learning that the woman he loved was a sister of whose existence he had been kept ignorant.

Now Wilhelm's last problem was solved. Lothario took him by the hand and said: "What if your alliance with my sister were the secret article on which depended my alliance with Theresa? She has vowed that we two pairs should appear together at the altar." The baron then led Wilhelm to Natalia, who confessed her love for him.

"I know," said Wilhelm, "that I have attained a happiness undeserved, which I would not change for anything in life."

All Quiet on the Western Front

By ERICH MARIA REMARQUE

BORN ON *June 22, 1898, at Osnabrück, in the Westphalian Rhineland, Erich Maria Remarque was educated in the schools at Osnabrück and at the University of Münster. Then this youth of French descent fought in the German army in the World War, serving on the Western Front. After the war he successively became a teacher, a race driver, a test driver, a sport editor, a dramatic critic, and an author. In his novels he became a spokesman of the generation that felt itself lost after the war. His novels burned by the Nazis, he became an exile, and in 1939 he came to the United States.*

KANTOREK, the schoolmaster, talked the nineteen-year-old boys into enlisting. Joseph Behm was one who hesitated. He was one of the first to be killed; shot in the eye during an attack, he was cut down as he groped his way back. Now four from the same class remained in the company: Little Albert Kropp, a clear-thinking lance corporal, Müller, who still studied for his physics examinations; Leer, full-bearded, with a preference for girls from the officers' brothels; and Paul Baumer.

Their friends were two men of their own age, the skinny, huge-appetited Tjaden, a locksmith, and huge-handed Haie Westhus, a peat-digger; and Detering, a peasant who thought always of his farm, and the group's shrewd forty-year-old leader, Stanislaus Katczinsky, known as Kat, a hard-bitten man of the soil with a nose for good food and soft jobs.

The company, back from 14 days at the front, had lost heavily, so that there were only 80 men to eat food prepared for 150. For once they had enough, and afterward they went over to the dressing-station to see Franz Kemmerich, a classmate who had a wound in his thigh. His leg had been amputated, and there was a look of death on his face. Müller had his eye on Kemmerich's fine pair of boots; he was not callous—it was only that one learns to be practical at the front. Next morning Franz died as Paul stood at his bedside. The orderly merely seemed harassed; 17 had died that day, and the wounded were lying on the floor outside. Paul took the boots to Müller, and wrote a letter to Frau Kemmerich.

It was in barracks that the boys had got their first hardening for this kind of life. Undersized Corporal Himmelstoss, a postman in civil life, was the drillmaster of Paul's platoon. He drilled them in the mud, ran Paul up and down stairs barefooted at two in the morning, and invented all sorts of bullying tricks until they hated the corporal and became so tough that they could endure the front lines.

The company got reinforcements, including twenty-five boys of 17. Sent up on wiring fatigue, they were caught in an English bombardment. The recruits were terrified, and some were hit because they didn't know how to take cover. Lying in a graveyard, Paul was well-protected in a coffin burst open by a shell hit. One boy, his hip-joint a mass of mincemeat, was put out of his misery by Kat—at best, he would have had three days of howling torture.

Himmelstoss was sent to the company, and Tjaden and Kropp merely insulted him when he got officious. Reported to the company lieutenant, Bertinck, the two received a few welcome days of open arrest, and Himmelstoss got a lecture. That night Kat, with his genius for spotting food, went with Paul and stole a goose from a regimental headquarters. Then they cooked it in a deserted lean-to, ate their fill, and took the rest to the prisoners.

Going up to the front two days earlier than usual, the company passed a stack of a hundred fresh coffins—efficiently ready in advance. In the dugouts it was a matter of waiting under bombardment that went on day and night. Food was hard to come by, and they had to fight the rats. But ammunition became more plentiful, while there was an everlasting roll of trains and trucks concentrating something behind the enemy lines. The recruits soon became ill under the strain, and finally one had a fit. He was beaten to his senses, but later another ran out past Paul and was killed. Then suddenly the shelling lifted and the enemy attack began. Fighting like wild beasts against the French charge, the company was driven back to another trench. Then came the counter-charge, possible only for men who have momentarily become savages. A blow from a spade cleaved the face of a Frenchman who had lagged behind. The pursuing Germans reached the enemy lines, hurling grenades and stumbling over slippery lumps of flesh. Then they retired to their own trench again, taking tins of the famous French corned beef with them.

The incredible days went by, with attack and counter-attack alternating while the dead piled up. There was one wounded man they could not find; for two days he cried out before they heard his death-rattle. It seemed an eternity before they were relieved. Before then Haie Westhus went off with a great wound in his back. At roll-call, 32 men answered.

Taken far back for reorganization, Paul, Leer, and Kropp swam a little canal to visit three Frenchwomen who were pleased to share the boys' bread and sausage. It was far better than a soldiers' brothel. Then Paul got a six-week leave—14 days at home and the rest at a training camp. In the little town, Paul found his mother ill with cancer, his father tired from overwork, the whole family undernourished. Paul found it impossible to talk to anyone about the war—the women could not understand, the men only thought they could. Paul had been changed, crushed without knowing it; he should never have come back. His old schoolbooks meant nothing now. One pleasure was seeing Kantorek in an ill-fitting uniform; he had been called up as a territorial. But it was painful to leave; he could never again be indifferent at the front.

Back with his company, Paul went through an inspection by the Kaiser, who was rather disappointing. This led to a discussion of the war, in which they all agreed that it wasn't useful to any of them. Then they went back into the lines. Paul got lost on patrol, and spent a gruesome day in a shell hole watching the slow death of a Frenchman he had stabbed. After this eight of them were sent to guard a supply dump in a village that had been abandoned because it was being shelled too heavily. There they lived royally for three weeks, eating, drinking, and dodging shells.

A few days later Paul and Kropp collected leg wounds while evacuating a village. They were taken to a Catholic hospital, where Kropp's leg was amputated. The sisters were kind, but there was death all around. Paul recovered, had a few days at home, worse than the time before, and was sent back to the front.

Now life had worn thin. The men lived from minute to minute, like walking dead men. Detering walked away one day, madly trying to get back to his farm. The military police caught him; his comrades heard nothing more of him. Müller was shot point-blank in the stomach with a Very light; he lived half an hour in horrible pain. Leer and Bertinck fell in an attack.

It was the summer of 1918; the food was bad, the guns were bad, the ranks were filled with hopeless soldiers, and the enemy's tanks and troops were fresh and fit. Only Paul and Kat were left. Then Kat's shin was smashed and Paul carried him to the dress-

ing-station. Paul could not comprehend when an orderly said Kat
was dead; a shell splinter had entered his skull without Paul notic-
ing it.

It was a day in October, 1918, that Paul fell—a day so eventless
that the army report said merely: All Quiet on the Western Front.
Paul's face was so peaceful that he seemed almost glad that it was
all over.

Quo Vadis

By HENRY SIENKIEWICZ

HENRY SIENKIEWICZ *was born in 1846 near Lukow in Russian
Poland. He studied philosophy at Warsaw University. In 1876 he
visited America and upon his return to Poland published an account of his travels under the pseudonym of "Litwos." He won
rapid recognition and enjoyed a profitable career in journalism.
He lived in Krakow and Warsaw most of his life and edited the
Warsaw newspaper* Slowo. Quo Vadis *appeared in 1895 and won
instant acclaim. It was published in thirty languages. In 1905
Sienkiewicz won the Nobel Prize for literature. November 14,
1916, he died in Switzerland while engaged in war relief work for
Poland.*

OF ALL of Nero's dissolute court only Petronius, an aesthete
styled by the emperor himself "arbiter of elegance," led a life that
was not completely brutal and debauched. But Petronius' disgust
for the orgies and bloodshed of the court was based on the dictates, not of morality, but of good taste. So it was with cynical
amusement that this man of the world listened to the problems

of his love-sick young kinsman, Marcus Vinitius. Vinitius had become enamoured of one Lygia, the daughter of a conquered barbarian king. This girl was living at the home of the Roman general, Aulus—a hostage, but beloved as a daughter of the house. Petronius well knew that the moral and upright Auli would never give the girl up as a concubine to Vinitius, but he promised to use his court influence in behalf of the smitten young soldier.

Petronius was as good as his word. The next day the Auli received a communication from Nero. Lygia was to be removed to the court! Aulus, grief-stricken but fearing to imperil his family by a refusal, was forced to relinquish the girl. But he sent Lygia's retinue with her and among them was Ursus the Lygian, Lygia's friend and servant since babyhood, a gigantic barbarian with incredible strength and a heart gentle as a babe's. The Auli bade the girl farewell, knowing full well that she was going to dishonor if not death. But Lygia was upheld by a faith that comforted and sustained her and the many other Romans who secretly embraced it; she was a Christian.

For two days Lygia remained at the palace. On the first evening she was forced to attend a banquet which ended in a debauch. Vinitius, who at the home of the Auli had seemed to her an attractive and charming young man, now frightened her with his drunken love-making. Unable to resist his brutal advances further, Lygia was near to fainting when Ursus appeared and carried her back to the comparative safety of her private apartments. The next day Lygia abandoned hope; she learned that that evening she was to be taken to the house of Marcus Vinitius. But while she was being conveyed thence a street fight occurred and in the confusion Ursus was able to escape with his young mistress.

The headstrong young Vinitius grew nearly insane with frustration and rage when he learned that his prize had eluded him. He became unsociable to his friends and cruel to his household. Petronius offered him his slave-girl, Eunice; Vinitius rejected the offer and Eunice herself refused to leave Petronius' house. Surprised at this wilfulness in a slave, Petronius learned that Eunice's stubbornness was due to a passion for himself. He looked at her with new eyes and found in her beauty and love something in life he had missed.

In an effort to find Lygia for his young kinsman, Petronius employed the services of one Chilo Chilonides, a Greek spy. Chilo soon discovered that Lygia was a Christian and traced her to the home of one Crispus, also of that faith. Vinitius, impatient of delay, went to demand that the maiden be delivered up to him. But he reckoned without Ursus. The giant barbarian felled the young Roman, indeed wounded him nearly unto death. When Vinitius regained his senses he found that the Christians, true to their principles, were tending him as lovingly as though he had come as a friend. And his nurse in the slow convalescence that followed was none other than Lygia. Slowly into Vinitius' heart was creeping a purer love for the maiden than ever he had imagined possible. And he listened to the teaching of the Christians about him with new respect. A frequent visitor in the house was the Apostle Peter, who by his gentleness soon won the heart of the young Roman. But all was doubt and confusion in the heart of Lygia. She realized that she loved the pagan Vinitius and, counselled by Crispus, she fled the house. Vinitius, by now recovered, searched for her in vain. Finally he appealed to Peter; and the Apostle, moved by the young man's sincerity, sanctioned the match and sent Lygia to her lover's arms.

But no sooner had the betrothal taken place than Vinitius was called to Antium, where Nero was holding his revels. The emperor day by day grew more bestial and soulless; finally his madness reached its peak and he ordered that the city of Rome be burned to the ground that he might write an ode on its destruction. Enraged, the people demanded a scapegoat and the terrified emperor named the Christians as the incendiaries. Thousands of Christians were martyred and for days the slaughter reigned. Lygia was imprisoned and though Vinitius and Petronius brought ruin on themselves in order to save her, her fate seemed hopeless. Finally the day set for her martyrdom came and she was sent into the arena tied to the horns of a savage bull, which the giant Ursus must fight. Vinitius, despairing, prayed for a speedy death for his love, but Ursus vanquished the bull and the populace screamed that mercy be shown the giant and the maiden. Nero was forced to reprieve them, and Vinitius, now converted to Christianity, escaped the city with Lygia. But Petronius, fallen into disfavor for championing the Christians, died a suicide with his beautiful Eunice, at Nero's command. Nero himself did not long survive. His people, his court, even his friends, turned against him; and sick of his cruelty and madness, declared him no longer emperor. The senators decreed the death penalty against him; and, since he was afraid to commit suicide, a faithful servant mercifully slew him.

And St. Peter, too, had not much longer to live. Persuaded by his followers to flee the city he started away from Rome, but in a vision Christ came to him. Peter said, *"Quo Vadis,"* "Whither goest thou, Master?" Christ replied that he was going back to Rome again to be crucified. But Peter, realizing where his duty lay, turned back toward Rome, there to die with his flock.

Story of Gösta Berling

By SELMA LAGERLÖF

SELMA LAGERLÖF *was born on November 20, 1858, at Marbacka in Sweden, in the province of Värmland, which she describes so well in her books. She became a teacher in Landskrona and taught until her writing enabled her to give teaching in 1895. Gösta Berling was her first work. Excerpts from it won a prize in a literary contest. An accomplished linguist, she traveled in Italy, Palestine, and the East, but wrote best about her own country. In 1909 she won the Nobel Prize for literature. In 1914 she be-*

came the first woman member of the Swedish Academy. She died
March 16, 1940.

OLD STORIES cling to the bleak iron-bearing earth of Värmland in
Sweden, legends the old folks heard from their grandparents
who had them from their fathers' fathers. These near-myths tell
of an age when the iron-foundries were producing great wealth
and when rich families gladly supported "pensioners," merry
soldiers of fortune who were able to do everything but make a
living. These knights of merriment paid their way with wit,
music, and versifying, and lived as permanent guests in the
houses of the gentry. Such a one was Gösta Berling.

In a pulpit in Western Värmland stood a young priest. He was
drunk. Eloquent, brilliant of mind, blessed with faith in God,
beautiful as an angel, this young man yet found life in the barren
little parish so dreary and comfortless that brandy had become
his only solace. The bishop had come to dismiss him. But, suddenly inspired by faith, the young priest preached a sermon so
magnificent that his congregation could do naught but forgive
him. Cleansed by this experience the young man felt that he
was saved; but his chances of redeeming himself dwindled into
nothingness when a drunken companion of his threatened the
bishop's life.

Gösta Berling—for the drunken priest was he—determined to
die. He was saved from suicide by the rich and iron-willed Major's
wife who lived at Ekeby. This woman told Gösta her own sad
story. As a girl she had been forced by her parents into a loveless
marriage. Later the love of her youth returned and, become
wealthy, helped her and her shiftless husband. Her mother hearing of this dishonor cursed her. Now her wealthy lover was dead
and by his will the Major and his wife had inherited the vast
estates of Ekeby. It was here that Gösta Berling became a pensioner with a dozen other landless gentlemen.

Nowhere could Gösta Berling find happiness. He became tutor to the lovely and pious young Countess Ebba Donna and the two fell in love. When the devout girl found that Gösta was a dismissed priest she allowed herself to die of an illness so as to escape her love for him. Talented, popular, the leader of the pensioners, Gösta, who had devoted his life to the pursuit of pleasure, could still not find contentment.

It was said that ugly old Sintram, the wicked master of the ironworks, was in league with the devil. Sintram persuaded the pensioners that the Major's wife had sold their souls to Satan. Gösta made a bargain with the devil by which the pensioners were to have control of Ekeby for one year. If, by the end of that time, the pensioners had proven themselves true gentlemen, the devil's power over Ekeby ended; if not, Satan got the souls of all of them.

In revenge for her double-dealing the pensioners informed the Major of his wife's sinful past; the Major drove her out and gave Ekeby to the pensioners.

Women admired Gösta. Beautiful Anna Stjärnhök fell in love with him. Marianna Sinclair, beloved of many, was turned from her father's house because she looked with love on the dismissed clergyman. When the smallpox disfigured her beauty she returned to her father's home and Gösta lost her.

After an attempt to burn down Ekeby had been frustrated the Major's wife was put in jail. The townspeople felt that she had been mistreated, and their consequent coldness affronted the pensioners.

The pensioners were most indignant at the young Countess Elizabeth. The Young Countess was beautiful, gay and good. She was so very good and innocent that she did not realize that her husband, Count Hendrik, was a conceited, cruel blockhead. Feeling that the pensioners were responsible for the plight of the Major's wife, she refused Gösta a dance. In revenge Gösta carried her off in his sledge but, disarmed by her youth and sweetness, he returned her to her husband's home. What was the amazement of the assembled company when the pompous young Count made the Countess apologize for the insult she had offered Gösta. Ashamed of the humiliation he had caused her, Gösta fell deeply and truly in love with the girl. They became friends. Their relationship continued on the highest plane until Elizabeth learned of his evil past. Shocked, the Young Countess wished no more to see Gösta, but when she learned that, in despair, he planned to marry a mad, wandering girl, she crossed the frozen river to dissuade him.

Gossip reached the silly Count's ears. He accused his young wife. To the pure girl her secret love for Gösta seemed wickedness, and she confessed it. The Count and his cruel mother devised many humiliations and hardships which the Young Countess endured gladly in order to atone for what she felt was a sin. At last her strength started to fail, and, fearing for the health of the baby which would soon be born to her, she fled to live in obscurity with a peasant family. When Elizabeth learned that the Count had had their marriage annulled she begged Gösta to marry her so that her child should have a father. This he did, although the child soon died. Gösta loved Elizabeth but feared that marriage with him would ruin her life.

Gösta's last prank was a sad one. Captain Lennert had been newly released from jail where he had been sent by a false accusation. The pensioners plied him with brandy, and the captain, unused to liquor, was soon overcome. The pensioners painted a false face on him and sent him home thus to his wife. The woman turned him out. The Captain dedicated the rest of his life to wandering about helping the poor. Finally he was killed in a brawl defending the helpless.

Meanwhile hunger and hardship had inflamed the villagers and, sick of the pensioners' misdeeds, they tried to storm Ekeby. By the gentleness of Elizabeth and Gösta's eloquence they were deterred from wrong-doing.

Gösta attempted suicide in an effort to free his wife but was balked. Finally Elizabeth was able to make him see that, not by suicide, but only by forsaking his life of pleasure, could he redeem himself and make her happy.

Wicked Sintram lost his bargain and perished; the Major's wife made peace with the mother who had cursed her and came home to Ekeby to die; Gösta and Elizabeth prepared to rebuild their lives by devoting themselves to the service of other people.